RETHINKING VALUE-ADDED MODELS IN EDUCATION

Since passage of the No Child Left Behind Act in 2001, academic researchers, econometricians, and statisticians have been exploring various analytical methods of documenting students' academic progress over time. Known as value-added models (VAMs), these methods are meant to measure the value a teacher or school adds to student learning from one year to the next. To date, however, there is very little evidence to support the trustworthiness of these models. What is becoming increasingly evident, yet often ignored mainly by policymakers, is that VAMs are (1) unreliable, (2) invalid, (3) nontransparent, (4) unfair, (5) fraught with measurement errors, and (6) being inappropriately used to make consequential decisions regarding such things as teacher pay, retention, and termination. Unfortunately, their unintended consequences are not fully recognized at this point either. Given such, the timeliness of this well-researched and thoughtful book cannot be overstated. This book sheds important light on the debate surrounding VAMs and thereby offers states and practitioners a highly important resource from which they can move forward in more research-based ways.

Audrey Amrein–Beardsley, Ph.D., is an Associate Professor in Mary Lou Fulton Teachers College at Arizona State University. She is one of the top Edu-Scholars in the nation, honored for being an academic who is contributing substantially to public debates about the nation's educational system. She is also creator and host of the blog: VAMboozled! (vamboozled. com).

RETHINKING VALUE-ADDED MODELS IN EDUCATION

Critical Perspectives on Tests and Assessment-Based Accountability

Audrey Amrein-Beardsley

Routledge
Taylor & Francis Group

NEW YORK AND LONDON

First published 2014
by Routledge
711 Third Avenue, New York, NY 10017

and by Routledge
2 Park Square, Milton Park, Abingdon, Oxon OX14 4RN

Routledge is an imprint of the Taylor & Francis Group, an informa business

Library of Congress Cataloging in Publication Data
Amrein-Beardsley, Audrey, author.
Rethinking value-added models in education : critical perspectives on tests and assessment-based accountability / Audrey Amrein-Beardsley. – First published 2014.
  p. cm.
  Includes bibliographical references and index.
  1. Educational accountability–United States. 2. Educational indicators–United States. 3. Educational tests and measurements–United States. 4. Teachers–Rating of–United States–Mathematical models. I. Title.
  LB2806.22.A46 2014
  379.1'58–dc23   2013037411

ISBN: 978-0-415-82011-0 (hbk)
ISBN: 978-0-415-82012-7 (pbk)
ISBN: 978-0-203-40990-9 (ebk)

Typeset in Bembo
by Wearset Ltd, Boldon, Tyne and Wear

This book is dedicated to the orphaned children at the Assisting Cambodian Orphans and the Disabled Organization (ACODO) Orphanage of the Kingdom of Cambodia. All of my personal royalties from this book will go to this orphanage.

My husband, children, and I believe that the royalties from this book will add more "value" to these children's lives at ACODO than they ever would ours.

For more information about the ACODO Orphanage, or to sponsor a child, donate money, or even donate your time should you visit Siem Reap, Cambodia, please visit: www.acodo.org

Figure 0.1 My daughter Blythe, son Aidan, and some of their ACODO friends in Siem Reap, Cambodia.

CONTENTS

List of figures ix
List of tables xi
Foreword by Diane Ravitch xii
Preface xiv
Acknowledgments xx

PART I
Introduction 1

1 Socially Engineering the Road to Utopia 3

2 Value-Added Models (VAMs) and the Human Factor 19

3 A VAMoramic View of the Nation 50

PART II
Highly Questionable Yet Often Unquestioned Assumptions 77

4 Assumptions Used as Rationales and Justifications 79

5 Test-Based, Statistical, and Methodological Assumptions 105

PART III
Non-Traditional Concerns about Traditional Methodological
Notions **129**

6   Reliability and Validity 131

7   Bias and the Random Assignment of Students into Classrooms 157

PART IV
Alternatives, Solutions, and Conclusions **183**

8   Alternatives, Solutions, and Conclusions 185

References 215
Index 247

FIGURES

0.1   My daughter Blythe, son Aidan, and some of their ACODO friends in Siem
      Reap, Cambodia   v
0.2   A drunk man under a streetlight   xviii
1.1   Map of Cambodia   4
1.2   Measure and Punish Theory of Change logic map   10
2.1   An example of a statistical model used to calculate value-added   21
2.2   Teacher C's SAS® EVAAS® Teacher Value-Added Report for 2010 and
      Report for Teacher Reflection   27
3.1   State legislation requiring that teacher evaluation systems use growth or
      VAM estimates   55
3.2   Current and planned growth model and VAM use by type   56
3.3   The EVAAS® multivariate response model (MRM) teacher-level equation   58
3.4   The EVAAS® univariate response model (URM) projection equation   58
3.5   VARC's two-period value-added model for school/district (not teacher)
      purposes   63
3.6   Student Growth Percentile (SGP) equation   67
4.1   The feedback loop as conceptualized for common use   99
4.2   The feedback loop as conceptualized for VAM-based educational use   99
5.1   Example of a box-and-whisker plot   109
5.2   Distribution of IQ scores under a normal bell curve   111
5.3   Student achievement trajectories from year to year (assuming within school
      learning is parallel) including variable levels of the summer growth/decay 120
6.1   A simple framework to help interpret correlation coefficients in the social
      sciences   135
6.2   One teacher's fluctuation from value-added decile 1 (bottom 10%) to
      value-added decile 10 (top 10%), taking into consideration the types of
      students (s)he taught   138
7.1   Teachers teaching the same courses with high- and low-achievers
      respectively   159

8.1 A pie chart illustrating how MET researchers recommended value-added estimates might be used for weighted teacher evaluation systems based on multiple measures   188

8.2 A pie chart illustrating how college faculty are sometimes evaluated according to their three main professional responsibilities   201

8.3 A distribution of faculty members' evaluation scores ($n = 50$) within one college of education over three separate evaluation periods (2010–2012)   203

8.4 A pie chart illustrating how a better, more holistic, evaluation system *might* look for teachers who are VAM-eligible   204

8.5 A pie chart illustrating how a better, more holistic, evaluation system *might* look for teachers who are *not* VAM-eligible   204

8.6 A pie chart illustrating how a better, more holistic, evaluation system *might* look for all teachers   205

TABLES

2.1	Teacher A's SAS® EVAAS®, and PDAS scores and ASPIRE bonuses	29
2.2	Teacher B's SAS® EVAAS®, and PDAS scores and ASPIRE bonuses	30
2.3	Teacher C's SAS® EVAAS®, and PDAS scores and ASPIRE bonuses	31
2.4	Teacher D's SAS® EVAAS®, and PDAS scores and ASPIRE bonuses	32
4.1	General assumptions about VAMs	84
4.2	Assumptions used as rationales to justify VAM adoptions	92
4.3	Assumptions used as justifications to further advance VAM implementation	101
5.1	Assumptions often made about the large-scale standardized achievement tests used for value-added calculations	113
5.2	Other statistical and methodological assumptions about VAMs	125
6.1	Correct and incorrect interpretations (possibly leading to decisions) if $r=0.4$ and $r^2=0.16$	136
7.1	Statistically significant correlations among teachers' VAM estimates and classroom composition	170
8.1	The five core propositions of the National Board for Professional Teaching Standards (NBPTS)	191
8.2	Multiple measures that might be used in holistic evaluation systems and their strengths and weaknesses	198

FOREWORD

Diane Ravitch

Audrey Amrein-Beardsley has written a timely, useful, and important book. She describes and analyzes in great detail the imposition of test-based evaluation of teachers, the theory behind it, the real-life consequences of this strategy, and its fundamental flaws.

This is not just another academic book by a scholar. It is a book written by a highly qualified scholar who worked as a math teacher for several years and understands the connections between theory and practice. More than that, it is a book informed by research and fieldwork. More than that, it is a book in which the author's outrage simmers slightly beneath the surface and occasionally comes into full view, as when she equates the purposeful demoralization of classroom teachers as "intellectual genocide." These are strong words, but they are not used lightly.

Amrein-Beardsley documents the insanity of test-based evaluation, or value-added modeling (VAM). It has been in use in Tennessee for more than 20 years, and it has now been imposed on the nation's public schools by the Obama administration's *Race to the Top* program. Amrein-Beardsley demonstrates that research does not support the use of VAM. The public and educators, she says at one point, have been VAMboozled by the advocates of this method of evaluating teacher quality.

What is known about VAM, she writes, is that it lacks validity and reliability. Some educational researchers support its use, but about 95% do not. Their voices, like the voices of teachers, are ignored by policymakers who think they have found an easy way to judge teacher quality, to hand out bonuses to those with high rankings, and to fire those who have low rankings.

As Amrein-Beardsley shows, the rankings are inaccurate, unstable, and unfair. Those who teach special education or gifted students or English language learners are at high risk of "failing." Only approximately 30% of the teachers are subject to the rankings based on VAM, and many districts give those teachers ratings based on the performance of the whole school, which is unfair and irrational.

No one understands the rankings, least of all the teachers. They get a high score and a bonus one year, a low score and a warning the next year. From their perspective, they have changed nothing in their teaching, and they have no idea why they were better or worse.

As Amrein-Beardsley shows in her fieldwork, Houston relied on VAM and fired teachers who had been recognized as "Teacher of the Month" and "Teacher of the Year" in their school.

If anyone went in search of a way to demoralize teachers and principals and to harm American public education, they could not have found a more valuable tool than VAM. Where sensible nations seek ways to strengthen collaboration among teachers and to improve their practice, we have adopted a strategy that encourages teaching to the test, gaming the system, and setting teacher against teacher.

Audrey Amrein-Beardsley's book could not have arrived at a more propitious moment. It is time for researchers, educators, and the public to recognize the damage now inflicted by federal policy on our nation's teachers and public schools. It is time to end it.

Diane Ravitch

PREFACE

The important thing is not to stop questioning. Curiosity has its own reason for existing.
Albert Einstein

Within the pages of this book is a series of research-based accounts about how the American public education system has, for the past 30 years, been derailed by the same socially engineered theory of educational reform and change; a Measure and Punish (M&P) Theory of Change that has been successively reinvented over the past three decades as politicians and policymakers have tweaked this or that to reform America's purportedly failing public schools. The M&P Theory of Change suggests that by holding districts, schools, teachers, and students accountable for meeting higher standards, as measured by student performance on high-stakes tests, administrators will supervise America's public schools better, teachers will teach better, and as a result students will learn more, particularly in America's lowest performing schools. In this interpretation of utopia, students' test scores will increase, America's global prominence will be reclaimed, and the nation will achieve the rehabilitated educational system and global superiority the public, now, so deeply desires.

The M&P Theory of Change is based on a paucity of empirical research evidence, however. Very few scientific studies have evidenced that this theory of change works. Rather, countless scientific studies have evidenced that the numerous educational policies based on this theory of change have caused unintended consequences. In addition, numerous academic researchers suggest that the negative side effects altogether outweigh the few positive benefits that may have been realized, if at all, post policy.

As well, teachers and principals working in practice under this M&P Theory of Change have much to say about the theory's critical shortcomings, but their voices have often been marginalized, dismissed, or even rejected, particularly when they have been positioned as unprofessional or even recalcitrant when charged with protecting their own self interests or the status quo. While educators working day-to-day in America's public schools would certainly be the best to speak truth to power, particularly about such policies that in theory make sense but in practice make nonsense, their voices too often fall on deaf ears.

Correspondingly, policy attention has now turned to a new set of improved educational measurement systems that can, again in line with the same M&P Theory of Change, improve upon the precision with which we might evaluate teacher (and school/district) effectiveness and more accurately hold educators accountable for doing their jobs and meeting even higher standards (e.g., the new Common Core State Standards currently being implemented across the nation). The M&P Theory of Change continues to hold, but atypically this time as value-added models (VAMs) are simultaneously being positioned at the center of the operations more "scientifically" supporting this same theory of change. Put differently, VAMs are now to help us better navigate the familiar road to utopia, by more appropriately and accurately helping us hold educators responsible for supposedly veering too far off of the same route to reform.

VAMs by definition are designed to isolate and measure teachers' (or schools'/districts') contributions to student learning and achievement on large-scale standardized achievement tests as groups of students move through school from one grade level to the next. VAM statisticians attempt to measure value-added by mathematically calculating the "value" a teacher (or school/district) "adds" to (or detracts from) student achievement scores from the point at which students enter a classroom (or a school/district) to the point they leave. In more precise terms, VAM statisticians attempt to calculate value added by computing the difference between students' composite test scores at these two points in time, after which they compare the added/detracted value (or growth/decline) coefficients to what they predicted beforehand and to the coefficients of other "similar" teachers (or schools/districts) who posted "similar" value-added estimates at the same time. VAM statisticians then position teachers (or schools/districts) accordingly, and typically hierarchically along a categorical yet arbitrary continuum, assigning teachers (or schools/districts) high to low value-added categorizations with negative and positive differences yielding negative and positive value-added classifications respectively. From here, high-stakes decisions (e.g., merit pay, teacher tenure, teacher terminations) can more appropriately and accurately be made, again, so it is assumed.

Yet, here, there is also a paucity of research illustrating that VAMs work in the ways theorized. Rather, a plethora of studies exist in which researchers have evidenced that VAMs cause unintended, perverse consequences instead. Again, evidence indicates that this same M&P Theory of Change, even with its advanced VAM metrics, is still grossly flawed, misguided, and potentially harmful.

As social engineering theory would have it, the new and improved VAM metric systems are continuously bamboozling, or in this case VAMboozling us as a collective society keenly interested in the fate of the American public school system. At the same time, those marketing and selling their VAMs, often for profit, are raking in millions in federal, state, and district monies. That is, not only are we being VAMboozled, we are paying to be VAMboozled as our political leaders continue to use taxpayer revenues to further advance a tested, tried, and untrue, and highly deceptive socially engineered theory of change.

Accordingly, within this book I present everything I think everybody who cares about America's public education system, and in particular this educational accountability trend, needs to know about VAMs. In Part I, I introduce a historical frame and some foundational knowledge, as well as a poignant case in which this VAM-based theory was implemented in practice. More specifically, in Chapter 1, I provide the background to the aforementioned socially engineered theory of change and how this history has brought us to a newly found love affair with VAMs. In Chapter 2, I deliver a series of research-based tales about how VAMs have been adopted and used in practice. Also included is the series of tales about how this theory has thus far fallen short in practice, namely in the Houston Independent School District (HISD). In Chapter 3, I present a national overview capturing what states are doing in terms of adopting VAM-based policies and in terms of the uses and consequences being adopted or mandated as per such policies.

In Part II of the book, I describe a series of "heroic" assumptions (Rubin, Stuart, & Zanutto, 2004) that I believe all involved must understand, and with which all must agree should they buy into VAMs and the VAM-based estimates from which VAM-based inferences are being drawn. Specifically, in Chapter 4, I detail the assumptions that are typically used to rationalize and justify the adoption of VAMs, and in Chapter 5, I dig deeper into the particular test-based, statistical, and methodological assumptions that go along with VAM adoption and use. It should be noted here that these assumptions are widely used not only to promote VAM adoption and use, but also to sell for-profits' and sometimes non-profits' VAM-based systems to states, districts, and local schools. Whether the assumptions discussed are indeed research-based facts and truths is another topic of interest that I explore within both of these chapters as well.

In Part III of this book, I examine the non-traditional issues with the traditional notions of research in education and educational measurement. The notions of interest here include reliability, validity, bias, fairness, and use. More explicitly, in Chapter 6, I present what are, in my opinion, the most major issues that are still impeding the practicality and usability of VAMs. These issues are being caused, primarily, by the instabilities being observed across models and over time when examining VAM-based estimate consistency (i.e., reliability). In addition, I examine all types of validity evidence (e.g., content-, criterion-, construct-, and consequential-related evidence of validity) that also continue to be the source of concern, specifically in terms of how accurate and truthful the inferences being made using VAM estimates might in reality be. In Chapter 7, I present how issues with bias and the non-random assignment of students to classrooms (and teachers to classrooms) are both compounding and complicating these methodological and pragmatic issues further.

In Part IV and in the final chapter of this book, Chapter 8, I explore a series of conventional alternatives and solutions – conventional in the sense that these alternatives and solutions are often and customarily offered by other researchers conducting and disseminating research in this area. Counter-intuitively, I end with an even-more conventional solution that I believe, with some good research evidence in support, might be the best solution available for evaluating and holding teachers accountable for their effectiveness as the professionals they likely are, and we as taxpayers pay them to be.

In short, within this book is everything I have ever read about VAMs in education from both academic and popular outlets, provided here in context and depth for reader consumption.

Fittingly, because this is probably the hottest and most controversial topic surrounding current debates about educational reform, there is a lot to be said. Conducting a Google search for "value-added models," for example, yields approximately 40 million results, while searching for "value-added models in education" yields approximately 16 million results. While I have certainly not read everything available on the topic, as this would be an impossible task, I have read probably more than most educational researchers conducting research in this area (see, for example, the over 600 references in the reference list). In addition, not one day has gone by while I was writing this book during which two or three new research manuscripts, newspaper articles, blog entries, webinars, or other informational pieces about VAMs have been made public online (or on paper), on which I have also kept up to keep this book as current as humanly possible. While there will certainly be pieces of information that I have missed by the time this book is published, keeping up with the literature in this area has been a continual task, as has been condensing everything "of value" in terms of the literature on this topic.

Ultimately, these efforts should help allow consumers, including readers from the school-house to the White House, become better educated and empowered to make more informed decisions about the VAMs being adopted with rapidity across the country. It is imperative that the major and minor issues that pertain to VAMs, and the issues that continue to inhibit VAM practicality be understood before more educators and policymakers blindly buy into VAM-based systems. Without accurate, research-based, and unbiased information about both the intended and the unintended consequences of the VAMs ruling supreme over all other contemporary measurement and test-based accountability systems, Americans will continue to be VAMboozled by such VAM-based policies. That said, I hope to afford readers a user-friendly academic guide to help them navigate and better understand VAMs.

However, I do reserve the right to speak truth to power as I aptly, genuinely, justly, and *not* dispassionately see it. For in writing this book, I embrace my professional obligation and moral imperative as one of a handful of academic researchers analyzing the intended, and one of very few academic researchers analyzing the unintended, effects of VAMs. I also embrace this imperative as a former public school teacher, noting that not many people (if any) who are advocating for, advancing, or even working on VAM methods and the statistics used to capture educator/educational effectiveness have ever set foot in a classroom, much less attempted to understand the realities and complexities that come along with teaching, especially in some of the nation's highest needs schools. Just because many of the people advancing and promoting VAM-based policies for America's public schools have likely been students themselves in America's private or perhaps public schools, this does not an educational expert make! Not to mention a successful educational researcher, and certainly not a successful educational reformer.

I am proud and honored to say that I am a former mathematics teacher with seven years of grade 7–12 teaching experience, teaching mathematics in both public middle and high schools to students who were (and still are) highly at-risk. I also have 15 years of educational research experience, through which, given my background in mathematics, I also bring what I believe is an atypical scientific perspective, particularly in terms of using statistics and educational measurement techniques to understand and explain phenomena, especially in the social sciences of which education is a part. I believe that numbers are often socially constructed, but they are not nearly often enough understood or interpreted as such. This perspective also resonates throughout this book, as it should, because this is so often misunderstood. As Albert Einstein so brilliantly put it, "As far as the laws of mathematics refer to reality, they are not certain, and as far as they are certain, they do not refer to reality." With this assertion, I certainly align.

In the case of VAMs, it seems that our "excessive attention to quantitative data *impedes* – rather than aids – in-depth understanding of [these] social phenomena" (Quintero, 2012). When researchers look for answers where they believe the data are better, "rather than where the truth is most likely to lie," this has been otherwise called the "streetlight effect."

According to Freedman (2010):

> The fundamental error here is summed up in an old joke scientists love to tell. Late at night, a police officer finds a drunk man crawling around on his hands and knees under a streetlight. The drunk man tells the officer he's looking for his wallet. When the officer asks if he's sure this is where he dropped the wallet, the man replies that he thinks he more likely dropped it across the street. Then why are you looking over here? the befuddled officer asks. Because the light's better here, explains the drunk man.

Figure 0.2 A drunk man under a streetlight.

The drunk is in good company here. Researchers often do not question whether they are looking for the right answers in the right places, they just defer to where they might find what they perceive as the best, and in this case most objective answers available, regardless of where else perhaps better and more accurate answers might exist. "Many, and possibly most, scientists spend their careers looking for answers where the light is better rather than where the truth is more likely to lie ... [all the while] ... hoping it turns out to be relevant" (Freedman, 2010). With this contention I also wholeheartedly agree, particularly in the case of VAMs. Correspondingly, I continue to position my research given my beliefs about what mathematics and statistics can and cannot do, particularly when used in isolation of other related, valid, and supportive data.

That said, I write here, definitely with passion and I hope some lucidity, but with the honest goal to let the readers be their own judges on the usability of VAMs and what they promise and contend for America's public schools and public school students. Take in, understand, think critically, and (hopefully) engage!

ACKNOWLEDGMENTS

When thinking throughout the year while writing this book about whom I would like to acknowledge for helping me, the person in the first position never changed. While no longer with us in the physical world, I will forever acknowledge my father, Dr. Roy Amrein, as the person who has had the greatest influence on me as a person and as a scholar. I know he is still with me, watching over me, and providing me with his guidance, encouragement, support, and undying love. I know I have made him proud!

I would also like to acknowledge my mom, Sharon Amrein, for she too, with her kind heart, patience, sense of caring, cute sense of humor, unconditional love, and calm demeanor, has influenced me greatly; and my brother, Dr. Derek Amrein, who is so similar to my mom, and who likewise has positively influenced me throughout our years as siblings. I would like to acknowledge him specifically for his kindness, thoughtfulness, enthusiasm, sense of humor, and his enduring dedication to our family, especially since the loss of our dad.

I also want to acknowledge my husband of now 10 years, Richard Beardsley, who is not only an amazing husband, but a wonderful father to our two children, Aidan and Blythe, and my two stepdaughters, Jessica and Alicia. If it was not for him, and the inordinate amounts of time and energy he took to protect me and my writing throughout the year, in many instances taking on all parenting roles and responsibilities, I might have lost my sense of self, not to mention my sense of mind. Related, I would like to acknowledge Aidan and Blythe for being such wonderful children and always making me laugh and smile, sharing with me their warmth and love, and helping me also keep perspective of the things that really matter most in my life. The two of them are and forever will be my best and most favorite accomplishments! I would also like to acknowledge Jessica for her generosity and her spirit and flare, and Alicia for her selflessness, helpfulness, and genuine kindness. They have also helped me in their own unique ways, often keeping me stable and sane as well.

As for those who helped me more directly with the book, I would like to thank Dr. Tom Haladyna for his editorial assistance, and general advice, guidance, and prudence, especially in terms of his knowledge and expertise in educational measurement, testing and assessment, and statistics. In addition, I will forever acknowledge my main and everlasting mentor, Dr. David Berliner. He and I have now worked closely together for 15 years. I am sure those who know, or know of, David understand that I could not have asked for a better, wiser, more insightful, and more ardent mentor and friend. Similarly, I will forever acknowledge one of my other eternal mentors, Dr. Gene Glass. His brilliance I will continuously find inspiring. Thanks are also in order for Dr. Chris Clark who helped me find the strength and inspiration to get this book off of the ground.

Thanks also to former public school teacher and current value-added specialist, Dr. Sarah Polasky, who helped me edit every chapter herein, even one week after recovering from the birth of her second child. Thanks are also in order for former public school teacher (and soon to be Dr.) Jessica Holloway-Libell. As my graduate research assistant, she too offered me the prompt editorial assistance and intellectual insight that (hopefully) will also make this book what I have set it out to be. To my other graduate student, (soon to be Dr.) Noelle Paufler and her husband Tibor, thanks are in order for both of them and their creative assistance with many of the figures, images, and illustrations included herein. Thanks also go out to Dr. Kent Sabo and Dr. Shelby Maier for their similar contributions. And to my former graduate student, Dr. Clarin Collins, many thanks for sharing the same passion for this research, particularly in the Houston Independent School District (HISD) from which some of this research evolved.

Within the Mary Lou Fulton Teachers College at Arizona State University, I must acknowledge the colleagues whom I also admire and treasure. Most importantly, I would like to acknowledge Dean Mari Koerner. As the Dean she has supported me the most. Not only is she a great leader, she is also an amazing friend who always keeps me laughing. And thanks to my other good friends and colleagues at ASU: Drs. Anna Arici Barab, Wendy Barnard, David Carlson, Gustavo Fischman, David Garcia, Ida Malian, Suzanne Painter, Jeanne Powers, Joe Ryan, Frank Serafini, and Kate Weber. I honestly love what I do, in great part because I get to work with wonderfully smart, bright, enthusiastic, inspiring, and often-amusing colleagues like all of you!

Finally, to the three practitioners who have also helped me throughout this journey. To Robert Morse, also a local public school practitioner, who helped me make this book and its at times highly complex material as (hopefully) comprehensible as possible. To one of my best friends from the fifth grade, Andrea Stark, for keeping my academic perspective grounded in the current everyday situations of the American public school teacher every time we get together. And to my sister-in-law, Michele Amrein, a former public school teacher turned teacher educator who has also had a keen sense for "keeping it real."

My father would also have been so proud of the person she has become, as he was always so passionate about us contributing to America's public school system and, in particular, dedicating our lives to serve its purpose as per its Thomas Jeffersonian roots. As my father would have said, could he have said so himself, "An educated citizenry is a vital requisite for our survival as a free people." To acknowledge all public school teachers and what they continue to strive to do for us in service to, and in protection of, our democratic liberties, and despite the prevailing forces continuously working against them, thank you also for everything you do.

PART I
Introduction

1

SOCIALLY ENGINEERING THE ROAD TO UTOPIA

So long as there are men there will be wars.

Albert Einstein

The summer before I began writing this book I spent time with my family traveling in Asia, throughout the remarkable landmarks of China, the rainforests and rice fields of Vietnam, the pristine beaches and waters of Thailand, and the beautiful but war-ravaged and still war-recovering Cambodia. While the whole trip was indeed moving, what I found most inspiring was our time well spent in Cambodia. Walking the ancient temples of Angkor Wat, meeting some of the kindest people in the world, especially given their palpable Buddhist and Hindu principles and beliefs, and experiencing everything we possibly could of Cambodian culture.

To my chagrin, I did not know until my arrival (or recall from my courses in world history) that the country recently survived one of the bloodiest genocides in history, one that occurred as recently as 1975 at the end of the Vietnam War, following America's invasion of Cambodia and following Nixon's carpet bombing of the Viet Cong occupying the country's eastern borders (see Figure 1.1).

Soon after America withdrew its forces, the country's capital city, Phnom Penh, fell, and the communist regime of the Khmer Rouge ascended. If you recall the Academy Award winning movie, *The Killing Fields*, you might remember the story, and the true account of a Cambodian photojournalist, Dith Pran, who befriended the *New York Times* correspondent, Sydney Schanberg. Schanberg by happenstance abandoned Pran nearing tyrant Pol Pot's bloody "Year Zero" takeover and cleansing campaign (Putnam, Smith, & Joffé, 1984).

The idea behind the "Year Zero" crusade was that in order for the communist Khmer Rouge regime to rule supreme (1975–1979), everything including the country's cultures, traditions, and many of its people had to be purged. This led to "necessary violence" and mass genocide which claimed the lives of approximately two million objectionable civilians of the then nearly eight million who resided in the country. The "undesirables" who were targeted and ultimately executed (or died of starvation, disease, torture, or in labor camps in the killing fields) included the country's most educated, specifically Cambodia's professors and teachers,

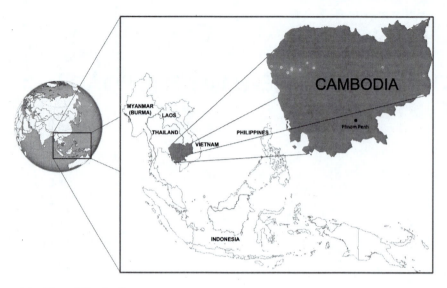

Figure 1.1   Map of Cambodia.

doctors, lawyers, police and businessmen and women, artists, musicians, writers, and the like. All who were deemed professionals, intellectuals, or even literate because they wore eyeglasses were pejoratively viewed as oppressive and subversive, and singled out for extermination. They were besieged for their alleged capacities to resist the Khmer Rouge's ultimate end – a utopian, self-sufficient, agriculturally focused, ethnically pure, and classless, communist-controlled state.

While the Cambodian photojournalist, Pran, was one of the "undesirables," he barely survived, undercover as his peasant alter ego – an uneducated taxi cab driver. He eventually escaped by walking his way out of the killing fields, only to discover that more than 50 of his family members had been killed. He lived the rest of his life working in the U.S. as a photographer for the *New York Times* and relentlessly promoting global awareness about the Cambodian Holocaust. He passed away in 2008 at the age of 65, with his horrific thoughts and memories "still alive to [him] day and night" (Dith Pran, 2004; see also Farrell & Rummel, 2008; Martin, 2008). In his "Last Words" interview with the *New York Times*, Pran noted that "in order to survive, you [had] to pretend to be stupid, because they [did not] want you to be smart. They [thought] that the smart people [would] destroy them … you [had] to show that you [were] not a threat to [survive]" (Farrell & Rummel, 2008). The Khmer Rouge's attempts to contrive and influence attitudes and social behaviors by cleansing (i.e., social engineering by genocide) still haunt the Cambodian people today.

What is resounding is that mass murder and methodical cruelty as preludes to utopia have occurred in many ways during many times and in many parts of the world in the past. Social engineering by genocide, whether via religious, racial, ethnic, or national group cleansing, is not a new historical phenomenon. In terms of religious cleansing, during the Middle Ages, a period generally fraught with intellectual obscurity and atrocity, inquisitional courts implicated, indicted, and burned at the stake perceived heretics who spoke out about or against, or thought differently from the politically dominant Catholic Church. With regards to racial cleansing, within the last century the Nazi-sponsored Holocaust aimed to completely exterminate the Jewish race, the race that according to Hitler was not a religion. This ultimately resulted in the execution of six million Jews and the slaying of five million other "undesirables" including homosexuals, gypsies, people with disabilities, and other political and religious adversaries. Regarding ethnic cleansing, just 20 years ago, nearly one million people in Rwanda were murdered due to ethnic tensions between the Tutsi and Hutu peoples. Concerning national groups, America's actions in the name of Manifest Destiny are also considered by many to qualify as social engineering by genocide. The numbers of Native Americans and Mexican nationals who perished during times of rationalized expansion and redemption are comparable to the fatalities recorded during the Nazi-sponsored Holocaust (Cesarani, 2004; see also Smith, 2013).

While all these persecutors used various forms of genocide to socially engineer the roads to their interpretations of utopia, however, none of these instances matched what occurred in Cambodia, not in terms of the sheer numbers of deaths or types of terror, but in terms of goals and objectives. The Khmer Rouge's deliberate and systematic efforts to destroy a group of perceived intellectuals (not to say that these groups were not intellectuals themselves) and the regime's efforts to extinguish their allegedly threatening and abhorred ideas, add much to our thinking about intellectual genocide and social engineering. In Cambodia, intellectual genocide was used to promote communism, thwart any hopes or prospects of a democratic state, and turn the country over to a state of the people, where the people were defined as the country's workers, farmers, laborers, and peasants. In the end, the Khmer Rouge's aims and actions to exterminate all intellectuals and socially engineer a totalitarian and utopian dictatorship devastated the country instead. The country is still in the process of healing and recovery (Jenkins, 2012).

Social engineering in the political sciences

However, while social engineering is often viewed negatively, particularly, for obvious reasons, in cases of social engineering by intellectual, religious, race, ethnic, or national group genocide), social engineering by other means is quite common in the political sciences. Most governmental and private groups, in their efforts to promote or protect private or the public's perceived interests, attempt to methodically sway or change public attitudes and behaviors in one way or another. While the goal remains the same – to control or influence society, the polis, or city-state by eliminating or reducing human agency or agents (Marx, 1995) – in the political sciences, social engineering relies on more subtle means. Here, social engineers use other powerful instruments to influence attitudes and social behaviors, ultimately to promote and promulgate a societal, oft-utopian ideal. Social engineering tools include scare tactics; propaganda and rhetoric often vetted through mass media outlets; generalizations, assumptions, and rationalizations; and incentives and disincentives to ultimately engineer the social behaviors desired.

It should be mentioned that social engineering is not always adversarial, however. For example, at the end of the Civil War, President Abraham Lincoln used highly controversial tactics to socially engineer the country's path to free the slaves of the Confederate South. His notorious actions, along with his remarkable leadership, led to his Emancipation Proclamation of 1863, which ultimately led to the adoption of the Thirteenth Amendment to the U.S. Constitution in 1865. This made slavery and involuntary servitude illegal throughout the U.S. This serves as a prime example of how governmental policies also constitute a powerful social engineering tool, again when control is the means and a utopian ideal the end.

The emancipation of the slaves in the South was certainly at the time utopian, while more often than not perceived as impractical and unreasonable.

By definition, a public policy is in itself a tool used by governments to define a course of action that will ultimately lead to a high-level, supreme, and desirable end. Sometimes public policies can be unwise, however, when seemingly principled means produce unintended, unanticipated, and perverse consequences instead. Often, the inadvertent effects outweigh the intended consequences for which the policy was engineered in the first place, as social engineers' attempts to control and alter their environments are imperfect and often contradict or distort what is virtuous, pure, and good (Campbell, 1976; Wheatley, 1992).

In 1962, for example, Rachel Carson published her acclaimed book *Silent Spring* – the book now widely credited with initiating the environmental movement and the founding of the Environmental Protection Agency. In it, Carson wrote lucidly and passionately about the U.S. Department of Agriculture's assault on the environment. She criticized the department for turning a blind eye, and disregarding the many empirical research studies from which she drew her conclusions but that were not new or inaccessible, just conveniently ignored (Griswold, 2012). She also criticized the department's ignorant and purchased acceptance of the chemical industry's oratorical, "research-based," and lobbied claims that their synthetic pesticides, from which they were profiting, were the best to control and kill agricultural pests. In fact, the government's excessive spraying of DDT (dichlorodiphenyltrichloroethane) was at one time so universally accepted that the public forgot to question its use. That is, until Carson wrote *Silent Spring*, which ultimately led to the banning of DDT in 1972, at least in the domestic U.S.A.[1]

Here, the public, having been socially conditioned, naïvely trusted that simply because the pesticide was familiar, it was safe and effective. The public's opinion had been socially engineered into believing DDT and other harsh pesticides were necessary and harmless. Unfortunately, however, what ended up being destroyed were the ecosystems into which the pesticides were introduced.

The culprits included those who socially engineered the severity of the problem, those who amplified public alarm about the problem, those who chemically manufactured the solution to the problem, those who marketed false promises about the solution to the problem, and those who subsequently profited by having provided the best, if not only solution to the problem turned severe. The unintended effect was that what the government and industrialists provided to control the problem caused effects markedly worse than the problem needing to be controlled in the first place (agricultural pests). Metaphorically speaking, the spring had gone silent because of the absence of the non-pest wildlife that the synthetic pesticides also killed (Carson, 1962; Griswold, 2012; see also Amrein-Beardsley, 2009b).

Social engineering via the use of federal and state tax policies to encourage or discourage societal behaviors has also become commonplace. This is especially true with the U.S. Department of the Treasury and its use of tax credits, breaks, deductions, and exemptions since the passage of the Tax Reform Act of 1986. The rationale is that via the tax system and its provisions, many societal behaviors and activities can be encouraged using incentives for things like charitable giving, homeownership, and the purchase of health insurance. Similarly, many societal behaviors and activities can be discouraged through disincentives like "sin" taxes to reduce alcohol and tobacco use or gambling. More recently "fat" taxes have been designed and introduced to curb the sedentary activities seen as contributing to America's obesity epidemic. Empirical evidence substantiating that the use of federal and state tax policies to encourage or discourage, or socially engineer these or other societal behaviors in fact works is scarce, however.

The most obvious of unintended consequences that come along with such (dis)incentive systems are tax distortions. Such distortions often come about as a result of system gaming techniques, whereby for those who are best equipped to understand and manipulate the incentives and disincentives put into place can exploit them to their advantage. Take, for example, the recent scandal with Apple Inc., whereby Apple CEO Tim Cook and associates have continued to use opposing taxation loopholes in Ireland and the U.S. to avoid paying billions in taxes. The U.S. Senate subcommittee investigating Apple also investigated Microsoft, Hewlett-Packard, and other multinational companies, charging that they too have exploited loopholes in the U.S. federal tax code avoiding billions in U.S. taxes as well (Associated Press, 2013).

The unintended effects that come along with such (dis)incentive systems then become cyclical. When the distortions are recognized and new tax policies are devised and implemented to offset and disincentivize the distortions discovered, the perceptibly more reasonable and sound tax remedies cause yet another series of unintended effects, and the cycle continues. This is precisely why many of the country's finest tax experts strongly discourage social engineering via federal and state tax policies (Lazear & Poterba, 2006; see also Chamberlain, 2005). The U.S. Department of the Treasury's attempts to control or influence society, the polis, or the city-state by using social engineering tools has not, for the most part, worked in the ways intended and has rather caused loopholes that simply cannot be closed.

City planning, housing, and transportation policies have also been devised to engineer the social world, namely to protect certain social environments and to reinforce the artificial borders within which various social classes reside. For example, the U.S. Department of Housing and Urban Development's strategies of the not-so-distant past were put into place to keep lower-income people out of certain areas via residential segregation. This has been supported by the strategic planning of urban and suburban areas, the U.S. Federal Housing Administration's former redlining policies, and the clever planning of public transportation systems, or more specifically city bus and subway routes and stops between, for example, Washington DC and Georgetown, Boston and Lexington, and New York City and Newark, New Jersey. Inter-area transports were once calculatedly devised to deter inter-neighborhood migration and to further segregate groups of (poor) people, and to keep them from other (wealthy) groups of people. This stimulated and resulted in residential segregation, which understandably led to other forms of segregation, racism, and classism given the other demographic variables that are still highly correlated with neighborhood and community characteristics (i.e., racial, ethnic, nationality, language, and social class characteristics). This also led to increased discrimination in that these groups became more susceptible to prejudicial treatment, having been increasingly defined by geographic borders and having become more concentrated and isolated than before.

Collectively, these interrelated conditions perpetuated even greater levels of un- and under-employment and, accordingly, higher levels of per capita poverty. This led to increased rates of violence, crime, and other anti-social behaviors over time (e.g., illegal drug use, non-compliance and disobedience, defiant behaviors toward authority, etc.). Likewise, those geographically marginalized unendingly had more difficulties gaining entry into decent jobs that would better help them "pull themselves up by their bootstraps," and increase their earning power and cultural and human capital, and improve upon their subsequent chances to succeed (see also Berliner, 2012). These conditions inhibited access to quality healthcare, typically as a result of a lack of or no medical or dental insurance, to affordable housing and other basic services and resources, and to early childhood and higher educational opportunities. All of these and other interrelated conditions contributed to the increased ghettoization of urban neighborhoods throughout the U.S. (Anyon, 1997; Kozol, 2005; Marx, 1995; see also Caro, 1975 for an account illustrating how Robert Moses used his power to (mis)shape the city and state of New York).

Combined with "white flight" (i.e., the movement of typically white, European American people from highly concentrated urban to suburban areas), this also contributed to the increased segregation of America's public schools in these neighborhoods. This has been most aptly illustrated in Jonathon Kozol's books (see, for example, Kozol, 1991, 1995, 2000, 2005).

Nonetheless, while policies and laws have been enacted since to counter the negative effects of these dystopian policies (e.g., fair housing laws, revoking "separate but equal" strategies, educational desegregation laws following *Brown v. Board of Education* in 1954), it is quite clear that these compensatory and restorative policies have had little consequence. In New York City, for example, half of the city's 1,600 schools currently have enrollments that are over 90% Hispanic/Latino(a) and black (Fessenden, 2012). It is certainly clear that racial segregation still exists and that current federal and local policies continue to perpetuate such problems (see also Berliner, 2012; Orfield, 2009).

Social engineering in American educational policy

It is also certainly clear that federal and local educational policies (e.g., district and school zoning, charter and magnet schools, open enrollment, vouchers and other choice policies, policies promoting the privatization of America's public schools) continue to perpetuate these societal problems (Boustan, 2011; Eaton & Rivkin, 2010; Kozol, 2005; Street, 2005). Added to the burden of such educational policies, it is also dauntingly difficult in poor communities to recruit and retain highly effective teachers, especially given inequitable teacher salaries and benefits. It is also difficult to secure, construct, and maintain sufficient educational facilities; to obtain and sustain quality resources and technologies and the highly effective teachers who know how to use such resources in instructionally relevant and efficacious ways; to hire and retain highly effective school administrators in progressive leadership positions; to promote decent levels of parent, family, and community support and involvement, and the like. The absence of these conditions clearly thwarts school achievement and inhibits the opportunities for students to learn in schools situated in poor, segregated communities (Anyon, 1997; Berliner, 2010, 2012; Biddle, 2001; Eaton, 2007; hooks, 2000; Katz, 1989; Kozol, 1991, 1995, 2000, 2005; Nieto & Bode, 2008). This is yet another tale of policies that have been socially engineered and implemented because they make sense, ideologically and theoretically, but that generate unintended, unanticipated, and perverse consequences instead.

Within education, there have also been federal and local educational policies many attribute to politically conservative governmental and private attempts at social engineering. The U.S. continues to reintroduce the teaching of phonics in classrooms, not based on the research evidence but driven by a back-to-basics ethos, eternally taking the country back to the Victorian era when phonics was first introduced. This concept has socially engineered itself so deeply into our thinking about reading/language arts instruction that the U.S. can hardly break free from its primitive logic. As well, politically conservative policies supporting the use of English-only in schools, and preventing various forms of bilingual education, have been attributed to governmental attempts to socially engineer an English-only, English-first society. Even school uniforms have been mandated at schools to deter or control materialism and gang affiliations or activities, and to increase student achievement. Yet, as Goodman (2006) notes, there is no scientific evidence whatsoever supporting the claim that dress codes increase student achievement or deter much of anything (see also Simonson, 1998). Yet the public still sees this as a rational approach to reach a commonsense end. As well, conservative public and private pundits immortalize these views using the same social engineering tools of the past, available at their discretion (e.g., scare tactics; propaganda and rhetoric; generalizations, assumptions, and rationalizations).

A paradigm case

The federal report *A Nation at Risk* serves as the paradigm case of social engineering by rationalistic means in American education. In 1983, the National Commission on Education released *A Nation at Risk* (U.S. Department of Education, 1983) in which the commission argued that schools in the U.S. were performing poorly in comparison to other industrialized nations and that our national security was therefore in jeopardy. This fear had been lingering since the Russians beat the Americans to space with their successful launch of Sputnik in 1957. However, in *A Nation at Risk*, the perpetrators of our national frailties – America's public schools – were at last named. Citing lower than expected national and international student test scores, deterioration in school quality, a diluted and diffused curriculum (particularly in mathematics and the sciences), and setbacks on other indicators of America's pre-eminence, the commission triggered a nationwide panic. They prompted anxiety and alarm about the weakening condition of the American public school system and, consequently, the nation's global supremacy and economic dominance.

Soon thereafter, Berliner and Biddle (1995) scientifically and effectively demonstrated that the claims made in *A Nation at Risk* were erroneous and grossly exaggerated (see also Berliner, 2011). They demonstrated that America's low but still above average test scores were more related to the demographics of the nation, as compared to the other industrialized nations that participated in the international tests. They exposed instead the very real problems impeding greater success in America's public schools and demonstrated that, despite the evidence, the federal government set out to "manufacture" or socially engineer a "crisis" about the American public school system.

Nonetheless, the commission's *A Nation at Risk* still had a massive impact. The report undeniably changed the general public's opinions and attitudes about the American public school system, for the first time in history, in line with the alleged desires of its social engineers. Its effects still echo today.

Increased accountability for results

Out of *A Nation at Risk* the stronger accountability movement was born. It resulted in a spirited move towards more rigorous standards and increased accountability mechanisms, both of which were to help bring the nation out of its perceived (and, as argued, socially engineered) educational crisis. The commission recommended that states institute higher standards to homogenize and improve curricula and administer large-scale standardized achievement tests more frequently to hold students and educators accountable for meeting those standards. It was at this time that Koretz (1996) noted that the nation began relying almost solely on measurement-driven educational policies to turn around what was perceived, and now tangibly feared, as America's failing public school system and slipping supremacy.

Thereafter, nearly every state developed its own enhanced standards, testing, and accountability policies, all of which focused primarily on increasing student achievement on states' large-scale standardized achievement tests, as well as requiring the kind of instruction (i.e., focused on basic skills and facts) that was thought necessary to increase student achievement on these tests (Center on Organization and Restructuring of Schools, 1995; Meyer, 1997). The Measure and Punish (M&P) Theory of Change was that by holding districts, schools, teachers, and students accountable for performance on the states' large-scale standardized achievement tests, administrators would supervise the schools better, teachers would teach better, and students would learn more, particularly in the nation's lowest performing schools. Soon thereafter, students' test scores would increase, the nation's prominence would be reclaimed, and the nation would achieve the utopian society that was now so deeply desired (see Figure 1.2).

Ironically, thanks to those who socially engineered and successfully engrained this rational systems theory of educational improvement into the minds of so many, and most importantly into the consciousness of policymakers on both sides of the partisan divide, the same M&P

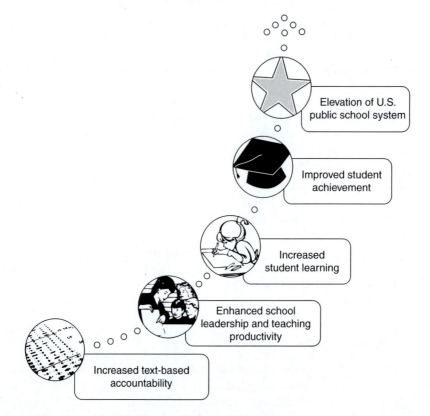

Elevation of U.S. public school system

Improved student achievement

Increased student learning

Enhanced school leadership and teaching productivity

Increased text-based accountability

Figure 1.2 Measure and Punish Theory of Change logic map.

Theory of Change continues to hold. In fact, it continues to shape the thinking of America's educational policymakers today.

This is likely because it is such an overly simplistic causal model, while a better, more fully explicated causal model would be much more difficult to understand and, more importantly, difficult to defend. A more realistic interpretation of the M&P logic would focus not just on teachers and administrators but the other agents of change at play. These include but are not limited to: (a) students' levels of intelligence, prior academic achievements and experiences, and aptitudes; (b) students' levels of social capital, as first defined by Hanifan (1916) as "those tangible substances [that] count for most in the daily lives of people" (p. 130); and (c) students' levels of risk. This last I define, here and throughout this book, as the populations of students in schools who, disproportionately to their low-risk peers, have emotional/learning disabilities and/or come from high-needs, high-poverty, English-language deficient, culturally isolated (e.g., inner-cities, hoods, ghettoes, enclaves, and American Indian reservations), and often racial/ethnic minority backgrounds; although, it should be noted that a large number of students at risk are not students of color. Such major factors unquestionably complicate the overly simplistic M&P Theory of Change, but these factors must be overlooked should simplistic solutions continue to be sought, not to mention perpetually pursued.

Since the turn of the millennium, this has been most notably evidenced through the passage of the No Child Left Behind Act (NCLB, 2002), the Obama administration's proposal to revise the Elementary and Secondary Education Act (ESEA) and to "reform" NCLB (U.S. Department of Education, 2010a), and most recently via the federal *Race to the Top* (RttT) initiative (RttT, 2011). Billions of dollars in federal stimulus monies have already been and continue to be awarded to states – $4.35 billion being the initial sum budgeted for RttT (Duncan, 2009a). In line with the same M&P Theory of Change, the states receiving RttT awards, in exchange for these desperately needed federal funds had to promise to use students' test scores for even more consequential purposes, especially for teacher evaluation, termination, and compensation. The 40 states that applied for RttT funds in the first year of funding also had to agree to adopt even stronger accountability mechanisms if they were to secure waivers excusing them from not meeting NCLB's improbable goal that 100% of the students in their schools would be academically proficient by the year 2014. This too was a utopian, albeit still distant target, one to which every state in the nation[2] was predicted to fall far short (Dillon, 2010b; Duncan, 2011; Layton, 2012).

Notwithstanding, within any of these documents one can find the familiar legends and myths of a golden age of American education: that schools in the U.S. were once internationally superior but no longer are; that other industrialized nations are outperforming the country that was once the best in the world; that America must raise its expectations of students, teachers, and administrators and hold them more responsible for doing their jobs and meeting even higher expectations; and that the nation must do a better job at penalizing failure and rewarding success (just as the marketplace penalizes laziness and rewards hard work). Paradoxically, these are the reasons still being used to justify America's newly "reenvisioned federal role in education" (U.S. Department of Education, 2010b), re-envisioned again just three years ago, despite the fact that a nearly identical version and nearly indistinguishable vision was introduced 30 years ago in *A Nation at Risk* (U.S. Department of Education, 1983).

Not-so-temporary insanity

According to Albert Einstein, the definition of insanity is to repeat the same behaviors over and over again in the hope that different results will materialize the next time, perhaps after this is fiddled with or that is fine-tuned. Here, it seems, educational policymakers propagating and regenerating policies based on the same M&P Theory of Change are epitomizing insanity. For the past 30 years they have repeatedly justified nearly the same policy actions while using nearly the same social engineering instruments as the means to justify their anticipated ends.

These tools include the same scare tactics (e.g., about America's accelerating inferiority); rhetoric (e.g., the titles *A Nation at Risk, No Child Left Behind,* and *Race to the Top* in themselves); propaganda (e.g., the federal education administration paying a prominent African American authority $240,000 to promote NCLB on a nationally syndicated television show; Toppo, 2005); generalizations, assumptions, and rationalizations (e.g., what is needed is greater authoritative control, higher standards and accountability, and an expanded application of business model thinking in education); and incentives (e.g., tuition waivers for students, salary bonuses for teachers and administrators) and disincentives (e.g., prevention of student grade-to-grade promotion or high school graduation, teacher dismissal, administrator termination, school closure).

Yet an overwhelming preponderance of empirical evidence indicates that this M&P Theory of Change is grossly flawed and misguided, and has not yielded its intended effects, ever! This theory of change has never improved the nation's global standing, nor has it positively impacted the ever-persistent achievement gap (i.e., the observed disparities between students with relatively low or high levels of poverty or who are typically Asian American and white versus their African American, Hispanic/Latino(a), and American Indian peers).

Nor has this theory of change ever improved the test scores used across the nation to determine college admissions decisions (e.g., SAT or ACT scores), high school graduation rates, college going rates or levels of preparedness, and the like (Amrein & Berliner, 2002; Au, 2009; Haney, 2000; Heubert & Hauser, 1999; Hursh, 2008; Johnson, Johnson, Farenga, & Ness, 2005; Klein, Hamilton, McCaffrey, & Stecher, 2000; Mathis, 2011; Nichols & Berliner, 2007; Nichols, Glass, & Berliner, 2012; Orfield & Kornhaber, 2001; Timar & Maxwell-Jolly, 2012).

Relatedly, many early proponents of this M&P Theory of Change have since become its strongest opponents. This has happened specifically since the passage of NCLB as they themselves observed the absence of NCLB's intended effects and the presence of (too many) unintended consequences in their place. For example, more than 50 Republican House and Senate members took issue specifically with NCLB's testing mandates, noting the mandates' lack of intended but abundance of unintended, perverse consequences instead (Weisman & Paley, 2007). Republicans in Texas, the state that then Governor George W. Bush used as a petri dish to culture NCLB for the nation (following former Texas Governor Ross Perot's lead), have recently turned against its high-stakes testing components as well (Pauken, 2013). Diane Ravitch, one of the ardent crafters of NCLB, and for years a devoted advocate, has since made it her mission in life to undo its effects. Not a day passes during which she does not contribute to the evidence base confirming that NCLB (2002), the reauthorization of the Elementary and Secondary Education Act (U.S. Department of Education, 2010a), the *Race to the Top* initiative (RttT, 2011), and the whole M&P Theory of Change are doing more harm than good (Ravitch, 2010a; see also Denby, 2012; Mathews, 2013).

It should be noted, however, that a few academic researchers disagree with the research majority who have collectively demonstrated that this theory of change does not work. They have empirically argued their points with counterfactuals (Chetty, Friedman, & Rockoff, 2011; Hanushek, 2011; Hanushek & Raymond, 2005; Raymond & Hanushek, 2003; Stotsky, Bradley, & Warren, 2005; Winters, Trivitt, & Greene, 2010). As well, a handful of other highly politicized proponents have argued (and continue to argue) that the theory of change works, although they have argued their cases on less scientific and more dogmatic grounds (Coleman as featured in Lewin, 2012 and in Rotherham, 2011;[3] Kress, 2011;[4] Phelps, 2011;[5] Rhee, 2011;[6] Spellings, 2012[7]).

Altogether, they continue to advance the theory's hyper-reliance on large-scale standardized achievement tests, the tests that along with high-stakes consequences are (still) to be used as both the positive and negative motivators (still) needed to increase the (still) substandard levels of student performance (still) at issue. The irony here is that, again, research evidencing that these policies have ever borne their intended fruit is (still) very much absent. We as a collective nation still have grave concerns about our international presence and dominance. These are the same grave concerns we had after the commission released *A Nation at Risk* (U.S. Department of Education, 1983) 30 years ago, and despite the fact that federal and state educational policymakers have relied on this M&P Theory of Change to improve America's education condition since. Actually, state-level policies aligned with this theory of change have been around even longer than 30 years.[8]

Intellectual genocide

What is worse is that, akin to the intellectual genocide witnessed in Cambodia, as a result of this M&P Theory of Change and the federal and state policies implemented to uphold it, large groups of students have been categorically stripped of their inalienable (yet not U.S. constitutional) rights to an equal, fair, appropriate, and proper education. Policymakers in nearly every state have now adopted even higher standards and even stronger high-stakes testing policies to keep the higher standards in check, although the seriousness of the state policies and the severity of the consequences or stakes attached to test output still vary by state (Nichols et al., 2012).

Notwithstanding, since the passage of NCLB annual state spending on large-scale standardized achievement tests rose from $423 million in 2002 to almost $1.1 billion in 2008. This represents a 162% increase compared to a 20% increase in inflation over the same time period (Vu, 2008). Most recently it was estimated that we now spend well over $1.7 billion on tests, although this is likely a gross underestimate given that such estimates traditionally account only for state- not district- or school-level tests. This also excludes the costs that come along with tests' associated resources (e.g., test preparation packets, workbooks, and materials) and other related costs (e.g., administrative and instructional time costs for test preparation; Cody, 2012). Most importantly, this illustrates that we as a nation, and our politicians on behalf of us as a nation, are placing a good amount of our taxpayers' bets on a bankrupt theory of change.

Furthermore, with the wide-scale adoption of these policies, many students, especially those being educated in the country's lowest performing schools, have been unremittingly deprived of opportunities to learn in ways that are not driven by large-scale standardized achievement tests. Since the passage of NCLB, many students, especially those in the country's lowest performing schools, have been increasingly susceptible to unprofessional test-based practices including teaching to the tests (not to be confused with teaching to the standards); teaching using scripted and prefabricated curricula to ensure that what is taught aligns with what is tested; teaching time being taken up by test preparation, test practice, and test rehearsals; hyper-emphasizing the rote memorization of facts and basic skills; narrowing the curriculum to match the content and concept areas tested; and, related, teaching the tested subject areas that "count" (i.e., mathematics and reading/language arts) while marginalizing or even eliminating other curricular areas and activities that do not "count" on high-stakes tests (i.e., social studies, sciences, art, music, physical education, library sciences, and recess).

As well, typically low-scoring students, including inordinate numbers of non-English proficient and special education students, have been purged (i.e., expelled, suspended, or simply excused) from school during test administrations to keep them, the "undesirables" when it comes to high-stakes tests, from participating and pulling test scores down. Students have also been counseled out of school, convinced to explore other options (e.g., alternative, "last chance," or adult education schools), or persuaded to strive for General Education Diplomas (GEDs) instead of traditional high school certificates. Eliminating undesirable students eliminates their scores: the scores that, if included or preserved, would pull composite test scores down.

Those students, mentioned above, whom educators have deemed the least likely to post high enough test scores, have also been academically shunned. This has occurred particularly during the weeks leading up to high-stakes tests as educators, who will be held accountable and potentially suffer punitive sanctions if test scores are low, may perceive certain students as hopeless, and hence, the most undesirable to take the tests. Undesirable students have been known to be retained in grade or credit hours to keep them from being eligible for high-stakes testing cycles (e.g., by thwarting progression in high school as sophomores/juniors might not be eligible for testing in their sophomore/junior year; see for example Haney, 2000). Some undesirable students have altogether disappeared from school rosters; that is, when administrators have created rosters and registered students for high-stakes testing purposes.

In other cases, underperforming students have been wrongly moved into exempt categories (e.g., special education and ELL categories), as misclassifying these students will prevent them from dragging down the performance of the teachers or the schools as a whole (Amrein & Berliner, 2002; Haney, 2000).[9] Recognizing this as an issue, the federal government started mandating minimum rates of test participation (NCLB, 2002), but it seems this still occurs. This was most recently evidenced in the state of Florida (Chakrabarti & Shwartz, 2013; see also Derby, 2013), the state often distinguished for the high-stakes testing policies put into place by former Florida governor Jeb Bush, brother of former President George W. Bush and potential contender for the 2016 presidential election. Ironically, like it was with the undesirables in Cambodia, undesirable students in America's public schools have had to demonstrate that they are not a threat in order to survive in high-stakes school systems, especially in the school systems most susceptible under America's increasingly distorted, stronger accountability policies.

Conversely, educators have focused inordinately on the students who are on the edge of passing high-stakes tests ("on the bubble"). The thinking here is that if educators teach to the test well enough these students just might clear the cut scores and pass, and help to bump composite test scores, even if ever so slightly, upwards. Educators have used "selective seating" practices in which the students expected to post high scores are seated among the students expected to post low scores, covertly encouraging cheating.

Educators have also overtly cheated, for example, by erasing and changing students' incorrect answers to correct ones, explicitly giving students correct answers, persuading students to revisit incorrect answers, and the like. Such cheating instances have been widely publicized, most recently in the cases disclosed in the public schools of Atlanta and Washington DC (Perry & Vogell, 2009; Rhee, 2011) as well as in the public schools of Arizona (Amrein-Beardsley, Berliner, & Rideau, 2010; see also Toppo, Amos, Gillum, & Upton, 2011; Upton, 2011).

Collectively, these are just some of the unintended effects that have come about due to this distorted, yet socially engineered, M&P Theory of Change, and the educational policies constructed in its likeness (Amrein & Berliner, 2002; Grodsky, Warren, & Kalogrides, 2009; Hursh, 2008; Nichols & Berliner, 2007; Ravitch, 2010a; Reardon, Atteberry, Arshan, & Kurlaender, 2009). In the end, these and other methods of "gaming" the system result in extra, albeit artificial, boosts in aggregate test scores (Haladyna, Nolen, & Haas, 1991). These are the boosts that those being held accountable via stronger accountability policies often desperately need, and these are the boosts that those across states who are promoting such educational policies often desperately need to preserve and prolong their political careers (see, for example, Slavin, 1989). The educators being held accountable often justify the actions in which they sometimes engage to yield such artificial boosts. They do this more so when they are under immense pressure to keep their jobs, keep their tenure, earn merit pay, and the like, and more so when they view that the accountability policies being devised to hold them accountable are unjust, unwarranted, and unreasonable (Amrein-Beardsley et al., 2010; see also Smith & Noble, 1997).

It is here that this M&P Theory of Change has not only used intellectual genocide as a Machiavellian means to an end, primarily by (a) purging undesirable students, (b) cleansing the curricula, (c) sterilizing the core subject and concept areas taught, (d) exterminating courses and activities that do not matter or do not matter as much when high-stakes tests approach, (e) shrinking students' time on the tasks that ultimately matter the most, (f) decimating students' other and often more important opportunities to learn, and (g) implementing other test-boosting practices well known to achieve higher, albeit artificial, test scores. It is here, too, that this theory of change has caused intellectual genocide primarily by denying many students proper, appropriate, fair, and equal opportunities to learn the things that will ultimately matter the most, versus the things that multiple choice test items normally included on large-scale standardized achievement tests typically reflect. It is here that this theory of change has thwarted many students' "pursuit of happiness" in America's public schools.

As demonstrated in Carson's *Silent Spring*, the ecosystems into which high-stakes tests are continuously being introduced, namely America's public schools, are what are being continuously destroyed. The culprits here, however, include those who continue to use social engineering tactics of the ever-present past to exaggerate the severity of the problem (e.g., politicians advancing such educational reform measures) and those who continue to amplify public alarm about the problem (e.g., conservative media outlets and think tanks). The culprits also include those who continue to refine and manufacture the solutions to the problem, lobby their solutions to those in political and policy-making positions, and profit by continuously providing the best if not only solutions to the educational problem (e.g., educational measurement, testing, and other educational research-based companies and non-profits).

As in the aforementioned examples of the U.S. Department of Agriculture, the U.S. Department of the Treasury, and the U.S. Department of Housing and Urban Development, the control measures put in place by the U.S. Department of Education and others are ultimately causing markedly worse effects than the initial troubles that needed to be controlled or reformed in the first place. Ironically, they too are working alongside and under the advisement of many of the industrialists with vested private and financial interests (e.g., CTB McGraw-Hill, the Educational Testing Service, Harcourt Educational Measurement, Pearson, Riverside Publishing). Yet they are buying into the products nonetheless. Metaphorically speaking, America's public schools are being silenced, because educational opportunities and experiences are being annihilated in many cases by high-stakes tests, particularly in the schools most in need of genuine guidance and support.

The 30-year road trip to nowhere

But why is it that this M&P Theory of Change has held so firm? Why is it that this theory of change has become commonplace when there is still virtually no scientific research evidence verifying that it works? Why is it that after 30 years of tinkering with this theory of change, we still have the ever-present grave concerns about America's public school system that so alarmed the public 30 years ago in *A Nation at Risk* (U.S. Department of Education, 1983)? If this theory of change, socially engineered and now so deeply engrained in the minds of many, indeed worked, why would we still have such concerns about America's public school system, after the implementation of 30 years of repeated educational policies aligned with the same theory?

Tyack and Cuban wrote about a similar saga in their book *Tinkering toward Utopia* (1995), arguing that in fact most educational reform initiatives are ahistorical and as such fail, for many reasons but particularly when bureaucratic controls become the means to bring about utopian ends (see also Slavin, 1989). This definitely resonates here as virtually all of the research evidence indicates that these unrealistic and highly bureaucratized goals, as governmentally fixed, will likely elude us forever. These goals are indeed illusions leading us down a socially engineered road to a non-existent idealized destination. In fact, the M&P Theory of Change and its policy derivatives might be viewed as the greatest failed social engineering project of our time (Jehlen, 2009).

The question remains whether in fact the road to utopia is really the road trip to nowhere. Thirty years of evidence would support the latter. It seems that the nation's educational policymakers' attempts to socially engineer the public's belief systems and values have indeed worked so well that, to the nation's detriment, it cannot successfully socially engineer its way out of this nonsense, and off this prolonged and futile path. Educational reform in this case is failing ironically due in part to a lack of accountability to its own history.

Box 1.1 Top 10 assertions

1 Governmental and private groups often attempt to methodically sway public attitudes and behaviors to achieve idealized ends. By definition, a public policy is a tool used to do this.

2 The U.S. Department of Education's release of *A Nation at Risk* in 1983 prompted a fear about America's "failing" public schools. Since then, scholars have not only discredited the report, they have produced evidence to show the report was intentionally used for politically charged purposes.

3 *A Nation at Risk*, regardless, resulted in three decades of measurement-driven education policies, fueled by a Measure and Punish (M&P) Theory of Change.

4 The M&P Theory of Change is that by holding districts, schools, teachers, and students accountable for performance on the states' large-scale standardized achievement tests, administrators will supervise the schools better, teachers will teach better, and students will learn more, particularly in the nation's lowest performing schools.

5 The most recent federally-backed *Race to the Top* (RttT) program follows the M&P Theory of Change, requiring that states receiving RttT awards use students' test scores for even more consequential purposes and adopt even stronger accountability mechanisms than those required by *No Child Left Behind* (NCLB).

6 The M&P Theory of Change is fundamentally flawed and misguided at its core. Accordingly, it has never yielded its intended effects. It has never improved the nation's global standing, nor has it positively impacted the ever-persistent achievement gap.

7 The U.S. currently spends well over $1.7 billion on tests. This excludes the costs that come along with tests' associated resources (e.g., test preparation workbooks) and other related costs (e.g., administrative and instructional time for test preparation and administration).

8 Because of the increased reliance on tests, the M&P Theory of Change has caused intellectual genocide, primarily by denying many students proper, appropriate, fair, equal, and equitable opportunities to learn the things that will ultimately matter the most.

9 Metaphorically speaking, public schools in the U.S. are being silenced, given the educational opportunities and experiences that high-stakes tests are in many cases annihilating, especially in the schools most in need of guidance and support.

10 Educational reform, in this case, is failing due in part to a lack of accountability to its own history.

Notes

1 As part of the negotiations and final agreement to ban DDT, the industrial companies producing it were permitted to export the pesticide outside the U.S. until the mid–1980s (Griswold, 2012).

2 The U.S. is not the only country buying into this theory of change. In Australia, the former Prime Minister, Julia Gillard, while Minister for Education was also vying for Australia to be ranked no lower than #5 by 2025 on the PISA (Programme for International Student Assessment) international tests. What is the road to utopia in Australia? Test preparation, teaching to the PISA tests,

and increased school choice. This is also the case in Great Britain, another country infected by what is being termed the GERM (the Global Education Reform Movement) advancing such initiatives (Sahlberg, 2012; see also Ravitch, 2012b).

3 David Coleman is the main architect and proponent of the Common Core State Standards. He is an original member of the board of Michelle Rhee's StudentsFirst organization (see note 6 below); he previously ran an educational data and assessment company, and he was recently appointed as the president of the College Board curriculum and testing company.

4 Sandy Kress served as an advisor to President George W. Bush with respect to NCLB, and is also credited as one of its crafters. Kress, however, is not an academic and has not conducted research on the topic.

5 The quality of the journal in which this article was published is suspect. For more information see www.nonpartisaneducation.org/.

6 Michelle Rhee, the former chancellor of Washington DC's public schools and founder and current CEO of StudentsFirst, enacted a strict testing policy to which high stakes were attached, after which noteworthy cases of cheating were uncovered. Rhee denied such cheating occurred, but this ultimately led to her undoing as well as that of the then DC mayor.

7 Margaret Spellings, another one of NCLB's architects, followed Rod Paige as the U.S. Secretary of Education in the George W. Bush administration. She continues to speak out in favor of NCLB and criticizes the current federal administration under President Obama for turning soft on the matter.

8 In the late 1970s, as part of the minimum competency movement, the state of Florida implemented the first recorded state policy aligned with this theory of change. In Florida, state policymakers implemented a statewide test on which students were required to show minimum competence prior to being graduated from high school. Early gains in Florida test scores were used as an example of how this theory of change could improve education. However, soon thereafter, the immediate gains hit a plateau and then returned to where they were before the testing policy was implemented, leading Florida to abandon its new and promising testing policy. It was also discarded because of differential pass rates among racial groups and a discernible increase in high school dropout rates, particularly among ethnic minorities and students from low socioeconomic backgrounds (Linn, 2000; Serow, 1984). As well, because the content that was tested for "minimum" competence became the "maximum" on which students, particularly in urban schools, became competent (Bracey, 1995; U.S. Department of Education, 1983), the testing policy backfired. This is essentially what we continue to witness today.

9 The authors of the AERA's (2000) position statement on high-stakes testing wrote:

> When schools, districts, or other administrative units are compared to one another or when changes in scores are tracked over time, there must be explicit policies specifying which students are to be tested and under what circumstances students may be exempted from testing. Such policies must be uniformly enforced to assure the validity of score comparisons. In addition, reporting of test score results should accurately portray the percentage of students exempted.

2

VALUE-ADDED MODELS (VAMS) AND THE HUMAN FACTOR

No problem can be solved from the same level of consciousness that created it.

Albert Einstein

It is argued here that the M&P Theory of Change continues to metastasize as educational policymakers and private and corporate organizations protecting their own interests continue to reinvent it. It is argued here, as well, that this has occurred largely because of basic flaws in the tenets of social engineering theory. Social engineers have used powerful instruments to influence attitudes and social behaviors, ultimately to reach idealistic ends.

Instead of discarding this M&P Theory of Change, particularly given the preponderance of 30 years of research evidence discrediting it, educational policymakers have held firm. They continue to preach about its alleged value, all the while tweaking this or tinkering with that, and all the while adding more of the tools deemed necessary for the desired social changes to finally take hold and yield their desired and commonsense ends (Slavin, 1989; Tyack & Cuban, 1995).

Most recently, along with RttT (2011) came even higher standards, in a highly predictable move but this time via the federal backing of a set of Common Core State Standards. These national standards are still being developed by the National Governors Association and the Council of Chief State School Officers, and they are currently being adopted state by state (NGA & CCSSO, 2010; see also Coleman as featured in Lewin, 2012 and Rotherham, 2011). In another highly predictable move, policy attention has turned towards even more accountability, but the focus this time has changed from student accountability to teacher accountability. Whereas in NCLB (2002) the focus was mainly on holding students accountable for meeting higher standards, in RttT (2011) the focus has shifted to holding teachers and administrators accountable for helping their students meet the higher standards being devised and implemented.

New and improved data systems

The guiding principle of RttT is that increased teacher (and school/district) accountability would be made possible by new and improved technologies yielding advanced data systems that could link students' test scores to their teachers (and schools/districts), longitudinally over time, regardless of whether students moved within or across classrooms (or schools/districts), and as long as students were continuously educated within state borders. Once statisticians realized that such links could be made, of course following an a priori logic that technologies facilitating such links could only bring about benefits, policy attention turned to what could be done with such links (Haycock & Crawford, 2008).

Specifically, attention turned to how such links might work to improve upon the archaic accountability systems that at the same time were increasingly (and opportunely) positioned as the main barriers that had averted the M&P Theory of Change for the same 30 years past. Whereas holding students accountable for meeting higher standards did not work before, holding teachers (and schools/districts) accountable for meeting higher standards certainly would work now, given the new and improved data and linking systems being developed for wide-scale use. These could now drive a series of new and improved accountability policies.

New and improved metrics

Accordingly, a new and improved set of metric systems was also introduced to help improve upon the accuracy with which the U.S. could measure teacher (and school/district) effectiveness, now that the data systems and links needed to measure the gains students made on large-scale standardized achievement tests over time were in place. The new and improved metric systems would certainly help the U.S. improve upon the precision with which it might hold teachers (and schools/districts) accountable for meeting higher standards. The M&P Theory of Change now had the advanced statistical tools needed to make it work, so the logic continued.

Value-added models (VAMs)

After the implementation of NCLB (2002), researchers and statisticians, and in particular the researchers and statisticians working at local departments of education and in local districts, quickly determined that the Adequate Yearly Progress (AYP) measures being used to measure status changes were far from perfect. Status changes could not be appropriately used to measure changes in student achievement from one point or moment in time (e.g., like a photographer's snapshot) to the next, nor among and between different cohorts of students in the same grade levels from one year to the next.[1]

In fact, AYP measures could not and did not yield reliable or valid information about much of anything, besides verifying that different cohorts of students were indeed quite different as they progressed through school. Accordingly, teachers (and schools/districts) could not reasonably be held accountable for students' test scores because of the methodological issues with measuring AYP (Baker et al., 2010; Ballou, 2002; CCSSO, 2005; Cody, McFarland, Moore, & Preston, 2010; Glazerman & Potamites, 2011; Ho, Lewis, & Farris, 2009; Kim & Sunderman, 2005; Linn, 2008; Nelson, 2011; Sanders, 2003; Scherrer, 2011; Tekwe et al., 2004).

So educational researchers and statisticians, joined by a set of econometricians most interested in measuring educational inputs and outputs (i.e., in line with the expanded application of business model thinking in education) began promoting more sophisticated test measurement methods – value-added models (VAMs). VAMs frame educational issues as economic issues, "in much the same way the federal government has over the last thirty years" (Gabriel & Allington, 2011, p. 16). So, fittingly, the U.S. Department of Education (2006a, 2006b) sponsored a series of state pilots at a cost of $100 million a year for four years to test how VAMs might be integrated into statewide accountability policies and systems (see also Hoff, 2007).

Despite the mixed results found by the U.S. Department of Education themselves (see for example Schochet & Chiang, 2010), federal policymakers carried onward, funneling billions in taxpayer revenues to incentivize all states to adopt and integrate VAMs into their state accountability policies and systems (RttT, 2011). This occurred despite the concerns that other VAM researchers had already brought to bear about VAM-based inferences and uses at that time (Amrein-Beardsley, 2008a; Bock, Wolfe, & Fisher, 1996; Bracey, 2000, 2004a; Braun, 2005; Glass, 1995; Kupermintz, 2003; Linn, 2001; McCaffrey, Lockwood, Koretz, & Hamilton, 2003; McCaffrey, Lockwood, Koretz, Louis, & Hamilton, 2004a; Morgan, 2002; Popham, 1997; Raudenbush, 2004; Rivkin, 2007; Rubin et al., 2004; Walberg & Paik, 1997).

VAMs defined

In the simplest of terms, VAMs are statistical tools used to measure the purportedly causal relationships between having been instructed by teacher A (or in school B/district C) and achieving Z growth on large-scale standardized achievement tests in certain subject areas (e.g., mathematics and reading/language arts) as calculated from point X to point Y while controlling for E, F, G, etc. (whereas E, F, G, etc. include various student background characteristics and demographics and classroom- and school-level characteristics and variables).[2] Then, the VAM equation can be written out with the measure of achievement of interest (i.e., Z growth in achievement) on the left-hand side of the equation, as calculated by Y post-test score minus X pre-test score[3] on the right-hand side of the equation and as a function of all of the explanatory variables (i.e., E, F, G, etc.). If only it was this simple.

Accordingly, "the bulk of the [methodological] research literature on VAMs has been devoted to a careful consideration for how the right-hand side of the equation should be specified" (Briggs & Weeks, 2009, p. 385). This is illustrated in Figure 2.1, which provides

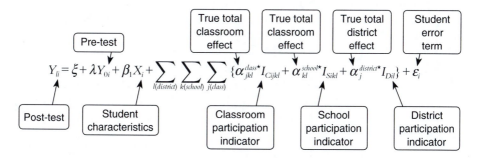

Figure 2.1 An example of a statistical model used to calculate value-added (source: Winerip, 2011, adapted with permission from original designer, R. Meyer).

an example of a typical VAM equation, whereby statisticians calculate value added by computing the average (or adjusted average) gain differences between students' composite test scores from pre- to post-test observation.

It is important to note here, however, that there are also student growth models that are related to but are not classified in the same way as VAMs. While the focus of this book is mainly on VAMs, many of the assertions apply to both student growth models and VAMs alike. The main differences between the two types of models are how precisely estimates are made and whether control variables are included (Goldhaber, Gabele, & Walch, 2012). This is discussed in more detail in the next chapter, but for now and throughout the rest of the book I will refer to both types of models as VAMs unless making distinctions is necessary.

In terms of producing estimates, VAM statisticians measure value added at the teacher (or school/district) level by either predicting the average student gains expected and then calculating the difference between the average gains made after the fact, with positive differences (usually above one standard deviation from zero) yielding "value added" and negative differences (usually below one standard deviation from zero) yielding the opposite. Or VAM statisticians measure value added by mathematically calculating the value a teacher (or school/district) adds to (or detracts from) average student growth scores after the fact, with no use of prediction in the model.

In terms of controls, VAM statisticians always control for at least one year of students' previous test scores (e.g., using covariates), allowing students to serve as their own controls.[4] This helps to "level the playing field," as students' prior test scores serve as strong proxy variables that help control for the impacts that other external variables have on student achievement over time (Sanders, Wright, Rivers, & Leandro, 2009, p. 4; see also Ballou, Sanders, & Wright, 2004; Ehlert, Koedel, Parsons, & Podgursky, 2012; Sanders, 1998; Sanders & Horn, 1998). Although the extent to which this works is yet another source of contention and dispute (Ballou, 2012; Cody et al., 2010; Dorn, 1994; Glass, 1995; McCaffrey, 2012; Rothstein, 2009).

Regardless, VAM statisticians only sometimes explicitly control for the external variables that we also know impact students' levels of growth on test scores over time (Ishii & Rivkin, 2009; McCaffrey, Lockwood, Koretz, Louis, & Hamilton, 2004b; Scherrer, 2011). These other variables include student risk variables (e.g., race, ethnicity, students' eligibility for free or reduced-cost lunches as a proxy for students' socioeconomic backgrounds, English proficiency, involvement in special education, gifted, or other programs). They can also include classroom- or school-level variables (e.g., daily attendance rates, prior teachers' residual effects, multiple teachers fractional effects), although these are more rarely used. These controls purportedly facilitate better model adjustments, to make such analyses more accurate (Ehlert et al., 2012; Harris, 2009, 2011; Hill, Kapitula, & Umlan, 2011).

The shortcoming here, however, is that these variables tend to be very rudimentary proxies of the true variables they are intended to represent. They do not capture all of the factors (e.g., the influence of parents' levels of education, after- and out-of-school learning opportunities, summer learning gains and losses, and other out-of-school factors) that also matter when measuring changes in student achievement over time. In addition, some of the influence of these variables is magnified when similar students go to similar schools within a district, attending schools in non-random patterns (i.e., given the neighborhoods in which they live and the social construction of school attendance zones). Or the influence of these variables is magnified when similar students are not randomly or even quasi-randomly assigned to classrooms, which is regularly the case (Paufler & Amrein-Beardsley, 2013), and then their scores are collapsed to indicate teacher (or school/district) effectiveness or quality (Briggs & Domingue, 2011; Rothstein, 2009, 2010b).

Nonetheless, statisticians ultimately compare the average (or adjusted average) gain value (or growth/decline) coefficients to other, "similar" teachers' (or schools'/districts') value coefficients. They then make relativistic comparisons and position teachers (and schools/districts) accordingly, typically hierarchically along a categorical (albeit highly arbitrary) continuum, including high to low value-added classifications. Because the average and adjusted average gains are in themselves normative, as are the continuums most often used to make final categorizations, by definition about 50% of teachers (or schools/districts) are typically categorized as adding value and the other 50% are typically categorized as subtracting it. As well, teachers (or schools/districts) can demonstrate growth but still yield a negative value-added estimate because a teacher's (or school's/district's) demonstrated growth is simply less than what was either predicted or demonstrated given the comparison groups (students across the district in the same grade and subject area). There are also ceiling and floor effects at play whereby high-achieving students consistently score high on tests and low achievers consistently score relatively lower, skewing the data in the extremes of the distribution as there is nowhere else to go besides down or up, respectively, in terms of regression to the mean[5] (see, for example, Cole, Haimson, Perez-Johnson, & May, 2011; Kelly & Monczunski, 2007; Koedel & Betts, 2007, 2010; Linn & Haug, 2002; Wright, Horn, & Sanders, 1997).

VAMboozled

Ultimately, the value-added estimates that result from these calculations should yield "tentative causal conclusion[s] based on partial evidence drawn from an uncontrolled study of schools and districts" (Braun, 2008). Yet again, we have empirical evidence indicating that this same M&P Theory of Change, even with its new and improved VAM-based systems and metrics, is still flawed and misguided. Before and since the federal value-added pilots, what has become increasingly evident, yet increasingly marginalized at multiple policy levels, is that VAMs are (1) unreliable (e.g., a teacher classified as adding value has approximately a 25–50% chance of being classified as subtracting value the following year); (2) invalid (e.g., there is very limited evidence that teachers who post high value-added scores are effective using at least one other correlated criterion); and (3) biased (e.g., teachers of certain students who are not randomly assigned to classrooms have more difficulties demonstrating growth).

It has also become increasingly evident, yet also increasingly marginalized at multiple policy levels, that VAMs are also (4) unfair (e.g., only teachers of mathematics and language arts with pre- and post-test data in certain grade levels are being held accountable using these systems); (5) fraught with measurement errors negating their summative uses (e.g., inordinate amounts of missing data, variables that cannot be controlled, measurement errors caused by non-traditional, non-isolated, non-insular, and "non-egg-crate" classrooms); and (6) inappropriate for formative use given their non-transparency (e.g., teachers and administrators do not understand the models being used to evaluate them) and limited instructional value (e.g., data estimates are difficult to understand or use for instructional decision-making).

Accordingly, VAMs are (7) being used inappropriately to make consequential decisions (e.g., on teacher termination, merit pay) while (8) their unintended consequences are going unrecognized (e.g., teachers leaving or refusing assignment to grades in which value-added estimates matter most, teachers leaving the profession altogether out of discontent or to protest, teachers choosing not to teach students who are most likely to hinder growth, principals "stacking" classes to make sure certain teachers can demonstrate value added or growth or vice versa).

These are the main things that many of those promoting and propagating VAMs are quick to forget or dismiss. Therefore, as social engineering theory would have it, the new and improved metrics are bamboozling, or in this case VAMboozling the public, polis, or city-state by eliminating or reducing human agency and, instead, using an alleged level of pseudo-mathematical precision to measure educational quality. Social engineers are convincing the public that we now have the powerful instruments to influence attitudes and drive out the social behaviors still feared in America's public schools (e.g., ineffective teachers and school/district leaders), as well as the powerful tools to influence attitudes and drive the social behaviors still needed to bring us to increased academic achievement and to reclaim the nation's preeminence.

Relatedly, we have private corporations (i.e., companies and non-profits providing educational measurement, testing, and other educational research) pushing their interests and selling their VAMs for profit (e.g., the SAS® Education Value-Added Assessment System [EVAAS®]). Yet these organizations are making promises that lack evidentiary warrant and proof, and are marketing these empty promises particularly to federal and state policymakers and district consumers willing – or in the case of RttT and its federal incentives – needing to buy into yet another, albeit related, theory of education reform and its associated tools. This is discussed next in the paradigm case of Houston Independent School District (HISD) and its high-stakes use of the SAS® EVAAS®.

The human factor

The purpose of the remaining section of this chapter is to highlight the human factor as we collectively continue to think and read about VAMs, and specifically their intended and unintended effects when VAMs are used in applied settings in schools. While in the remaining chapters and sections of this book, more technical, methodological, and statistical issues are discussed, it is important first to highlight the real VAM-based conditions, in this case, in the district using VAM-based estimates more than any other district across the nation for increased accountability purposes – HISD (Corcoran, 2010; Harris, 2011; Mellon, 2010; Otterman, 2010; Papay, 2011). I will illustrate the intended and unintended consequences that I, along with my former doctoral student, Clarin Collins, have uncovered when researching the use of the SAS® EVAAS® in HISD for highly consequential purposes (e.g., merit pay and teacher termination).

It is particularly important to highlight this research, here in this section of the book, as the educators who are working within and under these systems, day to day, I believe, are the best to speak truth to power, particularly about how such policies translate in practice. These are also the teachers whose voices are often marginalized, dismissed, or even rejected, particularly when they are positioned as insubordinate, unprofessional, or even recalcitrant when charged with not wanting to be held accountable, purportedly protecting their self-interests, or preserving the status quo.

It is also important to highlight this research here in this section of the book to help readers frame the more theoretical, conceptual, and technical issues discussed throughout the rest of the book. Existing VAM research tends to focus largely on the models and model specifics versus the intended and unintended consequences that come as a result of VAM use. I believe that, by focusing first on the intended and unintended consequences in an applied setting, putting a human face on the issues, it will be easier for readers to understand why things like reliability, validity, and bias matter so very much.

The SAS® Education Value-Added Assessment System (EVAAS®) in the Houston Independent School District (HISD)[6]

HISD is the largest, highest-needs district in Texas and the seventh largest district in the country. The district consists of 300 schools, over 200,000 students, and approximately 13,000 teachers. The majority of the students in the district are from high-needs backgrounds, with 63% of students labeled at risk, 92% from racial minority backgrounds, 80% qualifying for federal free or reduced-cost lunches, and 58% classified as English Language Learners (ELLs), Limited English Proficiency (LEP), or bilingual. Since 2007, HISD has contracted with the SAS® Institute, Inc., the world's "powerhouse in big data analytics,"[7] to use its EVAAS® system for district-wide increased accountability purposes.

In 2007, HISD created the Accelerating Student Progress and Increasing Results and Expectations (ASPIRE) program to recognize and celebrate great teaching as measured by students' progress (HISD, 2010). District administrators contracted with SAS® Institute, Inc. to measure this progress via their EVAAS® system. While Tennessee, North Carolina, Pennsylvania, and Ohio use EVAAS® statewide, and other states, districts, and schools are currently using or are planning to implement EVAAS®, again, at the time of this writing, no other school, district, or state used EVAAS® or any other VAM for more consequential decision making than HISD (Corcoran, 2010; Harris, 2011; Mellon, 2010; Otterman, 2010; Papay, 2011).

With over 20 years of development, EVAAS® is the largest, most widely implemented, and most widely used VAM in the country. While there are at least eight entities developing such models (Banchero & Kesmodel, 2011), like the model coming out of the Value-added Research Center (VARC) in Wisconsin and the Colorado Growth Model developed by Betebenner, which are discussed in more depth in the next chapter, EVAAS® is "the most comprehensive reporting package of value-added metrics available in the educational market." It is "the most robust and reliable" system available, more than the "other simplistic models found in the market today" (SAS®, 2012a). As well, it "provides valuable diagnostic information about [instructional] practices," helps educators become more proactive and make more "sound instructional choices," and helps teachers use "resources more strategically to ensure that every student has the chance to succeed" (SAS®, 2012c). It was these assertions that we used to frame this research.

In addition, it stands to reason that the VAM most deserving of further investigation is the EVAAS®, especially given the claims EVAAS® developers have made regarding what the system can do and deliver. The EVAAS® claims are used to secure millions of federal and state taxpayer revenues yearly (e.g., $500,000 per year via HISD alone), so it makes sense to examine these claims in more depth.

HISD, EVAAS®, and teacher termination[8]

In the spring of 2011, HISD decided not to renew 221 of its teachers' contracts (HISD, 2011). According to one of the lead lawyers retained in some of these teachers' defenses (A. Reichek, personal communication, June 8, 2011), a substantial number of HISD teachers' contracts were not renewed at least in part due to "a significant lack of student progress attributable to the educator," or "insufficient student academic growth reflected by [EVAAS®] value-added scores." According to the vice-president of the Houston Federation of Teachers, this number was greater than 50% of HISD teachers whose contracts were not renewed that year (Z. Capo, personal communication, April 6, 2012). HISD did not respond to our Open Records Request (submitted September 15, 2011) soliciting the actual number of unnamed teachers whose contracts were not renewed at least in part due to EVAAS® scores in spring of 2011, however, so it is uncertain how many teachers were actually terminated for these reasons.

We are also unaware of how many teachers pursued due process hearings, how many of them followed their due process hearings through to culmination, and how many were actually terminated after their due process hearings concluded. We are, however, aware that attaching such high-stakes decisions to VAM output in general is expected "to lead to a flood of litigation challenging teacher dismissals" as "value-added modeling as a basis for high-stakes decision making is fraught with problems likely to be vetted in the courts" (Baker, 2012a; see also Baker, Oluwole, & Green, 2013; Pullin, 2013). What we examined in this study are four such cases on which due process hearings were followed through.

Specifically, there were four teachers for whom I was invited to serve as the expert witness and testify on their behalves, after examining each of their EVAAS® data. I was specifically retained to testify regarding (1) the EVAAS® in general, (2) whether in fact the measure of value added for each teacher accurately evidenced that the teacher positively or negatively impacted student learning and growth, and (3) whether the grounds and reasoning on which their contracts were not renewed were justifiable and sound.

The practical experiences of these four teachers should help others better understand how this value-added system is being used within HISD, and attach human faces to such abstraction.

The four terminated teachers

The terminated teachers were four female, elementary school teachers, all of whom were from racial minority backgrounds (three were African American and one was Latina). Their ages ranged from 28 to 51. They averaged 11.8 years of teaching experience and 7.5 years teaching in HISD. Two were certified via a traditional teacher certification program and the other two were certified via HISD's Alternative Teaching Certificate program. All teachers taught core subject areas (reading/language arts, mathematics, social studies, and science) in grades 3 to 7, and they all taught in different schools under different school administrations.

In order to testify on their behalves, I had to work backwards, collecting historical information about the four teachers. I analyzed archival data for each case, and documented the teachers' stories to add context, all the while capturing these teachers' lived experiences up to the point of their termination.

Specifically, I collected each teacher's EVAAS® Teacher Value-Added Reports (see, for example, Figure 2.2[9]). These reports are used to evaluate how well individual teachers facilitated student achievement on Texas's Assessment of Knowledge and Skills (TAKS and TAKS Accommodated) and Stanford/Aprenda achievement tests, which are used in non-TAKS grades and subject areas. These reports are used to compare how well teachers influence student progress as compared to similar teachers within the district. Scores reported include an individual teacher's normal curve equivalent (NCE)[10] gain, a measure of standard deviation for confidence; a district reference gain, also expressed as an NCE, indicating how the district did compared to the state average each year; and the score of interest here – the gain score index. The gain score index compares each teacher to other similar teachers across the district and this is the score that HISD uses for determining ASPIRE awards. Note that according to the statistical rules and policies put in place by EVAAS®, comparisons are made based on one standard deviation. Teachers with a score above 1.0 are deemed as adding value, teachers with a score between 1.0 and −1.0 are deemed as not detectably different (NDD) from average, and teachers with a score below −1.0 are deemed as detracting value, comparatively.

Such reports, alongside SAS® EVAAS® Reports for Teacher Reflection (see also Figure 2.2), are provided to teachers yearly through an online portal. These reports include a color chart intended to offer teachers a graphical display of how different students (e.g., low, middle, and high-performing) progressed in their classrooms as compared to the district average. The reports also include a table to complement the chart and quantify the colors displayed. Resource guides are available to help consumers understand these reports as well (see, for example, SAS®, 2007).

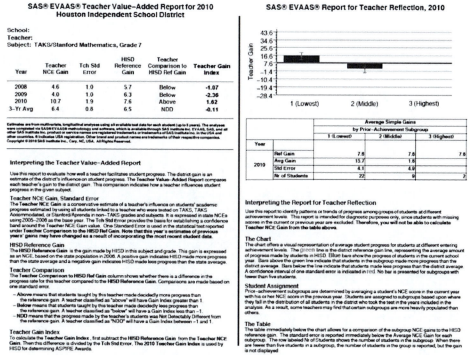

Figure 2.2 Teacher C's SAS® EVAAS® Teacher Value-Added Report for 2010 and Report for Teacher Reflection.

I also collected each teacher's Professional Development and Appraisal System (PDAS) supervisor evaluation scores as they are also valued in HISD's ASPIRE system. I collected these for the same historical time period as other contextual data to further contextualize and better understand each teacher's EVAAS® data. On the PDAS, I collected both numerical scores marked for each of the eight domains included on the PDAS instrument and overall (e.g., learner-centered instruction, classroom managment; see Region 13, 2004) and supervisors' written comments (also by domain and overall) for subsequent analyses.

Note that while it is likely that observational scores are often inflated (Weisberg, Sexton, Mulhern, & Keeling, 2009; see also Gates, 2012), and this is in large part why more objective measures of teacher effectiveness like VAMs are being adopted and implemented, it is important to examine whether in fact observational measures correlate with value-added estimates to assess validity (i.e., in terms of concurrent-related evidence of validity). This is important because evidence is still lacking to indicate that measures of teacher value-added are substantively related to at least one other correlated criterion (Hill et al., 2011; Kane & Staiger, 2012; Kersting, Chen, & Stigler, 2013; Sass & Harris, 2012). I also collected other indicators teachers might have had for the same years of analysis, especially about their general effectiveness as teachers (e.g., honors, awards, accolades).

I collected these data via extensive phone interviews that averaged 2.5 hours, although short follow-up phone calls necessary for verification purposes followed on occasion. During each phone interview, I first asked teachers a set of demographic questions (i.e., teaching certification, number of total years teaching and teaching in HISD, age, and racial backgrounds). I then asked them to explain their corpus of EVAAS® and PDAS data per school year, as aligned with the aforementioned documents collected. I also asked them four additional questions:

1   Is there anything else you can think of in terms of reasons why you are being terminated (e.g., excessive abseentism, insubordination, other test scores)?
2   Do you understand your EVAAS® value-added scores?
3   Have you received training on how to understand your EVAAS® reports/scores?
4   Have you received professional development as a result of your EVAAS® scores?

I analyzed the transcribed interview data alongside all numerical data, year by year, to establish a longitudinal chain of evidence (Yin, 1994). I then verified results and findings with the actual teachers themselves, via both a series of member-checks (Guba & Lincoln, 1981; Lincoln & Guba, 1985) and by giving the final report to the four teachers to check for accuracy and authenticity, to clarify misunderstandings and misconceptions, and to verify the overall viability of my interpretations of their professional stories. As well, these data were all vetted and examined, piece by piece, during a seven-hour deposition at which approximately five lawyers representing both sides, one court reporter, and myself were present.

Data and results

Teacher A

Teacher A, a university-certified teacher for more than 10 years, had been an elementary school teacher in HISD since 2000. Illustrated in Table 2.1 is a summary of Teacher A's

Table 2.1 Teacher A's SAS® EVAAS®, and PDAS scores and ASPIRE bonuses

	2006–2007	2007–2008	2008–2009	2009–2010	2010–2011
	Grade 5	Grade 4	Grade 3	Grade 3	Grade 5
Math	−2.03	+0.68*	+0.16*	+3.46	n/a
Reading	−1.15	−0.96*	+2.03	+1.81	n/a
Language arts	+1.12	−0.49*	−1.77	−0.20*	n/a
Science	+2.37	−3.45	n/a	n/a	n/a
Social studies	+0.91*	−2.39	n/a	n/a	n/a
PDAS: % of total	98.0	98.4	98.4	89.0	53.7
ASPIRE bonus	$3,400	$700	$3,700	$0	n/a

Notes
Scores shaded as light gray with a (+) sign indicate that the teacher added value according to EVAAS® data and in comparison to other similar teachers across the district. Scores shaded as dark gray with a (−) sign indicate the opposite. Scores with asterisks (*) do not signify statistical significance, but the opposite. They signify that the scores were not detectably different (NDD) from average. This means that the progress Teacher A's class made was not detectably different from the reference gain scores of other teachers across HISD given one standard deviation; however, the scores are still reported to both the teachers and their supervisors as they are here.

EVAAS® and PDAS scores and ASPIRE bonuses since 2007, the first year of HISD's ASPIRE system.

Across all years and subject areas for which Teacher A had EVAAS® data, she added value to her students' learning (relative to all other HISD teachers) 50% of the time (8/16 of EVAAS® observations) and detracted value (relative to all other HISD teachers) the other 50% of the time (8/16 of EVAAS® observations). Given her EVAAS® estimates, the probability that Teacher A was truly an effective or ineffective teacher was no different than the flip of a coin. Additionally, looking at Teacher A's most recent years of activity, she added more value than before, making termination unreasonable and indefensible at that time, especially on the grounds that there was "a significant lack of student progress attributable to the educator" or "insufficient student academic growth reflected by [EVAAS®] value-added scores," as referenced in her nonrenewal letter.

Analyzing Teacher A's EVAAS® scores alongside her PDAS scores, it is not only visually obvious that there is something peculiar about the relationship between Teacher A's performance on the EVAAS® and her supervisor evaluation scores, it is also statistically evident.

It is statistically evident given a series of correlations demonstrating the numerical relationships between two measures where $-1.0 \leq r \leq +1.0$. The closer the correlation coefficient r gets to either a positive or negative 1.0, the stronger or more perfect the relationship. If r is positive, this indicates that both numerical indicators move together in the same direction. That is, when one indicator increases (e.g., students' test scores) so does another related indicator (e.g., students' household levels of income). This does not mean that one causes the other, but simply that the two indicators are positively correlated. This has been the source of spirited debates for decades, for example, when postulating whether smoking indeed causes lung cancer given the high correlations that indicate that there is a strong relationship but that do not, especially as tobacco companies argue, suggest causation. If r is negative, this indicates that either of the two numerical indicators are negatively related. More specifically, when one indicator increases (e.g., one's levels of education) the other related indicator decreases (e.g., years one might have spent in jail). Correlations close to zero in value indicate little to no relationship between the variables or indicators of interest.

The correlations here, between Teacher A's EVAAS® and PDAS scores across reading/language arts ($r=-0.51$), mathematics ($r=-0.83$), and language arts ($r=-0.11$) from 2007 to 2010 suggest that beyond no correlation, the better Teacher A did on the EVAAS® the worse she did in the eyes of her supervisor(s), and vice versa. In addition, Teacher A was monetarily rewarded in a way that did not make sense. The worse she did the more money she received ($r=-0.42$). Until 2010–2011, Teacher A "exceeded expectations" across every PDAS domain, and she was given a "Teacher of the Year" award in 2008 and a "Teacher of the Month" award in 2010. Both were awarded by her colleagues.

Teacher A was only familiar with EVAAS® given the score reports distributed each year and because her colleagues and supervisors used to talk about something called "value added." Nobody ever explained her EVAAS® scores to her, and she never fully understood what the numbers meant, how they could impact or "hurt" her, or how she could use her EVAAS® scores to help her improve her own instruction. Additionally, she never received professional development as a result of her value-added scores, although whether she needed professional development to help her improve her value-added scores is questionable.

Teacher B

Teacher B, a career-changer with a bachelor's and master's degree in mathematics, was certified as a mathematics teacher for grades 2–12 via HISD's Alternative Teaching Certificate program in 2007. Since then, she had been a teacher in HISD. Illustrated in Table 2.2 is a summary of Teacher B's EVAAS® and PDAS scores and ASPIRE bonuses since 2008.

Teacher B's relative value-added scores were negative for mathematics for two years, and positive for the most recent year for which she had EVAAS® data. In her most recent position for which she had EVAAS® data she seemed to have added value to her students' learning. Note that she taught alongside another mathematics teacher who taught nearly half of her

Table 2.2 Teacher B's SAS® EVAAS®, and PDAS scores and ASPIRE bonuses

	2007–2008	2008–2009	2009–2010	2010–2011
	Grade 7	Grade 7	Grade 7	Grades 9 and 10
Math	−1.07	−2.36	+1.62	n/a
PDAS: % of total	58.0	55.3	59.2	n/a
ASPIRE bonus	$1,750	$0	$4,700	n/a

Notes
Scores shaded as light gray with a (+) sign indicate that the teacher added value according to EVAAS® data and in comparison to other similar teachers across the district. Scores shaded as dark gray with a (−) sign indicate the opposite. Scores with asterisks (*) do not signify statistical significance, but the opposite. They signify that the scores were not detectably different (NDD) from average. This means that the progress Teacher B's class made was not detectably different from the reference gain scores of other teachers across HISD given one standard deviation; however, the scores are still reported to both the teachers and their supervisors as they are here.

students mathematics an equal amount of time per week all year. Whether she alone demonstrated "a significant lack of student progress attributable to the educator," or "insufficient student academic growth reflected by [EVAAS®] value-added scores" (again, per her non-renewal letter) is debatable. In addition, her most recent year was demonstrably her best.

Analyzing Teacher B's EVAAS® scores alongside her PDAS scores, there is a strong relationship between Teacher B's EVAAS® and supervisor evaluation scores ($r = 0.91$). The better Teacher B did on the EVAAS® the better she did in the eyes of her supervisor(s), and vice versa. This yields the type of positive correlation coefficient we would expect to see if both indicators reliably and validly measured teacher effectiveness. In addition, Teacher B was rewarded in a way that made sense; the better she did the more money she received ($r = 0.93$).

The knowledge that Teacher B had about the EVAAS® was also sparse. She did not understand how "they" calculated her value-added scores. She would "just see the scores." She also knew that "they" compared her scores "to everybody else's in the district." She did not receive training to understand, nor professional development to improve her value-added scores, although whether her most recent scores were in need of improvement is also unclear.

Teacher C

Teacher C graduated with a bachelor's degree in early childhood education in 1999, and she received her master's degree in school counseling from the same university in 2000. Thereafter, she served as a long term substitute in HISD until she took a full-time teaching position in HISD teaching sixth grade in 2003. Illustrated in Table 2.3 is a summary of Teacher C's EVAAS® and PDAS scores and ASPIRE bonuses since 2007.

Teacher C's overall EVAAS® scores across years and subjects evidence that Teacher C detracted value from her students' learning (relative to all other HISD teachers) 100% of the

Table 2.3 Teacher C's SAS® EVAAS®, and PDAS scores and ASPIRE bonuses

	2006–2007	2007–2008	2008–2009	2009–2010
	Grade 6	Grade 6	Grade 6	Grade 6
Math	−1.67	−2.58	n/a	n/a
Science	n/a	n/a	n/a	n/a
Social studies	−1.72	−0.16*	−1.14	n/a
PDAS: % of total	84.6	86.3	88.6	78.0
ASPIRE bonus	$1,000	$100	$475	$1,225

Notes
Scores shaded as light gray with a (+) sign indicate that the teacher added value according to EVAAS® data and in comparison to other similar teachers across the district. In this table, there are no such scores. Scores shaded as dark gray with a (−) sign indicate the opposite, that the teacher detracted value instead. Scores with asterisks (*) do not signify statistical significance, but the opposite. They signify that the scores were not detectably different (NDD) from average. This means that the progress Teacher C's class made was not detectably different from the reference gain scores of other teachers across HISD given one standard deviation; however, the scores are still reported to both the teachers and their supervisors as they are here.

time across three subject areas. This was likely because Teacher C taught some of the highest needs students, possibly across the district. The ages of the sixth grade students in her remedial classes ranged from 10 (the typical age of a sixth grader) to 15 (the typical age of a high school freshman). Almost half of Teacher C's students, over time, had been retained in grade between one and four times at some time.

Analyzing Teacher C's EVAAS® scores alongside her mathematics PDAS scores was not possible as only a maximum of two EVAAS® scores were available, and her social studies EVAAS® and PDAS scores were mildly related ($r = 0.26$). Teacher C's monetary bonuses and PDAS scores were also mildly related ($r = 0.29$). Until 2010–2011, she "exceeded expectations" across almost every domain in terms of her supervisor evaluations. She was also given a "Teacher of the Year" award during the 2007–2008 school year by her teacher peers.

The knowledge that Teacher C had about EVAAS® was also limited. She understood that she was being compared to other HISD teachers who taught the same subject areas to students who were "very different than her students." She never received training to understand, or professional development to improve, her value-added scores.

Teacher D

Teacher D graduated with a bachelor's degree in business and administration in 2005 and in 2007 was certified as a teacher for grades 4 to 8 via HISD's Alternative Teaching Certificate program. She took a full-time teaching position in HISD in 2006. Illustrated in Table 2.4 is a summary of Teacher D's EVAAS® and PDAS scores and ASPIRE bonuses since 2007.

Up until 2009–2010 Teacher D, like Teacher A, flip-flopped back and forth across subject areas, adding value overall from 2006 to 2009 50% of the time (3/6 EVAAS® observations) and detracting value 50% of the time (3/6 EVAAS® observations). According to her EVAAS® estimates, like Teacher A, the probability that Teacher D was an effective teacher up to 2009–2010 was no different than the flip of a coin. Given Teacher D's most recent year of EVAAS® data

Table 2.4 Teacher D's SAS® EVAAS®, and PDAS scores and ASPIRE bonuses

	2006–2007	2007–2008	2008–2009	2009–2010	2010–2011
	Grade 4	Grade 3	Grade 3	Grade 4	Grade 3
Reading	+0.36*	−0.17*	−2.28	−3.88	n/a
Language arts	−1.60	+1.28	+0.39*	−3.25	n/a
Social studies	n/a	n/a	n/a	−2.36	n/a
PDAS: % of total	65.5	71.4	74.5	61.6	43.5
ASPIRE bonus	$1,500	$2,900	$2,150	$1,250	n/a

Notes
Scores shaded as light gray with a (+) sign indicate that the teacher added value according to EVAAS® data and in comparison to other similar teachers across the district. Scores shaded as dark gray with a (−) sign indicate the opposite. Scores with asterisks (*) do not signify statistical significance, but the opposite. They signify that the scores were not detectably different (NDD) from average. This means that the progress Teacher D's class made was not detectably different from the reference gain scores of other teachers across HISD given one standard deviation; however, the scores are still reported to both the teachers and their supervisors as they are here.

(2009–2010), however, she seemingly detracted from student learning across all three subject areas. In 2009–2010 Teacher D was assigned to teach an inordinate number of ELLs who were transitioned into her classroom. Whether Teacher D demonstrated "a significant lack of student progress attributable to the educator," or "insufficient student academic growth reflected by [EVAAS®] value-added scores" (per her nonrenewal letter) is still disputable.

In terms of the relationship between Teacher D's performance on the PDAS and her students' EVAAS® scores in reading/language arts, there is a mild correlation ($r=0.29$), and in terms of her performance on the PDAS and her students' EVAAS® scores in language arts, there is a strong correlation ($r=0.92$). In addition, the better Teacher D scored on the EVAAS® the more money she received ($r=0.79$). Until 2010–2011, she "exceeded expectations" or was "proficient" across every domain in terms of her supervisor evaluations.

In terms of Teacher D's knowledge about the EVAAS®, she reported not understanding how "they" could use different tests to evaluate her value added. She also did not trust whether "they" could really account for the types of students she had her in classroom, especially when she taught a disproportionate number of ELLs in comparison to her colleagues. While she reported having tried to figure EVAAS® out on her own via the district's online resources, she found it very confusing. It just "did not hit home."

Overall findings are presented next, and these include findings from the cases of these four teachers (see also Amrein-Beardsley & Collins, 2012), findings from focus group interviews that we conducted with HISD teachers excluding the four involved in the termination hearings (Amrein-Beardsley & Collins, 2012), and findings from a large-scale survey research study during which Collins (2012) surveyed HISD teachers about these topics. Findings across these three studies are described next, organized around more conceptual themes. I start first with the findings that pertained to issues with reliability, validity, and bias.

Findings – reliability, validity, and bias

Reliability

"Reliability" is the statistical term used to represent the degree to which a set of test scores have random error. Random error can be positive or negative and large or small, although it cannot be directly observed. Instead, what is observed, particularly here, is the extent to which a measure produces consistent or dependable results over time (i.e., reliability), especially in terms of supporting accuracy (i.e., validity). In terms of VAMs, reliability should be observed when VAM estimates of teacher (or school/district) effectiveness are consistent over time, from one year to the next, regardless of the type of students and perhaps subject areas teachers teach. If VAM estimates of teacher effectiveness are reliable, consistent results are observed. This is typically captured using reliability coefficients as well as confidence intervals that help to situate and contextualize VAM estimates and their (often sizeable) errors. This is also done to help others better understand the errors that come along with VAM estimates and to better contextualize the VAM-based inferences that result.

EVAAS® developers suggest that their system "assess[es] and predict[s] student performance with precision and reliability" and it is "the most robust and reliable" value-added system available, more than the "other simplistic models found in the market today" (SAS®, 2012a). In terms of what we found in Houston, however, it is clear that inconsistencies were a consistent problem.

Across the four cases discussed above, issues with reliability, or a lack thereof, were most evident. In three of the four cases, the probability that the teachers added or detracted value from year to year was roughly the same as the flip of a coin. Given that these teachers were removed from their teaching positions "at least in part" due to unreliable EVAAS® data, this is pragmatically, methodologically, and morally of great concern. These data did not signal that these teachers demonstrated "a significant lack of student progress attributable to the educator," or "insufficient student academic growth reflected by [EVAAS®] value-added scores." In addition, researchers agree that at least three years of value-added data are needed to make such judgments (Brophy, 1973; Cody et al., 2010; Glazerman & Potamites, 2011; Goldschmidt, Choi, & Beaudoin, 2012; Harris, 2011; Ishii & Rivkin, 2009; Sanders as cited in Gabriel & Lester, 2013), let alone make judgements well – remembering that 25% to 50% of teachers are at risk of being misclassified (Au, 2011; NGA & CCSSO, 2010; Otterman, 2010; Schochet & Chiang, 2010, 2013; Shaw & Bovaird, 2011). This recommendation is very troublesome given that not one of the four teachers had three years of consistent data (i.e., that were detectably different from other similar teachers) to warrant termination. It is important to note here that while research suggests three years of data are needed to make such decisions, many state's tenure laws already have provisions allowing states or districts to terminate or untenure teachers using, instead, two consecutive unsatisfactory evaluations (e.g., Delaware, Florida, Indiana, Pennsylvania), and, in the case of Louisiana, one unsatisfactory evaluation alone (Baker et al., 2013).

Other teachers in Houston noted concerns about the lack of consistency they themselves observed, comparing the receipt of merit monies based on EVAAS® data to "winning the lottery," given the random, "chaotic," year-to-year instabilities they also saw, and that are also prevalent in the literature (Amrein-Beardsley & Collins, 2012; see also Baeder, 2010; Baker et al., 2010; Haertel, 2011; Koedel & Betts, 2007; Papay, 2011). As well, teachers do not understand why they are being rewarded, especially because they profess that they are doing nothing differently from year to year as their value-added rankings "jump around." Along with the highs come rewards, but what they did differently remains unknown (Amrein-Beardsley & Collins, 2012, p. 4; see also Banchero & Kesmodel, 2011; Harris, 2011).

One teacher noted:

> I do what I do every year. I teach the way I teach every year. [My] first year got me pats on the back. [My] second year got me kicked in the backside. And for year three my scores were off the charts. I got a huge bonus, and now I am in the top quartile of all the English teachers. What did I do differently? I have no clue.
>
> *(Amrein-Beardsley & Collins, 2012, p. 15)*

Another teacher classified her past three years as "bonus, bonus, disaster."

Another noted:

> We had an 8th grade teacher, a very good teacher, the "real science guy," [who was a] very good teacher ... [but] every year he showed low EVAAS® growth. My principal flipped him with the 6th grade science teacher who was getting the highest EVAAS® scores on campus. Huge EVAAS® scores ... now the 6th grade teacher [is showing] no growth, but the 8th grade teacher who was sent down is getting the biggest bonuses on campus.

Collins' (2012) more recent survey research evidence supports this further, evidencing that inconsistent EVAAS® scores year to year are of concern among HISD teachers about half of the time (46.2%). One teacher explained, "In three years, I was above average, below average and average" (p. 96). Another wrote, "I have taught 4th grade for the last 8 years. My scores have been 'green' some years and 'red' other years" (pp. 96–97). While the other half (53.8%) did not note issues with inconsistencies over time, it seems that inconsistencies were "ironically, an inconsistent reality ... just like one would expect with the flip of a coin" (pp. 134–135).

EVAAS® developers claim they have evidence that teachers who move from one environment to another, even if radically different, continue to perform the same and are classified the same in EVAAS® terms over time (LeClaire, 2011). Research evidence presented herein has not demonstrated this as the case. About half of the responding HISD teachers (49.6%) also reported inconsistent EVAAS® data across the subject areas they taught. Respondents also reported moving to different grade levels and switching value-added ranks after the move, moving from "ineffective" to "effective" or vice versa, even across grade levels that are adjacent. This is problematic as the EVAAS® system is supposed to measure the teacher effectiveness construct consistently, and Sanders, the developer of the EVAAS®, claims he has evidence that this does not occur within his system. He claims that teachers who move from one environment to another, even if radically different, continue to do just as well (LeClaire, 2011).

Validity

"Validity" is the statistical term used to describe the accuracy of an interpretation that is derived from some use of a test score, or rather "the degree to which empirical evidence and theoretical rationales support the adequacy and appropriateness of interpretations" (Messick, 1995, p. 741). Validity describes the extent to which an assessment measure produces authentic, accurate, strong results and yields acceptable inferences about that which the assessment tool is intended to measure.

Validity is an essential of any measurement, and reliability is a necessary or qualifying condition for validity (Brennan, 2006, 2013; Kane, 2006, 2013; Messick, 1975, 1980, 1995). That said, validity almost always follows reliability, as without consistency (i.e., reliability) one cannot typically achieve any certain level or sense of truth (i.e., validity). Put differently, if scores are unreliable, it is virtually impossible to support valid interpretations or uses (see also Brennan, 2006; Popham, 2011).

In terms of VAMs, validity might be observed when VAM estimates of teacher (or school/ district) effectiveness relate, or more specifically correlate well with other measures (e.g., supervisor evaluation scores) that are developed to measure the same construct (e.g., teacher effectiveness; Hill et al., 2011; Kane & Staiger, 2012; Kersting et al., 2013; Sass & Harris, 2012). If VAM estimates of teacher effectiveness are valid, there should be research-based evidence (and some commonsense) that proves that all indicators are together pointing towards the same proverbial target of truth.

In the case of Houston, I examined whether the four teachers terminated for their subpar EVAAS® scores also seemed to be ineffectual according to their PDAS scores, specifically to determine if these teachers' supervisors also observed that these teachers were inadequate (i.e., criterion-related evidence of validity). Analyzing the four teachers' EVAAS® scores alongside their PDAS scores, however, it was visually and statistically apparent that the two indicators were not measuring the teaching effectiveness construct accurately and consistently across teachers. The better Teacher A did on the EVAAS®, the worse she did in the eyes of her supervisor(s) ($r=-0.51$, $r=-0.83$, $r=-0.11$). These results do not suggest validity, because the two measures did not point in the same direction, so to speak. Yet for Teacher B, the better she did on the EVAAS®, the better she did on the PDAS ($r=0.91$). This yields the type of correlation we would expect to see if in fact both indicators pointed in the same direction, yielding valid results. Analyzing Teacher C's mathematics EVAAS® scores alongside her PDAS scores was not possible, but her social studies EVAAS® and PDAS scores were mildly related ($r=0.26$). For Teacher D there were weak to strong results ($r=0.29$, $r=0.92$). The level of variability within these results, in terms of both the valence of correlations (positive or negative) and the magnitude (small to large), make it relatively impossible to call the relationship between EVAAS® estimates and PDAS scores a valid one. Collins (2012) substantiated this finding, demonstrating that more than half (57.6%) of HISD teachers who participated in her survey research study indicated their EVAAS® estimates did not typically match their PDAS observational scores.

Relatedly, analyzing all four teachers' EVAAS® scores alongside their bonuses, it was apparent that both of these measures were also not measuring the teaching effectiveness construct accurately and consistently across teachers. The worse Teacher A did on the EVAAS®, the more money she received ($r=-0.42$), but the better Teacher B did the more money she received ($r=0.93$). Teacher C's monetary bonuses and EVAAS® scores were mildly related ($r=0.29$), and Teacher D's monetary bonuses and EVAAS® scores were more strongly related ($r=0.79$). Again, the highly variable relationships between these indicators, across teachers, makes valid inference-making relatively impossible.

In addition, three of four teachers were honored with teaching awards (e.g., "Teacher of the Month or Year" awards) during the same timeframe for which they posted EVAAS® data that, at least in part, led to their termination. Teacher C ironically received a "Teacher of the Year" award from her peers at the same time she detracted the most value from her students' learning, according to her EVAAS® data. This raises additional concerns about whether these indicators are capturing teacher effectiveness validly.

In terms of the validity of the EVAAS® system taken at face value, Collins (2012) illustrated teachers' concerns about how they viewed the ways in which EVAAS® estimates were split across co-teachers, teacher aids, departments, or teams using overly simplistic ratios to account for proportional levels of instructional time and effort. Evident were issues with teachers being evaluated while teaching alongside other teachers who were teaching the same students the same subjects at the same time (e.g., Teacher B splitting mathematics instruction with another teacher). Others noted issues with not receiving EVAAS® estimates for students they had taught, or being provided EVAAS® estimates for subject areas or students they had not taught, or had not taught for any substantial period of time.

One teacher wrote:

> I'm not sure how I get evaluated for a student who is only in my class for one month and then goes into CEP [community education partners for disciplinary alternative education]. I'm still considered the teacher of record even though he spent 5–6 months out of my classroom.

(p. 104)

Teacher B, whose scores were negative for two years and positive for the most recent year for which she had EVAAS® data, taught for the same years alongside a mathematics enrichment teacher, who taught almost half of her students at the same time and an equal amount of time per week. Teacher A was not a teacher of record for approximately 50% of one of the years for which she was held accountable using the EVAAS® as she was moved from teaching the third to the fourth grade mid-year. Another Houston teacher taught alongside a reading/language arts specialist four days per week, and then posted the most growth and received the largest bonus she ever had (Amrein-Beardsley & Collins, 2012).

These instances all raise concerns about whether teachers can, in reality, be held responsible for 100%, or even 90%, 80%, or 70% of their students' scores, as implied. EVAAS® developers claim that through a linking verification process (during which teachers mark for what percentage of each student's instruction (s)he should be held accountable) they can partition out different teachers' effects (Derringer, 2010; Sanders & Horn, 1994). However, there is no research evidence demonstrating that numerically splitting or dividing teacher effects into simple proportions actually works. Not only is such a practice counter-intuitive, breaking up effort across teachers using percentages and ratios is nonsensical given the interaction effects that we also know occur among and between students and teachers (Bausell, 2013; Braun, 2005; Darling-Hammond & Haertel, 2012; Graue, Delaney, & Karch, 2013; Monk, 1987; Reardon & Raudenbush, 2009; Schafer et al., 2012). Teachers are situated in complex learning environments, and they do not teach in vacuum-sealed classrooms as most of these value-added models imply. This is well founded in the research on value added and also on peer effects (Baker et al., 2010; Bosworth & Caliendo, 2007; Braun, 2005; Monk, 1987; Corcoran, 2010; Ishii & Rivkin, 2009; Lazear, 2001; Linn, 2008; Nelson, 2011; Misco, 2008; Monk, 1987; Newton, Darling-Hammond, Haertel, & Thomas, 2010; Reardon & Raudenbush, 2009; Rothstein, 2009). Determining what percentage of value-added scores can be attributed to teachers is very difficult, if not impossible (Campbell & Stanley, 1963; Corcoran, 2010; Ishii & Rivkin, 2009; Kane & Staiger, 2008; Kennedy, 2010; Linn, 2008; Nelson, 2011; Papay, 2011; Rothstein, 2009). These issues might also play into why such inconsistencies are evident when examining VAM-based levels of reliability.

Finally, in terms of content-related validity evidence, teachers in Houston also reported having issues with using different large-scale standardized tests that, while manufactured by the same or similar testing companies, were designed to align to either national or state standards from year to year (Amrein-Beardsley & Collins, 2012; Collins, 2012). The main issue here was that the pre-test scores often being used to calculate teachers EVAAS® estimates were not linked to state standards (e.g., Stanford tests) and came from altogether different tests than the post-test scores, and vice versa. For example, in Collins (2012) one teacher noted that "ELL students usually don't [show progress] especially if they have taken the Aprenda[11] the year before," and the Aprenda is used as the pre-test score. "The Aprenda test really inflates their scores" making it more difficult to show progress on the TAKS post-test occasion (p. 102). While these tests and their scores can be normed, this still raises issues with content alignment and content-related validity evidence.

All of this greatly diminishes validity, or more precisely the extent to which valid inferences might be made given the faulty (and often inconsistent) VAM-based estimates so often observed. The conclusion specifically in Houston, however, is that there is not yet any substantive evidence to show that a valid system that yields valid inferences based on EVAAS®

and PDAS scores is in operation (see also Hill et al., 2011; Kane & Staiger, 2012; Kersting et al., 2013; Sass & Harris, 2012).

Bias

"Bias" is a huge threat to validity, as influential factors can increase or decrease test scores or test-based estimates, even though they are unrelated to what tests or test-based indicators are meant to represent. Bias, therefore, is any factor that affects test scores yet is unrelated to what the test score represents. In terms of VAMs, bias occurs when estimates derived systematically differ given the varying characteristics of the populations being examined. More specifically, bias is observed when VAM estimates of teacher (or school/district) effectiveness correlate too strongly with indicators (e.g., students' racial or socioeconomic backgrounds) other than those that are of interest (e.g., teacher effectiveness).

Bias is also known as construct-irrelevant variance (CIV), a term used by Messick (1989) to describe factors that falsely inflate or deflate the measurement of a variable and therefore distort its interpretation or its validity. As bias is the more commonly used term for CIV, although some argue the term is too general as it does not capture the complexity of variables that ultimately threaten validity (see, for example, Haladyna & Downing, 2004), bias is the term more popularly used in the VAM-based literature (Capitol Hill Briefing, 2011; Darling-Hammond, Amrein-Beardsley, Haertel, & Rothstein, 2012; Newton et al., 2010; Rothstein, 2009, 2010b).

Across cases in Houston, teachers not receiving merit monies attributed the lack of rewards to the types of students they taught, and how teaching particularly diverse groups of students might have biased their scores (Amrein-Beardsley & Collins, 2012; Collins, 2012; see also Hill et al., 2011; Newton et al., 2010). Teachers noted that the "chaos" or lack of consistency they observed across their value-added scores could be credited to the different students they taught, and to factors external to their classrooms, including students' home lives and family situations, levels of motivation, behaviors, disruptions, and the like. HISD teachers echoed what Newton et al. (2010) empirically found, that "A teacher who teaches less advantaged students in a given course or year typically receives lower effectiveness ratings than the same teacher teaching more advantaged students in a different course or year" (p. 2).

While Teacher C's EVAAS® data illustrated that Teacher C consistently detracted value from her students' learning, and did so across subject areas, this was likely because Teacher C taught some of the highest needs students, possibly across the district. According to Teacher C, her students "just came [to school] because they had to come, not necessarily because they wanted to be there." While Teacher C's traditional, 10-year-old sixth graders "did seem to care about their success in school," almost half of their classmates (e.g., those who had been held back one or more times) had "become complacent" and "no longer cared much about or took pride in their test scores." These students did not take the tests seriously, yet these tests were still used as a critical component in the evaluation of Teacher C.

Here is an interesting case, however, where consistency across Teacher C's scores was observed, which would lend itself to validity, but bias interfered. Teacher C's scores were demonstrably stable, yet invalid, given the types of students consistently placed in Teacher C's classroom – the same types of students year after year, characteristically different from their peers, who consistently biased Teacher C's EVAAS® estimates. The point here is that teachers who work with certain populations of students should not be negatively impacted by bias, but they sometimes are, especially when teaching inordinate numbers of homogeneous groups of students who are often low-achieving or, in particular, ELLs, gifted and special education students, children from racial minority backgrounds, students receiving free or reduced-cost lunches, students who have been retained in grade for multiple years, students in remedial or other tracked programs, or even when teaching small classes (Amrein-Beardsley & Collins, 2012; Baker et al., 2010; Capitol Hill Briefing, 2011; Carey & Manwaring, 2011; Goldhaber et al., 2012; Hermann, Walsh, Isenberg, & Resch, 2013; Hill et al., 2011; McCaffrey et al., 2004b; Newton et al., 2010; Rothstein & Mathis, 2013; Stacy, Guarino, Reckase, & Wooldridge, 2012).

HISD teachers teaching in grades in which ELLs were transitioned into mainstreamed classrooms reported being the least likely to add value and the most likely to be deemed "ineffective" (Amrein-Beardsley & Collins, 2012).

One teacher noted:

> I went to a transition classroom, and now there's a red flag next to my name. I guess now I'm an ineffective teacher? I keep getting letters from the district, saying "You've been recognized as an outstanding teacher" … this, this, and that. But now because I teach English Language Learners who "transition in," my scores drop? And I get a flag next to my name for not teaching them well?
>
> *(p. 16)*

Another teacher added:

> I'm scared to teach in the 4th grade. I'm scared I might lose my job if I teach in an [ELL] transition grade level, because I'm scared my scores are going to drop, and I'm going to get fired because there's probably going to be no growth.
>
> *(p. 16)*

Another teacher concluded, "When they say nobody wants to do 4th grade – nobody wants to do 4th grade! Nobody" (p. 16).

This was evidenced as well with Teacher D. Teacher D, like Teacher A, flip-flopped across subject areas, until her last year during which she detracted value across subject areas. This was the year she was assigned to teach an ELL transition year, during which an inordinate number of ELLs entered her classroom. Another teacher in Collins (2012) also noted that (s)he felt (s)he was being "punished" for teaching ELL students (p. 123). Had it been possible, (s)he would have "refuse[d]" to teach ELL students (p. 123).

This likely occurs for obvious reasons, in that these students are not proficient in the language in which the TAKS tests are written (i.e., English), and they are more likely to opt out of or skip questions they simply do not understand, all of which puts ELL teachers at risk. Until EVAAS® developers can evidence that teachers teaching inordinate numbers of ELLs, particularly in transition years, and teachers teaching disproportionate numbers of other diverse students are not disparately impacted by the non-random placement of these students into their classrooms, terminating teachers on these grounds is remiss and morally indefensible.

Teachers teaching inordinate numbers of special education students expressed similar concerns (see also Hill et al., 2011; Newton et al., 2010; Rothstein, 2009).

In Collins (2012), a teacher elaborated on this by writing:

> I had 11 special [education] kids last year with no co-teacher [or] assistance of any kind. The kids' disabilities ranged from emotional disturbances to learning disabilities to borderline retardation. I had a higher failure rate with them than with my other classes.
>
> *(p. 124)*

Similar reports came from teachers teaching the same students over consecutive years, regardless of whether the students they continuously served were diverse. Specifically, teachers who "looped" (e.g., teachers teaching the same cohort of students for two or more consecutive years or grade levels) reported receiving bonuses for the first year and nothing the next as they were "maxing out" on growth, and actually "competing with themselves." A teacher in Collins (2012) noted this as well, writing, "I teach many of [the] same students in 7th and 8th [grades]. In 7th I show growth, then in 8th [I] suffer" (p. 124).

Another teacher wrote:

> In 2nd grade my students scored so high (90th percentile), it was almost impossible to show growth with the same students in third [grade]. After realizing this, the next year in third [grade] I gave my student[s] twice as much test prep as I had the year before when they did not show any growth, preparing them for tricky multiple choice questions. The result was outstanding! I received a huge bonus and showed so much growth, but sad to say [it was] because of more test prep.
>
> *(p. 124)*

While this might not count as a traditional form of bias, that is, the bias we think about when inordinate numbers of students from diverse backgrounds weigh down EVAAS® estimates, teachers who looped seemed to also yield biased EVAAS® estimates simply because they taught the exact same students from one year to the next.

There are also ceiling effects prevalent, where HISD teachers teaching gifted students also reported finding it very difficult to add value, much less get merit pay as a result (see also Cole et al., 2011; Kelly & Monczunski, 2007; Koedel & Betts, 2007, 2010; Linn & Haug, 2002; Wright et al., 1997). HISD teachers could only get the best and brightest of HISD students "up so much!" (Amrein-Beardsley & Collins, 2012, p. 16).

One gifted teacher noted:

> Every year I have the highest test scores, [and] I have fellow teachers that come up to me when they get their bonuses.... One recently came up to me [and] literally cried, "I'm so sorry." I'm like, "Don't be sorry.... It's not your fault." Here I am ... with the highest test scores and I'm getting $0 in bonuses. It makes no sense year-to-year how this works.... How do I, how do I, you know, I don't know what to do. I don't know how to get higher than a 100%.
>
> *(p. 16)*

Another gifted teacher explained:

> I have students [in a fifth grade gifted reading class] who score at the 6th, 7th, & 8th grade levels in reading. But I'm like please babies, score at the 9th grade level, cause if

you don't score at the 9th or 10th grade or higher in 5th grade with me, I'm going to show negative growth. Even though you, you're gifted, and you're talented, and you're high! I can only push you so much higher when you are already so high. I'm scared.

(p. 16)

Another gifted teacher explained:

The first year, [my scores] were ok. Then as I began to teach the gifted students, the scores continued to show negative growth. For the 2010–2011 school year, the principal even told me that my scores revealed that I was one of the worst teachers in the school.

(Collins, 2012, p. 97)

Collins (2012) found that across HISD almost one in five teachers (17.4%) viewed gifted and advanced students as problematic when it came to EVAAS® growth.

Again, however, EVAAS® developers claim that student background factors do not impact students' ability to grow year to year in the EVAAS® model, mainly because the system uses students' previous years of data as "blocking factors" to prevent such variables from biasing or distorting growth (Sanders & Horn, 1994, 1998; Sanders et al., 2009; Wright, White, Sanders, & Rivers, 2010). Appropriately, particularly as demonstrated here, this is one of the most highly contested claims made by EVAAS® developers (Ballou et al., 2004; Braun, 2005; Cody et al., 2010; Kupermintz, 2003; McCaffrey et al., 2003; McCaffrey et al., 2004b; Sanders & Wright, 2008; Sanders et al., 2009; Tekwe et al., 2004).

That said, until EVAAS® developers can evidence that teachers teaching inordinate numbers of ELLs, particularly in transition years, as well as those teaching special education, back-to-back classes, or gifted students[12] are not disparately impacted by the non-random placement of these students into their classrooms (Amrein-Beardsley, 2008a; Ballou, 2012; Cody et al., 2010; Dorn, 1994; Glass, 1995; McCaffrey, 2012; Monk, 1987; Paufler & Amrein-Beardsley, 2013; Rothstein, 2009, 2010b), terminating teachers on these grounds is, again, remiss and morally indefensible.

Findings – fairness, transparency, and VAM-based use

Fairness

Issues of "fairness" arise when a test, or more likely its inference-based use, impacts some more than others in unfair yet often consequential ways. In terms of VAMs, the main issue here is that VAM-based estimates can be produced for only approximately 30–40% of all teachers across America's public schools (Gabriel & Lester, 2013; Harris, 2011; see also Thomas, 2012). The other 60–70%, which sometimes includes entire campuses of teachers (e.g., early elementary and high school teachers), cannot altogether be evaluated or held accountable using teacher- or individual-based value-added data (Collins & Amrein-Beardsley, 2014). What VAM-based data provide, in general, "are incredibly imprecise and inconsistent measures of supposed teacher effectiveness for only a tiny handful [30–40%] of teachers in a given school" (Baker et al., 2013, p. 12).

It should be noted that the fairness issues presented here are issues because EVAAS®, and other VAM-based estimates for that matter, only involve teachers of the core subject areas that are currently tested using large-scale standardized achievement tests. In HISD this includes teachers of mathematics, reading/language arts, and science and social studies, although in the latter two subject areas calculating VAM estimates is not as easily done given these two subject areas are not tested consistently from one grade to the next nor every year.

However, and unfortunately, because the teachers typically marginalized by the EVAAS® system in HISD were not directly targeted research participants in any of the research studies we have conducted thus far in HISD, no substantive findings about fairness can be presented that are specific to HISD only. All that is known comes from Collins (2012) who found evidence of issues with fairness. For example, one of HISD's core subject teacher respondents wrote that the district's lower grade teachers "feel like they are chopped liver compared to the testing grades" and "feel unappreciated and disenfranchised" (p. 130). More research on issues with fairness, and the approximately 60–70% of all teachers who are most often marginalized when most if not all VAM-based systems are put into place, is certainly needed.

Transparency and formative use

"Transparency" can be defined as the extent to which something is easily seen and readily capable of being understood. Along with transparency comes the "formative" aspects key to any, in this case, VAM-based measurement system. First, VAM-based estimates must be made transparent in order to be understood, so that they can ultimately be used to "inform" change, growth, and hopefully future progress in "formative" ways. In terms of VAMs, the main issue here is that most VAM-based esimates, and in this case certainly most EVAAS® estimates, do not seem to make sense. Data reports are confusing and in HISD (and in Tennessee, the state in which EVAAS® was first developed and is still used) they are often received months after students leave teachers' classrooms. This "lag time" sometimes causes scores to be returned months into the next school year (Gabriel & Lester, 2013, p. 7).

Teachers in HISD specifically express that they are learning little about what they did effectively or how they might use their EVAAS® data to improve their instruction. Eckert and Dabrowski (2010) also demonstrated this in Tennessee with teachers under the related TVAAS system (the scheme from which the EVAAS® system was derived). They illustrated that there was no explanation of how teachers or schools were to use their VAM data to improve much of anything (see also Harris, 2011). This is problematic in that the main purported strength of the EVAAS® is the "wealth of positive diagnostic information" accumulated for formative purposes (Sanders et al., 2009, p. 9). The question here is still, according to Darling-Hammond (1990), "How, and under what conditions ... policies intended to change teaching actually do so?" (p. 341).

In the case of Houston, Teachers A, B, C, and D were only familiar with EVAAS® and their EVAAS® data and reports. They understood that they were being compared to other similar teachers within the district, and they understood their scores were available each year via the district's online portal system, but that was about it. Nobody had explained their EVAAS® data to them, and none of them understood what their EVAAS® numbers meant, how they were calculated, how their EVAAS® scores could be "used against [them]," or how they could use their EVAAS® scores to help improve their instruction. Teacher D took steps to figure out her EVAAS® scores on her own, but her EVAAS® scores still "did not hit home" (see also Eckert & Dabrowski, 2010). In addition, the four terminated teachers did not receive professional development as a result of their value-added scores, although given the scores illustrated in Tables 2.1 to 2.4 whether Teachers A, B, C, and D needed professional development to improve their value-added scores is disputable. Because they were terminated at least in part due to their EVAAS® scores, and because they were reportedly not given professional development to improve their scores, the lack of feedback and formative action based upon the scores is quite troublesome.

Collins (2012) found that over one third (37.2%) of the HISD teachers who participated in her study were unaware of the EVAAS® training sessions provided by the district to help teachers understand the EVAAS® model and EVAAS® data and reports. Of those who attended such sessions, the majority (62.1%) found them unhelpful in terms of helping them better understand the EVAAS® model and their individual EVAAS® estimates. While about half of HISD teachers (48.6%) responded that their principals discussed their EVAAS® results with them, for example during their professional reviews, these teachers also indicated that their principals shared with them their EVAAS® scores in a manner that was "vague," "not in depth," and "not discussed thoroughly" (p. 116). HISD teachers also indicated that they believed the "very basic discussions" (p. 116) in which they engaged with their supervisors were likely due to the fact that their principals did not understand EVAAS® either (see also Amrein-Beardsley & Collins, 2012; Eckert & Dabrowski, 2010). One teacher wrote, for example, that "He looks at [the EVAAS® scores], but [he] is unable to explain them" (p. 116). Another teacher noted that his/her principal "goes over the data, without much comprehension on how scores are derived. [The principal] cannot suggest improvements" (p. 116). Another teacher wrote, "Our principal does not know how they get the score and has tried many times to get someone to come and explain it to us. No one can" (p. 116).

Collins (2012) also found that while SAS® claims to provide "easily understandable reporting" (SAS®, 2012b) that can be used by teachers to modify their teaching practices, this might not be the case in practice, either. When teachers were directly asked if they used their EVAAS® information to inform their instruction, 58.9% indicated that they did not. They replied that their EVAAS® reports were "vague" and "unclear" (p. 141), and they were "not quite sure how to interpret [them]" (p. 141) nor did they know how to use the EVAAS® data to change or improve their instruction. One teacher wrote that (s)he looked at the EVAAS® data "only to guess as to what to do for the next group in my class" (p. 110). Another wrote, "[I] attempted [to use them] but the reports are not helpful at all" (p. 111). Another wrote, "Since I don't find the reports consistent with my instruction, effort and quality of practice, I don't trust EVAAS® reports" (p. 128). Likewise, none of the four terminated teachers noted that they used EVAAS® data to inform their instruction either.

Those who indicated that they did use their EVAAS® data, however, could not effectively express how they used their EVAAS® data in any articulate ways, unless perhaps to plan for remedial instruction with future, yet different, students. One teacher, for example, described how (s)he used EVAAS® reports to look at subgroups, but then (s)he revealed (s)he was not quite sure what to do beyond that. Another responded, "It is not specific enough to tell me exactly the strength or weakness in each area" (Collins, 2012, p. 111). While some teachers noted doing things like using their EVAAS® data to identify students for purposes of ability grouping, to individualize instruction, or to identify particularly low-scoring students for pull out and other remedial programs, respondents otherwise provided vague descriptions writing things like "yes" and "I use it" (p. 113).

Additionally, the majority of respondents (60.1%) indicated that they received their EVAAS® reports after the students responsible for generating EVAAS® information were no longer under their instruction. One teacher noted that the timing of the distribution of EVAAS® reports prevented him/her from using the EVAAS® data, writing, "By the time I get the scores the students are in another grade. I can look at the previous years' scores, but [the reports] have to be pulled by individual students.... This is too time consuming" (p. 110). Many others (45.4%) indicated that they actually used, and preferred to use, data other than their EVAAS® reports to inform and improve upon their instruction (e.g., classroom-based assessment measures).

In sum, none of the data for the four terminated teachers in HISD or the other HISD teachers included in our research to date (Amrein-Beardsley & Collins, 2012; Collins, 2012; see also Eckert & Dabrowski, 2010) suggest that the EVAAS® system "provides valuable diagnostic information about [instructional] practices," helps educators become more proactive and make more "sound instructional choices," or helps teachers use their "resources more strategically to ensure that every student has the chance to succeed" (SAS®, 2012a). This is not to say this is not occurring elsewhere, perhaps in other states, districts, or schools using the EVAAS® system, but I would doubt this more than I would trust, for example, the testimonials available on the SAS® Institute, Inc. website (SAS®, 2012a).

VAM-based use

Finally, Collins (2012) found that HISD teachers actually disagreed with all of the statements used by SAS® Institute, Inc. as rationales to justify the adoption, consumption, or use of EVAAS® (SAS®, 2012c). Teachers most often disagreed with SAS® Institute, Inc. statements, for example, like "EVAAS® will enhance working conditions" (75.5% disagreement), "EVAAS® will validly identify and help remove ineffective teachers" (72.9%), "EVAAS® will enhance the school environment" (72.5%), and "EVAAS® will identify excellence in teaching or leadership" (68.3%).

What is also important to note in terms of use, though, is that these teachers felt that their EVAAS® scores were being used against them. Teachers A, B, C, and D felt they were targeted for termination because of the performance of the schools in which they taught. The schools in which they taught were labeled "in need of improvement" under NCLB. Accordingly, administrators under district and state pressure set out to "come over," "restructure the school," and "start firing teachers." Teachers A, B, C, and D all felt that they were part of "a larger plan," and because they were perceived to have low EVAAS® scores, or lower EVAAS® scores than their colleagues, they felt that they had been put "on a list." This was when they believed that they became most vulnerable, and this was when their PDAS observational scores also plummeted.

Teacher A, for example, "exceeded expectations" on her yearly PDAS reports until 2010–2011 when a new principal arrived and ranked her "proficient" or "below expectations" across domains. Teacher B's PDAS scores dropped as well, but her supervisor wrote on her PDAS form that she could not have earned higher scores because the state classified the school's scores as "unacceptable." Teacher C was evaluated by three different administrators and consistently "exceeded expectations," but in 2010–2011, when she was evaluated by a short-term administrator hired to transform the school, she too was rated as either "proficient" or "below expectations" across PDAS domains. Similarly, Teacher D reported that her supervisor's actions became perceptibly more aggressive as time went on.

These and other HISD teachers also noted that their supervisors were skewing their observational scores to match their value-added scores given external pressures to do so

(Amrein-Beardsley & Collins, 2012; Collins, 2012; see also Baker, 2012a; Garland, 2012; Ravitch, 2012c).

One teacher stated:

> Here's the problem: No principal wants to be called in by the superintendent or another superior and [asked], "How come your teachers show negative growth but you have high evaluations on them? Are you doing your job? I don't understand. Your teacher shows no growth but you have [marked them] as exceeding expectations all up and down the chart?" Now it's not just this [*sic*] data over here that's gonna harm us, it's the principals [who are] adjusting our data over there to match the EVAAS®. So it looks like they're being consistent.
>
> *(Collins, 2012, p. 55)*

Another teacher agreed: "Well my evaluations were fine, but of course now they have to make the evaluation match the EVAAS®. We now have to go through that" (Amrein-Beardsley & Collins, 2012, p. 19).

Another teacher wrote:

> They're not about to go to bat [for us, although] a few of them will. But most of them are going to go in there, and they're going to create a teacher evaluation that reflects the [EVAAS®] data because they don't want to have to explain, again and again, why they're giving high classroom observation assessments when the data shows [*sic*] that the teacher is low performing.
>
> *(Collins, 2012, p. 56)*

Another noted:

> Our principal pressures us. You bet she pressures. If you don't [make EVAAS®], then it goes against you in your PDAS. In a roundabout way she finds a way to put that against you.
>
> *(Amrein-Beardsley & Collins, 2012, p. 19)*

Another noted:

> My boss had to go to the district superintendent and explain why we needed to be kept, when ultimately the data showed that we weren't good teachers. ... [However] you've got other good teachers who are being thrown under the bus because of this system.
>
> *(Amrein-Beardsley & Collins, 2012, p. 19)*

In Collins (2012), HISD teachers also described how principals would switch their PDAS scores to match their EVAAS® scores if dissimilar, mainly because they believed their administrators held the opinion that the EVAAS® estimates were superior and should trump the more subjective PDAS scores (Amrein-Beardsley & Collins, 2012; Collins, 2012; see also Baker, 2012; Garland, 2012; Glazerman et al., 2010; Harris, 2011; Ravitch, 2012c; Rockoff, Staiger, Kane, & Taylor, 2010).

For example, one teacher wrote:

> One principal told me one year that even though I had high TAKS scores and high Stanford scores, the fact that my EVAAS® scores showed no growth, it would look bad to the superintendent.
>
> *(Collins, 2012, p. 106)*

Another wrote, "I had high appraisals but low EVAAS®, so they had to change appraisals to match [my] lower EVAAS® scores" (p. 106). Another wrote, "Upon the arrival of the [EVAAS®] scores my students did exemplary [so the assistant] principal changed the [PDAS] rating before I met with her to 'exceeds expectations'" (p. 106). In addition, about 10% of all HISD teacher participants noted having been nominated for or awarded teaching honors or honorable teaching duties (e.g., serving as mentor teachers, department chairs, academic coaches) at the same time as they had received EVAAS® scores that were low given their otherwise perceived levels of teaching expertise and skill. This also occurred with three of the four teachers whose contracts were not renewed by HISD.

From HISD teachers' general perspectives, it seems that district administrators are more trusting of EVAAS® and are skewing PDAS scores accordingly, sometimes as explicitly advised or implicitly influenced by district supervisors. This makes sense, though, as the EVAAS® is the "objective" system that the district has purchased (at $500,000 per year) and that the district continues to use, in large part to replace or add to the traditional observational scores increasingly being dismissed as subjective. Measuring teacher effectiveness using value added seems to be trumping other indicators to capture what it means to be an effective teacher (Amrein-Beardsley & Collins, 2012; Collins, 2012; Baker, 2012a; Gabriel & Lester, 2013; Garland, 2012; Glazerman et al., 2010; Harris, 2011; Ravitch, 2012c; Rockoff et al., 2010).

Conclusions

In the end, Teachers A, B, and D pursued due process hearings, but they decided not to follow their due process hearings through to culmination. They decided to quit teaching in HISD or to quit teaching altogether instead. Teacher C (the teacher who according to her EVAAS® estimates had the poorest and most consistent value-added scores) took her case through her due process hearing. Her hearing officer noted that the types of students Teacher C typically taught most likely biased her capacity to show growth. The hearing officer also noted that Teacher C did not have three years of consistent data in the core subject areas she taught, which was considered necessary to warrant a decision regarding whether indeed she was an effective teacher. Teacher C was given her job back.

The point of including these four cases here was not to prove unequivocally that these teachers were wrongfully terminated. At focus was an examination of their EVAAS® data, how they correlated with other data meant to capture the same construct of teaching effectiveness, and their complementary stories, to better examine the EVAAS® system, which is arguably the "best" value-added system available. My intent was also to examine the effects of the system and the districts' use of the system for high-stakes consequences. This was and continues to be the purpose of all of the research I, along with my colleagues, have thus far conducted in Houston.

It still stands to reason that before consequences are tied to value-added estimates, a teacher should be classified similarly on at least one other, medium-to-highly correlated, unbiased measure to independently assess the same construct at the same time. This must happen before anyone can make the case that a teacher is effective or ineffective, or should be monetarily awarded or contractually terminated (Baker et al., 2010; Harris, 2011; Hill, 2009; Hill et al., 2011; Newton et al., 2010; Papay, 2011). The more that multiple indicators point in the same direction, and the more years over which the indicators yield the same results, the better the accountability system might be, and the more justifiable high-stakes decisions surrounding teacher evaluation might become. This is in line with the current *Standards for Educational and Psychological Testing* that were collaboratively written by the American Educational Research Association (AERA), American Psychological Association (APA), and the National Council on Measurement in Education (NCME) (2000; see also Capitol Hill Briefing, 2011).

However, systems based on multiple-measures are also showing limited promise; the strengths of the measures being used (e.g., the VAM-based and observational measures) are not nearly strong enough to offset the weaknesses of the same measures being combined in such systems (see, for example, the Bill and Melinda Gates Foundation, 2013). The one thing that is absolutely certain here is that high-stakes decisions should *not* be made on the basis of VAM-based measures alone.

HISD is violating this recommendation, as principals seem to be skewing at least some teachers' PDAS scores to match what they seem to view as the superior scores derived via EVAAS®, making HISD's teacher evaluation system one that is, at least in some cases, ultimately based on one measure. Just recently, at the end of the 2012–2013 school year, for example, the district fired another set of teachers using only, and in isolation, teachers' EVAAS® scores. This illustrates well the increasing "value" HISD is increasingly "adding" or attributing to this "more objective" system. This time, it should also be noted, the district offered each teacher to be terminated one year's severance pay; that is, if the teacher agreed to reject his/her due process rights and avoid litigation (M. Owen, personal communication, May 24, 2013).

That said, whether HISD should be held responsible, particularly in court regarding the (ab)use of the system and/or whether those at SAS® Institute, Inc. should share in the responsibility to ensure that their system is being properly used, might be a debate for another day. Perhaps, in general, the focus here might shift from discussing how this and other VAM systems are being used towards who should be responsible for ensuring VAM estimates and VAM-based inferences are used correctly and with reliability and validity intact.

While it might be easiest to place blame for not ensuring proper use of the EVAAS® system on the for-profit institution, perhaps it is not SAS® Institute, Inc.'s responsibility. SAS® Institute, Inc. does, however, have the responsibility of identifying effective teachers, schools, and systems, in a precise, unbiased, and reliable manner, as marketed. These deliverables are advertised in the EVAAS® literature and marketing materials. Yet these claims have been countered with empirical, albeit case-based evidence as illustrated here. SAS® Institute, Inc. and the other companies working most closely with states, not to mention securing tax-subsidized contracts to continue and support their VAM-based initiatives, are discussed in more depth next.

Box 2.1 Top 10 assertions

1 The U.S. Department of Education sponsored pilot studies to test how value-added models (VAMs) might be integrated into statewide accountability policies. Despite problematic results, and the warnings of most VAM researchers at the time, federal policymakers funneled billions in taxpayer revenues to incentivize states to integrate VAMs regardless.

2 There are two main model types – VAMs and growth models (e.g., Student Growth Percentiles [SGPs]). The main differences among models are how estimates are calculated, whether control variables are used, and for what purposes estimates are generated.

3 It is becoming increasingly evident that all models, regardless of their specifics and levels of sophistication, are unreliable, invalid, and to varying degrees biased.

4 They are also unfair. Most teachers (i.e., 60% to 70%) are not eligible to receive teacher-level value-added scores because their students do not take large-scale standardized tests or because scores are missing to measure value-added on both pre- and post-test occasions.

5 Of the VAM-eligible teachers, 25–50% are at risk of being misclassified.

6 Teachers of certain students who are not randomly assigned to classrooms have more difficulties demonstrating growth.

7 VAM data have limited instructional value because VAM estimates are often difficult to understand and interpret for formative uses, and they are not as instructionally sensitive as often assumed.

8 Despite issues with reliability, validity, and bias, VAM estimates are being used to make consequential decisions about teachers (e.g., merit pay, tenure, termination).

9 Teachers are situated in complex learning environments, and they do not teach in vacuum-sealed classrooms as most VAM statisticians and consumers assume.

10 Even though research suggests three years of VAM data are needed to make still-imperfect decisions, many state policies have provisions allowing them to pay, untenure, or terminate teachers using, instead, one or two consecutive unsatisfactory VAM-based evaluations.

Notes

1 Status models are typically used to measure student achievement at one point in time, typically when states' large-scale standardized achievement tests are administered, once per year. These models illustrate a snap-shot indicator of student achievement but are incapable of capturing where students were, in terms of their academic achievement, before entering a classroom or school. Hence, the only thing snapshot scores can typically be used for is setting goals, that are often arbitrary, and then measuring whether the goals are met on the following years' tests. This might be useful when, for example, a teacher wants to know how many students are labeled below a predetermined definition of average, but because the teacher would not have much of an idea regarding how far below students were before his/her instruction, the test scores are more easily disregarded. All tests mandated via NCLB required such status models, but as stated above, they were increasingly dismissed, especially when they were used to measure AYP over time because they did not effectively measure student growth. While AYP measures helped to measure the statuses of different cohorts of students as they progressed across the same grade levels (and classrooms/schools) over time, facilitating

investigations about, for example, whether this year's fourth graders did better in reading/language arts than last year's fourth graders, what still could not be determined were the innate differences among cohorts and whether cohorts in fact grew from the point they entered the same grade levels (and classrooms/schools) to the point they left.

2 The best and most concise definition of VAM I have found in the literature follows:

> VAMs predict individual student achievement based on the student's characteristics, including baseline achievement, and compare this prediction with the actual achievement of a teacher's students. The prediction is derived using data on other students in the state or district and represents what we would expect the student to achieve if the average teacher taught him/her. The difference between how a teacher's students actually performed and how they were predicted to perform represents the estimate of the teacher's value-added to student achievement.
>
> *(Hermann et al., 2013, p. 2)*

3 The pre-test score used to represent the point at which students "enter" the classroom is taken from each student's test scores, typically a few months before exiting or a month or two before summer. The post-test score represents the point at which students "leave" the classroom and is taken from each student's adjacent test score, which is approximately one year after the initial pre-test score was measured and a few months before the student leaves the classroom of the current teacher's for whom value added is calculated.

4 In statistics, when students "serve as their own controls," this helps to reduce the amount of error that would have otherwise arisen given the natural variance between students. That is, when all students receive "treatments" in these studies, they experience different teacher (or school/district) effects. The "controls" (e.g., student's own pre-test scores that are used to help account for prior academic achievement) help to "level the playing field," given the rarity with which students are randomly assigned to classrooms (and schools) and the rarity with which teachers are randomly assigned to classrooms.

5 Test scores "regress to the mean" when the scores are extremely high on their first observation (e.g., in the case of gifted students), and because there is no place higher to go in the test score distribution, the scores hit a ceiling and regress backwards towards the mean or average. Inversely, test scores "regress to the mean" when the scores are extremely low on their first observation (e.g., in the case of very low-performing students), and because there is no place lower to go in the test score distribution, the test scores hit a floor and regress forward towards the mean or average instead.

6 The major pieces of this research were first published in Amrein-Beardsley & Collins, 2012.

7 See www.sas.com/.

8 For more information about this section of the study, and in particular the methods used to develop and warrant these assertions, see Amrein-Beardsley & Collins, 2012.

9 See also the SAS® EVAAS® "Teacher Effect Data for Jon Eckert 2007" in Eckert & Dabrowski, 2010, p. 90.

10 In statistics, converting test scores to normal-curve equivalents (NCEs) helps to standardize test scores in a way similar to percentile ranking while preserving equal intervals across the 0–100 point scale.

11 The Aprenda is the Spanish equivalent of the Texas Assessment of Knowledge and Skills (TAKS) standardized test used in HISD.

12 Just recently both SAS® EVAAS® and HISD's Chief Human Resources Officer acknowledged via email that ceiling effects adversely impacted some teachers working with gifted students in their capacities to demonstrate value added (A. Best, personal communication, January 21, 2012; see also Amrein-Beardsley & Collins, 2012; Cole et al., 2011; Kelly & Monczunski, 2007; Koedel & Betts, 2007, 2010; Linn & Haug, 2002).

3

A VAMORAMIC VIEW OF THE NATION

Whoever undertakes to set himself up as a judge of Truth and Knowledge is shipwrecked by the laughter of the gods.

Albert Einstein

For the past 30 years our policymakers have repeatedly justified nearly the same policy actions based on the same M&P Theory of Change (see Figure 1.2 in Chapter 1). Throughout this time they have also used nearly the same social engineering tools to justify their anticipated, yet still highly illusive ends. These include scare tactics (e.g., about America's accelerating inferiority); rhetoric (e.g., the titles *A Nation at Risk*, *No Child Left Behind*, and *Race to the Top* in themselves); propaganda (e.g., the federal education administration paying a prominent African American authority $240,000 to promote NCLB on his nationally syndicated television show [Toppo, 2005]); generalizations, assumptions, and rationalizations (e.g., what is needed is greater authoritative control, higher standards and accountability, and an expanded application of business model thinking in education); as well as incentives (e.g., tuition waivers for students, salary bonuses for teachers and administrators, etc.) and disincentives (e.g., prevention of student grade-to-grade promotion or high school graduation, teacher dismissal, administrator termination, school closure, etc.).

Coincidentally, we are also at the end of the 30-year post-Reagan era. This is an era that is credited (and blamed) for the soaring income of America's top 1%, and an era that led to dramatic governmental corruption, irresponsibility, and financial excess. During this generation the set of America's richest, greediest, and unrestrained, primarily chief executive officers (CEOs) of the most powerful corporations across the nation (i.e., America's top 1%), climbed their way to unprecedented levels of wealth and power. They ultimately contributed to the recent downfall of America's economy with which the country continues to cope, by reaping ill-gotten gains from plundering retirement funds and the vanishing home equity of the remaining 99%.

These events inspired the Occupy Wall Street demonstrations across the nation during which, on behalf of the 99%, demonstrators peacefully protested, and continue to protest, social and economic inequalities, the dramatically unequal distribution of wealth and power, and the recent financial collapse and economic downturn fueled by Wall Street (Sachs, 2011). In opposition to the top 1%, the occupiers use as their slogan "We are the 99%." Their only demand is that President Obama and the nation's political leaders confront the influence that big money, big business, and lobbyists have over its oft-corrupt government and its resultant agendas and policies, and "re-establish the supremacy of people votes over dollar votes in Washington" (Sachs, 2011). Thirty years after the Reagan era began we are now a nation of even more intolerable inequalities, inequities, uncertainties, and immoralities. During few other times in American history have both political parties served the interests of corporate magnates in such brazen and unapologetic ways.

Education's iconic charging bull

In education, value added is the equivalent of Wall Street's iconic charging bull. As noted, educators across the country are witnessing and falling victim to the hyper-implementation and wide-scale overuse (and abuse) of VAMs and their associated accountability systems, all of which have been spurred via federal, state, and local educational policies.

In addition, about 95% of the educational scholars researching value added are academi-cally protesting the misuse of VAMs, informing the public through their scholarly writing, and shaping policy decisions whenever possible (Amrein-Beardsley, Collins, Polasky, & Sloat, 2013; Au, 2011; Baker, 2011; Baker et al., 2013; Berliner, 2013; Bracey, 2007; Braun, 2008; Capitol Hill Briefing, 2011; Corcoran, 2010; Darling-Hammond et al., 2012; Gabriel & Lester, 2012, 2013; Hill, 2009; Hill et al., 2011; Ho et al., 2009; Ishii & Rivkin, 2009; Jen-nings & Corcoran, 2009; Linn, 2008; Newton et al., 2010; Pallas, 2012; Papay, 2011; Pullin, 2013; Ravitch, 2010a, 2012b, 2012d; Reardon & Raudenbush, 2009; Rothstein, 2009, 2010b; Rothstein & Mathis, 2013; Sparks, 2012a).

In other words, the 95% of those protesting VAM-based evaluation systems do not by any means include just teacher unions, as is sometimes assumed (Gabriel & Lester, 2013; Lowrey, 2012), although they too have taken at least their first turns at protest, namely in Chicago (Ahmed-Ullah, Hood, & Mack, 2012; Keen, 2012) and in Los Angeles (Watanabe, 2013). In Washington DC many concerned union and non-union educators, citizens, and again aca-demics, including Nancy Carlsson-Paige (Lesley University), Stephen Krashen (University of Southern California), Deborah Meier and Diane Ravitch (New York University), and others, similarly "occupied" the U.S. Department of Education. Collectively, they protested a batch of related ideas, including the adoption of the Common Core State Standards and their accompanying Partnership for Assessment of Readiness for College and Careers (PARCC) Consortium and the Smarter Balanced Assessment Consortium (SBAC) tests. These are the tests on which growth will likely be measured in the future. Again, these tests are to be con-cretized as federally incentivized, cleverly backed, and corporately funded (Johnson, 2013). By "occupying" the department, this group continues to demonstrate resistance towards "the destructive influences of corporate and for-profit education reforms" on America's public schools (United Opt Out National, 2013).

Yet the other 5% continues to fuel the value-added firestorm. This group continues to promote a propositioned level of pseudo-mathematical precision to better measure educa-tional quality, all the while convincing policymakers that we now have the powerful instru-ments (often their powerful instruments) needed to influence attitudes and drive the social behaviors still needed to bring us to increased academic achievement in America's public schools. The 5% here includes VAM statisticians and economists underscoring VAM's purported strengths (Ehlert et al., 2012; Gordon, Kane, & Staiger, 2006; Hanushek, 1970, 1971, 1979, 2009, 2011; Hanushek & Rivkin, 2010). It also includes VAM statisticians and economists who are accentuating and overstating VAM's powers and potentials (Branch, Rivkin, & Hanushek, 2013; Chetty et al., 2011), especially if and when positioned against other subpar educational measurement alternatives (Harris, 2008, 2009a, 2009b, 2009c, 2010, 2011; Harris & Sass, 2009; see also Gabriel & Lester, 2012; Glazerman et al., 2011; McCaffrey, Sass, Lockwood, & Mihaly, 2009; Wright, Sanders, & Rivers, 2006). The " 'it's not perfect, but it's the best we have' logic pervades pro-VAM arguments … even in the absence of a discussion of the implications of its admitted faults" (Gabriel & Allington, 2011, p. 7; see also Gabriel & Lester, 2012, 2013).

The 5% also includes politicians, policymakers, and business savvy philanthropists who continue to "drink the Kool-Aid," and hang their education reform initiatives on the lips of the lobbyists and researchers associated with the biggest businesses competing for value-added contracts.

At the top of this list sits President Obama (2009), who in a speech stated:

> Success should be judged by results, and data is [sic] a powerful tool to determine results. We can't ignore facts. We can't ignore data. That's why any state that makes it unlawful to link student progress to teacher evaluations will have to change its ways if it wants to compete for a [RttT] grant.

Also at the top of this list sits President Obama's Secretary of Education, Arne Duncan, who even as a Democrat has made it abundantly clear that, in line with the M&P Theory of Change, high-stakes testing and public accountability are key to any effective educational accountability system (see, for example, Au, 2011; Ravitch, 2012b; J. Roberts, 2012). Secretary of Education Duncan, has also made it clear, in both his words and actions (i.e., in terms of the states who received RttT funding), that states that did not (or did not intend to) link student achievement data to students' teachers, schools, and districts would not be eligible for the federal reform dollars on which states typically rely, and that they desperately need in order to operate (Duncan, 2009a). In addition, when the *Los Angeles Times* published teachers' names, value-added scores, and rankings on its website for public accountability purposes (Felch, Song, & Smith, 2010; see also Briggs & Domingue, 2011; Durso, 2011; Felch, 2011; Song & Felch, 2011), Duncan congratulated the newspaper and its reporters for their noble efforts, noting that "silence is not an option" (Santos & Gebeloff, 2012) and stating that their actions facilitated an "exercise in healthy transparency" (Dillon, 2010a). With Duncan's universal endorsement (Goldstein, 2012), the events in Los Angeles were replicated in New York City when the *New York Post* published similar information on about 18,000 teachers, which also prompted a strong response from the press, mainly producing articles about the city's worst teachers (Roberts, 2012; see also Campanile, 2012; *Chicago Tribune*, 2012; Darling-Hammond, 2012; Santos & Gebeloff, 2012).

Both Obama and Duncan, in fact, continue to advance educational reform initiatives based on measuring and holding educators accountable for growth or value added. They have thus far backed such initiatives to the tune of $290 million in Teacher Incentive Funds (TIF; Sparks, 2012a) and $4.35 billion in RttT funds (Duncan, 2009a). Many Republican politicians also support such initiatives, including Jeb Bush,[1] current Florida governor Rick Scott, U.S. representative from Minnesota and chairman of the House Education Committee John Kline, and others, many of whom are also involved in Chiefs for Change.[2] All of this is occurring in large part despite the research, however, and in many cases with controversial financial backing (see, for example, Fang, 2011, 2013).

At the top of the business "philanthropist" list sit corporate, Wall Street, and billionaire funded organizations like the conservative American Legislative Exchange Council (ALEC)[3] and Jeb Bush's highly controversial Foundation for Excellence in Education (FEE), that supports and finances Chiefs for Change and also came under recent fire for "using donations from for-profit companies to lobby for state education laws that could benefit those companies" (March, 2013).[4] Other individuals advancing policy initiatives in this area include the former chancellor of Washington DC's public schools and leader of StudentsFirst[5] Michelle Rhee; Microsoft mogul Bill Gates (whose Microsoft company is also competing for massive grants providing technology systems to support the implementation of the Common Core State Standards *and* the complementary, technology-based assessment systems meant to measure and assess these standards) and his wife Melinda and their Bill and Melinda Gates Foundation (Tomassini & Venugopal, 2012); and the leaders of Battelle for Kids (an independent non-profit organization established by multi-billion-dollar per year national defense contractor Battelle).

Other backers include the Broad Foundation, the Thomas B. Fordham Institute, the NewSchools Venture Fund, The New Teacher Project, and the Walton Foundation, to name a few (see, for example, McNeil, 2012). Others' names could certainly be added to these lists, including, for example Netflix's Reed Hastings, who financially backs pro-accountability movements, or Facebook's Mark Zuckerberg, who donated $100 million to support similar reforms in Newark, NJ (see, for example, McKenna, 2012; Strauss, 2013). All of the aforementioned players come from places of privilege. Their experiences are far removed from the realities of most of America's public schools, much less the research-based realities informing school reform. As intelligent as they may be in their specific areas of expertise, here they have succumbed the temptation to perpetuate the same scare tactics, propaganda, rhetoric, and generalizations, assumptions, and rationalizations about America's public schools.

As well, these big businesses leading the "reform" initiatives in this area continue to advance their claims via their lobbying and other marketing-type efforts (Banchero, 2013; Bill & Melinda Gates Foundation, 2013; Sawchuck, 2013b; Strauss, 2013). This is occurring so much so that we might

> someday view this era as one in which the nation turned its back on its public schools, its children, and its educators … [and] rejected the nation's obligation to support public education as a social responsibility [but instead] accepted the unrealistic, unsustainable promises of entrepreneurs and billionaires.
>
> *(Ravitch, 2012b)*

Others who promote value-added testing include the entrepreneurs, statisticians, and economists affiliated with the biggest testing, research, and educational measurement companies and non-profit organizations offering their value-added services, models, and systems to state and district leaders. While those involved here are doing this for what they may perceive as the betterment of America's public schools, they are selling their educational measurement and accountability systems for sizable profits and gains using public monies (Takahashi, 2012). Particularly when the services to be provided are pitched to potential consumers as overwhelmingly scientific, complex, arduous, and even intimidating, and often above and beyond districts' or state departments' human or financial resource capacities, external contracts seem the most appropriate, if not only choice to help districts and states meet these new federal and state policy demands (CCSSO, 2005; Ewing, 2011; see also a related debate in Hill, 2009 and Harris, 2009b).

These companies largely depend on the relationships they build with political leaders at national, state, and local levels. In addition, the integrity of the educational policies advanced by the same political leaders depends on the services the companies provide in response. The companies continue to profit by overselling their new and improved accountability systems to organizations with publicly subsidized funds, and the companies continue to profit by gaining these funds to evaluate the VAMs continuously being tested and implemented. In other words, not only are these companies developing and selling their models, they are evaluating them as well, further supporting their private interests and sustainability efforts.

This exemplifies crony capitalism in the educational economy, by which "ties between businessmen and the government influence the economy and society to the extent that it corrupts public-serving economic and political ideals" (Crony capitalism, n.d.).[6] To many, this is a familiar story. In education we have for decades witnessed the insatiable power of textbook companies working along with their political allies to not only define curricula but design and deliver the materials needed to teach the curricula as designed (Flynn, 2012). An example was revealed publicly when the *Los Angeles Times* uncovered a similar saga about former President George W. Bush's brother, Neil Bush, as well as their parents, former President George H.W. and first lady Barbara Bush, greatly profiting from the NCLB policies enacted by G.W. (Roche, 2006; see also Fang, 2013). University of Wisconsin researchers also recently exposed how ALEC members, including state legislators, collectively draft legislation and then introduce the same legislation across states almost verbatim. When the legislation is adopted, this directly benefits the private and corporate interests of ALEC's business members (Underwood & Mead, 2012).

Here, not unlike the case described in Rachel Carson's *Silent Spring* (1962), the culprits include those who continue to help socially engineer the severity of a problem, those who continue to amplify public alarm about the severity of the problem, and those who continue to manufacture and refine the main, if not only, solution to the problem. These are the folks who also continue to market false promises about the solution to the problem, secure governmental contracts based on such promises, and subsequently profit by having provided the best solution to the problem that has now (and for the last 30 years) turned severe. The CEOs of some of the most influential testing, research, and educational measurement corporations and non-profits, like those on Wall Street, have certainly had much to do with this highly profitable, yet highly uncertain, big business-in-education trend (Fang, 2013; Flynn, 2012; Roche, 2006; Underwood & Mead, 2012).

The national landscape[7]

To date, only six states across the U.S. have *not* applied for a federal NCLB waiver (Philips, 2012). The other 44 states and the District of Columbia (DC) are (or will soon be) using either a VAM or growth model (if not both) to evaluate and make consequential decisions about teachers (and schools/districts). In addition, 30 states and DC (61%) now have state legislation or regulations that require student achievement data be used to *substantively* inform both the evaluation of teacher effectiveness and subsequent decision-making efforts (see Figure 3.1).

Given the local control that states still constitutionally maintain, even despite new federal requirements, the aforementioned 44 states and DC (and possibly others) are still grappling with how they will align with the new federal mandates in their own ways. Districts within many states that also still maintain local control are doing the same. Collectively, and specifically, they are contending with how they might "meaningfully differentiate performance" with an evaluation "including as a significant factor, data on student growth for all students" (U.S. Department of Education, 2012). As well, many are still struggling with whether they should seek an external contractor's help or construct these systems using in-house human and technical resources, although a plurality of states have already chosen to use a pre-existing growth model or VAM statewide or as an "official" statewide model (Collins & Amrein-Beardsley, 2014).

At the time of writing this book, 40 states and DC (80%) are developing and implementing some type of model as part of a pilot program or are in the process of developing their own models. These same states either are using or are planning to use their state's large-scale standardized achievement tests in mathematics and reading/language arts to generate these accountability outputs. Eighteen states (35%)[8] are piloting or currently developing unspecified models. The Student Growth Percentiles (SGP) model is being used most often in 12 states (24%).[9] Eight states and DC (18%)[10] are using or piloting a "commercial" VAM like the Education Value-Added Assessment System (EVAAS®) or the Value-Added Research Center (VARC) model. In three states (6%),[11] model choice is still being left to local decision-makers, and in

Figure 3.1 State legislation requiring that teacher evaluation systems use growth or VAM estimates.

seven states (14%)[12] there are no current plans to develop such a model for evaluating effectiveness (see Figure 3.2[13]). Information about the most popular growth models and VAMs is provided next, starting with the EVAAS® – the VAM discussed in detail in Chapter 2 in terms of its use in Houston.

The SAS® Education Value-Added Assessment System (EVAAS®)

SAS® Institute, Inc.,[14] the world's "powerhouse" in big data analytics (Gualtieri, p. 13), advertises and sells the proprietary Education Value-Added Assessment System (EVAAS®). The EVAAS® is the best known, most widely implemented, widely used, and likely most controversial VAM available (as detailed in Chapter 2).

History

Dr. William L. Sanders first developed the EVAAS® model in the 1980s when he was an adjunct statistics professor at the University of Tennessee at Knoxville. Sanders taught advanced statistics and had studied and consulted with others about the use of advanced statistics, specifically mixed model selection methods (Kennedy, 1991) and best linear unbiased prediction (BLUP) methods[15] (Henderson, 1973; Hermann et al., 2013), to model genetic and reproductive trends among livestock (Sanders, 2004; Sanders, Saxton, & Horn, 1997). Sanders fell into the education field "practically by accident" (Gabriel & Lester, 2012, p. 4; see also Sanders, 1994) when a group of advanced statistics students literally prodded his thinking about transferring his methodological logic and expertise into education, mainly to help with the educational measurement and accountability challenges facing the state of Tennessee at the time. Sanders contemplated how he could help solve education's measurement quandaries. He concluded that he could help by using student achievement data and advanced

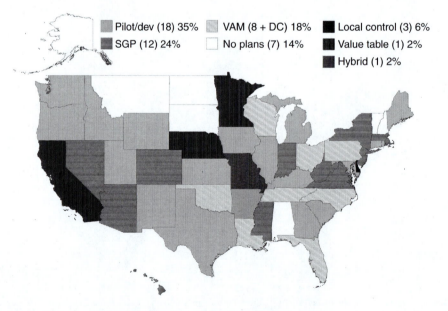

Figure 3.2 Current and planned growth model and VAM use by type.

statistics, similar to those he used for agricultural genetics, to link student tests scores with their teachers (or schools/districts). This would help to procedurally, systematically, and "objectively" make causal determinations about teacher (or school/district) effectiveness and their impacts on student learning and achievement.

Sanders subsequently developed the earliest version of the EVAAS®, the Tennessee Value-Added Assessment System (TVAAS). His focus was (and still is) to focus on the "product of [the] educational experience rather than the process by which it was to be achieved" (Sanders & Horn, 1994, p. 300). The TVAAS was used for state-level educational accountability in Tennessee for district-wide accountability purposes in 1993 and for school- and teacher-level accountability in 1994 and 1996, respectively (Sanders & Horn, 1998; Wainer, 2004). TVAAS was eventually moved to the SAS® Institute, Inc. for wider-scale sales, implementation, and distribution in 2000, where it assumed the more generic EVAAS® name and acronym. However, Sanders/SAS® Institute, Inc. continues to hold an exclusive contract with Tennessee to date (Gabriel & Lester, 2013).

Even though VAMs had been used in economics since the 1960s (Baird, 1987; Briggs & Weeks, 2009; Fincher, 1985; Pickering & Bowers, 1990), and VAMs had been used periodically for educational research since the late 1960s with the Coleman Report (Coleman et al., 1966) and occasionally in the 1970s (Boardman & Murnane, 1979; Hanushek, 1970, 1971, 1979), Sanders is widely credited as the one who popularized the use of VAMs for educational accountability (Stephens, 2008). Sanders (2006), in fact, identifies himself as "one of the first to invoke the label 'value-added assessment'" (p. 1) and "perhaps the leading authority on the value-added assessment of schools and teachers" (*Carolina Journal Weekly Report*, 2003; see also Bracey, 2007; Sanders, 1994; Sanders, Ashton, & Wright, 2005; Stephens, 2008).

Model specifics

Technically, the EVAAS® probably uses the most sophisticated statistical approaches to calculate value-added scores of all VAMs, with over 20 years of development already invested. EVAAS® does not use one single VAM across educational settings, but instead, given the unique characteristics of the standardized achievement test and other variable data that are available (or unavailable), EVAAS® statisticians typically employ one of two types of linear mixed (value-added) models. This may be the preferred multivariate response model (MRM),[16] which essentially entails a multivariate repeated-measures analysis of variance (ANOVA) approach[17] (see Figure 3.3).

Or it may be the less ideal univariate response model (URM)[18] that essentially entails a traditional analysis of covariance (ANCOVA) approach[19] (see Figure 3.4). This approach resembles certain hierarchical linear model (HLM) approaches[20] (Sanders, 2006; Sanders et al., 2005; Sanders et al., 2009; Wright et al., 2010).

The better the standardized achievement test data available, even if taken from different types of standardized achievement tests (e.g., large-scale standardized tests that are aligned to either national or specific state standards), the better the model used (Sanders, 2003, 2006; Wright et al., 2006; Wright et al., 2010). Although it should be noted that the word "better" does not imply great, or even good, just better.

To calculate EVAAS® estimates, in the simplest of terms, students' levels of growth are measured by changes in students' standardized achievement test scores over time. Included are

$$y = X\beta + Zv + \varepsilon$$

Figure 3.3 The EVAAS® multivariate response model (MRM) teacher-level equation (source: Copyright © 2010 SAS Institute, Inc., Cary, NC, USA. All Rights Reserved. Reproduced with permission of SAS Institute, Inc., Cary, NC).

Note

With the EVAAS® "y ... is the $m \times 1$ observation vector containing test scores (usually NCEs) for all students in all academic subjects tested over all grades and years (usually up to five years). X is a known $m \times p$ matrix which allows the inclusion of any fixed effects. β is an unknown $p \times 1$ vector of fixed effects to be estimated from the data. Z is a known $m \times q$ matrix which allows for the inclusion of random effects. v is a non-observable $q \times 1$ vector of random effects whose realized values are to be estimated from the data. ε is a non-observable $m \times 1$ random vector variable representing unaccountable random variation" (see Wright et al., 2010, pp. 4–5). These equations "do not represent the actual SAS® EVAAS® models, only basic statistical models used within the EVAAS® model" (Van Asch, personal communication, June 13, 2013). For more information see Wright et al., 2010, pp. 4–9.

$$C_i = \hat{\mu}_y + \hat{\beta}_1(x_{i1} - \hat{\mu}_1) + \hat{\beta}_2(x_{i2} - \hat{\mu}_2) + \ldots$$

Figure 3.4 The EVAAS® univariate response model (URM) projection equation (source: Copyright © 2010 SAS Institute, Inc., Cary, NC, USA. All Rights Reserved. Reproduced with permission of SAS Institute, Inc., Cary, NC)

Note

C_i represents prior achievement, before the purported effect of the current district, school, or teacher for students who have at least three prior test scores. "The 'projection' C_i is [otherwise] nothing more than a composite of all the student's past scores (thus the letter C). It is a one-number summary of the student's level of achievement prior to the current year. The different prior test scores making up this composite are given different weights (by the regression coefficients, the βs) in order to maximize its correlation with the response variable" (Wright et al., 2010, p. 14). These equations "do not represent the actual SAS® EVAAS® models, only basic statistical models used within the EVAAS® model" (Van Asch, personal communication, June 13, 2013). For more information see Wright et al., 2010, pp. 4–9.

all eligible students with preferably at least three and up to five years of prior test scores across multiple subject areas, grade levels, and years (even if incomplete or coming from fragmented databases – yes, incomplete sets of data are sometimes used to measure students' growth). Thereafter, growth scores are aggregated to yield teacher-level (or school-/district-level) value added.

Controversially, however, EVAAS® statisticians typically do not make adjustments for the other risk variables (e.g., student background variables including race, ethnicity, poverty, levels of English language proficiency, special education status, etc.) that when available can also be used to account for the biasing elements that impede VAM-based analyses. EVAAS® statisticians argue, instead, that the model is "unimpaired" by students' backgrounds (Ballou et al., 2004). Many argue that this is a fatal flaw, however, because these background variables are highly significant determinants of student learning (Amrein-Beardsley, 2008a; Braun, 2005; Kupermintz, 2003; McCaffrey et al., 2003, 2004b; Tekwe et al., 2004). Regardless, as a rule, EVAAS® statisticians do not make model adjustments for any variables other than students' prior test scores.

The EVAAS® is, in fact, the only large-scale VAM that intentionally excludes statistical controls for student risk variables and uses students' test score histories, instead. By doing this, EVAAS® statisticians effectively bury the effects of these variables within the model and implicitly control for these variables by exploiting students' test histories in the model. "To the extent that [the] influences [of student risk variables] persist over time, these influences are already represented in the student's data. This negates the need for [such] adjustment[s]" (Sanders et al., 2009, p. 4; see also Sanders, 1998; Sanders & Horn, 1998).

Again, many VAM researchers argue that such adjustments must be made if statisticians are going to even begin to account for the influences of student characteristics, and especially the non-random assignment of students to classrooms (Amrein-Beardsley, 2008a; Ballou, 2012; Cody et al., 2010; Dorn, 1994; Glass, 1995; McCaffrey, 2012; Paufler & Amrein-Beardsley, 2013; Rothstein, 2009). Such adjustments make comparison groups more uniform, and they do eliminate more bias from the sample than conducting these analyses without (Ferguson & Takane, 1989; Fraenkel & Wallen, 1996; Glass & Hopkins, 1989).

Without resolution on this point of controversy, others, including EVAAS® statisticians, also argue that controlling or accounting for student background and other environmental variables is not only unnecessary, but that such practices would create inequitable learning expectations for the very students who are at risk (e.g., students from racial minority or high poverty backgrounds). These are the students about whom the aforesaid "to control or not to control" debate continues. EVAAS® statisticians and others argue that adjustment practices (i.e., "to control") would perhaps cause teachers to focus relatively less on such students because the students who are in need of the most attention would have already been given a statistical accommodation, or artificial boost, given their backgrounds and related life circumstances (Ballou et al., 2004; Ross et al., 2001; Sanders, 2003; Tekwe et al., 2004).

EVAAS® statisticians and others also argue that even if class assignment placements are not made at random (as is the case with most quasi-experimental studies), complex statistics (e.g., student fixed effects, nesting data, blocking strategies, etc.) can tolerably adjust for the non-random effects that the non-random placement of students ultimately have on VAM estimates anyways (Ballou et al., 2004; Glazerman & Potamites, 2011; Harris, 2011; Rosenbaum & Rubin, 1983). They argue that with methodological sophistication they can ultimately make such effects "ignorable" (Rosenbaum & Rubin, 1983; see also Anderman, Anderman, Yough, & Gimbert, 2010; Raudenbush, 2004; Reardon & Raudenbush, 2009; Rubin et al., 2004).

However, without such controls, and actually even with them, there is no way of guaranteeing that such adjustments will eliminate bias to the degree needed, particularly when highly consequential decisions are to be made about teachers (or schools or districts). Solid research evidence already exists indicating that using statistics to eliminate bias does not work, especially as theorized (Capitol Hill Briefing, 2011; Darling-Hammond et al., 2012; Hermann et al., 2013; Newton et al., 2010; Rothstein, 2009, 2010b; Stacy et al., 2012). What is certain, for now, is that the use of such adjustments "has been largely discouraged among statisticians and policymakers involved with value-added modeling" (Sanders et al., 2009, p. 5). In fact, quite the contrary is true (see, for example, Branch et al., 2013).

Model use

Notwithstanding, depending on where teachers' (or schools'/districts') EVAAS® estimates fall as compared to other similar teachers (or schools/districts) to whom they are compared, value-added determinations are made. This also depends on where teachers' (or schools'/districts') EVAAS® estimates fall as compared to whether they exceeded or fell below the projected expectations that are typically made beforehand using the more advanced MRM models (Sanders, 2003, 2006; Wright et al., 2006). EVAAS® statisticians then make relativistic comparisons and categorize teachers (or schools/districts) hierarchically along a continuum including high value-added, statistically insignificant, and low value-added classifications.

In other words, "effectiveness is assumed to be the average of the population" (Sanders, 2000, p. 334; see also Wright et al., 2006). Teachers (or schools/districts) whose students grow more than the average teacher (or school/district) or surpass their projected or antici-pated levels of growth are identified as adding value. Inversely, teachers (or schools/districts) whose students grow less than the average teacher (or school/district) or fall short of their projected or anticipated levels of growth are identified as detracting value. Teachers (or schools/districts) whose students grow at rates that are not statistically different (i.e., falling within one standard deviation of the mean) from the average teacher (or school/district) are classified as "not detectably different" (NDD). While NDD scores are not to be used for evaluative purposes, they are still reported and used in overall value-added calculations.[21] This is another point of controversy, as evidence suggests that once these scores are reported they are used despite their statistical insignificance (Amrein-Beardsley & Collins, 2012).

Model claims and realities

Regardless, the EVAAS® is promoted as likely the best, or "the least bad" of all value-added systems available in the market (Walberg & Paik, 1997, p. 171; see also Amrein-Beardsley, 2008a). Again, it is also the largest, most widely implemented, and most widely used, despite its proprietary nature. The states of Tennessee, Ohio, Pennsylvania, and North Carolina all use the EVAAS® statewide, by law, as do multiple local districts and schools across the nation (SAS®, 2012a; see also Collins & Amrein-Beardsley, 2014).

Another point of controversy, however, is that the EVAAS® is also sold, marketed, and promoted as much more than it really is. The EVAAS® is advertised as "the most comprehen-sive reporting package of value-added metrics available in the educational market" and "the most robust and reliable" system available, better than the "other simplistic models found in the market today" (SAS®, 2012a).

The EVAAS® promotional literature includes other, exaggerated statements. These state-ments include but are not limited to: the EVAAS® "eliminates the possibility of a distorted view of effective schooling"; it helps educators become more proactive, make more "sound instructional choices," and "use their resources more strategically to ensure that every student has the chance to succeed"; and it "provides valuable diagnostic information about [instruc-tional] practices." The EVAAS® also provides "a clear path to achieve the US goal to lead the world in college completion by the year 2020" (SAS®, 2012c). This last claim was recently added to EVAAS® marketing claims to align with President Obama's most recently intro-duced goal to lead the world in college readiness and completion by 2020 (U.S. Department of Education, 2010b).

Yet all of the aforementioned claims are entirely void of supporting research. If anything, researchers have demonstrated that these claims are largely untrue (Amrein-Beardsley, 2008a; Amrein-Beardsley & Collins, 2012; Ballou, 2002; Bracey, 2004a, 2007; Collins, 2012; Corcoran, 2010; Eckert & Dabrowski, 2010; Kupermintz, 2003; McCaffrey & Hamilton, 2007; Morgan, 2002). Although limited internal and anecdotal research conducted by Sanders and his colleagues (Sanders, 1994; Sanders et al., 1997; Sanders & Horn, 1998), and very limited internal survey research conducted by one of the largest districts using the EVAAS®

system (i.e., HISD) suggest the opposite (Harris, 2011), external research has put the afore-mentioned claims and declarations into serious question. Researchers external to the EVAAS® have evidenced quite well that what is being pitched by EVAAS® is indeed different than what is being realized by educators using the EVAAS® in practice.

EVAAS® data are hardly "invaluable," as is still being maintained (Sanders & Horn, 1998; SAS®, 2012c). In addition, while the EVAAS® is certainly the most sophisticated system, it is by no means effective or useful. It, like the other large- and small-scale VAMs, and even with its 20 years of development, is still plagued and inhibited by major methodological issues (i.e., reliability, validity, and bias).

In addition, the larger academic community that is best equipped to review and validate the EVAAS® model was not provided complete and open access to the model's inner work-ings, until perhaps recently in Wright et al. (2010). Accordingly, the community of external VAM scholars has still not returned a fair-minded and objective stamp of approval, largely because of the lack of evidence supporting model reliability, validity and bias (Amrein-Beardsley, 2008a; Bracey, 2004a, 2007; Dorn, 1994; Glass, 1995; Kupermintz, 2003; Linn, 2001; Popham, 1997), with the exception of a handful of earlier micro-analyses (Bock et al., 1996; Harville, 1995; Stroup, 1995) and some larger-scale validation studies in which research-ers validated model estimates. However, they also noted grave concerns about the model, model implementation, and model use (see, for example, Braun, 2005; Corcoran, 2010; Kupermintz, 2003; Linn, 2001; McCaffrey et al., 2004b; Popham, 1997; Stroup, 1995; Topping & Sanders, 2000).

In fact, the EVAAS® is still more popularly recognized as the "black box" model (see, for example, CCSSO, 2005), and Sanders is still popularly seen as "being vague and elusive when it comes to explaining his calculations and methods. He routinely tells audiences that he could explain TVAAS to them, but they would not understand it," further positioning himself and his system as the ultimate sources of authority, the cornerstones of objectivity, and the arbiters of accuracy (Gabriel & Lester, 2013, p. 20). Such secrecy should not be tolerated in a public system (Harris, 2011; Nelson, 2011), especially as schools are a publicly financed and sup-ported function of a democratic state (Dewey, 1916), one where trust is expected and should never be abused.

Notwithstanding, when recently prompted to provide evidence of EVAAS® model valid-ity, specifically, Sanders referred to the U.S. Department of Education's approval of Tennes-see's use of the EVAAS® (or the TVAAS as it originated in Tennessee) for the RttT competition as all the validation he and his EVAAS® model needed. Another source of validation he cited was the shopping $502 million in federal RttT funds sent to the state of Tennessee to advance TVAAS implementation and use (LeClaire, 2011; see also Derringer, 2010; U.S. Department of Education, 2011). What seems to matter more with the proprietary EVAAS® system is not external, scientific, or empirical validation, but "market validation" instead (SAS®, 2012c). The TVAAS was mentioned over 50 times in the text of Tennessee's RttT application, and was by all accounts the main, if not major, reason that Tennessee was a first-round RttT winner, or, as they self-identify, the state that was "First to the Top" (Gabriel & Lester, 2013, p. 7).

At any rate, EVAAS® representatives have worked vigorously to counter the warnings and cautionary tales that have come from VAM scholars external to the EVAAS® (Sanders & Horn, 1998; Sanders et al., 1997; Sanders et al., 2009; Sanders & Wright, 2008; Topping & Sanders, 2000; Wright et al., 2010; see also Harbaugh, 2011; LeClaire, 2011). In EVAAS®

supporters' words, they have "taken the brunt of the *detractors*'[22] criticisms" (Sanders et al., 2009, p. 1 [emphasis added]).

Education policy implications

Yet, despite EVAAS®'s countless condemnations, including its strongest criticisms derived via the academic research at that time (Bracey, 2004a; Dorn, 1994; Glass, 1995; Kupermintz, 2003), in 2007 Sanders shared his (largely internal, unpublished, non-reviewed) research[23] with a U.S. Senate working group discussing the promotion of teacher incentives. One year earlier, Sanders did the same but this time he provided testimony at the U.S. House of Representatives Committee on Education and the Workforce's hearing on educational improvement (*Education Week*, 2006). Sanders has also shared his research with other educational policymakers, as well as countless practitioners, at multiple levels on multiple occasions for multiple years past (see, for example, New York State Educational Conference Board, 2004).

The Value-Added Research Center (VARC)

The Value-Added Research Center (VARC) is affiliated with the Wisconsin Center for Education Research at the University of Wisconsin–Madison. As it too is one of the most popular and most widely implemented and used VAMs across the nation's schools, it also deserves similar attention as the EVAAS®.

History

Dr. Robert H. Meyer, a "bowtie-wearing economist" (Banchero & Kesmodel, 2011) who began conducting value-added research in the late 1980s, founded VARC in 2004. He currently serves as VARC's research director. Meyer oversees all VARC operations, contracts, and the nearly 50 affiliated academics and full-time researchers, analysts, project managers, graduate students, and other educational professionals working under his direction. Accordingly, VARC's value-added model is now also known as Meyer's model, just as the EVAAS® is also known as Sanders' model.

As with the EVAAS®, VARC has a mission to perform ground-breaking work on value-added systems, as well as to conduct value-added research to evaluate the effectiveness of teachers (and schools/districts) and educational programs and policies.[24] Unlike SAS®, however, VARC describes its methods as transparent, although, there is actually more information about the inner workings of the EVAAS® model on the SAS® website and via other publications than there is about the VARC model and its methods. It is likely that this is due to the relative youth of the VARC model, however, as VARC is currently at year three in terms of model development and implementation (VARC, 2012c).

Nonetheless, VARC has a "research-based philosophy," and VARC officials have stated that one of their missions is to publish VARC work in peer-reviewed, academic journals (Meyer, 2012). VARC has ostensibly made publishing in externally reviewed journals a priority, possibly because of the presence of the academics within VARC, as well as its affiliation with the University of Wisconsin–Madison. However, very few studies have been published to date, again likely given its infancy. Instead (like with the EVAAS®), the Center has disproportionally produced and disseminated technical reports, white papers, and presentations, all of which (like with the EVAAS®) seem to be disseminated for marketing and other informational purposes, including the securing of additional contracts (see, for example, Meyer, 2012). Unfortunately, a commonality across the two models is that they seem bent on implementation before validation.

Regardless, VARC defines its methods as "collaborative" given that VARC researchers have worked with school districts, mainly in Milwaukee and Madison, to help them better build and better situate their value-added model within the realities of districts and schools (VARC, 2012c). As well, VARC defines its value-added model as "fair." What this means remains unclear, however, as the VARC model, like all other VAMs currently in operation, very likely has the same issues with fairness in that its use applies to only approximately 30–40% of all teachers in America's public schools – the teachers who teach reading/language arts and mathematics primarily in grades 3–8 (Gabriel & Lester, 2013; Harris, 2011; see also Thomas, 2012). Otherwise, little is yet known about the VARC model itself, including its strengths and weaknesses.

Model specifics

What is known is that the VARC model is analogous to the EVAAS®. The VARC model uses generally accepted research methods (e.g., hierarchical linear modeling) to measure and evaluate the contributions that teachers (and schools/districts) make to student learning and achievement over time. In their words, the VARC model uses "a generalized value-added model (which [they] refer to as a differential effects value-added model) that captures differences in value-added productivity (by student subgroups) across schools, classrooms, and teachers (and over time)" (Meyer & Dokumaci, 2011, p. 7). VARC researchers also use their value-added model to make projections about where students should be achieving at the end of each school year, within and across classes, as based on multiple years of students' individual test histories. VARC then compares their statistical projections to realities, after each post-test occasion (see Figure 3.5).

Like the EVAAS®, VARC also compares individual students to students who are like them but unlike the EVAAS®, however, VARC does this by adjusting the statistical models using student background variables that are outside of a teacher's (or school's/district's) direct control. VARC controls include approximately 30 variables including the standard race, gender, ethnicity, levels of poverty, students' levels of English language proficiency, and

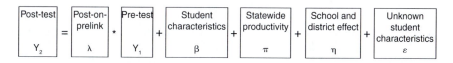

Figure 3.5 VARC's two-period value-added model for school/district (not teacher) purposes (source: adapted with permission from Meyer & Dokumaci, 2011).

Note

The model indicates that achievement at the end of a period (post-test Y_2) is the sum of: student achievement at the beginning of the period (pre-test Y_1) times a post-test-on-pre-test link parameter (λ); student characteristics, such as income, English Language Learner (ELL) status, and race/ethnicity (β); statewide productivity (π); school and district productivity (η); and student growth that is due to unknown student characteristics and random test measurement error (ε) (for more information see Meyer & Dokumaci, 2011, p. 7).

special education statuses. The VARC also uses other variables, when available, including, for example, student attendance, suspension, retention records and the like. "Classroom effects are estimated separately for each grade, subject, and year, as are within-school and across-school variation in classroom effects. Univariate and multivariate shrinkage estimations[25] are used to obtain more precise estimates, especially for classrooms with small class size" (Graue et al., 2013, p. 6). According to Meyer, this helps to make the VARC model "arguably one of the best in the country in terms of attention to detail" (Campanile, 2012), particularly as such statistical controls help to satisfy "the counterfactual assumption that all schools serve the same group of students" (Meyer & Dokumaci, 2011, p. 1).

Model use

Then (like with the EVAAS®) whether students whose growth scores are aggregated at the teacher (or school/district) levels statistically exceed, meet, or fall below their growth projections (i.e., above or below one standard deviation from the mean) helps to determine teachers' (or schools'/districts') value-added scores and subsequent rankings and categorizations. Again, these are relatively determined depending on where other teachers (or schools/districts) ultimately land,[26] and they are based on the same assumption that effectiveness is the average of the teacher (or school/district) population.

Like the EVAAS®, VARC also does this work with publicly subsidized monies, although, in contrast to SAS®, VARC is a non-profit organization. VARC is currently operating 25 projects exceeding a combined $28 million (i.e., $28,607,000) given federal (e.g., from the U.S. Department of Education, Institute for Education Sciences, National Science Foundation), private (e.g., from Battelle for Kids, The Joyce Foundation, The Walton Foundation), and state and district funding. VARC is currently contracting with the state departments of education in Minnesota, New York, North Dakota, South Dakota, and Wisconsin. VARC is also contracting with large school districts in Atlanta, Chicago, Dallas, Fort Lauderdale, Los Angeles, Madison, Milwaukee, Minneapolis, New York City, Tampa/St. Petersburg, and Tulsa (Meyer, 2012; VARC, 2012b).

Funding for the 25 projects currently in operation ranges from the lowest, short-term, and smallest-scale $30,000 project to the highest, longer-term, and larger-scale $4.2 million project. Across the grants that have been funded, regardless of type, the VARC projects currently in operation are funded at an average of $335,000 per year with an average funding level just under $1.4 million per grant. If all 25 of the aforementioned projects were in operation at the same average rate, this would yield an operating budget of approximately $8.5 million per year. Though this is likely less than EVAAS®'s annual operating budget within SAS®, it is no trivial amount, especially when considering that taxpayer funds are being used to fund such doubtful deliverables and uncertain ends.

Regardless, when examining the projects in which VARC has been and is currently engaged (VARC, 2012b) it is evident that VARC is expanding its business rapidly across the nation. In 2004 when the center was first established, VARC was working with fewer than 100,000 students across the country. By 2010 this number had increased 16-fold; VARC was then working with approximately 1.6 million students in total.

Model claims and realities

In terms of marketing, VARC delivers similar sales pitches in similar ways, although those affiliated with VARC do not seem to overstate their advertising claims quite like those affiliated with EVAAS® (see, for example, VARC, 2012a, 2012c). For example, VARC statements suggesting that their value-added analytics "can increase student success" (VARC, 2012c) are different than EVAAS® statements suggesting that their value-added analytics will provide "a clear path to achieve the US goal to lead the world in college completion by the year 2020" (SAS®, 2012c). While neither statement has research-based evidence to support its merit, the VARC intends to increase student achievement, while the EVAAS® tends to insist that increased achievement will come as a result of EVAAS® use. Perhaps VARC is at the least pitching something more realistic, although, like the EVAAS®, VARC's product is not without a lot of controversy (Campanile, 2012; *Chicago Tribune*, 2012; Otterman, 2010; Rutkoff, 2012; Watanabe, 2012). Such controversy can still be good for business and marketing purposes, however, and VARC has at least attempted to make good on bad press (News section of VARC, 2012a).

Additionally, like with the EVAAS®, VARC officials are greatly focused on the use of value-added estimates for data-informed decision-making. "All teachers *should* be able to deeply understand and discuss the impact of changes in practice and curriculum for themselves and their students" (VARC, 2012c [emphasis added]). Educators might increase their capacity to do this via VARC's train-the-trainer model for professional development. However, while there are some data use projects under way (see, for example, Graue, Gawade, Delaney, Karch, & Romero, 2011); there are many data use projects listed on the VARC website that are pending (e.g., a professional development series that VARC is developing with Milwaukee public schools).

In addition, VARC has information to help educators understand and use value-added estimates (VARC, 2012e), although this information is still fairly limited. And whether educators will ever actually use VARC's value-added information for instructionally relevant purposes is still unknown. Although VARC continues to make claims that it is providing "school and district staff with information that can be credibly used to set high performance expectations (or standards) and guide efficient allocation of resources to at-risk students" (Meyer & Dokumaci, 2011, p. 14), this is being said thus far, as with the EVAAS®, without research evidence or support.

Education policy implications

As with the EVAAS®, VARC also seems to have helped stimulate a marked increase in value-added activity, in no small part via its promotional efforts. Like Sanders, VARC officials also met with Arne Duncan about its VAM and its potential, even before President Obama selected Duncan as the U.S. Secretary of Education (VARC, 2012e). Fittingly, VARC recently contracted with the U.S. Department of Education to evaluate the value-added systems put into place by 175 districts across the country that were awarded Teacher Incentive Fund (TIF) federal grants (Sparks, 2011). VARC is providing recipients of TIF grants (34 grantees nationwide with $95 million in annual funding for performance pay systems) with assistance in the development and implementation of their value-added programs (VARC, 2012d). VARC is also venturing into analyzing the value added of teacher education programs

(Brooks, 2012; Hawkins, 2012), despite the newness of the VARC model and regardless of the reservations academics, educators, and others have about such VAMs, for even the simplest of purposes (i.e., measuring teacher versus college of teacher education effectiveness). This is yet another contemporary yet highly controversial trend in educational measurement and accountability.[27] Nevertheless, and despite the research, the trend is increasing.

However, ultimately, whether either the EVAAS® or the VARC value-added model does a better job at "get[ting] the story right" (VARC, 2012c) is something that has yet to be determined. Whether the VARC model is indeed a "well-crafted recipe," or whether Sanders' claim that Meyer is one of many who "smell the money" and who is in response pitching an "unsophisticated formula," is also something that has yet to be determined (see Rutkoff, 2012 and Banchero & Kesmodel, 2011, respectively).

The Student Growth Percentile (SGP) Model

Last, the Student Growth Percentile (SGP) model is the one being used most often throughout the nation. It is, at the time of writing this book, being officially used in 12 states as well as in other districts and schools at more local levels (Collins & Amrein-Beardsley, 2014; Harris, 2011). The SGP is not a value-added model by traditional standards and definitions, however, mainly because the SGP model does not use as many sophisticated controls as do its VAM counterparts.

History

Dr. Damian Betebenner developed the SGP model while he was a researcher affiliated with the University of Colorado–Boulder and while he was working in Denver with the Colorado Department of Education. Hence, just as the EVAAS® was developed in Tennessee and was formerly known as the TVAAS, the SGP was developed in Colorado and was formerly known as the Colorado Growth Model. This model is now supported and advanced by the New Hampshire-based National Center for the Improvement of Educational Assessment (NCIEA).

Unlike a typical VAM, however, the SGP model was purposefully designed to serve as a normative method for describing student growth during an academic year, facilitating discussion and reflection more than consequential decision-making. The SGP model was, and still is, designed to serve *not* as an absolute or supreme but as a descriptive measure of student growth during an academic year. As well, it was and still is not meant to facilitate high-stakes decisions (Betebenner, 2011; Betebenner & Linn, 2010; Briggs & Betebenner, 2009; Linn, 2008).

Model specifics

Different than the typical VAM, the SGP model is more simply intended to measure the growth of similarly matched students to make relativistic comparisons about student growth over time. Students are directly and deliberately measured against or in reference to the growth levels of their peers. Determinations are made in terms of whether students increase, maintain, or decrease in growth percentile rankings[28] as compared to their peers who are academically similar.

Within the SGP model, individual students are compared to peers who have similar testing histories in the same years and subject areas tested. Students who score similarly on each of the prior tests available form an academic peer group, and within each peer group each student's growth is compared to the growth of the other students in the same peer group, year-to-year. This means that an English Language Learner (ELL) might be compared to another ELL, a gifted student might be compared to another gifted student, or a student receiving special education services might be compared to another special education student. This also means that an ELL might be grouped with a gifted student if their test histories are near to the same. While peer groups are adjusted every year to establish a more accurate percentile ranking for each student within each group every individual year,[29] ultimately each student's final percentile rank demonstrates his/her growth as compared to his/her peers with similar test-score histories.

Similar to the VAMs as well, the SGP uses statistical methodologies to regress each student's test scores on their prior year test scores to calculate actual growth. More specifically, a student's SGP is calculated based upon the probability of the student achieving their current year score given their history of prior achievement scores on the same state's test. The underlying statistical methodology is quantile regression,[30] which uses B-spline functions[31] to account for any non-linearity[32] and heteroskedasticity[33] of student achievement data sets, including ceiling and floor effects (e.g., high achievers consistently score high on the test and low achievers consistently score low, skewing the data in the extremes of the distribution; see for example Cole et al., 2011; Kelly & Monczunski, 2007; Koedel & Betts, 2007, 2010; Linn & Haug, 2002). The regression curves produced by the B-spline technique (as opposed to the regression lines produced without the B-spline technique) better fit the data in the "tails" of the distribution of scores and therefore are a better fit for the estimation (Betebenner, 2009b). The model fits the equation illustrated in Figure 3.6.

To do this, like with the EVAAS® and VARC models, the SGP model uses large-scale standardized achievement test data on at least two and up to six separate occasions, per subject area and across years, to measure changes in student achievement over time. Growth is also quantified in a norm-referenced manner, after which SGPs can be collapsed and aggregate comparisons can be made at the teacher (or school/district) levels.[34] Because the SGP is more of a normative model, however, different tests (e.g., norm- and criterion-referenced tests) and their different testing scales purportedly contaminate SGP analyses less, making the SGP relatively more test- and metric-neutral (Barlevy & Neal, 2012; Betebenner, 2009b; Briggs, 2012; Goldschmidt et al., 2012).

In addition, whereas all other VAMs, with the exception of the EVAAS®, set out to separate the contributions of individual teachers (or schools/districts) from other confounding

$$Q_{Y_t}(\tau | Y_{t-1}, \ldots, Y_1) = \sum_{j=1}^{t-1} \sum_{j=1}^{3} \phi_{ij}(Y_j)\beta_{ij}(\tau)$$

Figure 3.6 Student Growth Percentile (SGP) equation (source: adapted with permission from Betebenner, 2009a).

Note
Given test scores for t occasions, $(t \geq 2)$, the τ-th conditional quantile for Y_t based upon $Y_{t-1}, Y_{t-2}, \ldots, Y_1$ is given by where $\phi i,j$, $i = 1,2,3$ and $j = 1, \ldots, t-1$ denote the B-spline basis functions (Betebenner, 2009a, p. 9; see also Betebenner, 2009b).

variables, the SGP model does not. Like with the EVAAS®, no specific controls are used in the SGP model to adjust for the student background variables that impact student learning and growth over time but that are out of the control of the teacher (or school/district) being evaluated (Goldhaber & Theobald, 2012; Goldschmidt et al., 2012; Nelson, 2011; Reckase, 2004). As with the EVAAS®, some of these variables are mediated by including up to five years of students' test score histories in the model; in fact, the more years the better. In addition, like the EVAAS®, the SGP model implicitly controls for the impact these variables have on student growth over time, although "SGPs can be hybridized with VAMs, by conditioning the descriptive student growth [percentile] on student demographic characteristics" (Baker et al., 2013, p. 8; see also Ehlert et al., 2012).

Model use

Students' actual progress, expressed as SGPs, is then used to make value-added determinations along a set of categorizations including *low, typical,* or *high* or *less than, typical,* or *more than typical growth.* Thereafter data can be aggregated at the teacher (or school/district) level, and yield median growth percentile scores. Just as the other VAMs make projections, the SGP model can also be used to make projections to specify what it will take for a student to make sufficient progress and meet certain sets of growth targets (e.g., at the 50th percentile) via separate goal-setting activities (Betebenner, 2008; Cody et al., 2010; Lefly, 2012).

Although the SGP model is not a true VAM, particularly when criticized by VAM developers who rightly insist their models are more statistically sophisticated, particularly if causative conclusions are *ever* to be made about teacher (or school/district) effectiveness (Baker, 2011, 2012a; Harris, 2011; McCaffrey, 2012; Reckase, 2004), the results of SGP analyses can be used to make appropriate, reasonable, and reasonably more cautious VAM-based inferences (Betebenner, 2011). "In really simple terms SGPs aren't even designed to identify [and isolate] the teacher's effect on student growth. VAMs are designed to do this, but fail" (Baker, 2012a).

Because SGP developers understand and acknowledge the issues with their own SGP model, VAMs in general, and all of the models' collective shortcomings and defects, SGP model developers, VAM scholars, and most users understand and agree that SGPs should not be used to make highly consequential decisions (Baker, 2011, 2012a; Nelson, 2011; Reckase, 2004). The SGP model is meant to be descriptive and non-causative and used only with other data derived via other evaluative measures to make more holistic determinations about teachers' (or schools'/districts') value added, appropriately so. This is the only model that is presented in accordance with the guidelines for high-stakes testing as developed by the *Standards for Educational and Psychological Testing* that were collaboratively written by the American Educational Research Association (AERA), American Psychological Association (APA), and the National Council on Measurement in Education (AERA et al., 2000).

Model claims and realities

In as much as external researchers have "validated" the other VAMs, they have validated this model, noting that the SGP too is more or less as effective, as well as more or less limited, imperfect, and inadequate as the other VAMs currently being used across the nation (Ehlert et al., 2012; Goldhaber et al., 2012; Goldhaber & Theobald, 2012; Goldschmidt et al., 2012;

Gottlieb, 2011; Ho et al., 2009). Again, however, some argue that the SGP model is even less perfect than its VAM counterparts (Baker, 2011, 2012a; Baker et al., 2013; McCaffrey, 2012; Reckase, 2004). These researchers argue these points mainly because the SGP model does not account for the confounding variables that prevent causal conclusions, again assuming VAMs yield causality with even acceptable levels of accuracy and without a series of extreme, unrealistic, and even "heroic" sets of assumptions (Rubin et al., 2004; see also Amrein-Beardsley, 2008a; Harris, 2011; Scherrer, 2011; Wainer, 2004).

Otherwise, "Scholars have not critiqued the usefulness of SGPs for inferring teacher effectiveness, [and they] have not evaluated their reliability or validity for this purpose, because scholars understand *full well* that [SGPs] are neither designed nor intended for this purpose" (Baker, 2012a [emphasis added]; see also Baker et al., 2013). As well, it should be noted that limited external research, namely that which has been published in peer-reviewed journals as opposed to technical reports, has been conducted to alleviate concerns about the model's reliability and validity. Though this is also the case with both the EVAAS® and VARC models and their methods.

Nonetheless, in general, VAMs are more strongly represented in the research literature (Ehlert et al., 2012), although preliminary evidence suggests that the SGP's levels of reliability and consistency, or a lack thereof, are comparable to other VAMs (Baker, 2011, 2012a; Goldhaber & Theobald, 2012; Linn, 2008). In addition, educational researchers and statisticians have similar warranted concerns about bias with SGPs, particularly when student background variables are not controlled for directly or explicitly, as is the case here (Ehlert et al., 2012; Goldhaber et al., 2012; Goldhaber & Theobald, 2012; Harris, 2011).

Finally, in terms of formative use, there is comparatively more evidence that the SGP model is easier for practitioners to understand, particularly because of the transparency and usability of the resulting student growth percentile estimations and rankings (Barlevy & Neal, 2012; Bonk, 2011).

According to Lozier (2012):

> In order to be useful, the data need not pinpoint what teachers are doing well or poorly nor must they strip out the myriad non-instructional factors that can influence learning. Neither must they be used for high stakes decisions, such as counting for half of a teacher's evaluation. Rather, they may be most useful for their utility in shining a light on areas that merit further inspection.

Model developer Betebenner echoed this sentiment, noting that the beauty of the SGP model lies in its formative potential, especially because the SGP model "sidestep[s] many of the thorny questions of causal attribution [to] instead provide descriptions of student growth that have the ability to inform discussions about assessment outcomes and their relation to education quality" (Betebenner, 2009b, p. 43; see also Linn, 2008).

Indeed it seems that stakeholders who opt into the SGP seem more interested in description and low-stakes decision-making versus making high-stakes decisions about educators (Betebenner, 2009b). Model transparency, alone, might be the reason that across the nation the SGP seems to be the preferred choice (Amrein-Beardsley & Collins, 2013; see also Betebenner & Linn, 2010). A recent survey of 91 districts in Colorado (more than 50% of the state's public school districts) revealed that over 75% of districts are using SGP growth data for official district purposes (Bonk, 2011). However, as with the EVAAS® and VARC models, no peer-reviewed, empirical evidence supports that any of the aforementioned assertions are indeed true. Aside from a few anecdotes, we otherwise know virtually nothing about the extent to which the SGP model (or any VAM for that matter) improves instructional practice or student learning and achievement.

It should be noted, however, that some also position the transparency of this model as a compromise worth considering, whereas with increased clarity and an improved potential for comprehension and use come more simplicity, less accuracy, less precision, and increased chances for making misleading interpretations and faulty decisions. This is a "devil's bargain" (Sanders et al., 2009, p. 7; see also Reckase, 2004), and again assumes that an even close to tolerable level of precision and correctness exists when using the "more sophisticated" VAMs (Gottlieb, 2011; Goldhaber & Theobald, 2012).

Education policy implications

Like with SAS® EVAAS® and VARC, NCIEA does this work with publicly subsidized monies and, like VARC, NCIEA is also a non-profit organization. Although, it should be mentioned that the SGP model also has its critics, particularly in terms of its goodness and fit, its greater potential for lawsuits over other VAMs (see below), and its financial not-for-profit gains (Baker, 2011; Baker et al., 2013). However, in stark contrast to the EVAAS®, VARC, and other off-the-shelf VAMs being used less frequently (Collins & Amrein-Beardsley, 2014), the SGP is the least expensive choice for districts and schools because it is essentially a free, open-source tool. It is publicly accessible and available, and fees rendered usually come in the form of consulting monies to help build human resource capacity, for example, in terms of running analyses in R using the SGP package. R is the free, albeit highly complex, syntax-based, statistical software in which the SGP package operates (R Development Core Team, 2009; see also Lockwood, Doran, & McCaffrey, 2003). Model developer Betebenner is now housing the open source analytics to facilitate open comprehension and collaboration, as well as to openly facilitate the continuous and cooperative improvement of the SGP model.[35]

SGP model developers and sponsors have kept the model fully transparent and open to ongoing research and improvement. Any and all external researchers and statisticians can contribute to the verification, validation, and strengthening of the model; and any and all who have access to data are permitted to use the model in-house, rather than having to send off their data for VAM-based analyses and estimate generation.

As well, however, any and all have so much access that, regardless of the warnings and cautionary notices that come along with SGP model use, local consumers can still use SGP estimates for high-stakes accountability (Harris, 2011), potentially increasing the possibility of lawsuits. Baker (2012a), in particular, argues the SGP model may be even more susceptible to lawsuits than its VAM counterparts if educators erroneously use SGPs to make highly consequential decisions (see also Baker et al., 2013).

On this note, all VAM developers often advise against the high-stakes use of their model estimates, especially if value-added estimates are to be used in isolation of other indicators of educational quality. However, local users do not always acknowledge VAM or growth model developers' cautionary directions and advisory warnings. As it is with most "garbage in, garbage out" systems (Banchero & Kesmodel, 2011; Gabriel & Lester, 2010, 2013; Harris, 2011), these models are also often used, without question, to process questionable input and produce questionable estimates. It should be noted that VAM and growth model developers do not always follow through on consumer use either, nor, unfortunately, in many cases consumer abuse (e.g., termination decisions linked to faulty value-added or growth estimates). It is here where there seems to be the most potential for lawsuits, when highly consequential decisions are made after which both parties involved might point fingers of guilt and liability in opposing ways.

Other models

Highlighted above are the three primary growth or VAMs that most organizations are currently using, particularly at the state level, but there are at least two other external entities developing such models for contractual purposes (Collins & Amrein-Beardsley, 2014). Other external VAM modelers include, but are not limited to, the American Institutes for Research and Mathematica Policy Research (Banchero & Kesmodel, 2011; Goldhaber & Theobald, 2002). Neither of these is without controversy however, given that they both have more or less the same methodological issues and resultant errors in the estimates derived (see, for example, Schafer et al., 2012). Nonetheless, they collectively continue to sanctify and promote their models regardless (Baker, 2012b). These five represent the main external contractors (and competitors) taking up the most in federal, state, and local district funds, that is, in terms of public funds and grants generated via taxpayer revenues (Collins & Amrein-Beardsley, 2014).

There are also some local models worth mentioning. The Dallas Independent School District uses a homegrown VAM that accounts for student demographics or what they call "fairness variables" (Goe, 2008). The Milwaukee model is considered a local model, although Milwaukee worked extensively with VARC to construct it (Cody et al., 2010; Meyer & Dokumaci, 2011). The Delaware model represents another homespun version that distinctively uses a value table. Elsewhere, some states or districts are working on implementing hybrid versions that incorporate both growth and VAM components (e.g., Missouri; Collins & Amrein-Beardsley, 2014).

Model conclusions

Generally speaking, though, these are the current models that represent the choice sets from which states and districts might pick, especially if they go with an external contractor to help calculate value-added. That said, the information provided here should not be used to make any definitive decisions about which model is best or which one might be adopted, particularly if a district or state is to go beyond its own resources to accomplish this work. One might still weigh some strengths and weaknesses against the others, as provided, even if at just a cursory level, as all models definitely have serious shortcomings that cannot be casually or carelessly overlooked. What good is any statistical model that is not fully explicated or fully validated, especially when falsely pitched as a causal model?

The bottom line here is that the empirical evidence that already exists puts all current growth models and VAMs into serious question. Again, what has become increasingly evident, yet increasingly marginalized at multiple policy levels, is that all of these models are (1) unreliable (e.g., a teacher classified as adding value has approximately a 25–50% chance to be classified as subtracting value the following year); (2) invalid (e.g., very limited evidence that teachers who post high value-added scores are effective using at least one other correlated criterion); and (3) biased (e.g., teachers of certain students who are not randomly assigned to classrooms have more difficulties demonstrating growth). In general, they are also (4) unfair (e.g., only teachers of mathematics and language arts with pre- and post-test data in certain grade levels are being held accountable using these systems); (5) fraught with measurement errors negating their summative uses (e.g., inordinate amounts of missing data, variables that cannot be controlled, measurement errors caused by non-traditional, non-isolated, non-insular, and "non-egg-crate" classrooms); and (6) non-formative due to being non-transparent (e.g., teachers and administrators do not understand the models being used to evaluate them) and of limited instructional value (e.g., data estimates are difficult to understand or use for instructional decision-making). Accordingly, they are (7) being used inappropriately to make consequential decisions (e.g., teacher termination, merit pay) while (8) their unintended consequences are going unrecognized (e.g., teachers leaving/refusing assignment to grades in which value-added estimates matter most, teachers leaving teaching altogether out of discontent or to protest, teachers choosing not to teach students who are most likely to hinder growth, principals "stacking" classes to make sure certain teachers can demonstrate "value-added" or growth or vice versa, etc.). These are the main things that many of those promoting and propagating VAMs are quick to ignore, forget, or dismiss, especially if marketing their models for increased sales.

As Jennings and Corcoran (2009) titled a recent article about these models, all potential consumers should at the very least "beware of geeks bearing formulas" (see also Buffett, 2008, p. 15). Rather, not only should potential consumers *beware*, all should *be aware* (Amrein-Beardsley, 2009a). All, including potential consumers must ask questions and not take what is being assumed at face value, nor take at face value what is being pitched as the "solution" to what we collectively and increasingly assume most ails America's public schools. The highly questionable assumptions we continue to make are the same assumptions that continue to go unquestioned. These are discussed in more detail next.

Box 3.1 Top 10 assertions

1   To date, 44 states and DC have adopted some form of a VAM to evaluate and make consequential decisions about teachers, and 30 states and DC have adopted policies in support.

2   However, no states have yet focused efforts towards determining how value-added data might be used to improve schools, the quality of the teachers teaching, or student learning in general.

3   Nearly all (i.e., approximately 95%) of value-added researchers are protesting the misuse of VAM estimates given the research they are continuously conducting on all aspects of VAMs.

4   The other approximately 5% include VAM statisticians, econometricians, politicians, policymakers, and business savvy philanthropists, all of whom continue to promote VAMs' theoretical and oft-overstated powers and potentials for educational reform.

5   Also included in the 5% are entrepreneurs, statisticians, and econometricians affiliated with for-profit companies and non-profit organizations offering value-added services to state and district leaders for publicly subsidized albeit sizable profits and gains.

6   The SAS® EVAAS®, Value-Added Research Center (VARC), and Student Growth Percentile (SGP) models are the most widely used, although their goals and objectives
vary.

7   William Sanders is credited for popularizing VAM use for educational accountability
with a VAM initially developed in Tennessee, that is now popularly known as the
SAS® EVAAS®. SAS® is a large, private corporation that markets and sells its SAS®
EVAAS® for profit.

8   VARC is a non-profit organization affiliated with the University of Wisconsin-Madison,
making it a more academic model by both its affiliation and its general purpose (e.g.,
in terms of transparency, its "research-based philosophy," and its collaborative
initiatives).

9   The SGP model is typically less expensive, as it is a free, open-source tool. Unlike the
SAS® EVAAS® and VARC models, however, the SGP model was purposefully designed
not to isolate a teacher's impact on student growth but rather describe trends and
possibilities.

10 The bottom line is that the empirical evidence that already exists puts all current
VAM and growth models into serious question regarding reliability, validity, and
bias. This is ever more important the more estimates are used for consequential
decision-making purposes.

Notes

1 As a reminder, Jeb Bush is the former governor of Florida, former President George W. Bush's
brother, and potential contender for the 2016 presidential election.
2 Chiefs for Change is a coalition of politicians and leaders

> that share a zeal ... [and] a strong voice for bold [educational] reform on the federal, state and
> local level ... [to ensure that] each and every student achieves his or her God-given potential
> for learning ... [and] learn[s] at least a year's worth of knowledge in a year's time.
> *(Foundation for Excellence in Education, 2012)*

3 The American Legislative Exchange Council (ALEC) "works to advance the fundamental principles
of free-market enterprise, limited government, and federalism at the state level through a nonpartisan public-private partnership of America's state legislators, members of the private sector and the
general public." For more information see www.alec.org/; see also Underwood & Mead, 2012.
4 A recent Freedom of Information Act request revealed that the lobbying efforts led by the FEE,
again directed by Jeb Bush, confirm that the reform initiatives supported by the FEE are benefitting
the businesses financing the FEE non-profit. This includes one company in which Jeb Bush is highly
financially vested, but also many other companies that "are closely tied to the for-profit interests
who stand to gain from [the education] policies" being advanced by FEE (Fang, 2011, 2013). It also
includes a number of ALEC corporations including K12 and Connections Academy (now a Pearson
company), Charter Schools USA, and APEX Learning (Schneider, 2013).
5 StudentsFirst is a non-profit organization that in its messaging supports public schools but in actuality supports neo-conservative policies, such as school choice, charter schools, value-added, and
educational initiatives encouraging radical teacher accountability and discouraging teacher unions/
unionization. For more information see www.studentsfirst.org/.
6 For a more detailed discussion about how this sometimes works in social science research, where
social science statistics are manipulated and exaggerated to advance false claims and in some cases
financially benefit, see Shea, 2012: "Sloppy statistics are like steroids in baseball." Across the social
science fields in which statistics are used, "the less fastidious flourish."
7 The major pieces of this national research were first published in: Collins & Amrein-Beardsley,
2014.

8 Arkansas, Connecticut, Georgia, Iowa, Idaho, Illinois, Kansas, Kentucky, Maine, Maryland, Michigan, New Mexico, Oregon, South Carolina, Texas, Utah, Washington, Wyoming.

9 Arizona, Colorado, Hawaii, Indiana, Massachusetts, Mississippi, Nevada, New Jersey, New York, Rhode Island, Virginia, West Virginia.

10 Florida, Louisiana, North Carolina, Ohio, Oklahoma, Pennsylvania, Tennessee, Wisconsin.

11 California, Minnesota, Nebraska.

12 Alabama, Alaska, Montana, New Hampshire, North Dakota, South Dakota, Vermont.

13 For another highly useful map of the states and what they are currently doing as per legislation, see Sawchuck, 2013a.

14 See www.sas.com/.

15 Best linear unbiased prediction (BLUP) methods are a type of shrinkage estimation method (e.g., the Empirical Bayes approach) that helps to adjust teacher-level VAM estimates given their levels of (im) precision. Such methods yield shrinkage estimates (e.g., BLUPs) that minimize the expected mean squared error (MSE) between teacher-level VAM estimates and teachers' purported contributions to student achievement. Statisticians do this by using adjusted estimates in the weighted averages of teachers' initial VAM estimates in comparison to the VAM estimates of the average teacher, allotting more precise estimates more weight. Inversely, less precise estimates receive lesser weights and are shrunk towards the mean, yielding more conservative estimates. Evidence suggests, however, that while shrinkage in general works to reduce noise and bias (McCaffrey, Han, & Lockwood, 2008), using shrinkage estimations might make little difference in classifying teachers of hard-to-predict students (e.g., ELLs, special education and gifted students, students from some racial minority backgrounds [Latino/a or African American]). Shrinkage approaches intentionally introduce statistical bias into VAM estimates but might not yield more accurate rankings in effect, given non-random student placement practices, and in terms of select or extreme sets of students (Hermann et al., 2013; Guarino, Maxfield, Reckase, Thompson, & Wooldridge, 2012; Guarino, Reckase, & Wooldridge, 2012; Tate, 2004).

16 EVAAS® employs three different multivariate response model (MRM) analyses for districts, schools, and teachers. The district and school models are essentially the same and perform well with large numbers of students. The teacher model (illustrated in Figure 3.5) uses an approach more appropriate for smaller sample sizes, for example, per classroom. All three models essentially operate, however, as linear mixed models, although projected expectations are typically made beforehand using the more advanced MRM (for more information see Wright et al., 2010, p. 5).

17 An analysis of variance (ANOVA) approach is a statistical method used when the goal is to make comparison between two or more means, in this case from the pre- to post-test for making determinations about student growth over time.

18 The univariate response model (URM) model is the same as the EVAAS® projection model. But since the URM model may be used at the district, school, or teacher level, the categorical variable in the ANCOVA (see note 19) may be the district, school, or teacher. Accordingly, but unlike the projection model, the estimated parameters here are pooled-within-district, pooled-within-school, or pooled-within-teacher (for more information see Wright et al., 2010, p. 14).

19 An analysis of covariance (ANCOVA) approach is a more sophisticated statistical method than ANOVA that combines ANOVA and statistical regression techniques. ANOVA is used when the goal is to make comparison between two or more means, again in this case from the pre- to post-test, for making determinations about student growth over time. With ANCOVA, however, covariates or other extraneous variables that are not of primary interest are used to set all other things equal, or "level the playing field." In this case, using at least the pre-test score as a covariate helps to account for the extraneous effects that come along with high or low pre-test scores (e.g., student socio-demographics). This also helps to account for the effects external variables might have on the post-test occasion, effects that might bias the outcome estimates of interest.

20 A hierarchical linear model (HLM) approach is an even more sophisticated statistical method that is also meant to make comparisons between two or more means, in this case from the pre- to post-test for making determinations about student growth over time but also while taking into consideration the nested nature of the data. Data, particularly education data, are nested within multiple levels of influence, including classrooms, classrooms within schools, schools within districts, and districts within states, depending on the level of analysis. Using HLM, otherwise simplistic data are organized into data hierarchies so that estimates can be described as sums of the effects of the successive levels in which the data are situated. Accordingly, the HLM approach, because it is so much more advanced

than the other methods typically used to calculate value-added, provides the most realistic while the most (appropriately) conservative VAM-based estimates available.

21 For more information about the inner workings of the EVAAS® model, see Anderman et al., 2010; McCaffrey et al., 2004b; Sanders et al., 1997.

22 Detractor – one who disparages or belittles the worth of something (see www.thefreedictionary. com/detractor).

23 At least some of the research studies that might have been shared as the basis of Sanders' claims during any of these occasions likely came from any of the citations included in the references, in which Sanders served as either the primary or co-author.

24 For more information about VARC see http://varc.wceruw.org/.

25 See note 15.

26 For more information about the inner workings of the VARC model, see Meyer & Dokumaci, 2011.

27 The editors of the November/December 2012 issue of the *Journal of Teacher Education* dedicated an entire special issue to the topic of examining and evaluating teacher education programs for accountability (Knight, Lloyd, & Arbaugh, 2012; see also Amrein-Beardsley, Barnett, & Ganesh, 2013).

28 A percentile represents the proportion of test scores that fall above or below a reported percentile score. This illustrates the relative standing of an individual within a test distribution, whereas the test distribution is divided into a set of 100 equal parts, or 100 percentage marks.

29 According to the Arizona Department of Education, 2012:

> Conceptually, a student growth percentile represents how "typical" a student's academic growth is by examining their achievement relative to their academic peers – those students with comparable prior achievement. Simply put, for every student in the state, this measure selects students in the same grade level, with the same [test] scores over a number of years to determine a "peer group." Then, for each student, the current year [test] score is compared to the current year scores of the other students in his/her peer group. If the student's current year score exceeded the scores of most of their academic peers, the student has done well, comparatively. If the student's current year score was [lower] than the scores of their academic peers, the student has not done well, comparatively.
>
> *(p. 18)*

30 Quantile regression is used to measure the difference between a set of predictor variables, in this case pre-test scores, and quantiles (regular intervals within a distribution) of the response variable, in this case post-test scores.

31 B-spline cubic basis functions are piecewise polynomial functions that use a series of non-linear curve segments to account for non-linearity, heteroskedasticity, and skewness, such as is associated with student achievement data. Due to the flexibility afforded by these functions, they provide a better fit and better account for variation in the distribution of the data.

32 Non-linearity occurs when the equation to be calculated cannot be written in a linear fashion or using a linear combination of the variables to be captured and expressed.

33 A collection of random variables is heteroskedastic if there are subpopulations under examination that have variances that are distinctly different from other yet similar subpopulations. Differences may be due to true differences in student achievement but also the measurement errors inherent within large-scale standardized achievement test scores. Otherwise, subpopulations are considered homoskedastic (i.e. variances more alike or of one kind). Evidence suggests that with heteroskedasticity, the achievement of particular students (e.g., students eligible for free or reduced-cost lunches, students with lower levels of prior achievement, students from some racial minority backgrounds [Latino/a and African American]) is much harder to predict (Hermann et al., 2013; Stacy et al., 2012).

34 For more information about the SGP, see Betebenner, 2009b and Betebenner & Linn, 2010. The RAND Corporation also offers a comprehensive overview (www.rand.org/education/projects/measuring-teacher-effectiveness/student-growth-percentiles.html). For more information about the SGP as seen by SGP users, see the information constructed by states including Colorado, the state in which the SGP originated (www.schoolview.org/ColoradoGrowthModel2.asp); Rhode Island (www.ride.ri.gov/assessment/RIGM.aspx); and West Virginia (http://wvde.state.wv.us/growth/).

35 See the GitHub website, available at: http://schoolview.github.com/SGP/.

PART II

Highly Questionable Yet Often Unquestioned Assumptions

4

ASSUMPTIONS USED AS RATIONALES AND JUSTIFICATIONS

If people are good only because they fear punishment, and hope for reward, then we are a sorry lot indeed.

Albert Einstein

As stated in Chapter 1, those who continue to socially engineer rational-systems theories of educational improvement into the minds of so many, and most importantly into the consciousness of policymakers on both sides of the partisan divide, have brought us to rely on the same theory of change on which we have relied for the past 30 years. The principle is that by holding districts, schools, and teachers accountable for their performance on states' large-scale standardized achievement tests, administrators will supervise the schools better, teachers will teach better, and as a result students will learn more, particularly in the nation's lowest performing schools. Students' test scores will increase, the nation's prominence will be reclaimed, and the nation will achieve the utopian society so desired (see Figure 1.2 in Chapter 1).

As this is a rational approach to reach a commonsense end, (too) many policymakers, political pundits, and conservative philanthropists (and some academics) continue to immortalize these views. As well, they continue to hyper-utilize a series of unchecked assumptions to preserve their stands and promote their positions. These assumptions are described in more depth in this and the next chapter, both of which are about the highly questionable yet often-unquestioned assumptions many continue to make about VAMs.

As detailed in Chapter 2, these assumptions, mainly about how new and improved VAM systems will help bring us to our rational interpretation of utopia, were put to the pragmatic test. There I discussed how what district leaders in Houston assumed to be good for student learning was in actuality experienced by many of the teachers. I illustrated this in the district that serves as the paradigm case or petri dish for examining how stronger VAM-based accountability policies work in practice, considering again the presumably positive and negative consequences needed to incite desired and prevent undesired behaviors.

As further detailed in Chapter 3, it is *largely* assumed that VAMs will provide the statistical sophistication that has thus far eluded us and prevented this theory of change from working.

It is also *largely* assumed that VAMs will yield more accurate statements about the causal effects of educational inputs (i.e., teacher, administrator, school, or district quality); VAMs will accurately unveil those who are the most demonstrably effective when it comes to educational outputs (i.e., levels of student achievement); and VAMs will help to better penalize failure and reward success, just as the marketplace penalizes laziness and rewards hard work. According to Pies (2013) such market-based assumptions are highly appealing to the typical American psyche, especially in a capitalist society in which these familiar logic systems inform the ways we think about and believe social systems should work. Such market-based assumptions also help sales when "external contractors [sell] their services along with their highly refuted claims, to districts and states for publicly subsidized monies" (Takahashi, 2012). Riding sales on assumptions is a particularly powerful tactic when potential consumers take at face value the "value-added" of a product, and disregard questions not only about the product but also about the assumptions being used or exploited to sell it (Pies, 2013).

It is also assumed that when higher standards are not met, VAMs will help to illuminate and address the areas needing improvement. VAMs will also help to replace the arbitrary and subjective decision-making processes historically used when making consequential decisions about teacher quality (e.g., via supervisor observations). Although, here, it is also assumed that such consequential decisions have not been made nearly often enough, primarily because of teacher tenure, traditional salary schedules and compensation structures, and other conventional human resource practices and systems (e.g., transfers of ineffective teachers to other schools within the same district and other forced placement practices). When VAMs are advanced, these are typically the traditional systems denounced as thwarting educational reform (Ravitch, 2007; see also Baker et al., 2010; Brill, 2009; Goldhaber & Hansen, 2010; Jacob, 2011; Rockoff et al., 2010; The New Teacher Project [TNTP], 2012). These are also the traditional systems being blamed for the perpetual problems now being named as the enemy of the educated state. While the targets of fault have been altered over time – underperforming students were targeted via NCLB and now ineffective educators are being targeted via the federal government's new accountability initiatives (i.e., RttT) – the same theory of change and supportive assumptions continue to hold.

These are just some of the unchecked assumptions that are being used to further promote the adoption and implementation of VAMs across the nation. These are also some of the unchecked assumptions (too) many in the media (see, for example, *Chicago Tribune*, 2012); Felch et al., 2010; Felch, 2011; Song & Felch, 2011; (too) many in the general public who are often (mis)informed by the media, and (too) many policymakers, political pundits, and conservative philanthropists (and some academics) have unwisely embraced in the name of education reform.

These are also the unchecked assumptions some of the VAM statisticians and economists underscoring VAM's purported strengths continue to assert via their advertising, marketing, and, in particular, lobbying efforts. Even though, in 2008, President Obama promised to reform the White House, take it out of the hands of lobbyists in particular, and put it back into the hands of the public, lobbyists in this field and elsewhere (e.g., defense, healthcare, pharmaceuticals, big oil, gun control and the National Rifle Association [NRA], the American Association of Retired Persons [AARP]) continue to function as the third largest and most powerful business next to government and tourism. The iron law of reciprocity (i.e., "I'll help you if you help me") continues to be ingrained in politics (Attkisson, 2012).

The manufactured crisis

Recall the award-winning Broadway musical *The Music Man* (Wilson, 1957) in which a slick, fast-talking traveling salesman by the name of Professor Hill travels via train from one small town to the next. Hill's goal is to sell naïve townsfolk, who are "as green as their money," band instruments and uniforms to help breathe music into each town's troubled youth. When Hill arrives in River City, Iowa, his usual plot unfolds. He addresses everyone as his "friend" or "neighbor," suggesting to all that he is dutiful and reverent. He then manufactures a crisis in the town to set the scene for his sales pitch (see also Berliner & Biddle, 1995).

The town has trouble. Too many adolescents are loafing around, playing pool, and becoming mindless and corrupt in the process. Hill alarms the townspeople about the emergency they have on their hands and convinces them to jump on his figurative bandwagon. In response, the townspeople hastily begin singing Hill's praises. So startled have the townspeople become they panic that they do "surely got trouble" and have "gotta figure out a way to keep the young ones moral after school." Hill then pitches himself as the drum major who, along with the band equipment he is selling, is the solution to the town's ills and misfortunes. A marching band, as constructed and led by him, is the answer to River City youths' idleness and immorality. Hill can teach the kids music even though he does not know how to read or play one note. "The main thing is the music." How hard could it be to understand the instrument?

In the case of VAMs, we have a similar scenario but with a much more complex instrument. Here, VAMs are the instruments in which too many are unwisely trusting, and VAMs are the instruments many are pitching, and in some cases selling, for profit, to a similarly naïve, uncritical, and highly assuming public. Here, though, those who are pitching and selling VAMs are riding proverbial bullet trains from one state or district to the next, given VAMs are being federally incentivized. Trusting townsfolk who are also "as green as their money" are buying into both the VAMs and the assumptions behind them, mainly that VAMs work as conceptualized and sold. Even some of the most critical townsfolk are still opting to purchase simply because they cannot see beyond or work around the financial incentives being offered in support of VAMs.

While in *The Music Man* Hill is ultimately accused of selling "gold-painted watches and glass diamond rings," here we have what is being pitched as "the gold standard" for educational measurement and accountability (*Chicago Tribune*, 2012; Gabriel & Lester, 2013; Michie, 2012). In both scenarios, whether the gold label is indeed real or is for fools is about misguided trust and a series of assumptions that the unquestioning have been led to believe.

Gold-painted watches and glass diamond rings

By definition, assumptions appeal to people's emotions and they are used to sway peoples' thinking in desired and often socially engineered ways. Assumptions are often made about intangible ideas or tangible products, but often without proof or data to support the legitimacy of those assumptions. Correspondingly, according to Marx (1995) most governmental and private groups, in efforts to promote or protect their private or the public's perceived interests, attempt to methodically sway or change public attitudes and behaviors using assumptions. Such assumptions are often expressed via enthusiastic statements and bold claims, further engraining the assumptions and transforming them into accepted realities, so that, according to Pies (2013), with each assumption it is implied that everyone else agrees, and that to question or reject the agreed upon assumptions would be senseless if not absurd.

This is precisely why it is often said that to "assume" is to make an "ass" out of "u" and "me." Because when one makes an assumption, even if in good faith, one is creating an illusion that will likely frustrate if not outright disappoint. While there are times when making assumptions can be reasonable or even necessary or "essential ... if we are to make progress," what is most important is that the assumptions being made are transparent (Reardon & Raudenbush, 2009, p. 496). Those making assumptions must become more aware of what they are taking as facts or givens to become more prudent and to possibly contribute alternative viewpoints countering the assumptions being delivered as truths. "Most fallacies in presumptive reasoning involve the tacit acceptance of doubtful assumptions, and an important function of external critics and alternative interpretations is to make these assumptions explicit" (Kane, 2013, p. 65).

Discussed next are the most common assumptions being made, and in some cases being exploited, when it comes to understanding and buying into VAMs. These are the assumptions that are crucial for others to understand before blindly adopting VAMs, and these are the assumptions with which consumers must agree if they are to wholeheartedly adopt and accept the legitimacy of VAMs and VAM estimates. All VAMs are, after all, according to Jennings and Corcoran (2009) "only as good as the assumptions on which they are built" (p. 639). These are also the assumptions that must be made clear, transparent, and accordingly positioned within the current research evidence (Newton et al., 2010; Raudenbush, 2004; Reardon & Raudenbush, 2009).

In this and the next chapter, these common assumptions are discussed with more breadth and depth than elsewhere (see, for example, Amrein-Beardsley, 2012; Gabriel & Allington, 2011; Harris, 2009c; Reardon & Raudenbush, 2009; Scherrer, 2011). In this chapter, these assumptions are organized around (1) general assumptions about VAMs, (2) the assumptions being used and in some cases exploited as rationales to promote the adoption of VAMs, and (3) the assumptions advocates are using to pitch VAMs as the solutions to what ails America's public schools. In Chapter 5, these assumptions are organized around (4) the test-based assumptions being made about the large-scale standardized achievement tests currently being used to generate VAM estimates, and (5) the other statistical and methodological assumptions that go along with VAM adoption, implementation, and use.

General assumptions about VAMs

The grandest of all VAM-based assumptions is that *(1) VAMs should be used to measure teacher, school, or district quality.* In the 2007 Phi Delta Kappa/Gallup poll, members of the general public were asked the following question:

> One way to measure a school's performance is to base it on the percentage of students passing the test mandated by the state at the end of the school year. Another way is to measure the improvement students in the school made during the year. In your opinion, which is the best way to measure the school's performance – the percentage passing the test or the improvement shown by the students?
>
> *(Rose & Gallup, 2007, p. 35).*

Eighty-two percent of respondents stated that the best way to measure school performance is to measure the gains posted by students longitudinally; by extension, this implies that the best way to measure school performance is through a measure of the "value" the teacher (or school/district) "adds" to students' learning over time (Rose & Gallup, 2007). On this assertion, most if not all academics conducting research on this topic agree (Amrein-Beardsley, 2008a; Baker et al., 2010; Ballou, 2002; CCSSO, 2005; Cody et al., 2010; Glazerman & Potamites, 2011; Ho et al., 2009; Kim & Sunderman, 2005; Linn, 2008; Nelson, 2011; Sanders, 2003; Scherrer, 2011; Tekwe et al., 2004). The research-based truth is that VAMs can be used to measure changes in student achievement over time, but they should not be used to measure teacher, school, or district quality, especially in consequential ways. The facts of the matter are that VAMs are meant only to measure changes in student achievement over time but NOT to *attribute* this growth to some *cause* (i.e., teacher, administrator, school, district, state, or program quality). "Causal inference may well be the holy grail of quantitative research in the social sciences, but it should not be proclaimed lightly" (Briggs & Domingue, 2011, p. 21; see also Baker et al., 2010). The most powerful determinants of student learning are social capital, intelligence, prior and early learning experiences, etc., and these will likely forever inhibit VAM-based validity. As well, no single measure alone is adequate for measuring student growth over time given that achievement is a complex construct and VAM is a weak representative of the constellation of achievement indicators.

Regardless, from here, many take not one small step but one giant leap in the wrong direction. Riding on the tails of advanced and in some cases mind-blowing statistics (see, for example, Chetty et al., 2011[1]), some argue that *(2) VAMs should be used for educational accountability policies and high-stakes or highly consequential decision-making purposes.* Across the country we have some great and many not so great schools. Given the amount of money we spend on the nation's public schools, budgeted at over 100 billion dollars per year (i.e., around the same amount we spend on the nation's defense systems), there is still a lot to be desired (Denby, 2012). With this, most if not all agree as well (Berliner, 2010, 2011, 2012; Carter, 2004; Kozol, 2005).

In terms of how to better the education condition for students, particularly in America's subpar public schools, great divisions and disagreements coexist. There is wide research-based agreement and recognition that stronger accountability mechanisms will not work to eliminate the root causes of poor district, school, or teacher quality (Au, 2009; Bushaw & Lopez, 2012; Haney, 2000; Heubert & Hauser, 1999; Hursh, 2008; Johnson et al., 2005; Klein et al., 2000; Mathis, 2011; Orfield & Kornhaber, 2001; Timar & Maxwell-Jolly, 2012). Despite this, however, the majority of the nation's educational leaders have still chosen to advance VAMs for these purposes. They continue to assume that VAMs will further stimulate stronger accountability systems and further advance the same theory of change. Moreover, they continue to assume that VAMs, even in their current, imperfect forms, are already "good enough" to be used for stronger accountability policies and consequential purposes (Glazerman et al., 2011; Goe, 2008; Harris, 2008, 2011; Lozier, 2012; Weingarten, 2011; Wright et al., 2006; see also Amrein-Beardsley, 2012; Briggs & Betebenner, 2009; Cole et al., 2011; Freedman, 2010; Gabriel & Allington, 2011; Gabriel & Lester, 2012).

In fact, the "'it's not perfect, but it's the best we have' logic pervades pro-VAM arguments ... even in the absence of a discussion of the implications of its admitted faults" (Gabriel & Allington, 2011, p. 7; see also Gabriel & Lester, 2010, 2013). The research-based truth is that VAMs will not further stimulate stronger accountability systems. Even if they did, stronger accountability mechanisms will not work to eliminate the root causes of district, school, or teacher failure or ineffectiveness.

These two general assumptions along with their research-based truths are illustrated in Table 4.1. From here, however, it is important to analyze why these two assumptions stand, or when dissected, fall apart.

Assumptions used to justify VAM adoption

Of utmost importance are the assumptions being used, and in some cases abused, as rationales to promote the adoption of VAMs. These are the assumptions most often used to support the use of VAMs to evaluate and hold teachers accountable for their effectiveness in the classroom. Note that while the same logic certainly applies to administrators, schools, and districts, the focus hereafter is on VAMs for teacher (not school/district) evaluation and accountability purposes.

Teachers as protagonists

The first assumption here is that *(1) teachers are the most important factors that impact student learning and achievement.* All VAMs are based on this fundamental assumption. Student learning and achievement are linked first and foremost to the quality of the teachers providing instruction, particularly in core subject areas (i.e., mathematics and reading/language arts). Because these core subject areas are most often tested, they are the areas almost always used to assert this assumption (see, for example, Gordon et al., 2006; Hanushek, 1970, 1971, 1979, 2009, 2011; Hanushek & Rivkin, 2010; Sanders & Rivers, 1996). This implies that all research studies using large-scale standardized achievement test scores in mathematics and reading/language arts should generalize across teachers and subject areas.

In addition, it is implied that teachers of these two subject areas matter more than teachers of other subject areas (e.g., science and social studies, physical education, music, and the arts) because these are the subject areas most often tested. The greater notion is that teachers matter regardless of the subject areas they teach, as well as that they matter more than all other factors that impact student learning and achievement. Both of these notions are void of research evidence. Nonetheless, it is still widely believed, particularly among ordinary citizens and politicians (see, for example, Duffrin, 2011), and even some academics (Hanushek, 1970,

Table 4.1 General assumptions about VAMs

Assumptions	*Research-based truths*
1 VAMs should be used to measure teacher, school, or district quality.	VAMs can be loosely used to measure changes in student achievement over time, but they should not be used to measure teacher, school, or district quality, especially in consequential ways.
2 VAMs should be used for educational accountability policies and high-stakes or highly consequential decision-making purposes.	VAMs will not further stimulate stronger accountability systems. Even if they did, stronger accountability mechanisms will not work to eliminate the root causes of district, school, or teacher ineffectiveness.

1971, 1979, 2009, 2011; Hanushek & Rivkin, 2010; Rivkin, Hanushek, & Kain, 2005), that teachers have the greatest effects on student learning and achievement. In fact, it is assumed, strong teachers, if and when identified, can actually wipe out the educational issues that continue to ail America's public schools (Gordon et al., 2006; Hanushek, 2013; Hanushek & Rivkin, 2010; Sanders & Rivers, 1996; TNTP, 2012).

The research-based truth, however, is that teachers are strong *school-level* factors that influence student learning and achievement. Teachers operate alongside many other school-level factors that also impact student learning and achievement (e.g., class sizes, classroom resources, school finances and budget allocations), and these other school-level factors largely conflate determinations about the authentic effects of teachers. Furthermore, all school-level factors put together matter much less than what many, again, assume (Berliner, 2012; LeClaire, 2011; Mathis, 2012; Organization for Economic Cooperation and Development [OECD], 2005; Schochet & Chiang, 2010, 2013).

Variance in student test scores can, in fact, usually be attributed to only about 10–20% of all school level effects, *including* the oft-exaggerated teacher effects. The other 80–90% of the variance typically observed in student test scores can be more appropriately attributed to other student-level and out-of-school factors, over which teachers and school personnel often have very limited control (Berliner, 2012; LeClaire, 2011; Mathis, 2012; OECD, 2005; Schochet & Chiang, 2010, 2013).

The fact of the matter, as also demonstrated in the famous Coleman Report (Coleman et al., 1966), is that student background and out-of-school factors are significantly more important when defining educational outcomes (i.e., test scores) than in-school resources. Powerful explanations for educational outcomes include student risk factors (e.g., emotional/ learning disabilities, English-language proficiency, racial/ethnic minority backgrounds). Included here as well are levels of student motivation and students' desires to do well on tests, particularly if students are not being directly held accountable for their performance. Out-of-school explanatory factors include parents' attitudes towards education; domestic stability and support; access to books, resources, and technologies in the household; access to healthcare and dental care, healthy breakfasts, and other nutritious foods; exposure to arts, culture and travel, and the like, all of which are correlated with families' socioeconomic backgrounds or levels of poverty.

In addition, the related assumption that *(2) good teaching comes from enduring qualities that teachers possess and carry with them from one year to the next, regardless of context*, is also void of research evidence (Gabriel & Allington, 2011; Kennedy, 2010; Xu, Ozek, & Corritore, 2012). The research-based truth is that the teacher effect (i.e., 10–20% of the variance in test scores) is not strong enough to supersede the powers of the student-level and out-of-school influences and effects (i.e., 80–90% of the variance in test scores) from one year to the next. A good teacher under condition X might not be an equally good teacher under condition Y, given the differences in students, resources, and the like that might (or might not) be present in a teacher's classroom from year A to year B (Amrein-Beardsley & Collins, 2012; Berliner, 2013; Newton et al., 2010). Teachers are only a small part of producing student achievement, especially when student achievement is defined and measured by large-scale standardized achievement tests that narrowly measure a very partial sample of the curriculum (which is almost always the case).

This is not to say teachers do not matter, however. They do! Every person reading this book right now can certainly recall at least one, if not a handful, of teachers for whom they are eternally grateful. Rather, the fact of the matter is that those teachers only influenced about 10–20% of our academic lives if defined by student achievement on large-scale stand-ardized achievement tests.

Between the ages of five and 18 children spend 10–25% of their wakeful hours with teach-ers and in schools.[2] Might we more reasonably attribute student achievement also to the outside factors that influence students' academic lives? Might the factors that are valued outside of the schoolyard, in students' homes with their parent(s) and sibling(s), and with friends and acquaintances in their neighborhoods and communities, matter more? Research suggests this is so, as do most teachers; although, they continuously, for the most part, give and live their professional lives to have the greatest impact possible, regardless (Berliner, 2012; Coleman et al., 1966; LeClaire, 2011; Mathis, 2012; OECD, 2005; Schochet & Chiang, 2010, 2013; Yuan et al., 2013).

Whether teachers have the abilities to convey ideas in creative ways and help students become caring individuals, critical thinkers, self-directed and eternal learners, or whether some teachers even save students' lives (e.g., in Newtown, Connecticut) is a question for another day. For the most part, teachers' effects and our collective assumptions about teach-ers' effects are almost always overstated and exaggerated. Inflated teacher effects estimates are almost always used to pitch stronger teacher quality and accountability policies.

Likewise, it is assumed that teachers matter so much that we should focus our policy efforts almost entirely on them. Because teachers matter so much, it only makes sense to hold them accountable for doing more. Because the teacher effect is (falsely) believed to be so strong, we must hold them even more accountable if they are to increase their collective efficacy. Without VAMs, never will we be able to effectively capture the prodigious promises that come along with effective teachers and their effects. Without VAMs, never will we be able to objectively identify effective (and ineffective) teachers and allocate human resources accordingly. Without VAMs, we will not be able to help more students realize the powerful effects of effective teach-ers for themselves (Sanders & Horn, 1998) … so the assumptions go.

Again, this is not to oversimplify the educational conditions in some of America's highest needs schools, namely the inordinate lack of opportunities students in such schools typically have to access relatively high-quality teachers (Berry, 2004, 2008; Boyd, Lankford, Loeb, Ronfeldt, & Wyckoff, 2011; Darling-Hammond, 1995; Ingersoll & May, 2012). However, we cannot continue to assume that the quality of the teacher is the most important factor in students' academic lives, nor that the teacher effect generalizes across teachers, subject areas, varied contexts, and over time. Teachers matter, but not in the way we are often led to assume, particularly when simplistic educational policies are pitched to convince, motivate, or incentivize teachers to make themselves matter even more.

Teachers as antagonists

Ironically, it is also often assumed that many of America's public school teachers are also vil-lains, acting in deceptive and disingenuous roles behind school curtains. The assumption here is that *(3) too many of America's public school teachers are unqualified, unskilled, lazy, or uninspired, and they are the ones who are hindering educational progress.* This assumption was well illustrated when the *Los Angeles Times* published teachers' names along with their value-added scores and rankings on its website, allegedly for public accountability purposes (Felch et al., 2010; see also Briggs & Domingue, 2011; Durso, 2011; Felch, 2011; Song & Felch, 2011).

As explained by Gabriel and Lester (2010):

> Throughout the series, the newspaper set up teachers as either one thing or another: effective or ineffective, good or bad, a detriment or a savior. With McCarthy-era tactics, the paper's series flooded us with profiles of extreme-case formulations – examples so good, bad, or surprising that they almost seduced us into believing that "ineffectiveness" could be lurking anywhere, unbeknownst even to the teacher himself or herself, regardless of certification, reputation, or experience.

In fact, some have likened recent VAM-based trends to modern-day witch-hunts (Ravitch, 2012c; Santos & Gebeloff, 2012) in pursuit of teachers who are sitting idle in malfunctioning schools (Duncan, 2009a) and preserving low expectations for low-achieving students (Sanders et al., 2009). Proponents argue that if the crisis in America's public schools is to be solved, these are the teachers who must be identified, labeled, and purged from America's public education system. While Bill Gates, a recognized proponent of VAMs, has publicly criticized practices that name, blame, and shame teachers (Gates, 2012, 2013), many of America's politicians and some academics overtly support such practices (see, for example, Dillon, 2010a; Duncan, 2009a; Goldstein, 2012; Rhee, 2011). Without such practices, they presume, schools will likely never improve (Gordon et al., 2006; Hanushek, 2013; Hanushek & Rivkin, 2010; Sanders & Rivers, 1996).

Hanushek (2009), for example, expressed his research-based opinions on this topic. He advised that allowing such teachers to remain in teaching is outright harming students, "doing damage," and "dragging down the nation" (see also Hanushek, 2013). While bad teachers certainly exist, using such sweeping generalizations to chastise teachers as a whole is certainly remiss. Such actions are especially inappropriate given the marginal effects that research evidence suggests teachers actually have on the student achievement demonstrated on large-scale standardized achievement tests, discussed above.

Hanushek has nonetheless been arguing for a few years that if we are to improve America's public education system we must purge the bottom 5–10% of America's public school teachers using VAMs. He did so quite publicly, for example, in the documentary *Waiting for "Superman"* (Chilcott & Guggenheim, 2011; see also Chetty et al., 2011; Friedman as cited in Lowrey, 2012; Gordon et al., 2006; Ravitch, 2012c; TNTP, 2012). This assumes that the bottom 5–10% is both easily identifiable and consistent from one year to the next. These assumptions overlook the very real issues with reliability and consistency, or the lack thereof, for example whereby there still exists a one in four chance that teachers will be misclassified even if three years of data are included when generating VAM estimates (Au, 2011; Kersting et al., 2013; NGA & CCSSO, 2010; Otterman, 2010; Schochet & Chiang, 2010, 2013; Shaw & Bovaird, 2011). Identifying and replacing these teachers, Hanushek (2011) assumes, would be enough to make America's public education system the world leader in mathematics and science (Hanushek as cited in Duffrin, 2011).

The research-based truth is that not nearly as many teachers as is often assumed are in fact ineffectual, particularly when "teacher effectiveness" is quantified in normative terms; the ways in which VAM estimates are calculated position 50% of any set of teachers as relatively ineffective (i.e., below average effectiveness via comparison to the mean). Thus, by statistical design, there will always be some teachers who will appear relatively less effective simply because they fall on the wrong side of the bell curve. Moreover, because the "value" that teachers "add" is not calculated in absolute terms, the normative approach taken by VAM analysts continuously precludes us from exacting our approximations about how many of America's public school teachers are in fact ineffectual. The VAM approach will not help us exact such classifications.

However, even if VAM approaches could help, the assumption here is also that *(4) if enough ineffective teachers are fired, test scores will increase.* The research-based truth is that we have no empirical evidence to suggest that such purgative policies work. Again, the greater academic community asserts that there is insufficient research evidence to support the accurate identification of such teachers using VAMs (Baker et al., 2010, 2013; Bock et al., 1996; Bracey, 2000, 2004b; Braun, 2005; Kupermintz, 2003; Linn, 2001; Raudenbush, 2004; Rivkin, 2007; Rubin et al., 2004; Walberg & Paik, 1997). Ineffective teachers often exit voluntarily anyways thus self-selecting themselves out of teaching (Weisberg et al., 2009, p. 35). Lastly, there is no evidence to support the idea that these teachers, if purged, would be replaced by more effective teachers. "Is there a large pool of average, good, or great teachers waiting in the wings?" (Ravitch, 2012d; see also Baker et al., 2010; Briggs & Domingue, 2011; Jacob, 2011; Ravitch, 2010a). There is no evidence indicating that there are qualified teachers knocking down classroom doors, waiting to teach or replace the teachers that VAMs, so it is assumed, are to identify and help to purge from the system. While there are some teachers who enter teaching through alternative routes (e.g., Teach for America [TFA]), research evidence continues to suggest that these teachers remain in teaching only for the short term (e.g., three years on average) and their effects compared to other new and career teachers are no different from average (see, for example, Darling-Hammond, Holtzman, Gatlin, & Heilig, 2005; Laczko-Kerr & Berliner, 2002; Ravitch, 2012a; Strauss, 2011). Thus, we have no evidence that there is a surplus of even more highly qualified people waiting to become teachers.

While it is not unreasonable to fire ineffective teachers, aligning ourselves with this series of assumptions will certainly not yield what is imagined via such purgative policies (Boyd, Grossman, Lankford, Loeb, & Wyckoff, 2008). While teachers matter, they do not matter as much as accountability proponents might like to believe. Purging teachers from the education system would have unknown effects, but the effects would likely be far less than anticipated. Might individual teachers be terminated? Sure! How (or how not) to do this, however, is still another point of controversy around which exists another set of assumptions.

Faulty human evaluation systems

Most conventional evaluation systems used in education are faulty. Our current teacher evaluation systems are in need of improvements, especially because these systems are limited given the very social complex phenomenon that is to be evaluated (i.e., quality teaching). Because of this, and the lack of viable (or relatively inexpensive) alternatives, however, the objective quantification of teaching quality is now more than ever the desired end (Glazerman & Potamites, 2011). Objective teacher evaluation systems are so much desired, in fact, that the quantification of the teacher effectiveness construct (i.e., via VAMs) is increasingly being positioned to supersede if not replace traditional evaluation systems based, even in part, on human judgment (Gabriel & Lester, 2013; Garland, 2012; Ravitch, 2012c).

The New Teacher Project's "Widget Effect" report, for example, found that 99% of teachers whose evaluation reports were examined received ratings of "satisfactory" when supervisors evaluated them using the binary options of "satisfactory" and "unsatisfactory." Only 1% of teachers examined received ratings of "unsatisfactory" (Weisberg et al., 2009; see also Brill, 2009; Gates, 2012). While binary constructions of complex data such as these are often used to ground simplistic ideas and push simplistic yet definitive ideas and agendas, particularly in the media, this tactic certainly worked here (Gabriel & Lester, 2010, 2013).

This report was widely publicized given the assumed improbability that only 1% of America's public schoolteachers are, in fact, ineffectual. Conversely, it is certainly possible that high scores and ratings might be more typical than assumed, simply because those seeking licenses are often well trained and able. So, teachers might in fact get high observation ratings because they are competent, not because the system used to evaluate them is flawed.

Regardless, this report (and others like it) has since been repeatedly used as evidence that the systems typically used to evaluate teachers, even the new and improved systems, are unacceptably subjective and flawed (Sawchuck, 2013d). This has also caused increased concerns about the biased natures of traditional evaluation systems, their "meaningless" results and the "negligent" decisions that continue to be made, or worse, continue *not* to be made using such systems (TNTP, 2012, pp. 21–22).

All of the above assertions are assumptions, of course, that underlie VAM-based logic. Nonetheless, the main assumption here is that *(5) more than 1% of America's public school teachers are ineffective.* Do we have "a K–12 system that remains hesitant to differentiate between the best and the weakest performers," or might we work with a counter-assumption that many more teachers than many people would like to believe are, in fact, effective (Sawchuck, 2013d)?

The research-based truth is that, according to Graue et al. (2013), we really have no idea how many teachers are (or are not) effective because how one defines teacher effectiveness varies widely. If one is to use VAM estimates, as discussed, scores are typically manipulated to represent a normal distribution (i.e., a bell curve). This would presume that 50% of all of America's public school teachers are ineffectual as compared to the other 50% who are not, but are on the other side of the mean. Although, because teachers typically have to be statistically different from the mean in order to be classified accordingly, sometimes only approximately 2% to 15% end up being deemed as distinctly worse than the average, also depending upon whether controls for student socioeconomic and demographic background variables are used (Ballou, 2002; see also Braun, 2005; Dorn, 1994). Again, however, this does not necessarily mean "bad," but "worse than the average" in that these are all based on normative not absolute distinctions. Teachers who demonstrate added value might fall below the mean, placing them on the wrong half of the curve. If one is to use observational data alone, as in the "Widget Effect" report or more recent analyses of states' new and improved observational systems (Weisberg et al., 2009; see also Anderson, 2013; Sawchuck, 2013d), estimates suggest that only approximately 1% of America's public school teachers are ineffective. Yet again, others presume this estimate is far removed from reality given the subjective evaluation methods used to define and classify teacher effectiveness.

The truth of the matter is that nobody knows where the real number falls or to what extreme it is closer. Teacher effectiveness is simply a difficult construct that is not easily reduced and quantified for such simplistic purposes,[3] unless of course a series of heroic assumptions are used as means to justify oft-political ends. The real number probably falls somewhere in between, if not closer in the favor of teachers. Recent evidence suggests, for example, that even with the new and improved teacher evaluation systems coming into play, teachers are still faring quite well. In Florida, a state revered for its reform-minded educational policies and a state that received $43 million in federal RttT monies to support its reforms, 97% of teachers were recently deemed effective or highly effective under its new VAM-based evaluation systems. In Tennessee, the state in which the EVAAS® system is used statewide for stronger accountability purposes, 98% of teachers were judged to be, at a minimum, "at expectations." "Advocates of education reform concede that such rosy numbers, after many millions of dollars developing the new systems and thousands of hours of training, are worrisome" (Anderson, 2013). Perhaps all this "reform" has been in vain.

Yet the overarching assumption remains, suggesting that *(6) VAMs will improve upon, if not solve, that which is wrong with the faulty evaluation systems traditionally used in education.* Here, there are really three camps of folks. The first group believes that VAMs should replace the faulty human resource systems we have used for decades past, wiping out the methods with which we have grown familiar (e.g., supervisor observations) when evaluating teachers.

The second group sees a need for teacher evaluation systems that are based on multiple methods and measures. Such systems would include indicators based more on human judgment (typically qualitative; e.g., supervisor evaluations) along with quantitative indicators that are based on more seemingly objective data (e.g., student test scores). This group sometimes believes, however, that the data derived via the seemingly more scientific, objective, statistical methods (i.e., using VAMs) should supersede the other, seemingly "less scientific" indicators included (see, for example, Gabriel & Lester, 2013; Garland, 2012; Glazerman et al., 2010; Harris, 2011; Ravitch, 2012c; Rockoff et al., 2010). These advocates sometimes argue that VAM estimates should trump other output, particularly when disparities and inconsistencies are prevalent between and among the multiple measures used, which is currently almost always the case.

The third group believes in systems that include multiple measures, based on multiple data collection methods, from which data might be used in supplementary ways or to trigger further investigation. However, this further investigation will almost always require human judgment, which purists in this arena want to suppress. Members of this third group are the people least likely to be misled by illusions of objectivity, the same illusions that VAM-based purists have yet to confirm. These are the people most likely to trust research before theory, and these are the people who cautiously understand that the research warranting the use of VAMs to accurately identify teachers is thus far, disappointingly underwhelming. The research-based truth is that there is no strong research evidence to support the accurate identification of teachers using VAMs (Baker et al., 2010; Capitol Hill Briefing, 2011; Hermann et al., 2013; Hill et al., 2011; Newton et al., 2010; Rothstein, 2009, 2010b; Rothstein & Mathis, 2013; Stacy et al., 2012). In addition, while the implementation and use of VAMs for high-stakes purposes is increasing across the country, there lingers a paucity of research evidence to support the attachment of significant consequences to value-added output, and using VAMs in isolation or as the dominant indicator in evaluative systems based on multiple measures is not yet warranted and should not be done or encouraged (Au, 2010; Braun, 2005; Capitol Hill Briefing, 2011; Darling-Hammond et al., 2012; Eckert & Dabrowski, 2010; Haertel, 2011; Hill et al., 2011; Ho et al., 2009; Newton et al., 2010; Papay, 2011; Rothstein, 2009, 2010b; Schochet & Chiang, 2010, 2013). According to Baird (1987), "[Value-added] is, above all, not a panacea, or even a solution to be recommended widely" (p. 214; see also Scherrer, 2011; Yeh, 2011).

School administrators as co-conspirators

Related, the final assumption here is that *(7) if ever our teacher evaluations systems were made stronger (e.g., via the use of VAMs), the barriers preventing teacher termination would still be too substantial and burdensome to permit the terminations assumed necessary.* Barriers include teacher tenure policies, teacher union affiliations and oppositions, and other onerous (although once considered protective) dismissal rules and regulations (Baker et al., 2013; Brill, 2009; Underwood & Mead, 2012). These barriers contribute to the "institutional inertia of public school systems" (Goldhaber, 2009, p. 2; see also TNTP, 2012). Moreover, these barriers make it very difficult to fire ineffective teachers, unless under the most extreme circumstances given teachers' due process rights (Baker et al., 2010, 2013; Pullin, 2013; see also Goldhaber, 2009).

Yet the research-based truth is that even if all barriers and blockades preventing ease in teacher dismissal were torn down, whether administrators would fire ineffective teachers – those who many believe exist in greater numbers than might be the case – is uncertain. The assumptions many have about breaking down barricades to further strengthen school leaders' incentives to make such decisions might be false and again overstated (see also Toch & Rothman, 2008).

In a study conducted in Chicago, for example, researchers found that approximately 42% of elementary school principals and 30% of high school principals, including principals in some of Chicago's lowest-achieving schools, still chose not to dismiss any of the teachers whom they supervised when these barriers were removed (Jacob, 2011). This could have been due to the unwillingness of some school leaders to make difficult decisions. This could have also been due to the possibility that not nearly as many teachers as some would have expected were in fact ineffective (see also Sawchuck, 2013d). Or this could have been due to another raw assumption, that *(8) ineffective school administrators are part of the problem. Ineffective school administrators do not really care whether good teachers stay or bad teachers leave, and this has been evidenced by their lack of action, as they are the ones ultimately responsible for firing ineffective teachers* (TNTP, 2012).

The research-based truth here is that, for the most part, school administrators are not a part of the problem. While ineffective school administrators certainly do exist, we really have no idea about how many school administrators are or are not effective either. Defining school administrator effectiveness is even less developed than defining teacher effectiveness. With the exception of using school-level VAM estimates and the evaluations of school administrators' supervisors (i.e., district superintendents), there is a marked shortage of indicators to evaluate school administrators, especially if school administrators are to be "objectively" evaluated as well (Branch et al., 2013). Nonetheless, we can state with some certainty (without having counter-evidence) that school administrators are not co-participants in the same alleged plot to maintain average levels of student learning and performance. We can also state with greater certainty that, as demonstrated here, people make assumptions, not research-based statements, when exaggerated claims are needed to advance false truths and assertions (Pies, 2013; Takahashi, 2012).

In sum, these are just some of the assumptions that we as a public must keep in check about our schools and the teachers and administrators within them. However, these are also the assumptions that are most often being used to rationalize why VAMs are so desperately needed in America's public schools (summarized here in Table 4.2).

In sum, this yields evidence that the assumptions some make about America's public school educators, in general, are somewhat reckless and stretched beyond reason, and sometimes

Table 4.2 Assumptions used as rationales to justify VAM adoptions

Assumptions	Research-based truths
1 Teachers are the most important factors that impact student learning and achievement.	Teachers are strong school-level factors that influence student learning and achievement, but teachers operate alongside many other school-level factors that also impact student learning and achievement, and these other factors largely conflate determinations about the authentic effects of teachers. Furthermore, all school-level factors put together matter much less than many assume.
2 Good teaching comes from enduring qualities that teachers possess and carry with them from one year to the next, regardless of context.	The teacher effect (i.e., 10–20% of the variance in test scores) is not strong enough to supersede the powers of the student-level and out-of-school influences and effects (i.e., 80–90% of the variance in test scores) from one year to the next.
3 Too many of America's public school teachers are unqualified, unskilled, lazy, or uninspired, and they are the ones who are hindering educational progress.	Not nearly as many teachers as is often assumed are in fact ineffectual, particularly when "teacher effectiveness" is quantified in normative terms (i.e., below average effectiveness via comparisons to the mean). Thus, by statistical design, there will always be some teachers who will appear relatively less effective simply because they fall on the wrong side of the bell curve.
4 If enough ineffective teachers are fired, test scores will increase.	We have no empirical evidence to suggest that such purgative policies work. Ineffective teachers often exit voluntarily anyways by self-selecting themselves out of teaching. Lastly, there is no evidence to support the idea that these teachers, if purged, would be replaced by more effective teachers.
5 More than 1% of America's public school teachers are ineffective.	We really have no idea how many teachers are (or are not) effective because how one defines teacher effectiveness varies widely.
6 VAMs will improve upon, if not solve, that which is wrong with the faulty evaluation systems traditionally used in education.	There is no strong research evidence to support the accurate identification of teachers using VAMs. In addition, using VAMs in isolation or as the dominant indicator in evaluative systems based on multiple measures is not yet warranted and should not be done or encouraged.
7 If ever our teacher evaluation systems were made stronger (e.g., via the use of VAMs), the barriers preventing teacher termination would still be too substantial and burdensome to permit the terminations assumed necessary.	Even if all barriers and blockades preventing ease in teacher dismissal were removed, whether administrators would fire ineffective teachers is uncertain in that realities about how many teachers need to be fired are still uncertain.
8 Ineffective school administrators are part of the problem. Ineffective school administrators do not really care whether good teachers stay or bad teachers leave, and this has been evidenced by their lack of action.	School administrators are not a part of the problem. While ineffective school administrators certainly do exist, school administrators are not co-participants in the same alleged plot to maintain average levels of student learning and performance.

even decency. Yet we continue to let others (e.g., U.S. Secretary of Education Arne Duncan) make false assumptions about the objectionable conditions of America's public schools, the objectionable quality of the teachers working within them, and the objectionable quality of the school administrators looking over them, not to mention the objectionable colleges of education preparing teachers and school administrators (Duncan, 2009b; see also Constantine et al., 2009). The question remains as to whether there are really teachers and administrators out there working not for the lives of the students in their schools but to preserve mediocrity and to protect their self-serving interests. Perhaps there are some who fall into this category, but overall, teachers and administrators are not involved in some demonic plot to allow America's high-needs public schools to continue their record of poor performance and lower than average levels of student learning. Teachers and administrators are, instead, working on a daily basis on all of our behalves, most importantly to positively impact the lives of their students about whom the large majority of them deeply care.

Assumptions used to further advance VAM implementation

Along with the aforementioned assumptions that are used as rationales to justify VAM adoption come assumptions used as justifications to further advance VAM implementation as well. Next are the assumptions frequently positioned when pitches are made regarding how we might move forward with VAMs to instill and ensure education reform.

Economics-based beliefs about education reform

In economics, the added value of a product is determined by calculating the difference between the price of a finished product and the labor and raw material costs of producing it. Like a net benefit, this value-added difference serves as a useful index when determining the profit the product has garnered for its manufacturer. The manufacturer's collective set of products that "add value" then add further value to the greater economy if the products jointly yield greater profits than losses each year. The products that yield higher returns and add relatively more value are the most likely to survive in and contribute to the greater economy. Conversely, the products that do not yield returns worthy of their costs perish for having detracted value from the manufacturer's overall gains. Obvious financial incentives support to further the production of the products that add value and obvious financial disincentives exist to halt the production of the products that do not. This is how value-added is defined and, well, valued in "an ideal economy characterized by perfect capital markets, rational behavior, and perfect certainty" (Miller & Modigliani, 1961, p. 412; see also Baird, 1987; Fincher, 1985). Increased wealth is always the desired end, and the end is rationally achieved in the most objective and certain of terms.

The logic-based thinking about how value-added systems should work to improve America's public schools is essentially the same. As captured by Miller and Modigliani (1961) years ago, this thinking exists in a perfect and rational system in which certainty is assured as long as *something* is objectively measured in the most certain of terms, that is, via VAMs. The only real difference here is that the value-added commodity of interest is the "knowledge added" by America's public school teachers (Tekwe et al., 2004, p. 28; see also Baird, 1987). Value-added is to be objectively calculated in terms of student achievement after knowledge is delivered (assuming students are vessels whose brains are to be filled with information) and minus the level of student achievement before the knowledge was delivered (Berliner, 2005; Fincher, 1985; Misco, 2008).

Likewise, in order to increase productivity, representing the quality of the input variables, teachers must be enticed to escalate their output. This can be done using incentives (e.g., via bonus monies and merit pay) to boost teachers' levels of knowledge production, using punishments (e.g., teacher termination or revocation of teacher tenure) to discourage laziness, inertia, ineptness, incompetence, unskillfulness, unwillingness, or any other reason used when thinking about why teachers might lack knowledge production (Yuan et al., 2013), if not applying both tactics. Outcomes (i.e., students' standardized achievement test scores) are then used to filter valuable feedback back into the educational system to complete the cause-and-effect education production function that will then work to stimulate further improvements or corrective action where needed (Braun, 2008; Linn, 2008). It is really as simple and straight-forward as that, based on economic models and theories. Or is it?

The assumption here is that *(1) to reform America's public schools, we must treat educational systems as we would market-based corporations. Educational corporations produce knowledge, the quality of which can be manipulated by objectively measuring knowledge-based outcomes (i.e., via VAMs).* It is widely assumed that in order to improve our schools, we must measure what we are doing well to stimulate and expand upon measurably effective practices (e.g., good teaching). Elsewhere, we must halt what we are not doing measurably well to disincentivize caustic practices (e.g., bad teaching). To achieve either of these goals, we must measure the quality of the system's assumingly "most important" inputs (i.e., teachers) by measuring the system's most objective outputs (i.e., students' test scores). Likewise, attaching incentives (and disincentives) to the things that are valued the most (i.e., improvements in students' test scores) will ultimately work to guarantee reform. Unfortunately, mainly conservative, business-savvy philanthropists (e.g., those affiliated with ALEC, Chiefs for Change, FEE, etc.) sustain this seductive logic, largely because they believe that the ways in which they think about their businesses aptly apply to the ways we should think about school improvement (Flynn, 2012; Gabriel & Allington, 2011; McNeil, 2012).

The research-based truth is that schools are social institutions that do not operate like mechanistic corporations. Teaching is one of the most complex occupations in existence, and thinking about teacher effects in economic terms is misleading, unsophisticated, disingenuous, and obtuse (Berliner, 2005; Braun, 2008; Gabriel & Allington, 2011; Harris, 2011; Linn, 2008; Misco, 2008; Tekwe, et al., 2004). The real world of education is much more complicated than we would like to believe, and it cannot be simplistically positioned or investigated in terms of inputs that cause quantities of outputs to change (Hanushek, 1979; see also Berliner, 2002; Bracey, 2004b). Teaching is highly complex, and so it is true that student learning is equally complex and cannot be reduced to one or a set of test scores.

Nothing that matters in education can be quantified or controlled for using even the most complex statistical or methodological approaches, especially not by "exploiting quasi-experimental variation in lieu of a randomized experiment" (Chetty et al., 2011, p. 3; see also Bausell, 2013; Gordon et al., 2006; Harris, 2009c; Ishii & Rivkin, 2009). Even the most advanced statistical and econometric approaches will likely never facilitate the apples-to-apples comparisons assumed when calculating value-added (see, for example, Meyer & Dokumaci, 2011). Solving complex problems in education cannot be simply addressed using numbers, nor can they be immediately resolved by tinkering with individual components of the process–product function (Hawkins, 2012; Miller & Modigliani, 1961; see also Berliner, 2005; Lockwood & McCaffrey, 2009; Rothstein, 2010b; Winerip, 2012).

Look at our current economy, for example. Is it not ironic that we would trust economics-based thinking to reform our educational system, given the country's and the globe's current economic crises, especially as economic researchers have themselves debunked the myths about their own econometric methods and findings in the business world (De Long & Lang, 1992)? In fact, given their recent admissions, "It's a wonder the global economic infrastructure is not in far worse shape" (Freedman, 2010). American business mogul Warren Buffett (2008) communicated with his shareholders about the economic models that *caused* the current financial crisis in America, writing:

> Investors should be skeptical of [economic]-based [and forecasting] models. Constructed by a nerdy-sounding priesthood using esoteric terms such as beta, gamma, sigma and the like, these models tend to look impressive. Too often, though, investors forget to examine the assumptions behind the symbols.
>
> *(p. 15; see also De Long & Lang, 1992; Freedman, 2010)*

This might serve as a lesson in wisdom in and of itself, particularly in terms of the ways we might *not* want to think about the principles, ideologies, and assumptions made about educational reform and how economics-based thinking might inform it (Banchero & Kesmodel, 2011; Hill et al., 2011; Jennings & Corcoran, 2009).

Age-old ideas about carrots and sticks

A related assumption many make about the best ways to reform our schools also has historical roots in economic theory (Andreoni, Harbaugh, & Versterlund, 2003). It has to do with carrots and sticks and the ways in which both hopes and fears might be manipulated to increase worker productivity. This translates into education when VAMs are positioned as the mechanisms that will provide the objective measure of desired and undesired teacher behaviors (Ames, 1992; Epstein, 1988). VAMs are thus advanced as the mechanisms that will help induce desired behaviors (i.e., increased levels of student growth on large-scale standardized achievement tests) if and when educational policies are put forth to potentially reward teachers (with carrots). Similarly, VAMs are advanced as the mechanisms that will help prevent adverse behaviors (i.e., substandard levels of student growth on large-scale standardized achievement tests) if and when educational policies are put forth to potentially punish teachers (with sticks).

Epstein (1988) and Ames (1992) worked on a framework to exemplify how this might work in education by proposing that learning environments can be strategically manipulated to motivate or dissuade teachers' instructional strategies and efforts, ultimately to improve student achievement. Anderman et al. (2010) adapted their framework to demonstrate how such a theory would hypothetically work to further enhance teaching and learning environments using VAMs (e.g., by using VAM estimates to arrange students into "traditional educational groupings"; pp. 132–133). Even the U.S. Secretary of Education Arne Duncan (2009a) believes that to boost teacher effectiveness, high-quality teachers should be identified and rewarded, low-quality teachers should be identified and penalized, and the incentives and threats, respectively, should be enough to improve America's public schools. No research studies are cited to support any of these propositions, however, which makes them, yet again, highly assumptive postulations.

Here the main assumption is that *(2) if educational goals are informed by VAMs, and the goals are then operationalized using incentives and disincentives, teachers will become more motivated to improve their instruction and student achievement will subsequently improve.* Using VAMs will induce teachers to work harder, and using VAMs will incite teachers who do not work hard enough to improve out of fear of being penalized or terminated (Harris, 2011). Such positive and negative motivators will increase the quality of the inputs (i.e., teaching) and subsequently enhance the quality of the outputs (i.e., student achievement) included in the aforementioned education production function.

The research-based truth is, however, that there is little to no research evidence to support this assumption.

For example, Johnson (2012) wrote:

> The truth is, teachers don't need elected officials to motivate us. If our students are not learning, they let us know. They put their heads down or they pass notes. They raise their hands and ask for clarification. Sometimes, they just stare at us like zombies. Few things are more excruciating for a teacher than leading a class that's not learning.

As one teacher stated, after being asked whether VAM-based incentives would increase his/her productivity: "I never needed an incentive to teach to do my best, I love to teach" (Collins, 2012). The research-based truth is that teachers are not altogether motivated to improve student achievement by the possibility of being monetarily rewarded for gains in student test scores (Baker et al., 2010; Ehlert et al., 2012; Goldhaber, 2009; Gratz, 2010; NGA & CCSSO, 2010; Springer et al., 2010; Toch & Rothman, 2008; Wells, 2011). Ask yourself if you have ever heard a teacher say they decided to teach because of the money.

In some ways the research-based truth is counter-intuitive, however, because it is commonly known that teachers are not paid particularly well. In addition, teachers across the country have recently experienced salary freezes, wage cuts, or stunted salary growth given current economic trends. In some cases, states and districts have limited or altogether halted conventional salary increases (e.g., those based on years of experience and/or earning advanced academic degrees), to offset the costs of putting in place performance-pay plans instead (Bell-wether Education Partners, 2011; Goldhaber, 2009; NGA & CCSSO, 2010). So it makes more sense now than ever before that, if teachers were given the opportunity to boost their salaries with bonuses, they might work harder to realize the monetary awards (Toch & Rothman, 2008).

The related assumption here is that *(3) the monies to be earned via merit pay and other monetary bonuses are substantial and worth enough to become the motivators conceptualized.* This overlooks the very important fact that merit pay, and merit-based policies meant to improve student learning and achievement, are not new. Rather, merit-based reforms have been proposed as a means to motivate teachers to work harder many times over. These reforms began with education reform trends in the 1920s, were repeated in the 1950s, and were seen again in the 1980s as well (Moore-Johnson, 1984). These commonsensical measures for reform are, therefore, by no means a new idea, yet in no way have they ever demonstrated that they indeed work. "Merit pay is the idea that never works and never dies" (Ravitch, 2013b); it is a "zombie" idea that "fails and fails and fails again, but legislators just want more of it" (Ravitch, 2013c). This continues to be the case with this current education reform movement.

For example, in the Houston Independent School District, the district using VAM estimates to inform teachers' performance pay more than any other district in the country (see Chapter 2), 92% of all district employees received a bonus in 2011, the maximum of which was $3,000 (Grier & Holcombe, 2008; Harris, 2011; Mellon, 2010, 2012; Sparks, 2011). This is a moderate yet typical bonus amount for a classroom teacher (Wells, 2011). At the same time, however, the district superintendent received an $18,000 bonus (*Education Week*, 2011).

Ask yourself whether receiving a maximum award of $3,000 alongside approximately nine out of every 10 of your colleagues would be a significant motivator to improve upon your instruction. Ask yourself, if you taught students similarly to another teacher who received $3,000 and you earned $300 (which happens frequently given the inconsistencies prevalent across year-to-year VAM estimates and also across teachers who teach core and non-core subject areas), would that motivate you to teach better or work harder? People in the business world would likely scoff at such "incentives." Yuan et al. (2013) evidenced that a large reason these types of reforms typically do not work is that the financial motivators are rarely large enough to motivate much of anything. Instead, they might provoke levels of job-related stress or perhaps more focus on tested content, especially when teachers do not understand the merit systems or reject them as unfair or impossible unless they engage in increased test preparation, particularly given the out-of-school influences over which they have no control. This also assumes that a teacher is not already motivated to improve upon his/her instruction, without a monetary incentive.

The district is currently revising its pay-for-performance plan to motivate its teachers with greater but fewer awards, assuming again this might work and, again, without any research evidence whatsoever that any of their VAM-based reforms over the past five years have indeed worked to improve student achievement as theorized (see, for example, Duffrin, 2011; Yuan et al., 2013; see also Corcoran, 2010; Mellon, 2012; Papay, 2011). If anything, research suggests their concerted efforts have caused deleterious effects instead, including, for example, disincentives to teach certain students; cheating or teaching to the test; the narrowing of the curriculum when certain subject areas count more on tests; general distrust, disillusionment, and low morale among teachers; administrators manipulating school rosters to advantage some teachers over others; etc. (Collins, 2012; Player, 2010; Vogell, Perry, Judd, & Pell, 2012; see also Amrein-Beardsley & Collins, 2012; Capitol Hill Briefing, 2011; Darling-Hammond et al., 2012). Other cases of this exist in Tennessee (Springer et al., 2010), in Denver with the "ProComp" pay-for-performance reform initiatives still ongoing (Gratz, 2010), and elsewhere (Yuan et al., 2013).

Nonetheless, the research-based truth is that pay-for-performance bonuses are not nearly large enough to act as motivators, especially when considering the cuts in pay and halted levels of salary growth that teachers have realized at the same time (Ehlert et al., 2012; Gratz, 2010; Springer et al., 2010; Yuan et al., 2013). In addition, for the most part, teachers are already exerting a lot of effort in their classrooms. Maximum levels of teacher effort have been reached more often than assumed, which also inhibits teachers' capacities to further advance and *continuously* demonstrate VAM-based growth over time (Ehlert et al., 2012; Yuan et al., 2013).

This way of thinking also assumes that *(4) teachers, who for the most part became teachers because they wanted to have an impact on the lives of children, are more motivated by money than they are by the interests of the students in their classrooms. When teachers are faced with choices between serving their own needs and serving the needs of others, they will on average choose themselves* (see, for example,

Harris, 2011; Weisberg et al., 2009). The research-based truth is that, as discussed, pay-for-performance bonuses are not nearly large enough to motivate much of anything (Ehlert et al., 2012; Gratz, 2010; Springer et al., 2010). In addition, when teachers view such systems as neither accurate nor fair, they see little to no value in the performance-based systems to which the seemingly important rewards and sanctions are attached (Amrein-Beardsley & Collins, 2012; Baker et al., 2010; Koedel & Betts, 2009; Mellon, 2010; Sass, 2008; Sparks, 2011; Weisberg et al., 2009; Wells, 2011). What is worse is that implementing pay-for-performance plans may trigger adverse consequences that well outweigh the intended, yet illusive, benefits of the plans. All of the negative effects that come along with competition do not offset the relatively small financial gains to be earned or realized with such pay-for-performance schemes (Gratz, 2010; Kohn, 1986; Layard & Dunn, 2009).

For example, evidence suggests that when the merit monies to be distributed are finite, one teacher's gain becomes another teacher's loss. When teachers are pitted against one another this overemphasizes competition and creates a zero-sum situation in which an individual teacher's gains or losses are balanced by the gains or losses of the other teachers up for the same, finite pot of money. When "competitors are placed in competition with players against whom they have no hope of winning, incentives [then] weaken for everyone" (Ehlert et al., 2012, p. 16; see also TNTP, 2012). One teacher captured this by saying that VAMs, and the EVAAS® specifically, "trades 'it takes a village' for 'every man for himself.'" Another noted that it "undermines collaboration, a cooperative work place, and pits administration against the staff" (Collins, 2012, p. 134).

If monies are infinite this is less of an issue. This is also less of an issue when team-level awards are distributed instead, for example, given grade-level or school-level VAM-based scores (Buddin & Zamarro, 2008). As well, because teaching is so complex, and the effects of one teacher are extremely difficult to disentangle from the effects of other teachers (and other school personnel), it makes more sense to award team-based bonuses when salaries are on hold or cautiously controlled.

I say this simply to get monies back into the hands of those who I believe deserve them, not necessarily in support of such VAM-based decision-making at the school or district levels. If anything, for now, it might be cautiously prudent to invest only in group-based performance pay schemes, especially if standard salary structures are a thing of the past. Although, this too can cause reverse effects whereby team members might be otherwise incentivized to work less and ride on the efforts of others (Buddin & Zamarro, 2008; Harris, 2011).

Otherwise we will have to wait to pay teachers for their specific knowledge and skills, until (if ever) they can be demonstrated, perhaps using more holistic, research-based systems that may or may not include VAM estimates. While it would be great to increase the salaries of teachers, this should not be done unless it can be done in fair, equitable, and transparent ways that cause the fewest of unintended, perverse consequences.

The formative feedback loop

When outcomes-based information is delivered back to the input(s) level for interpretation and use, the act of interpreting and using the outcomes-based information to improve upon subsequent outcomes completes the "feedback loop." This assumes that the information being fed back into the system is of value, as well as that the information can be used within and to improve upon the system in meaningful ways (see Figure 4.1).

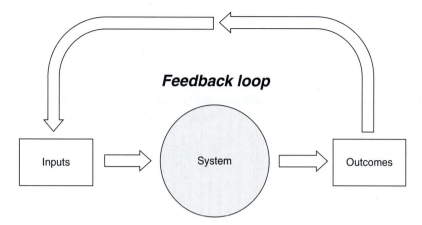

Figure 4.1 The feedback loop as conceptualized for common use.

In the education production function, this feedback loop is expected to occur when VAM-based information (i.e., test-based outcomes about student growth) is sent back to the teachers who are the key inputs in the econometric models conceptualized so that they can act upon the feedback. This assumption is best illustrated by U.S. Secretary of Education Duncan (2009a) who notes that, "When teachers get better data on student growth, it empowers teachers to tailor classroom instruction to the needs of their students and boost student achievement" (p. 4).

Teachers, once empowered with VAM-based data, are expected then to interpret and use the information to improve upon their instruction. Using the VAM-based information in meaningful and important ways will therefore improve upon subsequent outcomes (i.e., increased levels of growth on large-scale standardized achievement tests) as long as the feedback loop continues to function as designed. Again this assumes that the VAM-based information being fed back into the system "adds value" or at least has the potential to add value (see Figure 4.2). That said, the overarching assumption here is that *(5) teachers can both understand*

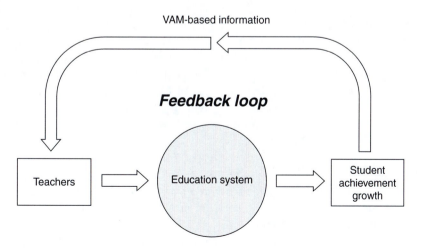

Figure 4.2 The feedback loop as conceptualized for VAM-based educational use.

VAM-based information and use VAM-based information to diagnose needs and improve upon their instruction. Then increased levels of student achievement and growth will come as a result.

According to Popham (2013), "Ample research evidence is now at hand to indicate emphatically that when the [formative feedback loop] is used, students learn better – lots better." However, the research-based truth is that, to date, there is no evidence to suggest that using general assessment information (especially from district- and classroom-based assessments) generalizes when using VAM-based information in the same ways (i.e., via the feedback loop). There is no research evidence to demonstrate that if teachers are provided increased access to VAM-based information, their abilities to understand or use this information in instructionally meaningful ways will be enhanced. This is largely because VAM-based information is based upon large-scale standardized achievement tests, tests that are in no way up to such a task. These tests survey the domain of knowledge and skills included in the curricular standards used to guide instruction, but they do not have nearly enough depth to be diagnostically or instructionally useful.

Likewise, there is no research evidence whatsoever to suggest that using VAM-based information will increase levels of student achievement or growth by "feed[ing it] back into the system as a lever to prompt action" (Braun, 2008; see also Briggs & Domingue, 2011; Graue, Delaney, Karch, & Romero, 2011a; Kraemer, 2011). While, according to Popham (2013), using assessment data for (in)formative purposes is an "ends–means" process by which teachers should "rely on assessment outcomes (the ends) to decide whether any adjustments are warranted in what they're doing (the means)," no evidence yet exists that such a feedback loop works with VAMs and VAM-based estimates as based on large-scale standardized achievement tests.

Every person who makes any of the above assumptions *never* cites research evidence in support (see, for example, Anderman et al., 2010; Buddin, 2011; Harris, 2011; Lander & Pautsch, 2011; Witham, 2011). Again, this is simply because no research evidence exists to support the prevailing assumptions about the formative functions of VAMs. This is also because VAM-based data are typically designed for summative and not formative purposes (Baker et al., 2013; Callendar, 2004; Carter, 2004; Briggs & Domingue, 2011; Goe, 2008; Graue et al., 2013; Harris, 2009c, 2011; Kraemer, 2011; Medina, 2009; NGA & CCSSO, 2010; Raudenbush, 2004).

Whether using VAM-based data will ever yield instructionally relevant or useful information is certainly unclear. Accordingly, those who make statements about such possibilities should certainly be more careful until research evidence supports such claims. The adoption of the Common Core State Standards and their related tests, as affiliated with both the Partnership for the Assessment of Readiness for College and Career (PARCC) Consortium with approximately 20 states involved and the Smarter Balanced Assessment Consortium (SBAC) with approximately 30 states involved, should (in theory) help to improve upon the extent to which teachers might use more relevant and sensitive data to improve their instruction (Popham, 2013). It is still, however, unknown how these tests, to be released in the spring of 2015, might be used in VAM-based formative ways. With these tests come a "devil's bargain," by which adding more tests with more formative potential will ultimately create excessively more standardized achievement testing than there already is. Current estimates sit at between 200 and 300 total tests with the upper estimate including tests for all subject areas from kindergarten through grade 12 (Gabriel & Lester, 2013; Richardson, 2012).

In sum, these are the assumptions currently being used as justifications to further advance VAM implementation. These are the assumptions also tightly or loosely linked to corporate-based ways of thinking about how schools should operate, and these are the assumptions currently being used to justify the steps it will presumably take to reform America's public schools (summarized below in Table 4.3).

Table 4.3 Assumptions used as justifications to further advance VAM implementation

Assumptions	Research-based truths
1 To reform America's public schools, we must treat educational systems as we would market-based corporations. Educational corporations produce knowledge, the quality of which can be manipulated by objectively measuring knowledge-based outcomes (i.e., via VAMs).	Schools are social institutions that do not operate like mechanistic corporations. Teaching is one of the most complex occupations in existence, and thinking about teacher effects in economic terms is misleading, unsophisticated, disingenuous, and obtuse.
2 If educational goals are informed by VAMs, and the goals are then operationalized using incentives and disincentives, teachers will become more motivated to improve their instruction and student achievement will subsequently improve.	There is little to no research evidence to support this assumption. Teachers are not altogether motivated to improve student achievement by the potential to be monetarily rewarded for gains in student test scores.
3 The monies to be earned via merit pay and other monetary bonuses are substantial and worthy enough to become the motivators conceptualized.	Pay-for-performance bonuses are not nearly large enough to motivate much of anything, especially considering the cuts in pay and halted levels of salary growth that teachers have experienced at the same time. In addition, for the most part, teachers are already exerting a lot of effort in their classrooms. Maximum levels of teacher effort have been reached more often than is assumed, which also inhibits teachers' capacities to further advance and continuously demonstrate VAM-based growth over time.
4 Teachers, who for the most part became teachers because they wanted to have an impact on the lives of children, are more motivated by money than they are the interests of the students in their classrooms. When teachers are faced with choices between serving their own needs over the needs of others, they will on average choose themselves.	When teachers view such systems as neither accurate nor fair, teachers see little to no value in the performance-based systems to which seemingly important rewards and sanctions are attached. What is worse is that implementing pay-for-performance plans may trigger adverse consequences that well outweigh the intended, yet illusive, benefits of the plans.
5 Teachers can both understand VAM-based information and use the information to diagnose needs and improve upon their instruction. Increased levels of student achievement and growth will come about as a result.	There is no evidence to suggest that the research about using general assessment information generalizes when using VAM-based information in the same ways. There is no evidence that demonstrates that if teachers are provided increased access to VAM-based information, this enhances teachers' abilities to understand or use this information in instructionally meaningful or relevant ways. There is no evidence to suggest that doing so will increase levels of student achievement or growth.

Conclusions

Discussed in this chapter are the assumptions used to support and advance VAMs, VAM implementation, and VAM-based educational policies. My goal in this chapter was to help others better understand the commonsense assumptions on which VAMs are based, as well as to better understand these assumptions as situated and deconstructed within the research literature. Discussed first was that the oft-exaggerated teacher effect is not everything it is often assumed to be. Furthermore, not nearly as many teachers as is frequently assumed are, in fact, ineffectual. In addition, while ineffective school administrators certainly do exist, as do ineffective teachers, school administrators are not co-participants in the same alleged plot to maintain average levels of student learning and performance in America's public schools.

As well, schools are social institutions that do not operate like mechanistic corporations. So thinking about teacher effects in economic terms is unsophisticated and simpleminded. Carrots and sticks do not motivate most teachers, but for those who do care, sometimes implementing such plans triggers adverse consequences instead (e.g., gaming the system). These unintended consequences often outweigh the intended, yet still illusive, benefits of the VAM-based policies implemented.

Finally, there is no research evidence to demonstrate that if teachers are provided increased access to VAM-based information, this will enhance their abilities to understand or use VAM estimates in instructionally meaningful or relevant ways. In addition, there is no evidence to suggest that even attempting to use VAM estimates for formative purposes will increase levels of student achievement or growth as a result.

In sum, the large majority of assumptions surrounding VAMs, particularly VAMs that are to be used for teacher evaluation and accountability purposes, are rejected by empirical evidence, as well as theory, logic, and common sense. VAMs fail on all of these considerations. While some argue that the violations of these assumptions are "not severe" enough to prevent VAM use (Harris, 2008, 2009c; Stroup, 1995), others argue the opposite, especially if VAMs are to be used for high-stakes purposes (Briggs & Domingue, 2011; Rothstein, 2009, 2010b, 2011). These assumptions are too "heroic," and because they are unwarranted and rejected by the research evidence, or a lack thereof, they should not be casually made or blindly adopted (Rubin et al., 2004; see also Amrein-Beardsley, 2008a; Kupermintz, 2003; McCaffrey et al., 2004a; Wainer, 2004). Yet, these are the assumptions that continue to perpetuate the socially constructed and highly deceitful beliefs that the underlying causal questions (i.e., about how teachers directly impact student learning and achievement) can be accurately and legitimately answered using VAMs.

Illustrated in the next chapter are the assumptions about the large-scale standardized achievement tests and the statistics and methods used to generate VAM estimates. While VAM proponents and technicians argue that these particular assumptions are of little consequence, I will demonstrate that these assumptions cannot be blindly or ignorantly adopted either. The tests, statistics, model controls, and methods about which the next assumptions are made are also grossly flawed.

Box 4.1 Top 10 assertions

1   VAM advocates continue to immortalize the view that VAMs can effectively measure teacher impacts on student learning and achievement. They do so by utilizing a series of unchecked assumptions to preserve their stands and promote their positions.

2   VAMs are the instruments in which too many are unwisely trusting, largely because VAMs are the instruments VAM advocates are pitching, and in some cases selling for profit, to an often very naïve, uncritical, and highly assuming public.

3   Educational researchers generally agree that VAMs can be used to measure changes in student achievement over time, but they should not be used to measure teacher, school, or district quality, especially in consequential ways.

4   However, objective teacher evaluation systems are so much desired that the quantification of the teacher effectiveness construct is increasingly being positioned to supersede, if not replace, traditional evaluation systems based, even in part, on human judgment.

5   Teachers have powerful effects on student learning and achievement, but they do not have nearly the amount of impact as is commonly assumed and perpetuated. In-school factors, including teachers, account only for 10–20% of the variation in achievement scores.

6   Related, not nearly as many teachers, as is also often assumed, are ineffectual. This is particularly true when teacher effectiveness is quantified in normative terms whereby VAM estimates position 50% of any set of teachers as relatively ineffective, and vice versa.

7   No research evidence supports the widely endorsed assumption that if ineffective teachers were removed from schools, they would be replaced by more effective teachers.

8   Merit-based reforms have been proposed to boost student achievement many times during the past century, yet there is no evidence to suggest that merit-based systems work. Rather, research suggests that merit-based systems have detrimental effects instead.

9   No research evidence suggests that using VAM-based data will increase student learning, for example, by helping teachers make more informed instructional decisions.

10 No research evidence suggests that using school-level VAM estimates to evaluate and hold administrators (e.g., principals and superintendents) accountable, given the lack of other indicators, supports the Measure and Punish (M&P) Theory of Change.

Notes

1 In this study researchers famously found that students of high-value-added teachers were more likely to go to college, go to higher-ranked colleges, earn higher salaries when adults, live in better neighborhoods using income as an indicator of "better," etc. President Obama cited this study in his 2012 State of the Union Address, it continues to be cited by Michelle Rhee, and it made print and

television news headlines across the country once released. However, this study was not peer-reviewed; it still has not been published in a highly esteemed journal; it was not based on a randomized control trial or an appropriate research design with comparable samples, it was based on archival data that were collected before high-stakes tests were a standard part of educational policy. For major critiques of this study, see Adler (2013), Baker (2013b), Hawkins (2012), Institute of Education Sciences (IES; 2012), and Winerip (2012).

2 Students typically attend 180 days of school per year for six hours per day for 13 years from full-day kindergarten through grade 12 ($=14,040$ hours). This time includes lunch, recess, extracurricular and core subject courses, and certain other school-related activities. If students are awake approximately 14 hours per day, they also typically spend 8 hours awake but out of school during the school year ($=18,720$ hours). As well, students typically spend 185 days outside of school entirely, over weekends, holidays, and summer breaks ($=33,670$ hours). Given the hours students spend in school throughout their K–12 careers ($=14,040$) and the total hours they are awake throughout the whole year but not in school ($18,720+33,670=52,390$ hours), it can be approximated that at the very most students spend 26.8% of their K–12 lives, from ages five to 18, in school. If one assumes that classroom instruction in core academic areas constitutes approximately 50% of every academic day, it can be estimated that at the very most students spend 13.4% of their K–12 lives, from ages five to 18, in classrooms learning core academic content (see also Berliner, 2012).

3 Polarizing teacher effectiveness into either "effective or not" dichotomous categories allows for no variance in distinction. Classifying teachers along categories that include more variance (e.g., excellent, above average, average, and satisfactory) would certainly yield better, albeit still imperfect, estimates of how many teachers in America are in fact good teachers. But distorting the construct of interest (i.e., teaching effectiveness) in dichotomous ways trivializes the issue, as does reducing highly complex phenomena into binary categories in general. Regardless, both are effective schemas to help perpetuate (often false) assumptions, simply by having reduced the data into clear and comprehensible categories.

5

TEST-BASED, STATISTICAL, AND METHODOLOGICAL ASSUMPTIONS

Not everything that counts can be counted, and not everything that can be counted counts.
Albert Einstein

In the previous chapter, I examined (1) the general assumptions about VAMs, (2) the assumptions being used, and in some cases exploited, as rationales to promote the adoption of VAMs, and (3) the assumptions advocates are using to pitch VAMs as the solutions to what ails America's public schools. In this chapter I examine another series of related assumptions organized around (4) the assumptions being made about the large-scale standardized achievement tests currently being used to generate VAM estimates, and (5) the statistical and methodological assumptions that go along with VAM adoption, implementation, and use. These assumptions are mostly made about the precision with which VAM estimations are made and the sophistication of the statistical models and methods on which VAM estimations are based.

While a high level of precision is almost always implied by those advocating VAM use, the actual precision with which VAM estimations are made is almost never made transparent, for example, in terms of statistical errors, bias, or levels of reliability (i.e., inconsistencies in teacher classifications over time; Baker et al., 2013; Kelly & Downey, 2010; see also Braun, 2005). VAM estimations are, by definition, rough calculations that are largely imperfect. So "users of VAM[s] must resist the temptation to interpret estimates as pure, stable" or even "true" measures of teacher effectiveness (Lockwood, McCaffrey, Hamilton, et al., 2007, p. 61; see also Raudenbush & Jean, 2012; Rubin et al., 2004), especially when policymakers and promoters continue to endorse them in these ways.

Standardized achievement tests as measurement tools

I will start first with the assumptions about the large-scale standardized achievement tests that are being used across the country to yield the raw numerical data from which VAM estimations are being made (Collins & Amrein-Beardsley, 2014; see also Braun, 2005). All VAM methods and statistics are based on large-scale standardized achievement test scores, so it only makes sense to examine these tests and the assumptions that go along with using and interpreting large-scale standardized achievement tests. Understanding the tests and their assumptions is foundational to understanding the greater methodological assumptions that come along with VAMs.

Werner Heisenberg's Uncertainty Principle explains that when measuring atomic and subatomic particles, measuring one unyieldingly distorts the measurement of the other. Thus, neither particle can be measured with certainty because the very act of being measured changes the behavior of that which is being observed (*Stanford Encyclopedia of Philosophy*, 2006).[1] This principle generalizes beyond research in physics to other areas of scientific inquiry, especially in what Berliner (2002) termed the "harder" social sciences in which humans are involved. For example, many would assume measuring the physical properties of people (e.g., weight, height, blood pressure) would yield near perfect and precise computations. Uncertain measurements still result, however, as people stretch their spines to be taller, stand off center on a scale to weigh less, or become anxious simply by the act of being measured, causing a rise in blood pressure.

What distorts all measurements systems, to a lesser or greater degree, is that the accuracy of the tools being used to measure the phenomena is confounded by the actions of the people being measured (see also Stone, 1997). Human error is present in almost every measurement made (Marder, 2012, p. 159). However, the assumption here is that *(1) because measurements typically yield a mathematical and assumingly highly scientific value, an appropriate level of certainty or exactness comes along with the numerical scores that result.* The fact of the matter is that "Even though measurement is scientifically based and rooted, measurements function much more like language – they are essentially arbitrary designations that have no inherent value. Rather their values are constructed given there is mutual agreement about how to use and interpret the numbers derived" (Amrein-Beardsley & Barnett, 2012, p. 2).

In most traditional educational research studies, as in the case here, measurement is operationally defined as a numeric value representative of student learning, using student achievement on the large-scale standardized achievement tests mandated in NCLB as a proxy for student learning (Marder, 2012). However, large-scale standardized achievement tests are not all they are assumed to be, nor do they reveal what it is they are assumed to disclose.

Contrary to popular belief and assumptions about what standardized achievement tests measure, scores taken from these tests do *not* provide accurate indicators of educational effectiveness, nor in this case teacher effectiveness. This is because of five main reasons: (a) the errors that are inherent in standardized achievement tests distort standardized test output; (b) the very construction of standardized achievement tests and their limited content coverage; (c) the assumptions required for test score conversions and manipulations; (d) the bias inherent in standardized achievement tests, which confounds what test scores demonstrate about student learning and achievement; and (e) the very fact that large-scale standardized achievement tests are not designed to measure teacher effectiveness, nor to make causal statements about teacher effects, even though they are being used for both of these purposes, regardless.

Errors

The assumption here is that *(2) large-scale standardized achievement tests serve as precise measures of what students know and are able to do.* This is the belief held firm, particularly by most people without experience of the realities and fine intricacies that come along with educational measurement and testing. Unfortunately, large-scale standardized achievement tests come with two forms of error: random and systematic error. Random errors are often associated with measurement noise, for example, when idiosyncratic factors (e.g., a student's mood) distort test scores and falsely inflate or deflate scores away from the "true" value that is to be observed and captured (Linn & Haug, 2002; Miller & Modigliani, 1961). Systematic errors are often equated with measurement bias or construct-irrelevant variance (CIV) when outside factors consistently, albeit falsely, inflate or deflate the measurement of a variable and therefore distort its interpretation and validity (Haladyna & Downing, 2004; Messick, 1989). This occurs, for example, when teachers tell students that their test scores will determine whether the teacher gets fired or gets paid a bonus, to which students then respond in unnatural or abnormal ways. This also occurs when students have no reasons besides "just doing well" to do their best on tests and test scores yield underestimates of what students actually know and can do, simply because the students do not value the tests as much as we assume they do, or we think that they should.

The assumption here is that *(3) regardless of whether student-level consequences are attached to tests, students inherently want to perform well on large-scale standardized achievement tests.* I, for one, recall at least a few times when I was in public school taking large-scale standardized achievement tests and randomly filled in the answer bubbles on test forms instead of reading and answering the questions, particularly those questions that took the most work (e.g., the test items with the longest reading passages or the most complicated mathematical processes). Remember for yourself the type of test-taker you were when you were in elementary or high school; that is, when the test did not count for a grade or another laudable reason.

The research-based truth is that because of this, and other reasons, students may believe that large-scale standardized achievement tests are of no consequence (Davis, 1994; Pallas, 2012; Zeis, Waronska, & Fuller, 2009). Inversely, when serious consequences are attached to tests students may perceive the tests to matter more than they really do (Amrein & Berliner, 2002; Carey, 2006; Corcoran, 2010; Grodsky et al., 2009; Haladyna et al., 1991; Haney, 2000; Hursh, 2008; Koretz, 2002; Koretz, McCaffrey, & Hamilton, 2001; Nichols and Berliner, 2007; Papay, 2011; Ravitch, 2010a; Reardon et al., 2009; Rothstein, 2011; Zeis et al., 2009). Either scenario typically yields underestimates or overestimates, respectively, pulling test scores away from the "true" scores of interest (Rubenstein, 2012b; Vogell, Perry, Judd, & Pell, 2012) and making interpretive errors more likely. This has nothing to say of human scoring errors, which also have notable and sometimes alarming consequences (see, for example, FairTest, 2013; see also McCaffrey et al., 2008; Rhoades & Madaus, 2003; Santos & Gebeloff, 2012).

Nonetheless, when the students' scores and random and systematic (and human) errors are reported, the resultant units and numerical values are designed to approximate, at best, and then designate students' assumingly "true" understandings of the tested subject and concept areas. With VAMs, the assumingly "true" values are then combined to yield "truer" measures of achievement via the measures of growth over time. The truth of the matter is that while VAMs might be able to reduce some of the systematic errors, although likely none of the random errors, lingering errors lend themselves to decision errors, which only makes things worse if the outcome data are used for highly consequential decision-making purposes. This is especially true when errors "mean the difference between merit pay, promotion, or job termination for a percentage of teachers every year" (Gabriel & Lester, 2013, p. 4; see also

Harris, 2011; Schochet & Chiang, 2010, 2013). As advised by Cronbach and Gleser (1965), these errors cannot be ignored as "they alter the goodness of whatever decisions are to be made" (p. 137; see also Baker et al., 2013).

Problems with standardized achievement test construction

The very design of most large-scale standardized achievement tests actually makes it impossible to meet most if not all of the assumptions so many have about large-scale standardized achievement tests (Ballou, 2002; Gabriel & Allington, 2011; Sparks, 2012b). As expressed by esteemed scholar Edmund Gordon at the annual meeting of the National Academy of Education "With only few exceptions, [large-scale standardized achievement tests] systematically overrepresent basic skills and knowledge and omit the complex knowledge and reasoning we are seeking for college and career readiness" (as cited in Sparks, 2012b; see also Toch & Rothman, 2008). The assumption here is that *(4) large-scale standardized achievement tests yield highly objective numbers based on complex statistics and therefore yield "true" scores about student learning.* The research-based truth is that statistics are being used to convey authority and intimidate others into accepting VAMs simply because VAMs are based on statistics and their mystique, despite statistics' gross limitations when used to make what are presumed to be highly scientific inferences derived via large-scale standardized achievement tests (Ewing, 2011; Gabriel & Lester, 2013). The fact of the matter is that large-scale standardized achievement tests offer very narrow measures of what students have achieved, and they do not effectively assess students' depth of knowledge and understanding, their ability to think critically, analytically, or creatively, solve contextual problems, or even accomplish authentic, performance-based tasks (e.g., solving mathematical problems by collecting and manipulating real data, conducting experiments, etc.; Baker et al., 2010; Corcoran, 2010; Harris, 2011; Toch & Rothman, 2008). Accordingly, whether tests that typically test a total of 40 to 50 items that are meant to represent hundreds of more complex items can in fact capture the breadth and depth of information students have learned, is also suspect (Amrein-Beardsley, 2008a; Pallas, 2012; Raudenbush & Jean, 2012). These tests survey the domain of knowledge and skills included in the standards, but they do not have nearly enough depth to fulfil what they are increasingly being tasked with (e.g., to make high-stakes inferences about whether teachers might be terminated or might receive merit pay).

Also doubtful is whether using tests that assess student learning and achievement in mathematics and language arts as an indicator of teacher (or school/district) value-added is measuring the things we value the most in education. Along with this comes another set of assumptions, as well as implications pertaining to what we value and what we collectively think is most worth knowing and doing. The assumption here is that *(5) the subject areas that are tested using large-scale standardized achievement tests matter more than the subject areas not tested.* Sometimes science, and more often social studies, music, physical education, and the arts, are marginalized by the fact that it is very difficult to construct large-scale standardized achievement tests to assess student learning in these subject areas, not to mention to do so well (Corcoran, 2010; Toch & Rothman, 2008). Thus, what is tested often dictates what is taught, implying that the tested subject areas matter more than the others. This is particularly true when test administration times approach. The research-based truth is that this alone has led our country (and other countries, for that matter) to marginalize the "value" that non-tested subjects "add" to our educated lives. Even the forthcoming tests that are to be used to assess student learning of the Common Core State Standards – the tests the federal government is funding to the tune of approximately $350 million – are still primarily narrowly focused on assessing mathematics and reading/language arts, but this time with more rigor, so it is assumed (Robelen, 2012; see also Harris, 2011; Richardson, 2012).

However, when test developers aim to make their tests appropriately rigorous, typically they more specifically work to make sure that neither too many difficult, nor too many easy test items are included. They work to ensure, literally, that their tests are "just right." Test developers use statistical tools (e.g., *p*-values that are calculated to determine the proportion of students who answered items accurately) to remove the test items that too many people answered correctly or incorrectly.

The assumption here is that *(6) the test items used to construct large-scale standardized achievement tests are included to measure things that students should know and should be able to do.* What ends up being left on the tests after measurement specialists work their magic to perfect their tests, however, are the items that "discriminate" well, or that discriminate between those who seemingly know unique concepts and particulars and those who do not. Contrary to popular belief, the test items that therefore typically remain on large-scale standardized achievement tests are often the items that are not taught as often or in as much depth by teachers. They are not taught as much simply because they often matter less in the real world and other applied settings. Yet, these are the items that help make large-scale standardized achievement tests function well, mainly because they discriminate between those with and those without specific expertise in specific content area knowledge.

For example, on the high school graduation exam that has been used for years in the state of Arizona, there is a test item that involves interpreting data displayed on a box-and-whisker plot (see Figure 5.1 for an example of a box-and-whisker plot[2]). Few statisticians whom I

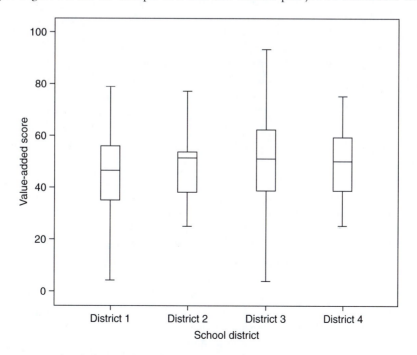

Figure 5.1 Example of a box-and-whisker plot.

know use box-and-whisker plots anymore, but this item is included nonetheless, implying that high school students need to know this to graduate high school.

Might students understand and be able to interpret data that are displayed using bar, column, or circle graphs instead? Might this in actuality be more important? The answer to both of these questions is likely "Yes," but none of these more practical items discriminate as well as the more difficult box-and-whisker plot. So the assumption is that students who answer this item correctly know more about statistics and data displays in general. So what ends up being valued more on large-scale standardized achievement tests are the things that students might not normally do or use in the real world, which are the things that teachers are certainly less likely to teach, even if all of the topics and concepts are included in the state standards. Large-scale standardized achievement tests do not measure much that is practical.

Finally, with the advent of VAMs and using large-scale standardized achievement tests to measure growth, it is assumed that *(7) the large-scale standardized achievement tests being used to measure growth are set on equal interval scales*, that is, that the scale used to measure growth from one year to the next is on a scale of equal units (Nelson, 2011). So a 10-point difference between a score of 50 and 60 should mean the same thing as a 10-point difference between a score of 80 and 90. Yet "even the psychometricians who are responsible for test scaling shy away from making this assumption [about equal intervals]" (Harris, 2009c, p. 329). If the scale is not an equal interval scale, VAM consumers must overlook this technical hazard as well. VAM consumers must nonetheless agree to make problematic inferences, despite the scale being much more arbitrary than is almost always assumed (Ballou, 2009), and despite the variability in measurement error that scaling issues cause (Cole et al., 2011). Although, some might argue that to counter for this, one might use item response theory with scales transposed into logits or log-odds.[3]

The bell curve

The standard response to account for tests that are not on an interval scale is to norm the test scores before using them. Most, although not all VAMs, are fundamentally normative in nature (Schafer et al., 2012). This too comes with another series of unchecked assumptions discussed earlier. These assumptions primarily align with the assumptions many make about the bell-shaped curve (see Figure 5.2) historically used to display intelligence quotients (IQs) and the economic and social conditions correlated with IQs (see, for example, Herrnstein & Murray, 1996).

The main assumption here is that *(8) a normal distribution (i.e., a bell curve) of teacher effectiveness exists and can and should be used to norm large-scale standardized achievement test scores for VAM analyses. Half of all of America's public school teachers are above and the other half are below average.* Accordingly, every ineffective teacher who crosses the statistical mean in the middle of the bell curve to the ineffective side, slightly or dramatically, is categorized as such. Similarly, teachers exceeding the statistical mean, slightly or dramatically, are categorized as effective. Given the normative nature of this curve, as some teachers get better, other teachers must get worse, and vice versa; that is, again, if you are to abide by the bell curve and the arbitrary assumptions that go along with it, despite the fact that using bell curves to define organizational complexities is highly misleading and rarely reflects reality, particularly in social systems like education (Gould, 1996; see also Baker et al., 2013).

The research-based truth is that VAM estimates do not indicate whether a teacher is good

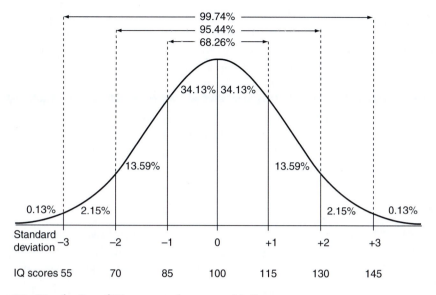

Figure 5.2 Distribution of IQ scores under a normal bell curve.

or highly effective, as is often assumed, but rather whether a teacher is better or worse than other, "similar" teachers to whom (s)he is compared, again assuming this all reflects upon teachers and not just students (Baker et al., 2013; Goe, 2008). Teachers' value-added scores are not absolute, but relative, having been determined by comparing teachers' growth trajectories to other, "similar" teachers' growth trajectories (e.g., teachers within the same district teaching the same subject area at the same grade level at the same time). Each teacher's value-added estimate is assumed to be average unless pulled away from the mean at a statistically significant level, although this also presumes that all teachers start out at average (Bracey, 2004a; Braun, 2005; Briggs & Domingue, 2011; CCSSO, 2005; Eckert & Dabrowski, 2010). It is on these assumptions that all VAM analyses are based; that is, after students' messy test score data are converted and normed for VAM-based analyses.

Disparate impact and bias

In addition, with all large-scale standardized achievement tests, students who are educationally "at risk" (i.e., students who, disproportionately to their low-risk peers, are more likely to have emotional/learning disabilities and/or come from high-needs, high-poverty, English-language deficient, culturally isolated, and often racial/ethnic minority backgrounds, although a large number of students at risk are not students of color) typically score the worst on large-scale standardized achievement tests. In fact, the correlations between student test scores and students' demographic and environmental backgrounds are so strong that one (i.e., students' demographics) can effectively be used to predict the other (i.e., students' test scores), even before students take the tests, with almost perfect precision (Ballou, 2002; Berliner, 2012; Meyer, 1997). This ties back to the earlier discussion regarding the plausibility of the strength of teacher and school effects, or the lack thereof.

The greater problem here involves confounded causation whereby students' standardized achievement test scores capture not only what the students have learned or achieved in school, but also their levels of motivation (over which educators have at least some influence), what they learn outside of school (over which educators have little to no control), and their innate intellectual abilities (over which educators have no control).[4] While the assumption here is that *(9) test scores derived via large-scale standardized achievement tests yield strong indicators about what students learn in school*, the reality is that test scores capture many factors inside *and* outside of school, such as the out-of-school variables that are related to students' backgrounds, peers, parents, families, neighborhoods, communities, and the like. However, it is important to note, again, that test scores provide weak signals about educational quality and often much stronger signals about what students bring with them every year to the schoolhouse door, from their family, home, and neighborhood experiences.

Attribution and causation

Lastly, with the advent of VAMs we are now beginning to use large-scale standardized achievement tests in even more consequential ways. Now, more than ever, we are overlooking the fact that large-scale standardized achievement tests have always been, and continue to be, developed to assess levels of student achievement and *not* levels of teacher effectiveness. They were never designed to estimate teachers' causal effects. Yet regardless, with the advent of VAMs, we are now using large-scale standardized achievement test scores, more than ever before, to make causative statements about the contributory effects teachers have (Au, 2011; Papay, 2011). We are doing this "under extreme and unrealistic assumptions" (Rubin et al., 2004, p. 113), assumptions that are "extraordinarily strong [yet] rarely tested" (Kane & Staiger, 2008, p. 1; see also Baker et al., 2010; Briggs & Domingue, 2011; Gabriel & Allington, 2011; Koretz, 2002; Linn, 2008; Meyer, 1997).

The assumption here is that *(10) because large-scale standardized achievement tests are "the best" and most objective educational measures we have, because we have them readily available and accessible, and despite the fact that they are designed to measure student achievement not teacher effects, we should use them to make causal distinctions about teacher quality.* As mentioned, the large-scale standardized achievement tests on which VAM analyses are based are inherently flawed for measuring student achievement in and of themselves. Using such faulty measures to make causal statements about teacher (or school/district) effects simply exacerbates the issues (see, for example, Baker et al., 2010, 2013; Ballou, 2002; Reckase, 2004). The fact remains that VAMs are meant only to measure changes in student achievement over time but NOT meant to attribute this growth to some cause (i.e., teacher, administrator, school, district, state, or program quality).

These are the "necessary assumptions" that provide mathematical convenience to support statisticians', econometricians', and others' tendencies to reduce complex phenomena into categories and numbers, in this case using large-scale standardized achievement tests. These are the assumptions often made about the large-scale standardized achievement tests used for such reductionistic purposes, particularly in the case of VAMs (summarized here in Table 5.1).

Statistical and methodological assumptions about VAMs continued

VAMs are based on a very imprecise science, although the precision with which estimates are made is assumed to be highly scientific (Santos & Gebeloff, 2012). I presented examples of this in the previous section and will present more examples of this next. In this section I

Table 5.1 Assumptions often made about the large-scale standardized achievement tests used for value-added calculations

Assumptions	Research-based truths
1 Because measurements typically yield a mathematical and, it is assumed, a highly scientific value, an appropriate level of certainty or exactness comes along with the numerical scores that result.	Even though measurement is scientifically based and rooted, measurements function much more like language – they are essentially arbitrary designations that have no inherent value. Rather, their values are constructed given there is mutual agreement about how to use and interpret the numbers derived.
2 Large-scale standardized achievement tests serve as precise measures of what students know and are able to do.	Tests offer very narrow measures of what students have achieved, and they do not effectively assess students' depth of knowledge and understanding, nor their ability to think critically, analytically, or creatively, solve contextual problems, or even accomplish authentic, performance-based tasks.
3 Regardless of whether student-level consequences are attached to tests, students inherently want to perform well on large-scale standardized achievement tests.	Students often believe that tests are of no consequence. Inversely, when serious consequences are attached to tests, students might perceive the tests to matter, possibly more than they really do. Either scenario typically yields underestimates or overestimates, respectively, pulling test scores away from the "true" scores of interest.
4 Large-scale standardized achievement tests yield highly objective numbers based on complex statistics and therefore yield "true" scores about student learning.	Statistics are being used to convey authority and intimidate others into accepting VAMs simply because VAMs are based on statistics and their mystique, despite statistics' gross limitations when used to make (presumed highly scientific) inferences derived via tests.
5 The subject areas that are tested using large-scale standardized achievement tests matter more than the subject areas not tested.	Sometimes science, and more often social studies, music, physical education, and the arts, are marginalized by the fact that it is very difficult to construct tests to assess student learning in these subject areas. Then, what is tested often dictates what is taught, implying that the tested subject areas matter more than the others.
6 The items used to construct large-scale standardized achievement tests are included to measure things that students should know and be able to do.	The items most often included on tests are those that "discriminate" well, but they are not representative of the test items we might value most or that are most often taught by teachers as written into state standards.
7 The large-scale standardized achievement tests being used to measure growth are set on equal interval scales.	The tests being used are typically not set on equal interval scales. Even the psychometricians who develop the tests that are used for value-added analyses hesitate to agree to such an assumption.

continued

Table 5.1 Continued

Assumptions	Research-based truths
8 A normal distribution (i.e., a bell curve) of teacher effectiveness exists and can and should be used to norm large-scale standardized achievement test scores for VAM analyses. Half of all of America's public school teachers are above and the other half are below average.	VAM estimates do not indicate whether a teacher is good or highly effective, but rather whether a teacher is better or worse than other "similar" teachers. Teachers' value-added scores are not absolute, but relative.
9 Scores derived via large-scale standardized achievement tests yield strong indicators about what students learn in schools.	Test scores provide weak signals about educational quality and often much stronger signals about what students bring with them every year to the schoolhouse door, including out-of-school variables that are related to students' backgrounds, peers, parents, families, neighborhoods, communities, and the like.
10 Large-scale standardized achievement tests are "the best" and most objective measures we have. Because they are readily available and accessible, and despite the fact that they are designed to measure student achievement not teacher effects, we should use them to make causal distinctions about teachers.	The tests on which VAM analyses are based are inherently flawed for measuring student achievement in and of themselves. Using such faulty measures to make causal statements about teacher (or school/district) effects simply exacerbates the issues (e.g., errors, bias, disparate impact).

examine the other statistical and methodological assumptions that go along with VAM adoption, implementation, and use. These are the assumptions frequently made about the general sophistication of the statistical models and methods from which VAM estimations are derived.

Statistical controls simplify chaos and disorder

All VAMs (including the SGP growth model) include students' test scores from prior years to "control for" the extraneous variables that we know impact student learning and achievement. Some VAMs also include other student background variables (e.g., eligibility for free or reduced-cost lunches as a proxy for students' socioeconomic backgrounds) to control for these outside effects as well. This was discussed previously, but the main assumption here is that *(1) once students' prior learning and other background variables are statistically controlled for, or factored out, the only thing left in terms of the gains students make on large-scale standardized achievement tests over time can be directly attributed to the teacher and his/her causal effects* (Andrejko, 2004; Chetty et al., 2011; Ehlert et al., 2012; Hershberg, 2004; Nelson, 2011; Nicholson & Brown, 2010; Sanders, 2000; Sanders & Horn, 1994). The assumption is that statistically controlling for previous achievement and combinations of other student background variables is enough to account for the impact these variables have on student learning and achievement over time.

The research-based truth, rather, is that the variables typically available in the databases used to conduct VAM analyses are very limited (see, for example, Briggs & Domingue, 2011) and, accordingly, cannot be used to work the statistical miracles assumed. Even the richest of variables (that are not typically available; e.g., that might account for daily attendance, after-school factors, tutoring, homework clubs, parental involvement, access to resources, prior teachers' residual effects, multiple teachers' fractional effects) would not liberate value-added analyses from the confounding effects students' backgrounds and other risk factors have on achievement growth over time (Ishii & Rivkin, 2009; McCaffrey et al., 2004b; Scherrer, 2011). The use of students' testing histories and other socio-demographic variables, even if abundant and sufficient, cannot effectively wipe out the things that ultimately matter when it comes to measuring student learning and achievement from one year to the next (Scherrer, 2011).

Assuming that these variables are constant across similar students is unfounded as well (Misco, 2008), as is assuming that the circumstances and events that are unique to students' lives average out when data are collapsed together for teacher evaluation purposes (Gabriel & Allington, 2011). Also unfounded is the assumption that by controlling for the variables that are available (e.g., eligibility for free or reduced-cost lunches), statisticians are also controlling for the related variables they cannot measure or control (e.g., student levels of motivation). These factors, together, considerably and markedly affect student growth, and controlling for some does not necessarily mean you are compensating for enough of what cannot be controlled.

The best that statisticians can do is to rely on the argument that because the unobservable variables are correlated with the observable variables, they can be included, and they can hope that this is enough to control for bias. However, the fact of the matter is that controlling for some variables will not control for the other variables, despite all of these variables being highly correlated. This has been shown across studies in which researchers have demonstrated that levels of bias caused by non-random placement practices continue to contaminate value-added analyses, even when the most sophisticated controls have been deployed (Capitol Hill Briefing, 2011; Darling-Hammond & Haertel, 2012; Hill et al., 2011; Newton et al., 2010; Rothstein, 2009, 2010b).

The research-based truth here is that even the most complex and sophisticated VAM will likely never be able to take into account enough of the factors that impact student achievement over time to yield valid enough inferences about teacher effectiveness (Ishii & Rivkin, 2009; McCaffrey et al., 2004b). This problem is compounded by many of the other issues (e.g., with large-scale standardized achievement tests) already discussed. Without accounting for the variables that are very rarely accessible (e.g., daily attendance, after-school factors, tutoring, homework clubs, parental involvement, access to resources, prior teachers' residual effects, multiple teachers' fractional effects), and without accounting for the variables that will likely never be accessible (e.g., students' innate abilities, levels of motivation and concern, access to online resources and technologies outside of school), the assumptions made about the statistical controls used with VAMs are highly unlikely to hold. They will likely never be "good enough" to remove all of the biasing elements that continue to hinder VAMs and effectively prevent valid VAM-based inferences.

Accordingly, without agreeing to these assumptions, it is nearly impossible to attribute gains in scores solely to teachers and their effects (Gottlieb, 2011; Kennedy, 2010; Linn, 2008; Rubin et al., 2004). "It is very difficult for the statistical machinery to disentangle these intrinsic student differences from true differences in teacher effectiveness" (Braun, 2005, p. 3) making causation "the most dangerous and shortsighted leap" that can be made using

VAM-based output (Misco, 2008, p. 13). Instead, according to Braun (2008), the best inferences these models might ever produce are "tentative causal conclusion[s] based on partial evidence drawn from an uncontrolled study of schools and districts." This is the reality that many, including America's policymakers, must begin to confront. While "causal inference may well be the holy grail of quantitative research in the social sciences," causal inference certainly cannot be proclaimed here (Briggs & Domingue, 2011, p. 21; Reardon & Raudenbush, 2009), particularly without random assignment.

Random assignment supports causative statements

Random assignment is the "gold standard" technique used most often with scientific experiments and experimental designs, particularly when one is to make causal claims and distinctions. It is used when assigning similar subjects (e.g., students who might be similar in terms of levels of achievement or another "like" variable) to different treatments (e.g., classrooms in which sets of students' teachers might be held accountable for their students' levels of achievement). Random assignment "helps to ensure that the participants in different experimental groups are initially equivalent and therefore have the same propensity to change relative to a specified variable ... [provided] every participant is afforded an equal chance of receiving any given treatment" (Bausell, 2013).

The well-founded theory behind random assignment is that randomizing the conditions under examination, value-added analyses in this case, helps to equalize or balance out the treatment(s), in this case teacher effects. Randomly assigning students to classrooms (and, ideally, teachers to classrooms) would ultimately make the inter- and intra-teacher value-added comparisons as rigorous as scientifically possible. Whatever differences might then be observed between and among teachers could then be directly attributed to the teachers under examination. By randomizing the conditions under examination, *besides the teacher effects*, all (or almost all) of the other reasons differences might have occurred could be reasonably explained away using logic or methodically explained given chance occurrences. What would be left would be a series of reasonable assertions that could, with increased confidence, be made about teacher quality (Bausell, 2013; Hill et al., 2011; Linn, 2008; Rothstein, 2010b).

The assumption here, though, is that *(2) the placement of students into classrooms occurs more or less at random as standard practice, so any effects that are observed among teachers can be reasonably attributed to those teachers provided effective statistical tools and techniques are used.* This is an assumption, for example, supported by the research and evaluation administrator heading one state's department of education (Paufler & Amrein-Beardsley, 2013). Others have also supported laxer versions of this assumption, however.

For example, Harris (2011) writes, "in elementary schools, there is typically little tracking across classes (though teachers do track within classes)" (p. 114), and "in middle school, tracking is more common; and in high school, it is almost universal" (p. 114; see also Rivkin & Ishii, 2008). VARC model developers make explicit the fact that their VAM "produces estimates of school productivity – value-added indicators – under the counterfactual assumption that all schools serve the same group of students. This facilitates apples-and-apples school comparisons rather than apples-and-oranges comparisons" (Meyer & Dokumaci, 2011, p. 1). The Bill and Melinda Gates Foundation (2013) advanced the final of $45 million dollars worth of its Measures of Effective Teaching (MET) studies – the best, most invested studies in the world on this topic – under the false, yet highly publicized, assertion that study results were based on a randomized trial. "It's sort of a big deal to be able to say that" but saying that was false in that a large majority of schools backed out of their agreements to ensure and follow through with the study's randomized plans (Sawchuck, 2013b; see also Banchero, 2013; Simon, 2013).

While this is discussed in greater depth in Chapter 7, the fact remains that, when constructing VAM estimates, it is methodologically necessary to assume that even if perfect random assignment practices are not used, for the most part any teacher is more or less as likely as any other teacher to be assigned any student who is more or less as likely as any other student to have similar backgrounds, abilities, dispositions, skillsets, and the like. Such assumptions, as nonsensical as they are, however, are necessary if VAM statisticians are to effectively (over)simplify the serious complexities that come about when random assignment of students to classrooms (and teachers to classrooms) is neither feasible, nor realistic, or outright opposed (Paufler & Amrein-Beardsley, 2013). As random assignment is a robust technique used to scientifically make distinctions, in this case about teacher effectiveness, it would make almost all of the serious issues discussed within this book null and void, if it could be actualized and more rigorous results realized.

Unfortunately, especially for research purists, the research-based truth is that true random assignment is likely impossible. The assignment of students to classrooms (and teachers to classrooms, as well as students and teachers to schools) is much farther from random than is often assumed (Bausell, 2013; Braun, 2005; Burns & Mason, 1995, 2002; Darling-Hammond & Haertel, 2012; Dills & Mulholland, 2010; Koedel & Betts, 2009; Monk, 1987; Paufler & Amrein-Beardsley, 2013; Praisner, 2003; Rivkin & Ishii, 2008; Rothstein, 2010b; Scherrer, 2011). In many schools parents influence where their children are placed, and in most schools current teachers influence which students will be placed with which future teachers (e.g., given students' aptitudes, behaviors, relationships with other students, types of learning styles, and the pedagogies and classroom management styles to which students seem to respond well). Administrative control over student placement practices is highly valued and is seen as being in the best interests of students, even if highly idiosyncratic (Burns & Mason, 1995; Dills & Mulholland, 2010; Monk, 1987; Paufler & Amrein-Beardsley, 2013; Player, 2010; Praisner, 2003). In fact, administrative control is valued substantially more than what administrators perceive as random or other "slipshod" student placement practices; practices that administrators might see as never in students' best educational or developmental interests and might forever reject (Paufler & Amrein-Beardsley, 2013).

Then, certain students (e.g., those with greater or lesser demonstrated aptitudes, skills sets, behavioral problems, learning challenges, levels of individual and collective motivation, assertive parents) might haphazardly find themselves in classrooms alongside similar peers. After which the teachers non-randomly assigned to the non-randomly sorted classes are to be credited or penalized accordingly based on VAM analyses, sometimes even despite the disparate differences any layperson could observe across classrooms (Amrein-Beardsley & Collins, 2012; Scherrer, 2011). This is extremely problematic as non-random sorting also biases VAM estimates and weakens arguments that teachers, not students, are responsible for the effects observed (McCaffrey, et al., 2004b; Reardon & Raudenbush, 2009; Rosenbaum & Rubin, 1983).

Yet here again it is assumed that *(3) the issues and errors caused by non-random placements either cancel each other out or can be cancelled out using complex statistics (e.g., student fixed effects, nesting data, blocking strategies, reduced-form coefficients) to make such non-random effects tolerable if not ignorable* (Ballou et al., 2004; Chetty et al., 2011; Glazerman & Potamites, 2011; Harris, 2009c,

2011; Reardon & Raudenbush, 2009; Rosenbaum & Rubin, 1983). Yet the research-based truth is that even the most complicated statistics cannot, and may never be able to, effectively counter for the deleterious effects caused by the non-random assignment practices (Ballou et al., 2004; Capitol Hill Briefing, 2011; Darling-Hammond & Haertel, 2012; Koedel & Betts, 2009; Kupermintz, 2003; McCaffrey et al., 2004b; Reardon & Raudenbush, 2009; Rosenbaum & Rubin, 1983; Rothstein, 2009, 2010b; Scherrer, 2011; Tekwe et al., 2004).

In addition, as previously noted, the variables most often used as controls and covariates only partially capture students' background characteristics (e.g., race, gender, prior levels of student achievement, family income). Yet statisticians must neglect the non-observable student characteristics (e.g., behaviors, motivational factors, support systems, access to resources) that likely outweigh the effects of the measured ones, simply because they are not available. Nonetheless, by controlling for some of the variables it must be assumed that the others that cannot be observed or measured can be effectively or de facto controlled for as well (Glazerman & Potamites, 2011; Koedel & Betts, 2010; Newton et al., 2010; Rothstein, 2009, 2010b).

Even though researchers continue to debate about how and to what extent the non-random placement of students into classrooms (and teachers to classrooms) biases value-added estimates, both sides agree this is a major, if not the most significant, methodological issue of concern when it comes to VAMs. How bias (or CIV) influences the accuracy (i.e., validity) of VAM-based estimates and inferences is still of considerable concern (Amrein-Beardsley & Collins, 2012; Darling-Hammond & Haertel, 2012; Newton et al., 2010; Paufler & Amrein-Beardsley, 2013; Rothstein, 2009, 2010b).

Learning is linear, consistent, and persistent

All VAMs are based on the assumption that test scores can be used to accurately measure educational "value" over time, from one test to the next; that is, if tests have sufficient stretch to permit accurate analyses of growth over time and if tests are vertically scaled. It should not come as a surprise that this too is very difficult to do and even more difficult to defend (Baker et al., 2010; Ballou, 2002, 2004; Braun, 2004; Briggs & Betebenner, 2009; Corcoran, 2010; Doran & Fleischman, 2005; Goe, 2008; Hill et al., 2011; Ho et al., 2009; Koretz, 2002; Kupermintz, 2003; Lockwood, McCaffrey, Hamilton, et al., 2007; Newton et al., 2010; Papay, 2011; Reckase, 2004; Rubin et al., 2004; Sanders et al., 2009). The assumption here is that *(4) bright students learn no faster than their less intellectually able classmates, and students with lower aptitudes for learning learn as fast as their peers.* This presumes that a teacher who is given a set of students with stronger relative aptitudes, and an equally effective teacher who is given a set of students with weaker relative aptitudes, will measure up the same in the end. The stronger students will learn no faster than the comparison students with lower average aptitude (and possibly motivation) levels (Alexander, Entwisle, & Olson, 2001, 2007a, 2007b; Amrein-Beardsley, 2008a; Ballou, 2002; Gabriel & Allington, 2011; Garlikov, 1995; Glass, 1995; Nelson, 2011).

While it is reasoned that students who begin at lower achievement levels should be expected to gain at the same rates as their peers who begin at higher achievement levels, and vice versa, into the future (Nelson, 2011), the research-based truth is that growth in learning is neither linear nor consistent (Glass, 1995; Stephens, 2008). Learning is generally uneven, unstable, and discontinuous, as well as often detected in punctuated spurts. Ask any parent and they can attest to the fact that learning spurts are certainly observable, but also that they often occur randomly, sporadically, and differently across children.

Accordingly, the learning trajectories of groups of students over time are not essentially the same, and students' individual and group learning trajectories often deviate from the linear, constant, unwavering forms statistically predicted. This occurs, again, largely because of students' academic backgrounds (e.g., foundations and literacies), developmental backgrounds (e.g., age-based curiosities, levels of motivation, and self-handicapping behaviors), and home backgrounds (e.g., poverty and risk factors that inhibit a rich and stable learning environment). Students from less affluent and racial/ethnic minority backgrounds typically learn at slower rates than their more affluent, racial/ethnic majority peers, and learning is not smooth, nor continuous, nor non-discriminating (Northwest Evaluation Association, 2006). The same differences that affect students' test scores also affect the rates at which students show progress over time (Alexander et al., 2001, 2007a, 2007b; Baker et al., 2010; Gabriel & Allington, 2011; Glass, 1995). Again, sophisticated statistical controls and blocking factors cannot effectively control for this.

Summer learning growth and decay

What also makes this problematic is summer learning gains and decay. The assumption here is that *(5) VAMs use large-scale standardized achievement test scores that capture student achievement while students are under the direct tutelage of the same teacher, within the same academic year, as if the pre-test was given in the fall (at the beginning of the school year) and the post-test was given in the spring following (at the end of the same school year).* If this were universally true, it would help facilitate causal statements. However, the research-based truth is that when large-scale standardized achievement tests are used to calculate value-added, this assumption is violated. In almost every case, these tests are administered annually, for example, from the spring of year X to the spring of year Y. Given this administration pattern, the summer months are *always* captured in the post-test score (Baker, 2011; Baker et al., 2010, 2013; Collins & Amrein-Beardsley, 2014). Yet VAM technicians must assume that summer learning growth and decay does not matter, or better yet, that it matters the same for all students despite the research-based fact that we know that different types of students lose or gain variable levels of knowledge over the summer months. These losses and gains account for between one half (Darling-Hammond, 2010) and one third (Harris, 2011) of the achievement gap that is persistently prevalent between high-and low-income students.[5]

Over the summers, students from less affluent and racial minority backgrounds lose significantly more (or gain significantly less) knowledge than their peers. Students from more affluent and racial majority backgrounds lose significantly less, and instead they often gain significantly more knowledge, having increased access to summer academic programs, national and international travel and tourism, and educational resources outside of school, including technologies and the like. In addition, during the school year, students from less affluent and racial minority backgrounds learn at the same or slower rates than their more affluent, racial majority peers, as described before. Each of these factors contributes to the ever-present achievement gap (Alexander et al., 2001, 2007a, 2007b; Fairchild, 2009; Gabriel & Allington, 2011; Harris, 2011; Northwest Evaluation Association, 2006).

This would not matter as much, however, if the pre- and post-tests that are used to measure value-added did not encapsulate the summer time, or rather these tests were administered, for example, at the beginning and end of the same school year during which students were under the tutelage of the same teacher all the while (see also Harris, 2011). Unfortunately, however, this is never the case. Students come to school with varying levels of knowledge, they learn more or less during the school year, and they gain or lose variable levels of knowledge over the summer months (see Figure 5.3).[6]

All of this, as well, is nonlinear, inconsistent, and highly deviant from what is often assumed (Alexander et al., 2001, 2007a, 2007b; Baker et al., 2010; Corcoran, 2010; Gabriel & Allington, 2011; Glass, 1995; Harris, 2009c; Northwest Evaluation Association, 2006; Papay, 2011). In addition, and as discussed, the statistics used to measure value-added will never be sophisticated enough to tease all of these complexities out or make value-added measurements "free of the exogenous factors that influence academic achievement" (Sanders & Horn, 1998; see also Bracey, 2004a; Harris, 2011; Meyer & Dokumaci, 2011).

Residual and interaction effects

In addition, it is assumed that *(6) the influences students' prior teachers have on student learning (i.e., teacher persistence effects) are negligible and if not negligible they can be statistically controlled for under the assumption that these effects do not last and decay quickly and at the same rate over time* (see, for example, Kane & Staiger, 2008; see also Harris, 2011; Rothstein, 2011). If a student has an excellent teacher X, the year before entering teacher Y's classroom, whatever lasting effects teacher X might have must either be assumed to be null, or statisticians must put into place

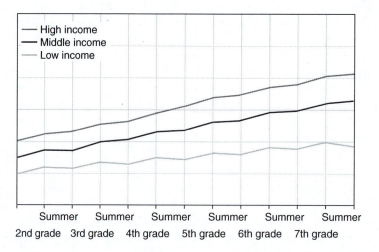

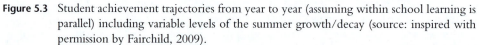

Figure 5.3   Student achievement trajectories from year to year (assuming within school learning is parallel) including variable levels of the summer growth/decay (source: inspired with permission by Fairchild, 2009).

Note
Fairchild (2009) developed a similar graph to demonstrate that students, particularly in reading, in kindergarten through Grade 5, and from low- and middle-income backgrounds, experience summer learning loss at a rate of approximately two months per year (see also Alexander et al., 2007a, 2007b; Cooper, Valentine, Charlton, & Melson, 2003). Cooper and Sweller (1987) also demonstrated this in mathematics. As researchers agree that summer learning loss is certainly an issue, dependent on subject area, grade level (particularly in early childhood and elementary grades), and student type (by income), this figure serves as a research-based illustration of what this summer learning loss might look like in the context of VAMs.

model parameterizations to counter or control for these effects (Briggs & Weeks, 2009; Lockwood, McCaffrey, Mariano, & Setodji, 2007; McCaffrey et al., 2004b). However, because the pre-test scores used to calculate teacher Y's value-added are collected in year X (usually the spring before students exit teacher X's classroom) and the value measured from point X to Y includes teacher X's prior effects, even with the most sophisticated statistics it is highly unlikely that statements can be made that the value teacher Y added or detracted to his/her students was entirely due to teacher Y's efforts. Approximately 30% of the student learning that is to be demonstrated on the post-test should be attributable to the previous year's teacher X given the mere fact that the student was still in teacher X's classroom after the test. Similarly, the value-added estimate does not account for the current year teacher Y's contribution during the last 30% of his/her instruction (Papay, 2011; see also Baker et al., 2013; Briggs & Weeks, 2011; Dorn, 1994).

Oddly, value-added analysts have presented research evidence that favors teachers' long-lasting and enduring effects (Chetty et al., 2011; Gordon et al., 2006; Hanushek, 2009; Sanders & Rivers, 1996; Wright et al., 1997; see also Grier & Holcombe, 2008; Lowrey, 2012). They have done this, though, while arguing that they can control for these everlasting effects (e.g., via stacked blocking) in their models as well (Baker et al., 2010; Bock et al., 1996; Briggs & Weeks, 2009; Kane & Staiger, 2008; Lockwood, McCaffrey, Mariano, et al., 2007; Lockwood & McCaffrey, 2009; Meyer, 1997; Misco, 2008; Nelson, 2011; Rothstein, 2010a; Sanders, 1994; Stroup, 1995). It seems that the degree to which prior teachers' effects conflate current teachers' value-added estimates varies, but teacher residuals are ever-present nonetheless.

Another related assumption here is that *(7) even though multiple teachers (and other instructional and non-instructional school personnel) teach and interact with students in multiple social and academic ways, value-added effects can be attributed solely to the teacher under examination, regardless of others' simultaneous efforts and effects* (Bausell, 2013; Gansle, Burns, & Noell, 2011; Scherrer, 2011). The research-based truth is that teachers do not work in isolation of other teachers, and student test scores cannot be attributable to individual teachers in isolation of others' efforts and effects. Teachers, school leaders, and other staff members (e.g., counselors, substitute teachers, teacher aids, teacher interventionists and specialists, librarians, student teachers, tutors, parent volunteers) all contribute to student learning in various ways. Thus their contributions contaminate the effects of the teachers singled out for value-added evaluations (Baker et al., 2010; Bausell, 2013; Croninger & Valli, 2009; Harris, 2009c, 2011; Schafer et al., 2012; Scherrer, 2011).

Social studies teachers who require reading and writing skills in their courses might contribute to students' reading/language arts scores. In fact, evidence demonstrated by Croninger and Valli (2009) suggests that teachers in all subject areas might collectively contribute most to students' growth in skills and aptitudes in reading/language arts. Reading teachers who teach reading/language arts alongside, but separately from, language arts teachers (as often occurs at the middle school level, McCaffrey et al., 2008) might contribute together to one another's value-added estimates. Science teachers who require mathematical computations as part of covering a concept area might contribute to students' knowledge of mathematics. These crossover effects are even more likely when large-scale standardized achievement tests approach, and out-of-subject teachers focus inordinately on the subject areas that are anticipated to count the most on the tests (Bracey, 2004a; see also Gabriel & Allington, 2011, 2013).

However, for the purposes of VAM analyses, all of this is conveniently assumed not to have occurred, or to have occurred only at negligible levels. To counter for this, weighted proportions accounting for various teacher effects can be used, allegedly to arbitrarily partition or average out these confounding effects (Corcoran, 2010; Gabriel & Allington, 2011, 2013; Harris, 2011; Lockwood & McCaffrey, 2009; McCaffrey et al., 2008; Sanders et al., 2009). In fact, the extent to which these weighted proportions work to tease out various contributory effects has been marvelously argued (Sanders, 2003; Sanders et al., 2009; see also Gansle et al., 2011).

The research-based truth is, again, that the mechanisms used to do this are as flawed as one would expect, especially when thinking about doing this in overly simplistic ways with percentages, ratios, or proportions. This cannot be done simplistically, for example, by calculating the number of days a student might have been present in a teacher's classroom, assuming presence in a classroom means engagement or that presence in any one classroom is the same in form and function as presence in any other classroom, or by allowing teachers to decide for how much time or what percentage they should "claim" to have been solely responsible for individual students' learning, or what proportions of instructional time they should share with one or more other teachers per individual student (Gabriel & Allington, 2013, p. 6).

In the same vein, another assumption here is that *(8) peer effects are negligible – that is, the extent to which students academically or socially influence other students (e.g., in terms of levels of motivation or efficacy) assigned to their classrooms or attending their schools in non-random ways is trivial.* There is limited interference among students who interact daily within and across classrooms and schools, and this interference does not influence students' peers' test scores. This too is grossly unrealistic.

The research-based truth is that students are not independent of one another; they interact inside and outside of their individual classrooms in academic and social ways, both positively and negatively. As well, they likely boost or take away from one another's achievement regardless of whether physically in the presence of or actively interacting with other high or low achievers, respectively. Students are not uncooperative or restrictive in their peer-to-peer interactions (Bausell, 2013; Kennedy, 2010; Rubin et al., 2004). Rather students impact other students' levels of learning, in both positive and negative ways, as their behaviors and personalities are situated and activated in social contexts (Graue et al., 2013). This is well founded in the research on value-added and also on peer effects, and this makes it all the more unlikely that peer effects, because they are both so significant and so difficult to measure, will ever be adequately accounted or controlled for. This too is a fatal flaw in terms of VAMs (Baker et al., 2010; Bosworth & Caliendo, 2007; Braun, 2005; Corcoran, 2010; Ishii & Rivkin, 2009; Lazear, 2001; Linn, 2008; Misco, 2008; Monk, 1987; Nelson, 2011; Newton et al., 2010; Reardon & Raudenbush, 2009; Rothstein, 2009).

Missing data are missing at random (or are they?)

There are also major issues with missing data that inordinately affect teachers of different types of students, particularly those who are relatively more mobile or absent from school. Missing data clearly affect longitudinal analyses in this case. Yet the assumption here is that *(9) VAM analyses and estimates are based on sufficient amounts of data, and any data that are missing are missing at random.* Both of these assumptions are certainly untrue (Bausell, 2013; Braun,

2004; Lockwood & McCaffrey, 2009; McCaffrey, et al., 2004b). Researchers in one study illustrated that approximately 20% of students had the five years of test scores that were necessary to run VAM analyses as per one model (Lockwood, McCaffrey, Mariano, et al., 2007). This is the ideal number of years of data needed to seemingly yield the best value-added results (Braun, 2005; Ross et al., 2001; Sanders & Horn, 1994). Researchers in another study found that nearly one half (45%) of the fifth grade teachers for whom they examined value-added had data for just one group of students they had taught, 23% of the teachers had data for two years of fifth grade students, and 14% had data for three years of fifth grade students (Kersting et al., 2013). A researcher in another study found that approximately 14% of the students residing in a large, high-needs school district were missing test scores in a typical year, as well as that African Americans, ELLs, and recent immigrants were missing data at even higher rates (Corcoran, 2010). Even Sanders, when working with his sophisticated EVAAS® system, noted that 11–12% of the students included in one of his studies did not have one of the two minimum test scores needed to calculate one year's worth of gains (Sanders, 2006).

Missing data cannot be ignored, especially as they impact different types of students differently. Nor can they be simplistically removed from the analyses to facilitate complete cases, under the assumption they are missing at random (Bausell, 2013; Braun, 2005; Briggs & Domingue, 2011; Harris, 2011; Linn & Haug, 2002; Lockwood et al., 2003, McCaffrey, et al., 2004b; Raudenbush, 2004). For example, dropping typically low-scoring students will certainly bias analyses by causing artificial inflation (Haladyna et al., 1991). In addition, missing data should not be replaced or "imputed" by inserting simulated scores for students who are missing them, typically using a measure of central tendency (e.g., using the mean scores of "similar" students' scores calculated from the same items) also under the assumption that the data are missing at random (Lockwood et al., 2003; Rubin et al., 2004).

Treating missing data in any of the above ways, under a "missing at random" assumption, is remiss, although statisticians argue that these approaches are necessary for value-added technicians to continue to run such analyses with appropriate levels of statistical power (Bausell, 2013; Raudenbush, 2004; see also Dunn, Kadane, & Garrow, 2003). The fact is that student data do not go missing at random, they go missing in highly non-random ways. This "missingness" is not ignorable (Rosenbaum & Rubin, 1983; see also Anderman et al., 2010; Raudenbush, 2004; Reardon & Raudenbush, 2009; Rubin et al., 2004). The students who are missing data are typically housed in relatively higher-needs schools with higher levels of mobility, poverty, and rates of absenteeism. In addition, the students who are missing data are typically those who tend to score lower than their peers, even after controlling for their test score histories (Lockwood, McCaffrey, Mariano, et al., 2007; see also Braun, 2005; Brophy, 1973; Corcoran, 2010; McCaffrey, et al., 2004b).

According to Sanders et al. (2009):

> Missing student test data jeopardize the validity of the analyses … statistics show that missing data do not happen at random but in a pattern that is consistent with the population of students served by the schooling entity. In particular, lower achieving students are more likely to have missing test scores. This missing data can create selection bias … the inclusion of students with certain test scores and the exclusion of students without certain test scores can seriously bias [value-added] estimates.
>
> *(p. 3)*

This says nothing of the fact that beyond missing data, data errors (e.g., students linked with incorrect teachers, students listed in incorrect grades, students no longer at school but still present in data records, students recently having entered school absent from data records, students receiving special education or English language services but not keyed accordingly) are also widespread (Bausell, 2013; Otterman, 2010). These errors, once cleaned up or cleared out of the dataset, are also assumed to be inconsequential and minimally impactful upon results and conclusions. Yet again, data accuracy *and* data completeness matter more than most too often assume, denoting yet another huge challenge when calculating value-added (Baker et al., 2010, 2013; Bausell, 2013; Bock et al., 1996; McCaffrey et al., 2003, 2008; Meyer, 1997; Rubin et al., 2004).

Think for a moment about data accuracy in itself and about how special education students are typically keyed in these data systems. While typically a "1" is used to signal that the student is receiving special education services and a "0" is used to signal the opposite, this alone hyper-trivializes the very important reality that special education students are unique in and among themselves. However, whether a "1" or "0" binary coding system effectively captures students who are distinctly classified as autistic, emotionally disabled, chronically or acutely ill, orthopedically compromised, or speech impaired is rarely, if ever, discussed among the econometricians and statisticians working with and manipulating these marginal codes (see also Baker et al., 2013).

(Sample) size does matter

Finally, not only does the amount of data that are missing matter, sample size matters as well. While related to missing data, sample size has some of the largest of all effects on value-added stability over time (Kersting et al., 2013; Lockwood, McCaffrey, & Sass, 2008; McCaffrey et al., 2003; Nelson, 2011). Yet the assumption here is that *(10) VAM accuracy is defensible across teachers' classrooms regardless of the sizes of the classrooms of students taught any given year.* This assumption suggests that VAM certainty is resistant to sample size issues, and as such we can be confident VAM estimates are authentic and true.

Even if no data are missing, the accuracy of all VAM estimates still depends on the size of the samples used to generate teachers' value-added estimates. Accordingly, estimates for teachers with fewer students are less accurate than estimates for their colleagues who teach more students to whom they might be compared. When sample sizes are small (e.g., under 15 or 20), which is also more common than often assumed (Santos & Gebeloff, 2012), the likelihood that the errors that come along with small sample sizes will bias VAM estimates will increase, as will the tendency for the VAM estimates to be pulled towards the mean (i.e., regression). This leaves consumers making erroneous conclusions that teachers with smaller class sizes are performing at average levels, although their average categorizations likely have more to do with the quantity of the students in their classrooms than their actual performance as teachers. This leaves it nearly impossible to generate accurate estimates for teachers of small class sizes (Sanders et al., 1997; see also Baker et al., 2010; Buddin, 2011; Goldhaber & Hansen, 2010; Kersting et al., 2013; Kupermintz, 2003).

This also makes it less fair for teachers of small classes (including special education teachers) to reap the positive consequences associated with posting higher relative value-added scores or, inversely, to be penalized for posting lower relative value-added scores. These issues also generalize to smaller schools in which small sample sizes impact higher proportions of classes

(Linn & Haug, 2002; Newton et al., 2010; Reardon & Raudenbush, 2009). This ultimately leaves teachers who teach smaller classes and teachers in relatively smaller schools more susceptible to the rewards and punishments being attached to VAM estimates (Ballou, 2002; Brophy, 1973; Harris, 2011). This is one reason why value-added technicians encourage the use of shrunken estimates to account for such measurement errors, as well as multiple years of estimates to theoretically generate more accurate classifications (Harris, 2011; McCaffrey et al., 2008; Sanders et al., 2009). Yet, if teachers' classrooms are unchanging, sample size will remain an issue, particularly for some more than others (Evans, 2008).

In sum, such are the "necessary assumptions" that provide mathematical convenience and statisticians', econometricians', (and others') tendencies to reduce complex phenomena to categories and numbers. Reviewed here were the other statistical and methodological assumptions that go along with VAM adoption, implementation, and use, and the assumptions frequently made about the general sophistication of the statistical models and methods from which VAM estimations are derived (summarized here in Table 5.2).

Table 5.2 Other statistical and methodological assumptions about VAMs

Assumptions	Research-based truths
1 Once students' prior learning and other background variables are statistically controlled for, or factored out, the only thing left in terms of the gains students make on large-scale standardized achievement tests over time can be directly attributed to the teacher and his/her causal effects.	The variables typically available in the databases used to conduct VAM analyses are very limited and, accordingly, cannot be used to work the statistical miracles assumed. Even the richest of variables would not liberate value-added analyses from the confounding effects students' backgrounds and other risk factors have on academic growth over time.
2 The placement of students into classrooms occurs more or less at random as standard practice, so any effects that are observed among teachers can be reasonably attributed to those teachers provided effective statistical tools and techniques are used.	The assignment of students to classrooms (and teachers to classrooms, as well as students and teachers to schools) is much farther from random than is often assumed, and this biases VAM estimates and greatly weakens arguments that teachers, not students, are responsible for the effects observed.
3 The issues and errors caused by non-random placements either cancel each other out or can be cancelled out using complex statistics to make nonrandom effects tolerable if not ignorable.	Even the most complicated statistics cannot, and may never be able to, effectively counter for the deleterious issues with VAMs caused by non-random assignment practices.
4 Bright students learn no faster than their less intellectually-able classmates, and students with lower aptitudes for learning learn as fast as their higher aptitude peers.	Learning is neither linear nor consistent. Learning is generally uneven, unstable, and discontinuous, as well as often detected in punctuated spurts. The learning trajectories of groups of students over time are not essentially the same, and they often deviate from the linear, constant, unwavering forms statistically predicted and used.

continued

Table 5.2 Continued

Assumptions	Research-based truths
5 VAMs use on large-scale standardized achievement test scores that capture student achievement while students are under the direct tutelage of the same teacher, within the same academic year, as if the pre-test was given in the fall (at the beginning of the school year) and the post-test was given in the spring following (at the end of the same school year).	In almost every case, the tests used to estimate value-added are administered annually, and meant to measure growth from the spring of year X to the spring of year Y. The summer losses and gains captured over this time account for between one half and one third of the achievement gap that is persistently prevalent between high- and low-income students, and they distort VAM-based estimates accordingly.
6 The influences students' prior teachers have on student learning (i.e., teacher persistence effects) are negligible. If not negligible, they can be statistically controlled for under the assumption that these effects decay quickly and at the same rate over time.	Because the pre-test scores used to calculate teacher Y's value-added are collected in teacher X's year, and the value measured from point X to Y includes teacher X's prior effects, it is highly unlikely that statements can be made that the value teacher Y added to or detracted from his/her students' learning was entirely due to teacher Y's efforts.
7 Even though multiple teachers teach and interact with students in multiple ways (as do administrators and others), value-added effects can be attributed solely to the teacher under examination.	Teachers do not work in isolation from other teachers (and administrators and other staff), and student test scores cannot be attributable to individual teachers in isolation of others' effects accordingly.
8 Peer effects are negligible. The extent to which students academically or socially influence other students in their classrooms or attending their schools is trivial.	Students interact inside and outside of their individual classrooms in academic and social ways, both positively and negatively, likely boosting or taking away from one another's achievement, respectively.
9 VAM analyses and estimates are based on sufficient amounts of data, and any data that are missing are missing at random.	Data are very frequently missing, data are missing more often for high-needs students, and the more years needed to conduct value-added analyses the more this becomes problematic. Missing data are not missing at random, and this too biases VAM estimates for some versus others.
10 VAM accuracy is defensible across teachers' classrooms regardless of the sizes of the classrooms of students taught any given year.	Even if no data are missing, the accuracy of all VAM estimates still depends on the size of the samples used to generate teachers' value-added. Estimates for teachers with fewer students are less accurate that their colleagues with more students to whom they might be compared.

Conclusions

Doug Harris, in his book (2011), the first written about what educators and others need to know and understand about VAMs, wrote: "Arguments against value-added-based accountability have been rooted in a researcher perspective that is really not appropriate for policy decisions" (p. 8). Evidenced throughout this and the previous chapter is that research does indeed matter. Research matters a lot when politicians, policymakers, journalists, and even academic researchers (who we might assume are the most likely to know better) deliver strings of unchecked assumptions and often deliver them covertly or explicitly as unconditional truths (see also Amrein-Beardsley, 2012). The fact remains that when calculating value-added, we are looking at a series of "high-stakes experiments conducted under extremely uncontrolled conditions" (Bausell, 2013).

We are not looking at a sure-fire way to improve America's public schools, even though, if we were to ride on the assumptions that go along with adopting and implementing VAMs, it might certainly seem that the possibilities that come along with VAM-based reforms are endless. Additionally, we cannot continue as a matter of public policy to focus on measuring teacher quality under these same false assumptions which, in theory, guarantee that this can be done in systematic ways.

Box 5.1 Top 10 assertions

1   VAM estimates are calculated using large-scale standardized test scores, scores that are assumed to be much more accurate indicators of educational effectiveness than they in fact are.
2   VAMs cannot eliminate all of the errors that are inherent when using large-scale tests, especially the random and systematic errors that grossly distort what scores are to infer.
3   Statistics, despite their limitations, are being used to convey authority and intimidate others into accepting VAM estimates as truth, simply because VAMs are based on mathematics and a mystique often used against the unknowing or unaware.
4   Since reading/language arts and mathematics are typically the only subjects tested using large-scale tests, other subject areas are often marginalized or ignored, despite what is also often assumed when using VAM estimates to make inferences about general teacher quality.
5   Test items on large-scale tests are probabilistically chosen for their ability to discriminate between students with and without specific knowledge or expertise in specific content areas. Test items are not typically chosen based on how valuable the content really is.
6   The correlations between student test scores and students' demographic and environmental backgrounds are so strong that one (i.e., student demographics) can almost perfectly be used to predict the other (i.e., student test scores), even before students take the tests.
7   Large-scale tests were designed to measure student learning and achievement. They were never designed to measure teachers' causal effects on student learning and achievement.

8   Though VAM statisticians claim that by controlling for certain factors they can isolate student learning and achievement and attribute both back to teachers, it is virtually impossible to account for all of the factors that affect learning and achievement to appropriately do so.

9   The random assignment of students into classrooms would be the most scientifically effective way to reduce VAM-based bias. However, students are rarely assigned randomly as, while scientifically beneficial, principals believe this would not be in students' best interests.

10   There are countless extraneous variables (e.g., home, community, and other teachers' and peer effects) for which even the most sophisticated VAMs will never fully control. This alone will likely make the quest for VAM reliability and validity forever elusive and intangible.

Notes

1   To learn more about Heisenberg's Uncertainty Principle, see "Dr. Quantum – Quantum Physics Simplified!" at www.youtube.com/watch?v=EpSqrb3VK3c.

2   The actual item from the Arizona test could not be included here.

3   Logits or log-odds are the inverse of the "logistic" function used in mathematics and statistics. They are an equal-interval unit of measurement, similar to NCEs. The use of logits ensures that a concept is measured in the same units as the test's difficulty and makes the distribution symmetrical around zero. For example, on a statewide student achievement test, student performance would be measured in the same units as the difficulty of test questions and would recenter the mean at zero (for more information see http://en.wikipedia.org/wiki/Logit).

4   To read more about what educators control or for what they might be reasonably held accountable and vice versa, see Harris, 2011. While Harris' logic becomes increasingly confusing as you read about what should or should not be attributed to teachers, reading through the confusion is a lesson in itself regarding how very difficult it is to make simple rules and decisions about VAM modeling and to derive valid value-added estimates accordingly (see also Collins & Amrein-Beardsley, 2011).

5   Bloom, Hill, Black, and Lipsey (2008) found that the achievement gaps are relatively small for gender (i.e., between male and female students). Affluence and race/ethnicity are the major variables to consider when examining the achievement gaps.

6   Northwest Evaluation Association researchers found in their value-added study "that for every group at every grade, students from poor schools grew less than students from wealthy schools and minority students exhibited less growth than their non-minority peers. In general, students enrolled in high poverty schools, African-American students, and Hispanic students begin school with lower skills, grow less academically during the school year, and lose more skill over the summer than their wealthier and European-American peers. In the case of the African-American students in these samples, the concern carries added emphasis. Their rate of change over the two-year projection was the lowest of all groups, suggesting that the achievement gap between student segments remains a significant problem" (NWEA, 2006, p. 1).

PART III

Non-Traditional Concerns About Traditional Methodological Notions

6

RELIABILITY AND VALIDITY

As far as the laws of mathematics refer to reality, they are not certain; and as far as they are certain, they do not refer to reality.

Albert Einstein

When using measurement tools, it is important to recognize that it is the meanings and inferences, or interpretations and uses derived from the tools that matter more than the numbers derived themselves (Cronbach & Meehl, 1955; Kane, 2006, 2013; Messick, 1975, 1980, 1989, 1995).

> Even though measurement is scientifically based and rooted, measurements function much more like language – they are essentially arbitrary designations that have no inherent value. Rather their values are constructed given there is mutual agreement about how to use and interpret the numbers derived.
>
> *(Amrein-Beardsley & Barnett, 2012, p. 2)*

Common numerically based measurement tools include scales when measuring weight and mass; meter sticks when measuring height, length, and depth; thermometers when measuring temperature; and clocks when measuring time. All of these can be interpreted in reference to some base unit of worth and magnitude. Interpretive metrics include pounds, kilos, and scruples; meters, feet, and inches; degrees in Fahrenheit or Celsius; and seconds, minutes, and decades, respectively. Measurements can be interpreted in absolute terms, whereas base units can be used to better understand fixed values. Similarly, measurements can be interpreted in relativistic terms, whereas values can be measured in comparison to other observations of the same discernable realities. Take, for example, the weight scale. The weight scale is a measurement tool that (some) use everyday. It is useful because it yields a level or sense of truth, that is, about one's heaviness. Repetitive use yields very personal inferences about the extent to which fluctuations in weight might occur due to high or low levels of exercise and consumption (e.g., fatty foods, carbohydrates, alcohol, etc.). It is also useful because the inferences that everyday people can draw from this complex yet comprehensible device can be used to control and monitor the construct of interest (i.e., one's weight) over time.

Take, as another example, the thermometer. The thermometer is also a measurement tool that many use, although not as often and typically only when one is feeling feverish or otherwise ill. It is useful because it also yields a level or sense of truth, that is, about one's body temperature and the probability that one might indeed have the flu or another fever-related illness. Repetitive use yields personal inferences about the extent to which certain treatments (e.g., medicine, cold baths, hydration, etc.) can be used to control, monitor, and even remedy the construct of interest (i.e., one's temperature). With the help of both measurement tools, the inferences that are drawn from the numbers derived, if the numbers are *reliable* and *valid*, can ultimately be used to improve one's health and overall wellness.

What would happen, though, if you stood on a scale in the bathroom, stepped off of the scale momentarily, and then stepped back on (without having done anything that would affect weight gain or loss in the meantime) to find that the number displayed on the first occasion was dramatically higher than the number registered the second time? Besides being temporarily hopeful, perhaps, any logical person would likely step on the scale at least once more to determine if the scale is indeed broken given its inconsistent or *unreliable* results, and given the likelihood that no *valid* interpretations could be made given the inconsistencies observed.

What would happen if you felt feverish and you could feel heat radiating from your forehead to the palm of your hand, but your thermometer indicated two or three consecutive times that your temperature was at a solid 98.6°F (37°C)? Would you trust the mathematics over your own (fallible) human judgment? While the thermometer might consistently read 98.6° Fahrenheit (37°C), suggesting *reliability*, only a fool would trust the tool over the other (less objective) indicator pointing in the opposite direction, indicating instead that there might be an infection to be fought. Here, even though *reliability* was observed, *valid* inferences could not be drawn given the indicator contradicting the mercury-based readings.

In both cases, here, neither measurement tool yielded a numerical indicator from which valid inferences could be made. The scale did not evidence consistency (i.e., reliability), making valid inferences about the construct of interest (i.e., weight) impossible. The thermometer yielded consistent readings (i.e., reliability), although they contradicted the readings of the other measures (i.e., invalidity) estimating the same construct (i.e., one's temperature). In both scenarios, no valid inferences could be drawn or used for any informational, inferential, or therapeutic purposes.

Relationship between reliability and validity

As discussed in Chapter 2, "reliability" represents the degree to which a set of indicators are falsely inflated or deflated by random error, systematic error, or both. With the bathroom scale example, daily fluctuations represent random error, while measurements higher or lower than true scale observations represent systematic error. Likewise, these types of errors cause test scores to increase or decrease, in large or small amounts, although neither type of error can be directly observed. Instead, what is estimated or observed is the extent to which a measurement tool produces consistent or dependable results, in this case over time (i.e., reliability). Increasing reliability reduces uncertainty (i.e., less random error) and vice versa, although the latter is of utmost concern if unreliable measures are to be used for consequential inference or decision-making purposes.

In addition, without adequate reliability, valid interpretations and uses are difficult to defend. Validity is an essential of any measurement, and reliability is a necessary or qualifying condition for validity. Put differently, if scores are unreliable, it is impossible to make or support valid, authentic, and accurate inferences (Brennan, 2006, 2013; Kane, 2006, 2013; Messick, 1975, 1980, 1995). This principle was demonstrated in the case of the weight scale.

In terms of VAMs, reliability (or a lack thereof) is the most major issue impeding all VAMs, especially when inordinately erratic estimates are used for consequential inference or decision-making purposes. Furthermore, because reliability is such a hindrance, valid inferences are very difficult to draw and even harder or impossible to defend, even with most lenient standards of scientific merit. However, even if reliability is supported (i.e., consistency or inter-temporal stability[1] is observed), validity will not simply or effortlessly follow.

In terms of VAMs, strong evidence of validity is never observed, mainly given VAMs' fundamental issues with reliability. According to the AERA, APA, and NCME (2000) standards on educational measurement and testing, "if high-stakes testing programs [such as these] are implemented in circumstance[s] where test or test uses lack sufficient *reliability* and *validity*, there is potential for serious harm" (AERA et al., 2000 [emphasis added]).[2] Hence, it is vital we focus in more detail on both reliability and validity, to further explore what we know from the VAM-based research in these areas. As mentioned, most, if not all, studies on this topic have thus far been conducted at the teacher level. Accordingly, I will present the research referring directly to teacher-level value-added research unless otherwise noted (e.g., where a study was conducted at the school level).

Research on reliability

Reliability is observed when VAM estimates of teacher effectiveness are consistent over time, from one year to the next. Put differently, if VAM estimates of teacher effectiveness are reliable, consistent results are seen over multiple observations over time. This is typically captured in numerical or statistical ways using reliability coefficients signified by r.[3] Sometimes r is converted for further ease in comprehension into estimates of R-squared (i.e., $r \times r = R^2$). R-squared helps to illustrate whether teachers reside within or move between value-added categories over time. Using confidence intervals is another common statistical technique used to help illustrate the (un)certainty or (non)standard error of measurement surrounding VAMs.

Confidence intervals

Confidence intervals are typically defined as the area within which one can be confident that a teacher's true value-added estimate has been effectively and accurately captured. To contextualize, the typical confidence intervals used in statistics give or take about 5 percentage points from the reported estimate (i.e., given standard 95% confidence intervals). However, in New York, for example, the confidence intervals around 18,000 teachers' ratings spanned 35 percentile points in mathematics and 53 percentile points in reading/language arts (Santos & Gebeloff, 2012). This meant that a mathematics teacher who ranked at the 50th percentile could have actually had a true score between the 33rd and 67th percentile ranks (rounding inwards). In reading/language arts, a teacher who ranked at the 50th percentile could have had an observed score anywhere between the 24th and 76th percentile rank (rounding inwards). While 95% confidence intervals are typically used, with VAMs these standard error ranges are typically much, much larger.

Reliability and r

Researchers agree that preferably three years of student achievement data (and up to five years of data, as is the case with the EVAAS®) are needed to analyze value-added over time, and to do it well.[4] The more data to which one has access, the more reliable the VAM estimates become, although at some level (e.g., after including three years of data) the strength that more years of data add to the reliability of the estimates seems to plateau (Brophy, 1973; Cody et al., 2010; Glazerman & Potamites, 2011; Goldschmidt et al., 2012; Harris, 2011; Hill et al., 2011; Ishii & Rivkin, 2009; Koedel & Betts, 2009; Loeb & Candelaria, 2012; Papay, 2011; Rothstein, 2010; Sanders as cited in Gabriel & Lester, 2013).

Given datasets in which at least two or more years of teacher-level value-added data are included, researchers have estimated year-to-year correlations. The parameters are simply set as the correlations between the VAM estimates for the same teachers, between and among the baseline and outcome years for which teachers who are VAM-eligible have VAM estimates (Glazerman et al., 2011). That said, researchers have found that these teacher-level VAM correlations typically fall within the range of near zero (i.e., $0 \leq r \leq 0.3$) or slightly higher (i.e., $0.3 \leq r \leq 0.5$), with most estimates falling somewhere in between (i.e., $0.3 \leq r \leq 0.4$; Brophy, 1973; McCaffrey et al., 2009; Sass, 2008; see also Baker et al., 2013; Glazerman et al., 2010; Glazerman et al., 2011; Hill, 2009; Kane & Staiger, 2012; Koedel & Betts, 2007; Linn & Haug, 2002; Lockwood & McCaffrey, 2009; Loeb & Candelaria, 2012; Newton et al., 2010; see also Di Carlo, 2013).

However, researchers in a few studies have either noted or found year-to-year correlations, mainly at the middle school levels (Hill et al., 2011; Goldhaber et al., 2012; McCaffrey et al., 2009), to be as high as $r = 0.6$ (Kersting et al., 2013; Loeb & Candelaria, 2012; McCaffrey et al., 2009). Conversely, others have found the opposite to be true at both the middle and high school levels (Goldschmidt et al., 2012; Jackson, 2012; Rivkin & Ishii, 2008; Sawchuck, 2012). In addition, Goldhaber et al. (2012) found that consistency is modestly greater for mathematics than reading/language arts (i.e., 0.4 vs. 0.3, respectively; see also Ballou, 2002; Bill & Melinda Gates Foundation, 2010; Chetty et al., 2011; Goldschmidt et al., 2012; Kane & Staiger, 2008; Rothstein, 2011), although others have found the opposite (Briggs & Domingue, 2011; Kimball, White, Milanowski, & Borman, 2004). What does all of this mean?

When answering questions about how reliable these estimates should be, the most appropriate answer might be as reliable or as close as possible to positive[5] one (i.e., $r = +1.0$). This would indicate that a teacher's value-added measure in one year would be perfectly related to the teacher's value-added score the following year. However, determining an adequate level of reliability is largely determined by the nature of the rewards and sanctions to be attached to the estimates, understanding that the stronger the consequences attached the more that statistical strength is necessary. Conversely, a zero correlation tells us nothing, as no consistent relationship was found between estimates.

Nonetheless, as perfect positive correlations (i.e., $r = +1.0$) are almost never attainable, researchers sometimes follow a set of commonly used, yet purposefully ambiguous set of categories to help guide their interpretations of correlation coefficients. These categories are more often associated with interpreting effect sizes (e.g., Cohen's d; Cohen, 1988; see also Bloom et al., 2008; Green & Saikind, 2010) and levels of internal consistency on instruments (e.g., Cronbach's alpha [α]; George & Mallery, 2003; Kline, 1999). But, particularly for beginning-to-intermediate researchers, such ubiquitous categories can help to construct reasonable (although often out of context and sometimes overgeneralized) explanations of these correlations.

As per Merrigan and Huston (2004), a representative interpretive framework to help interpret simple correlation coefficients in the social sciences (e.g., educational research) is as follows (see Figure 6.1).

That said, "even the most optimistic reliabilities reported in this literature are still far below the standards set by most organizations for using assessments in stakes-attached situations" (Hill, 2009, p. 712). Put more directly, as researchers have estimated year-to-year correlations to be in the range of near zero (i.e., $0 \le r \le 0.3$) or slightly higher (i.e., $0.3 \le r \le 0.5$), with most estimates falling somewhere in between (i.e., $0.2 \le r \le 0.4$), the best we can say is that VAM-based levels of reliability are very weak to moderate.

For all research-intensive purposes, strong or very strong correlations (e.g., $r \ge 0.6$) are most desired and most necessary, *especially* if these measures are to be used for high-stakes or highly consequential decision-making purposes. This is *especially* true if these estimates are to be used in isolation or used as the objective indicators capable of trumping more subjective indicators of teacher effectiveness. This is occurring across the nation per both explicit and implicit local policies (Amrein-Beardsley & Collins, 2012; Baker, 2012a, 2012b; Collins, 2012; Garland, 2012; Glazerman et al., 2010; Harris, 2011; Ravitch, 2012c; Rockoff et al., 2010).

Reliability and R^2

Otherwise, albeit related, we can also use R^2 to determine the extent to which VAMs might be capable of producing reliable estimates over time. R^2 is exactly what its title implies (i.e., $r \times r = R^2$). Even when used with negative correlation coefficients, R^2 turns the outcome statistic positive, yielding another useful interpretive tool. Here, for example, if $r = 0.5$ then $R^2 = 0.25$. In terms of VAMs, this means that about 25% of the observed variation between two estimates might be due to true stability in teacher effects. Inversely, this also means that the other 75% of the variance might be due to errors and unexplained effects other than the teacher's value-added that was to have been observed.

Take, for example, that $r = 0.4$ and $R^2 = 0.16$, an optimistic r and R^2 given the current research on VAM-based reliability. Here is an illustrated version of what this might mean in real terms and in terms of the correct and incorrect interpretations that might lead to correct and incorrect decisions, respectively, using VAMs (see Table 6.1).

- $0.8 \le r \le 1.0$ = a very strong correlation
- $0.6 \le r \le 0.8$ = a strong correlation
- $0.4 \le r \le 0.6$ = a moderate correlation
- $0.2 \le r \le 0.4$ = a weak correlation
- $0 \le r \le 0.2$ = a very weak correlation, if any at all

Figure 6.1 A simple framework to help interpret correlation coefficients in the social sciences.

Table 6.1 Correct and incorrect interpretations (possibly leading to decisions) if $r = 0.4$ and $r^2 = 0.16$

	Teachers truly below the 25th percentile	*Teachers truly above the 25th percentile*	*Total*
Teachers estimated to be below the 25th percentile	80 *(correctly identified as below the 25th percentile)*	80 *(falsely identified as below the 25th percentile)*	160
Teachers estimated to be above the 25th percentile	170 *(falsely identified as above the 25th percentile)*	670 *(correctly identified as above the 25th percentile)*	840
Total	250	750	1,000

Source: Adapted with permission and corrections from Raudenbush & Jean, 2012.

Raudenbush and Jean (2012) have illustrated with an $r = 0.4$ or $R^2 = 0.16$, that out of every 1,000 teachers 750 teachers would be identified correctly and 250 teachers would not. That is, one in four teachers would be falsely identified as either being worse or better than they were originally classified. Of concern here is the prevalence of false positive or false discovery errors (i.e., Type I errors), whereby an ineffective teacher is falsely identified as effective. However, the inverse is equally likely, defined as false negative or false non-discovery errors (i.e., Type II errors), whereby an ineffective teacher might go unnoticed. Some place value judgments about which type of error is worse. Raudenbush and Jean (2012), for example, wrote that, "Falsely identifying [effective] teachers as being below a threshold poses risk to teachers, but failing to identify [ineffective] teachers who are truly ineffective poses risks to students." Harris (2011) also made the case that Type II errors matter more, particularly in policy contexts in which the main goal is to keep incompetent teachers from teaching (see also Briggs & Domingue, 2011; Chester, 2003; Glazerman et al., 2011; Guarino, Reckase, et al., 2012; Harris, 2011; Rothstein, 2010b; Shaw & Bovaird, 2011; Yeh, 2011).

While I agree that Type II errors are in general less desirable, as this type of error damages students while the other damages teachers, I believe both types are of great concern given all who are interpreting and using such scores with higher than warranted levels of confidence. The more important issue here is that so many who are using VAM estimates' capabilities are overly ignorant about their faults and fallibilities, like those demonstrated above.

In probably the most oft-cited report to date, Schochet and Chiang (2010, see also Schoceht & Chiang, 2013), who conducted a similar analysis for the U.S. Department of Education, found that there was about a 25% chance that an average teacher would be misidentified as far below average if using three years of VAM estimates. If using one year of VAM estimates (e.g., as per Louisiana state policy), the probability increased to a 35% chance. This empirically demonstrates that, when VAMs are applied in practice, a teacher might have a one in four chance of being misclassified using three years of data and a one in three chance of being misclassified using one year of data.

Sass (2008) wrote in another study:

> About one quarter to one third of the teachers in the bottom and top quintiles[6] stay in the same quintile from one year to the next while roughly 10 to 15 percent of teachers move all the way from the bottom quintile to the top and an equal proportion fall from the top quintile to the lowest quintile in the next year. Thus, for example, if bonuses

were allotted to teachers ranked in the top 20 percent based solely on value-added, at most a third would get bonuses two years in a row and about one in ten who received a bonus one year would be ranked in the bottom 20 percent of teachers the next year.

Corcoran (2010) also explained this issue:

> [A]mong those in the bottom quintile of performance last year, 36 percent remain in the bottom quintile in the following year. Similarly, among those in the top quintile of performance last year, 38 percent remain in the top quintile in the following year … however, there are many inconsistencies. Twenty-three percent of last year's lowest performers are in the top two quintiles in the following year. Twenty-three percent of last year's highest performers are in the bottom two quintiles in the following year.
>
> *(p. 25)*

Guarino, Reckase, et al., (2012) noted that they too found, "substantial proportions of teachers can be misclassified as 'below average' or 'above average' as well as in the bottom and top quintiles of the teacher quality distribution, even in the best-case scenarios" (p. 3). It is clear that no matter how complex the statistics used, "every estimator has an Achilles heel (or more than one area of potential weakness)" (p. 15).

Altogether, researchers have found, more or less, that between 25% and 50% of the teachers in the top quintile (i.e., scoring higher than 80% of their colleagues) or in the top quartile (i.e., scoring higher than 75% of their colleagues) in one year remained in their group the following year. Between 5% and 30% of the teachers in the top quintile or quartile fell into the lowest quintile or quartile the following year. The remaining 20–70% of teachers fell in between (i.e., average performance) the following year (Aaronson, Barrow, & Sanders, 2007; Au, 2011; Ballou, 2005; Glazerman et al., 2011; Goldhaber & Hansen, 2010; Koedel & Betts, 2007; Lockwood et al., 2008; McCaffrey et al., 2009; Newton et al., 2010; NGA & CCSSO, 2010; Otterman, 2010; Schochet & Chiang, 2010, 2013; Shaw & Bovaird, 2011).

Complementary anecdotes

Teachers have reported living out these year-to-year instabilities in their classrooms as well. Recall the teachers from Houston (discussed in Chapter 2) who compared receiving merit monies based on EVAAS® data to "winning the lottery," given the random, "chaotic," year-to-year instabilities they themselves experienced and observed from one year to the next. Recall the teacher who classified her past three years of VAM-based merit as "bonus, bonus, disaster." Recall the teachers who reported not understanding why they were being rewarded especially because they professed that they were doing nothing differently from one year to the next as their value-added rankings "jump[ed] around."

Or the teacher who noted:

> I do what I do every year. I teach the way I teach every year. [My] first year got me pats on the back. [My] second year got me kicked in the backside. And for year three my scores were off the charts. I got a huge bonus, and now I am in the top quartile of all the English teachers. What did I do differently? I have no clue.
>
> *(Amrein-Beardsley & Collins, 2012, p. 15)*

Again, however, this is not unique to Houston (Baeder, 2010; Baker et al., 2010; Banchero & Kesmodel, 2011; Haertel, 2011; Koedel & Betts, 2007; Papay, 2011). One teacher from the Los Angeles Unified School District, another VAM-based case carrying with it considerable controversy, was rated above average one year after which his/her value-added scores plummeted. In the teacher's opinion, (s)he did nothing differently in terms of instruction to cause the dramatic decline. What changed? (S)he went from teaching "rock star" students to less skilled, less English-fluent students (Watanabe, 2012).

Newton et al. (2010) presented a similar case of a mid-career reading/language arts teacher whose value-added estimates also changed radically from one year to the next, in this case moving from the bottom to the top decile.[7] This occurred over two school years in which (s) he first taught 58% ELLs, 42% students eligible for free or reduced-cost lunches, and 75% Hispanic students. (S)he then taught 4% ELLs and about half of the students eligible for free or reduced-cost lunches and Hispanics. The education level of his/her students' parents in year two were also significantly higher (see Figure 6.2).

While teachers might be more effective in some years than others, we would not expect teachers to yield such inconsistent scores over time. "[T]eacher effects are not as stable from year to year as we would expect them to be if they were due primarily to enduring qualities within teachers themselves" (Kennedy, 2010, p. 592).

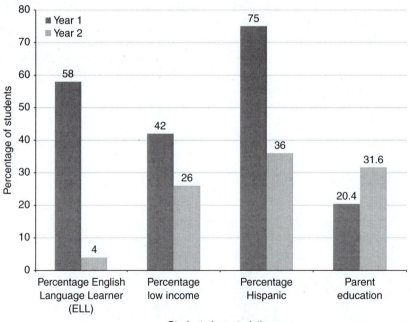

Figure 6.2 One teacher's fluctuation from value-added decile 1 (bottom 10%) to value-added decile 10 (top 10%), taking into consideration the types of students (s)he taught (source: adapted with permission from Newton et al., 2010).

Why so unreliable?

The complications causing these problems include the aforementioned types of error, the observed variations in teacher effectiveness that are often caused by the dissimilar students non-randomly assigned to teachers' classrooms, and the dissimilar subject areas teachers typically teach over time. Sanders, the developer of the EVAAS® system, claims he has research evidence that teachers who change teaching assignments continue to do just as well in terms of EVAAS® regardless of the grade levels or subject areas they teach (LeClaire, 2011). Once a good teacher, always a good teacher, so Sanders claims (see also Loeb & Candelaria, 2012).

As shown, recent research in Houston and New York suggests the opposite is evidently true. In Houston, Teacher A (see Chapter 2), flip-flopped back and forth across subject areas, adding value 50% of the time and detracting value 50% of the time across the subject areas she taught. Like Teacher A, Teacher D also flip-flopped across subject areas, until her last year. During this final year, she detracted value across all subject areas while teaching a new grade level, one in which an inordinate number of ELLs were transitioned into her English-only classroom. Similarly, in New York, hundreds of teachers were found to be both effective and ineffective in the same year, according to the different subject areas they taught. One teacher, for example, scored in the very top percentile in reading/language arts and in the very bottom percentile in mathematics, with the same students, in the same year (Rubenstein, 2012a; see also Baeder, 2010).

In addition, the students who take the tests that contribute to their teachers' value-added estimates might not perform in consistent or stable ways over time, contributing further to the instabilities observed. This might occur for a plethora of reasons, including that students, too, are human and rarely, if ever, perform the same on any academic exercise, including their tests (Papay, 2011). This might also occur given the very basic reality that students are not taking the same tests from one year to the next, and all of the tests that are being used on the pre- and post-test occasions have their own measurement errors that, when combined from the pre- to post-test occasions, in essence double the incidence of statistical errors (Baker et al., 2010; see also Bock et al., 1996; Braun, 2005). As well, these tests are often changed internally, perhaps to set new benchmarks and higher performance standards, or test items might be removed or added for various reasons, all of which decrease stability over time.[8] All of this occurs often enough so that consistent levels of teachers' value-added cannot be reliably observed with any standard level of certainty, making valid inferences about teacher effectiveness all the more impossible to infer (Au, 2011; Baker et al., 2010; Bausell, 2013; Bracey, 2004a; Glazerman & Potamites, 2011; Harris, 2011; Kersting et al., 2013; Lockwood & McCaffrey, 2009; McCaffrey et al., 2008; Milanowski, 2004; Nelson, 2011; Newton et al., 2010; Raudenbush, 2004; Raudenbush & Jean, 2012).

Reliability conclusions

While "[l]arger samples and statistical adjustment techniques can help 'smooth out' this imprecision ... they cannot eliminate it" (Di Carlo, 2013; see also Hanushek & Rivkin, 2010; Harris, 2011; Loeb & Candelaria, 2012; McCaffrey et al., 2009; Nelson, 2011). This is especially true if there is bias, which is discussed in the next chapter. Otherwise, if $r = 0.7$ or higher (i.e., $R^2 = 0.49$ or higher) we might be more comfortable trusting these measures as accurate representations of teacher effectiveness or, perhaps, even for high-stakes purposes. If r was even higher, perhaps we might even consider using these measures in isolation, pending evidence of validity, of course. Unfortunately, however, this is much more a utopian ideal or hypothetical scenario than the current VAM-based situation permits.

Some, however, argue that fluctuations in teacher effectiveness measures are not all that bad, particularly when positioned against reliability statistics that might be observed across other fields, such as worker productivity in sales, athletic prowess in sports (e.g., major league hitters in baseball), and instabilities in the economy (Baeder, 2010; Glazerman et al., 2011; Goldhaber & Hansen, 2010; Kersting et al., 2013; Loeb & Candelaria, 2012; McCaffrey et al., 2009; Raudenbush & Jean, 2012). As noted by Di Carlo (2013), "If instability is a deal-breaker, you'll have a tough time finding anything suitable."

Perhaps a reasonable compromise might be to keep these analyses at the school level so that at least lower error rates can be achieved with larger sample sizes (Schochet & Chiang, 2010, 2013; for a counterpoint see Evans, 2008). Another compromise might be to use these data only to distinguish among the extremes in performance, although the extent to which teachers in the extremes stay put over time (i.e., reliability) is still grossly suspect. In North Carolina, for example, of 1,600 teachers' value-added scores, 15% were rated as adding value and 18% were rates as detracting value, and only 2% were rated as detracting value for three consecutive years (Duffrin, 2011). The rate at which this occurs might be due to the sizeable random errors still prevalent, rather than "true" indicators of value-added (E. Sloat, personal communication, April 29, 2013).

This is highly problematic given that fewer than the expected number of teachers are consistently categorized as distinctly different from the mean (e.g., outside of one standard deviation in either direction; Ballou, 2002; Braun, 2005; Cronbach & Gleser, 1965; Dorn, 1994; Harris, 2011; Jacob & Lefgren, 2005, 2008; Kersting et al., 2013; NGA & CCSSO, 2010; Nicholson & Brown, 2010; Toch & Rothman, 2008; see also Corcoran and Hanuschek as cited in Duffrin, 2011; Corcoran as cited in Otterman, 2010). And, even if teachers were consistently categorized within either extreme, bias can distort these estimates and yield a false sense of reliability if, for example, teachers on the extremes teach similar students over time (e.g., ELLs,[9] students who are gifted,[10] students receiving special education services,[11] etc.). That said, when reliability is demonstrated, we must always check for bias before we can begin making valid inferences (Hill et al., 2011; Kersting et al., 2013; McCaffrey et al., 2004b).

Validity

Validity is an essential aspect of any measurement system as it captures "the degree to which empirical evidence and theoretical rationales support the adequacy and appropriateness of interpretations" (Messick, 1995, p. 741). When establishing evidence of validity, one must be able to support with quantitative and/or qualitative evidence that authentic and accurate inferences can be drawn from measurement data (Brennan, 2006, 2013; Cronbach & Meehl, 1955; Kane, 2006, 2013; Messick, 1975, 1980, 1995; Popham, 2011).

In terms of VAM validity, many VAM researchers are still "stuck on reliability," mainly because they cannot (and really should not) move past the aforementioned and ever-present issues with consistency, or the lack thereof. Inversely, others, including VAM developers in particular and those wanting to force the fit of VAMs, have adopted more of a separatist and also subliminal logic. Their logic is separatist in the sense that their actions suggest that reliability and validity should be observed independently, in more of a complementary versus conditional way; conditional in that one (i.e., reliability) should really precede the other (i.e., validity). Their logic is subliminal in the sense that the intent behind their actions is not made explicit. Their actions seem to occur below some threshold of methodological awareness or consciousness, or consciously but with false intent and an improper treatment of reliability, validity, and the relationship between them (see, for example, Harris & Anderson, 2013; Sanders, 2003[12]).

All of this is often overlooked in these kinds of VAM-based evaluation programs and in spite of prevailing measurement theory of the past half century (Brennan, 2006, 2013; Cronbach & Meehl, 1955; Kane, 2006, 2013; Messick, 1975, 1980, 1995; Popham, 2011); all of this implies that reliability is not a necessary or qualifying condition for validity. If scores are unreliable, which in the case of VAM estimates they are, it is still possible (and even preferable), they argue, to research whether making and supporting valid, authentic, and accurate inferences might otherwise occur. This, however, is faulty logic.

The truth of the matter is that if reliability is threatened, then we need not discuss validity. We, as researchers, should first investigate reliability and if, and only if, it is adequate, should we move forward. If it is inadequate, we should stop, because low reliability should prevent everyone, even Bill Gates or our U.S. Secretary of Education Arne Duncan, from attempting to make valid inferences and interpretations. All of those not following these time-honored rules as part of this long-standing theory are simply adding fuel to an already high-burning firestorm.

Following suit, VAM researchers of all sorts have delved into searching for evidence of four main sub-areas of validity, both in support of and against VAM use, and again regardless of the prevailing issues with reliability. They also continue to make both highly ambitious and cautious claims about what VAMs can and cannot do. I must admit that I too am guilty of having looked past the issues with reliability to prematurely examine evidence of validity (see, for example, Amrein-Beardsley & Collins, 2012).

Regardless, as per Messick (1989):

> [A] unified view of validity is required that comprehends both the scientific and the ethical underpinnings of test interpretation and use. This unified concept of validity integrates considerations of *content*, *criteria*, and *consequences* into a *construct* framework for testing rational hypotheses about theoretically relevant relationships, including those of an applied as well as of a scientific nature.
>
> (p. 5 [emphases added]; see also Cronbach & Meehl, 1955; Loevinger, 1957; Messick, 1995)

Next, I present VAM-based evidence of validity in terms of the same four sub-areas: (1) content-related, (2) criterion-related (predictive and concurrent), (3) consequence-related, and (4) construct-related evidence of validity.

Research on validity

Content-related evidence of validity

To collect content-related evidence of validity, it is necessary to examine whether test scores can in fact be used to make inferences about student learning and achievement. Messick writes (1995) that evidencing content validity is not about the properties of the tests, but the meanings of the inferences derived. "[W]hat is to be validated is not the test ... but the inferences derived from [the] test scores" (Messick, 1989, p. 5). Messick further writes (1975) that this should always be done, keeping in mind that the tests, in and of themselves, are "a function of the persons making them and of factors in the environmental setting and measurement context" (p. 956; see also Kane, 2013).

At issue here in terms of VAMs is that the large-scale standardized achievement tests on which current VAM-based estimates are almost always, if not always, based offer very narrow measures of what students know and are able to do. For the most part (with some test items as exceptions), large-scale standardized achievement tests do not effectively assess students' depth of knowledge and understanding, their abilities to think critically, analytically, creatively, or in highly cognitive ways, or their capacities to solve contextual problems, and the like (Baker et al., 2010; Corcoran, 2010; Harris, 2011; Toch & Rothman, 2008). Accordingly, whether tests that typically include 40 to 50 total tested items effectively represent the hundreds of complex items that capture the breadth and depth of information students should learn each year, as per the state standards, is also suspect (Amrein-Beardsley, 2008a; Pallas, 2012; Raudenbush & Jean, 2012). These tests survey domains of knowledge and skills, but they do not have nearly enough depth and breadth to be up to their newfangled duties, duties for which they are now being tasked within VAMs.

Researchers who have examined the content tested on the large-scale standardized achievement tests used by a number of states over time (i.e., the same tests used across the nation's current VAM systems) have found that much of what is valued across state standards is never tested or, at best, sometimes superficially tested, particularly if the standards to be tested are too advanced for even the most sophisticated of test-item formats. Messick (1989) called this construct under-representation, whereby these tests typically do not measure the state's fully vetted and accordingly valued curricula. Typically tested, rather, are the concepts that can be easily probed with multiple-choice questions of varying levels of complexity (Braun, 2005; Corcoran, 2010). Typically included are also those test items that "discriminate" well, or that distinguish between students who seemingly know unique concepts and particulars from those students who do not. This means that items appear on these tests that capture concepts that are not often taught or valued (e.g., the box-and-whisker plot Figure 5.1 explained in Chapter 5), simply because keeping items that discriminate well helps make large-scale standardized achievement tests function better, that is, better in their intended ways. More specifically, using such items helps to yield a normal (i.e., bell curve) distribution of test scores from which student-level distinctions can be more easily made.

To complicate this further, when one considers if and when teachers teach to the test,[13] particularly when high-stakes are attached to test output, this makes interpreting levels of student achievement (and teachers' contributions to student achievement, in the case of VAMs) all the more problematic. When teachers teach to the test, they isolate and teach, only or inordinately, the concepts they know will be measured on large-scale standardized achievement tests. What is tested then often dictates what is taught, which takes us even further away from making valid inferences about what students actually know and can do. This then increases the student's test score in a prejudiced way, falsely demonstrating that the student achieved (and learned by proxy) more than if the entire curriculum was fairly and properly taught and attended to.

In other words, not only are the tests limited in terms of how they capture that which is valued (i.e., the standards), when teachers teach to the test they further isolate that which is tested from that which is supposed to be taught. This distorts test-based inferences, and content-based validity, as the items that are tested become even less representative of what was supposed to have been captured in the first place.

As stated, the errors that are inherent in large-scale standardized achievement tests continuously complicate things. These errors cannot be ignored as "they alter the goodness of whatever decisions are to be made" (Cronbach & Gleser, 1965, p. 137) from the test-based inference perspective (see also Baker et al., 2013). Again, these errors come in two forms: (1) random errors that are often associated with measurement noise and (2) systematic errors that are often associated with measurement bias or construct-irrelevant variance (CIV) when outside factors consistently, albeit falsely, inflate or deflate the measurement and therefore distort test-based interpretations (Haladyna & Downing, 2004; Linn & Haug, 2002; McCaffrey, et al., 2004; Messick, 1989; Miller & Modigliani, 1961). CIV, in this case, is typically due to things like teaching to the test, narrowing of the curriculum,[14] cheating, and other such nettlesome but often willful activities. These errors are also caused by whether students are intrinsically motivated to do well on large-scale standardized achievement tests, especially if student-level consequences are not attached to the tests (Davis, 1994; Pallas, 2012; Zeis et al., 2009).

Related, and more specific to the case of VAMs, since teachers are not randomly assigned the students they teach, whether the students they teach are invariably more or less motivated, smart, knowledgeable, capable, and the like, can bias students' test-based data for better or worse. When students' test scores are aggregated, however, this can also bias teachers' VAM-based scores and the score-based inferences that are to be used to evaluate them. Kane and Staiger (2008), for example, wrote that "Teachers may be assigned classrooms of students that differ in unmeasured ways – such as consisting of more motivated students, or students with stronger unmeasured prior achievement or more engaged parents – [all of which] result in varying student achievement gains" (p. 1). VAM-based estimates, then, reflect more upon the students assigned to teachers' classrooms than the instructional and pedagogical talents of the teacher, even despite the sophisticated statistics that are supposed to control for bias interference (Capitol Hill Briefing, 2011; Darling-Hammond & Haertel, 2012; Hill et al., 2011; Koedel & Betts, 2009; Newton et al., 2010; Rothstein, 2009, 2010b).

Finally, most VAMs require that the scales that are used to measure growth from one year to the next land upon vertical, interval scales of equal units. These scales should connect consecutive tests on the same fixed ruler, making it possible to measure growth from one year to the next across different grade-level tests. Here, a ten-point difference (e.g., between a score of 50 and 60 in fourth grade) on one test should mean the same thing as a ten-point difference (e.g., between a score of 80 and 90 in fifth grade) on a similar test one year later. However, the large-scale standardized achievement test scores used in all current VAMs are grossly misaligned; their scales do not even come close to being vertically aligned as assumed (Baker et al., 2010; Ballou, 2009; Braun, 2004; Doran & Fleischman, 2005; Harris, 2009b; Ho, 2011; Nelson, 2011; Newton et al., 2010; Reckase, 2004; Scherrer, 2011). "[E]ven the psychometricians who are responsible for test scaling shy away from making [such an] assumption" (Harris, 2009c, p. 329).

Instead, the standard response is to normalize the test scores before using them (i.e., to a mean of zero and a standard deviation of one), as with the EVAAS® system where statisticians convert scores into normal curve equivalents [NCEs] that are interval-scaled. Other responses are to make the growth calculations and interpretations normative in and of themselves, like with the SGP model, or to counter for this using item response theory with scales transposed into logits or log-odds.[15] Doing any of this poses an entirely different set of problems and issues, however, in terms of content-related validity (Baker et al., 2013; Goe, 2008). One major issue is that some of the tests still being used are based on national versus state norms (when state tests do not exist in certain grade levels). For these few tests, which most states use for large-scale testing purposes, the national norms are not aligned with what is to be taught as per the state standards. This raises further concerns about content-related validity, or the extent to which these tests measure and represent the facets of the valued standards (i.e., construct representation).

Criterion-related evidence of validity

As per Messick (1989), "criterion-related validity is based on the degree of relationship between the test scores and [other] criterion scores" (p. 7). Ideally, to establish criterion-related evidence of validity, VAM estimates should be highly correlated with other criteria, all of which should point in the same direction to yield valid interpretations and uses. Criterion-related evidence of validity typically comprises two types: concurrent validity when test and criterion data are collected at the same time and predictive validity when test and criterion data are collected at different times, typically one in advance of the other (Messick, 1980).

Some consider criterion-related evidence of validity to be the gold standard of all types of validity. However, developing and using the proper measurement criteria to establish the extensive empirical evidence required to establish criterion-related evidence of validity can be exasperating (Kane, 2013). In terms of VAMs, it is very difficult to develop accurate measures that capture complex constructs (e.g., effective teaching). This is especially true if the goal is to improve upon the best we currently have available: VAM-based estimates, supervisors' observational ratings, and sometimes student or parent survey data meant to capture self-reported perceptions of teacher effectiveness. With that being said, all of the VAM-based evidence to date has been generated using these measures, along with their limitations.

In terms of VAMs' predictive-related evidence of validity, VAM-based estimates might be used to predict future outcomes on a related measure, after which predictions might be verified to evidence whether and to what extent VAM-based predictions come true. If predictions are detected as anticipated, predictive-related evidence of validity is present. If not, predictive-related evidence is void or deemed inessential (Kane, 2013).

In the case of VAMs, predictive-related evidence of validity is scant. This is because relatively few researchers have used VAMs to make predictions and even fewer have followed through on their predictions to determine if indeed their predictions came true. For example, in Tennessee in 2002, developers of the TVAAS system (from which the EVAAS® was conceived) used model estimates to help parents determine whether their children might eventually pass Tennessee's high school graduation exam, earn a high enough score on college-entrance exams to gain admissions into Tennessee's colleges or universities, and receive good, average, or poor grades once in college (Olson, 2002; see also Sanders, 2003). Wright et al. (2006) wrote four years later that, using the model, as EVAAS® developers "we are able to provide projections for every student in the state to a variety of endpoints, ranging from next year's test scores to high school end-of-course test scores to college entrance exam scores" as well (p. 11).

Nowhere, however, did any of the authors of any of the above quotes or claims provide empirical evidence demonstrating the extent to which the predictions they made were in fact realized with any degree of accuracy. When I overtly criticized them for their actions, or lack thereof (Amrein-Beardsley, 2008a), Sanders et al. (2009) responded, again without empirical evidence, that in one of the four predictive studies conducted using EVAAS® output, they found that "using all of each student's prior test scores from multiple grades and subjects to make the projections, one could predict three years in advance with more accuracy than predicting one year ahead using a single prior test score" (p. 8). Nowhere did they provide, nor have they yet provided, evidence of the EVAAS® system's predictive accuracy. They simply left their work incomplete by stating that accuracy is better with more years of data. While most if not all VAM scholars would agree that using more years of data for VAM-estimates is better than using less (Brophy, 1973; Cody et al., 2010; Harris, 2011; Sanders as cited in Gabriel & Lester, 2013), without the follow-up to determine whether their predictions were accurate, the arguments are relatively moot.

Notwithstanding, others have used prior VAM scores to project future VAM scores, for research- versus decision-based purposes (decisions exemplified in the above). At the same time or after, these researchers have also analyzed the predictions. They have found that VAM-based estimates are "incredibly weak" (Baeder, 2010) predictors of teachers' future performance in the same or different subject areas, as well as that they are particularly weak at the high school level (Jackson, 2012; Loeb & Candelaria, 2012; see also Sawchuck, 2012). While some counter this by asserting that VAM-based estimates are still, to date, the best predictors of future teacher performance (i.e., as compared to teachers' years of experience, certification status, degrees earned, courses taken, and prior supervisor observational scores), it stands that VAM-based estimates are only partially predictive of future teachers' performance, even with two or more years of data (Bill & Melinda Gates Foundation, 2010, 2013; Glazerman et al., 2011; Goldhaber & Hansen, 2010; Harris, 2010, 2011; Harris & Sass, 2009; Jacob & Lefgren, 2005; Koedel & Betts, 2007; Loeb & Candelaria, 2012). This too is likely and largely due to the aforementioned issues with reliability, or the lack thereof (Glazerman et al., 2011; see also Bill & Melinda Gates Foundation, 2010), and serves as yet another illustration of why reliability is so important and a necessary qualifying condition for validity (Brennan, 2006; Kane, 2006, 2013; Messick, 1975, 1980, 1995).

Otherwise, in terms of VAMs' concurrent-related evidence of validity (Messick, 1989), it is necessary to assess, for example, whether teachers who post large and small value-added gains or losses over time are the same teachers deemed effective or ineffective, respectively, over the same period of time using other independent quantitative and qualitative measures of teacher effectiveness (e.g., supervisors' observational scores, student or parent surveys). Evidence of validity increases as more sources of evidence point in the same direction or support the same inferences and conclusions (Nelson, 2011). If all measures line up and they validate one another (i.e., convergent evidence of validity), only then can our confidence in them as independent measures of the same construct increase (Messick, 1975, 1980, 1995; see also Hill et al., 2011; National Education Policy Center, 2011). If all indicators do not point in the same direction, this means something is likely wrong with the indicators being used. In the case of VAM-based measures, something is likely wrong with all of the indicators currently in use.

Unfortunately, however, and contrary to what some suggest (see, for example, Chingos & Peterson, 2011; Harris, 2012b), current research evidence suggests that VAM estimates of teacher effectiveness do not strongly correlate with the other measures typically used. While some argue that the other measures (e.g., supervisors' observational scores, student or parent surveys) are at fault, others argue that all of the measures, including VAM estimates, are at fault, largely because all of the measures typically used to examine teacher effectiveness are in themselves limited and insufficient.

Let us assume, as do most but not all researchers here, that there is such a thing as a general teaching effectiveness construct (see, for example, Braun, Goldschmidt, McCaffrey, & Lissitz, 2012; Harris, 2012b; Hill et al., 2011; Kennedy, 2010; Rothstein & Mathis, 2103). Let us also assume that this construct can be observed, measured, and captured consistently (i.e., with reliability), accurately (i.e., with validity), and independently from other biasing and exogenous variables (Berliner, 2013). If the large-scale standardized achievement test scores that contribute to VAM estimates and the other measures typically used to measure teacher effectiveness were reliable and valid measures of this construct, effective teachers would rate well more or less continuously from one year to the next, across the various indicators used. Inversely, ineffective teachers would continuously present themselves poorly across the indicators used. However, this does not occur, except in the slightest of patterns. The correlations being observed among both mathematics and reading/language arts value-added estimates and either teacher observational scores or student surveys of teacher quality are low to moderate[16] (e.g., $0.2 \leq r \leq 0.6$; see, for example, Baker, 2013a; Bill & Melinda Gates Foundation, 2013; Curtis, 2011; Graue et al., 2013; Harris, 2009b, 2011; Hill et al., 2009, 2011; Kersting et al., 2011; Kimball et al., 2004; Kyriakides, 2005; Milanowski, 2004; Nye, Konstantopoulous, & Hedges, 2004; Rothstein, 2009; Rothstein & Mathis, 2013).

Again, this indicates that across studies, using R-squared (i.e., $r \times r = R^2$), anywhere from 4% to 36% of the variance observed can be explained by the relationship between value-added and the other measures, but the other 64% to 96% of the variance observed is more likely due to things beyond the purview of that which is being measured. Again, this is largely caused by the errors that incessantly impact the more objective measures (e.g., causing unreliability) and the prejudicial issues incessantly impacting the more subjective measures. The former issues are due to the fact that VAMs limit definitions of student learning and purported teacher effects only to what large-scale standardized achievement tests can measure, along with their errors. The latter issues were illustrated in the "Widget Effect" (Weisberg et al., 2009; see also Brill, 2009; Gates, 2012) and they are largely due to score inflations and, accordingly, the decreased levels of variance needed to examine score distributions for these measures, as well as these measures' alignment with other criteria.

Regardless, probably the most recent, and to date the most publicized study that examined criterion-related evidence of validity was the most recent MET study (Bill & Melinda Gates Foundation, 2013). Gates researchers examined how states might best combine value-added scores, classroom observations, and student surveys when building their teacher evaluation systems. The study, despite how speciously it was positioned by the media, did not evidence that all three separate indicators reflected the same "teacher effectiveness" construct (Rothstein & Mathis, 2103). And despite the low correlations observed in this study ($r \approx 0.4$), Gates researchers still made recommendations that states look past the low correlations and use the different measures for summative (and consequential) purposes regardless.

In New York, after teachers' value-added estimates were publicly released, 73% of New York principals reported that the "ineffective" labels assigned to some of their teachers were inaccurate based on their observations, primarily given what they believed about the performance of the students in the particular teachers' classrooms and what they had consistently heard from parents and students about the allegedly ineffective teachers (Strauss, 2012b; see also Michie, 2012; Otterman, 2010). Around the same time, the *New York Post* identified and made public "New York City's Worst Teacher," overlooking the details that the teacher taught a large proportion of ELLs and that the teacher's principal, one of the city's most highly respected leaders, vouched for the teacher as being one of the best (Darling-Hammond, 2012; see also Pallas, 2012; G. Roberts, 2012; Winerip, 2011).

In Los Angeles, after teachers' value-added categorizations were made public by the *Los Angeles Times* (Felch et al., 2010; see also Briggs & Domingue, 2011; Durso, 2011; Felch, 2011; Song & Felch, 2011), one teacher who was advertised as detracting value from his students' learning, despite his students' expressed positive beliefs and his supervisors' praised performance reviews, both of which countered his value-added score, actually committed suicide (Ravitch, 2010b; Zavis & Barboza, 2010). There has been no higher consequence attached to value-added estimates – yes, estimates – to date. Sad as this is, this also illustrates an absence of concurrent-related evidence of validity.

Also relevant here is the extent to which value-added estimates derived from similar yet different tests correlate when given at the same time. Corcoran, Jennings, and Beveridge (2011), for example, compared value-added estimates taken from both high- and low-stakes testing data. They found low to modest correlations between high- and low-stakes measures used within reading/language arts ($r = 0.50$) and high- and low-stakes measures used within mathematics ($r = 0.59$). In other words, the same students who take similar subject area tests at the same time within the same grade levels might post vastly different scores by the mere fact that the tests are different. This also throws off concurrent-related validity if teachers' VAM-based estimates, which should be similar across tests based on the assumption that both tests measure the same content knowledge, are rather quite different just because of the individual test that is chosen and used for VAM-based evaluation (Baker et al., 2013; Harris, 2009b, 2011, 2012b; Hill et al., 2011; Lockwood, McCaffrey, Hamilton, et al., 2007; McCaffrey et al., 2009; Rothstein, 2011; Sass, 2008).

Within one of the initial Bill & Melinda Gates Foundation's MET study reports (2010), Gates researchers found even lower correlations between similar yet different tests in reading/language arts ($r = 0.37$) and mathematics ($r = 0.22$). In perhaps one of the best-known studies, Papay (2011) found that such estimates widely ranged across different tests as well (e.g., $0.2 \leq r \leq 0.6$), mainly given the aforementioned errors that come along with large-scale standardized achievement tests, the different concepts yet similar content areas being assessed, scaling and timing issues, and the like. This finding held true when the same student populations were tested and the same test developers developed the tests.

However, when holding the tests constant, the estimates derived via different VAMs and growth models (i.e., the SGP) seem to be, for the most part, much more strongly associated with one another across VAMs and subject areas (e.g., $0.5 \leq r \leq 0.9$). In other words, this means that while the choice of test can seriously diminish validity, the actual model that is used to estimate value-added, as long as it is sophisticated, may not matter all that much. This makes arguments and declarations about which VAM or growth model is "the best one" quite trivial, as they all seem to be correlating well with one another (Briggs & Betebenner, 2009; Glazerman & Potamites, 2011; Goldhaber et al., 2012; Goldhaber & Theobald, 2012; Goldhaber, Goldschmidt, & Tseng, 2013; Goldschmidt et al., 2012; Gottlieb, 2011; Hill et al., 2011; Schafer et al., 2012; Sloat, 2012). However, if one considers all such models as "garbage in, garbage out" systems, given the test data they all use to generate their estimates, the extent to which model outputs correlate with and across one another might also be expected (Banchero & Kesmodel, 2011; Gabriel & Lester, 2010, 2013; Harris, 2011).

Consequence-related evidence of validity

As per Messick (1989) "[t]he only form of validity evidence [typically] bypassed or neglected in these traditional formulations is that which bears on the social consequences of test interpretation and use" (p. 8). Neither content- nor criterion-related evidence of validity (concurrent or predictive) is sufficient for inferential purposes alone, as the social and ethical consequences matter as well (Messick, 1980; Kane, 2013). Accordingly, as per the *Standards for Educational and Psychological Testing* (AERA et al., 2000) "ongoing evaluation of both [the] intended and unintended consequences [of any test use] is essential" with any such testing program.

While this is an imperative that really should rest on the shoulders of the governmental bodies that mandate such test-based policies, as they are those who "provide resources for a continuing program of research and for dissemination of research findings concerning both the positive and the negative effects of the testing program" (AERA et al., 2000), this rarely occurs. The burden of proof here, rather, rests on the shoulders of VAM researchers to provide credible evidence about the positive and negative side effects that come with VAM use, to explain these effects to external constituencies including policymakers, and to collectively work to determine whether VAM use, given VAMs' intended and unintended consequences, can be rendered as acceptable and worth their negative consequences or the inverse if "negative consequences render [use of] a score unacceptable" (Kane, 2013, p. 1).

In terms of VAMs' intended consequences, one of the primary intents of VAMs, beyond their summative purposes, is to improve teaching and help teachers (and schools/districts) become better at educating students (Burris & Welner, 2011). The theory of action is clear: "(a) if you build strong data access structures and (b) enhance the ability of educators to use data, (c) better decisions will be made and, as a result, (d) student achievement will rise" (Graue et al., 2011a). Current U.S. Secretary of Education Arne Duncan (2009a) captured this in a speech: "When teachers get better data on student growth, it empowers teachers to tailor classroom instruction to the needs of their students and boost student achievement" (p. 4). Establishing evidence that demonstrates that VAM use helps to improve student learning and achievement is research priority number one. Whether VAMs effectively hold teachers accountable for what they do to promote student learning and achievement is also of interest, but this also directs attention back to intended consequence number one.

Whether VAM use helps to improve student learning and achievement is of acute interest, as well. Some VAM developers have made quite bold claims about their VAMs' intended consequences, and they have done so as part of their sales and marketing efforts. Recall, for example, that the EVAAS® is marketed for its capacity to provide "valuable diagnostic information about [instructional] practices," to help educators become more proactive, to increase educators' capacities to make more "sound instructional choices," and to help educators use "resources more strategically to ensure that every student has the chance to succeed" (SAS®, 2012a). The EVAAS® is also being advertised as providing "a clear path to achieve the US goal to lead the world in college completion by the year 2020" (SAS®, 2012c).

These are unrealistic goals, perhaps, but most would agree that the intents, or the intended consequences, are of collective value, at least in theory (see similar goals for VARC use in

Meyer & Dokumaci, 2010). However, in practice, whether these claims are (thus far) being realized is entirely unknown due to the void of supporting research. No independent research evidence exists whatsoever to support the contention that EVAAS® consumers, or other VAM and growth model users for that matter, are realizing the purported, marketed, advertised, and intended consequences that are to come with model adoption, implementation, and use (Amrein-Beardsley, 2008a; Amrein-Beardsley & Collins, 2012; Ballou, 2002; Bracey, 2004a, 2007; Collins, 2012; Corcoran, 2010; Dorn, 1994; Eckert & Dabrowski, 2010; Goe, 2008; Kupermintz, 2003; McCaffrey & Hamilton, 2007; Morgan, 2002).

Only one editorial, anecdotal piece of which I am aware has supported the contrary in terms of the EVAAS® (Haycock & Crawford, 2008). People continue to make unwarranted claims about VAMs, but the claims are all too often largely based on logic as opposed to research (Battelle for Kids, 2013; Bill & Melinda Gates Foundation, 2010; Derringer, 2010; Grier & Holcombe, 2008; Lozier, 2012; Nicholson & Brown, 2010; Sanders, 1994; Sanders & Horn, 1998; Sanders et al., 2007, 2009; Wilkins, 2010). The unfortunate truth remains that VAM estimates tell us nothing about how teachers might improve upon their instruction, how schools and districts might improve upon their educative services and social obligations, or how all involved parties might collectively improve student learning and achievement (Baker et al., 2013; Briggs & Domingue, 2011; Callendar, 2004; Carter, 2004; Goe, 2008; Graue et al., 2013; Harris, 2009c, 2011; Kraemer, 2011; Medina, 2009; NGA & CCSSO, 2010; Raudenbush, 2004).

This is due to issues with transparency. VAM formulas are often perceived as being overly obscure and complex, so that few teachers, few administrators, and few people in general, other than intermediate to advanced statisticians, understand the output or how to interpret and use it (Amrein-Beardsley & Collins, 2011; Ballou, 2002; Banchero & Kesmodel, 2011; Braun, 2005; CCSSO, 2005; Dorn, 1994; Glazerman et al., 2012; Harris, 2011; LeClaire, 2011; McCaffrey & Hamilton, 2007; Marder, 2012; Medina, 2009; Morgan, 2002; Nelson, 2011; Sass, 2008; Tekwe, et al., 2004). This is true when human resource and other support systems (e.g., financial, time, knowledge, and experience) are scarce, whereas "[D]ata reports [provide] little more than extra information" (Medina, 2009; see also Graue et al., 2011a; Harris, 2011; Kraemer, Geraghty, Lindsey & Raven, 2010; Lander & Pautsch, 2011; Raudenbush & Jean, 2011). This is true when there is a time lag between the tests being administered, scored, and transformed and when teachers (and schools/districts) receive VAM results (Amrein-Beardsley & Collins, 2012; Baker et al., 2010; Gabriel & Lester, 2013; Santos & Gebeloff, 2012). This is also due to the trust educators do or do not have in the estimates; educators struggle to use these data for (in)formative purposes because they do not view them as inherently useful in the first place (Amrein-Beardsley & Collins, 2012; Baker et al., 2010; Otterman, 2010; Sparks, 2011).

In addition, evidence from every state indicates that not one state has figured out how they might use VAM estimates to help teachers improve, largely because those beyond the statisticians who develop and run the actual models do not understand the models or how to use model output for such formative purposes (Collins & Amrein-Beardsley, 2014; see also Amrein-Beardsley & Collins, 2012; Gabriel & Lester, 2013). While there is some evidence that the SGP model is easier to understand than VAMs in general (Barlevy & Neal, 2012; Betebenner, 2009b; Bonk, 2011; Goldhaber & Theobald, 2012; Linn, 2008), there is no evidence to suggest that, even when made transparent and when understood, using VAM- or growth-based data would increase levels of student achievement whatsoever (Braun, 2008;

Briggs & Domingue, 2011; Darling-Hammond, 2012; Eckert & Dabrowski, 2010; Graue et al., 2011a; Kraemer, 2011).

Evidence is needed to evaluate whether VAMs cause unintended effects and whether their unintended effects outweigh their intended effects, all things considered. To be contemplated are the educative goals at issue (i.e., student learning and achievement), and the implications for both the science and the ethics of using large-scale standardized achievement tests for their intended purposes within VAMs (Messick, 1989, 1995).

The unintended consequences thus far tied to VAM use in the literature include research-based evidence or concerns about teachers teaching to the test, narrowing the curriculum, and cheating to manufacture whatever might constitute "enough" growth. The behaviors demonstrated here are commensurate with those demonstrated elsewhere in which research-ers have investigated the unintended consequences that come along with high-stakes testing (Amrein-Beardsley & Collins, 2012; Collins, 2012; Liu & Teddlie, 2005; Vogell et al., 2012; see also Braun, 2005; Corcoran, 2010; Gratz, 2010; Hanushek & Rivkin, 2010; Meyer, 1997; National Education Policy Center, 2010; Rothstein, 2010a, 2011; Sparks, 2012a).

Evidenced as well have been increased competition, decreased morale, and decreased trust among educators (Cody et al., 2010; Darling-Hammond, 2012; Dorn, 1994; Goldhaber & Theobald, 2012; Gratz, 2010; Liu & Teddlie, 2005; Scherrer, 2011; Wells, 2011). In terms of competition, for example, in Collins (2012), a teacher claimed that the "EVAAS® is creating a very competitive setting" (p. 126). Another wrote, "EVAAS® trades 'it takes a village' for 'every man for himself'" (p. 130). Another teacher wrote, "[EVAAS®] undermines collaboration, a cooperative work place, and pits administration against the staff" (p. 130). In terms of decreased morale, a teacher wrote that "EVAAS® and the bonuses attached to it are tearing down the morale of our school. Before, we worked as a team to get our kids where they needed to be" (p. 130). Another teacher pointed out the early childhood teachers as evidence of this, writing:

> The [early childhood teachers] feel like they are chopped liver compared to the testing grades. We need tutors to help out with our struggling kids in the testing grades, and usually we rely on our lower grade teachers to help out. This year, we can't beg, borrow, or steal anyone to stay after school or come in on Saturdays. Our upper grade teachers are barely running on steam, and our lower grade teachers feel unappreciated and disenfranchised, and say, "They're getting the big bucks [attached to EVAAS® output], let them earn it."
>
> *(p. 131)*

Not only have teachers reported increasingly not trusting one another, they have reported not understanding or trusting the systems in general. On the former (i.e., not trusting each other), one teacher wrote:

> Since the inception of the EVAAS® system [in the district], teachers have become even more distrustful of each other because they are afraid that someone might steal a good teaching method or materials from them and in turn earn more bonus money. This is not conducive to having a good work environment, and it actually is detrimental to students because teachers are not willing to share ideas or materials that might help increase student learning and achievement.
>
> *(p. 129)*

On the latter (i.e., not trusting the systems), another teacher wrote:

> Ultimately, there are no stated metrics and as such I don't trust that the people who assign this number are using this in my or my school's best interest. To use the lingo, the current system is not transparent. That makes me more resistant to data [or] a system that has the potential to be very useful for testing.
>
> *(p. 129)*

Another teacher reported being skeptical of its usefulness writing, "I don't completely believe in it or trust that the calculations are valid. And even if the whole EVAAS® operation is mathematically sound, I'm still not sure if it is all that important" (p. 129).

There is also evidence of teachers avoiding certain students whom they believe will drag down their growth scores over time (e.g., ELLs, gifted students, and special education students) or making sure such students do not participate in the tests when administered (Amrein-Beardsley & Collins, 2012; Collins, 2012; Sanders, 2003; see also Baker, 2011; Baker et al., 2013; Bracey, 2004a; Hill et al., 2011; NGA & CCSSO, 2010). In Collins (2012), for example, an ELL teacher wrote "Since I am teaching 5th grade ELL, I have been categorize[d] as ineffective because my students don't grow when coming from 4th grade all Spanish to 5th grade all English" (p. 98). Another teacher wrote, "The more ELL students I have, the lower my scores" (p. 124). A gifted teacher wrote:

> The first year [before I taught gifted students, my test scores] were ok. Then as I began to teach the gifted students, the scores continued to show negative growth. For the 2010–2011 school year, the Principal even told me that my scores revealed that I was one of the worst teachers in the school. The School Improvement Officer observed my teaching and reported that my teaching did not reflect the downward spiral in the scores.
>
> *(p. 98; see also Amrein-Beardsley & Collins, 2012; Hill et al., 2011;*
> *Newton et al., 2010; Rothstein, 2009)*

One teacher wrote that, if it were possible, "I would refuse to teach ELL and [gifted] students" (Collins, 2012, p. 124). A special education teacher wrote, "I had 11 special [education] kids last year with no co-teacher [or] assistance of any kind … I had a higher failure rate with them than with my other classes" (p. 139). See Collins (2012) for more instances of these situations and beliefs, or see other incidences of or discussions about this elsewhere (Amrein-Beardsley & Collins, 2012; Sanders, 2003; see also Baker, 2011; Baker et al., 2013; Bracey, 2004a; Hill et al., 2011; NGA & CCSSO, 2010).

Inversely, there is evidence of teachers befriending principals to stack their classes in their favor; that is, to fill the classes with students whom they believe have greater potential for growth (Banchero & Kesmodel, 2011; Burris as cited in Strauss, 2012b; Gabriel & Lester, 2013; Harris, 2011; Koedel & Betts, 2009; Kupermintz, 2003, Liu & Teddlie, 2005; Player, 2010; see also Bracey, 2004a; Rothstein, 2009). One teacher, for example, wrote, "The teachers want to recruit the best profiles. There are conversations 'during the summer' to obtain the best rosters" (Collins, 2012, p. 127). Another teacher described an opposite yet similar scenario about principals, writing "If they don't like you they stack [your roster with] the students with issues, give you no support and crucify you with EVAAS®. It's a set up" (p. 126).

It should be mentioned here, though, that no hard evidence exists to indicate that teachers are leaving the schools in which they teach due to their value-added scores, beyond anecdotal evidence (Mellon, 2010; Ravitch, 2013a, 2014). However, Weisberg et al. (2009), who authored The New Teacher Project's "Widget Effect" report, noted the likelihood of this happening is high. This will then "[set] off a game of musical chairs" (Ravitch, 2011), assuming these teachers do not leave teaching altogether.

Altogether, the unintended consequences here are similar to those that researchers have observed and evidenced for at least the last decade. Accordingly, "the insistence of the [U.S. Department of Education] to pursue initiatives involving highly controversial assessment methods continues to astound people who had expected President Obama to make a sharp break from the *No Child Left Behind* mentality rather than to exacerbate some of its worst effects" (Strauss, 2012a). This should cause us to pause and reconsider why we continue to rely on the same M&P Theory of Change discussed and explicated in the first few chapters of this book.

Construct-related evidence of validity

Finally, construct-related evidence of validity is "the whole of validity" (Loevinger, 1957, p. 636) or "the unifying concept of validity" (Messick, 1980, p. 1015). That is, construct-related evidence of validity is based on the integration of all "evidence that bears on the interpretation or meaning of the test scores" (Messick, 1989, p. 7; see also Messick, 1975) and helps us better define theoretical constructs (Cronbach & Meehl, 1955). To establish construct-related evidence of validity is a more significant undertaking, however, as this requires defining the construct to be measured (e.g., teacher effectiveness) and logically determining whether the instruments used to measure the construct represent and capture the construct well (Cronbach, 1971; Cronbach & Meehl, 1955; Messick, 1975).

According to Messick (1989) "the construct evidence accrued should be attuned to supporting the [overall] interpretive and action inferences to be drawn and to undercutting alternative interpretations and actions" (p. 6). Accordingly, of issue here first is confounded causation. This is of concern, particularly in this case, when students' scores are taken from large-scale standardized achievement test scores, which are expected to capture what students have learned and achieved in school *because* of their teacher(s). As discussed, confounding this construct are things like students' levels of motivation (over which educators have at least some influence), what students learn outside of school (over which educators have little to no control), and their innate intellectual abilities (over which educators have no control).[17] The reality is that test scores capture the influence of many factors inside, but also many factors from outside, of school, all of which are related to students' backgrounds, peers, parents, families, neighborhoods, communities, and the like, and most of which cannot be statistically controlled for in order to nullify the issues with confounded causation (Capitol Hill Briefing, 2011; Darling-Hammond et al., 2012; Newton et al., 2010; Rothstein, 2009, 2010b). Large-scale standardized test scores provide weak signals about educational quality and, instead, provide much stronger signals about what students bring with them every year to the schoolhouse door, from their families, homes, and neighborhoods. Accordingly, they cannot and should not be used to make inferences about what students know and are able to do academically, as well as about what teachers did or did not do to directly or causally impact changes in their students' performance over time.

The fact of the matter is that VAMs should be used only to measure changes in student achievement over time and *not* to attribute this growth to some cause (i.e., teacher, administrator, school, district, state, or program quality). Valid causal inferences do not come effortlessly, except in randomized, controlled experiments in which students would be assigned to treatment and control groups and the treatments themselves (i.e., teachers) would be randomly placed into classrooms (Ballou, 2012; Bausell, 2013; Cook & Campbell, 1979; Ehlert et al., 2012; Paufler & Amrein-Beardsley, 2013; Rubin et al., 2004; Wilkinson & Task Force on Statistical Inference, 1999).

Large-scale standardized achievement tests have always been and continue to be developed to assess levels of student achievement, *not* levels of teacher effectiveness. These tests have never been designed to estimate teachers' causal effects (Au, 2011; Briggs & Domingue, 2011; Kane & Staiger, 2008; see also Baker et al., 2010; Gabriel & Allington, 2011; Koretz, 2002; Linn, 2008; Meyer, 1997; Papay, 2011; Raudenbush, 2004; Rothstein & Mathis, 2013; Rubin et al., 2004). The assumption here is that because these tests are the best, most objective educational measures we have and because they are readily available and accessible, we should therefore use them to make causal inferences about teacher quality. This assumption is holding so strong, in fact, that it is becoming a universal truth that the only way to define teacher effectiveness is now with the use of VAMs (Gabriel & Lester, 2013). This "truth" goes forward without any evidence whatsoever that gains in these test scores can be empirically linked to teachers' causal effects; that is, the construct of interest. Are there slight signals that some teachers might indeed demonstrate added value over time? Yes, but the correlations, as illustrated and described earlier, are very low to moderate both in terms of consistency over time (i.e., $0.3 \leq r \leq 0.4$) and in terms of VAM estimates' relationships with other construct-related measures (i.e., $0.2 \leq r \leq 0.6$). These are certainly too low for high-stakes consequences to be tied to value-added output at this time.

Conclusions

The list of issues surrounding VAM-based reliability and validity all have major implications for both the science and the ethics of using tests for these purposes (Messick, 1989, 1995). All of this is also bound to be the source of the major and minor lawsuits, some now emerging (e.g., in Florida, see, for example, Postal, 2013), and others certain to follow (Baker, 2011; Baker et al., 2013; Pullin, 2013; Sawchuck, 2013c). Ultimately what matters most, though, especially for the time being, are the value judgments that come along with the measurements of such characteristics, in this case, about teacher quality and effectiveness, that are sometimes used against teachers themselves, even without evidence of reliability or validity. "Ambitious interpretations and uses (e.g., those involving causal claims or high stakes decisions) can require an extended research program for their validation" (Kane, 2013, p. 65). We simply do not have sufficient empirical evidence to support low-stakes decisions, let alone high-stakes decisions, using VAM-based estimates at this point. Causal inferences about teacher effectiveness are not, as evidenced by the research, currently appropriate using VAMs as sole sources of evidence.

Box 6.1 Top 10 assertions

1   Validity is essential for any measurement, and reliability is a necessary or qualifying condition for validity. That is, if scores are unreliable, it is impossible to make or support valid, authentic, and accurate inferences.

2   In terms of VAMs, there is very little evidence of reliability when examining teacher estimates from year to year, even when conditions (e.g., grade level and subject areas) are held constant.

3   Accordingly, strong evidence of validity has not yet been observed, given VAMs' fundamental and in many ways striking issues with reliability, or a lack thereof.

4   VAM-based estimates do not closely match other measures of teacher quality (e.g., classroom observation scores), inhibiting opportunities to make valid inferences using VAMs even more.

5   Students who take similar subject area tests within the same grade levels at the same time post vastly different scores given the fact that tests are different. This also distorts VAM validity.

6   Evidence of increased levels of competition, as well as decreased levels of morale and trust, has been linked to the use of VAMs in high-stakes teacher evaluation systems.

7   VAM formulas are often overly obscure and complex, so much so that few teachers and administrators understand how to interpret or use output for formative or beneficial purposes.

8   Related, VAM estimates tell educators little to nothing about how they might improve upon their instruction, how schools and districts might improve upon their educative services, or how all involved might collectively improve student learning and achievement.

9   While there is some evidence that some VAMs are easier to understand than others, no research evidence suggests that, even when understood, VAM data can be used to increase student achievement.

10   The reality is that test scores capture the influence of many factors both inside and outside of schools. Many of these factors are related to students' backgrounds for which statistical controls exist, but most of these factors cannot be controlled for well enough when attempting to make causal statements about teacher effects, as is the case with VAMs.

Notes

1   Inter-temporal stability, in the case of VAMs, can be defined as the stability or consistency with which past, present, and future events, conditions, or, in this case, VAM estimates, and perhaps the constructed categories that are based on VAM estimates, endure over time.

2   It should be noted that a revision of these standards was scheduled to begin in 2008. The new standards are still in development, but the sections cited here should not be too different than those to come. That said, the current professional standards are the standards put in place in 2000.

3   Recall that correlations demonstrate the strength of numerical relationships between, in this case one year's VAM-based estimates to the next, and then the next, and possibly back again in permutation form. Also recall that the correlation coefficient r can range $-1.0 \leq r \leq +1.0$, where the closer the value gets to either positive or negative 1.0 the stronger or more perfect the relationship. If r is

positive, this indicates that both measured variables are moving in the same direction. More specifically, while one indicator increases (e.g., students' test scores) so does another related indicator (e.g., students' household levels of income). If r is negative, this indicates that either of the two measured variables is negative when the other is positive. More specifically, while one indicator increases (e.g., one's levels of education) the other related indicator decreases (e.g., years one might have spent in jail). Correlations close to zero indicate no relationship between the variables or indicators of interest.

4 Whether states and districts are following the advice of researchers is still uncertain. Conversations continue to revolve around single-year estimates given the very real data limitations often overlooked when theorizing how these models should work in practice (e.g., missing test score data, nonexistent tests for teachers of certain grade levels and subject areas). As well, many states' tenure laws already have provisions allowing states or districts to terminate or de-tenure teachers when they have two consecutive unsatisfactory value-added evaluations (e.g., Delaware, Florida, Indiana, Pennsylvania). In the case of Louisiana, only one unsatisfactory value-added evaluation is needed (Baker et al., 2013).

5 While in this case these correlations are typically positive, demonstrating that both VAM-based indicators are positive (i.e., a teacher's VAM estimate for year X is at least somewhat related to the same teacher's VAM estimate for year Y), these correlations can also be negative. This indicates, instead, that individual teachers can demonstrate added value one year and the inverse the year following. If this occurs too often, the overall correlation coefficient (i.e., r) could be pulled even closer to zero.

6 A quintile is a 20% range used to divide 100% into five consecutive, essentially equal groups, where the bottom quintile includes all percentages between 1% and 20%, the second quintile includes all percentages between 21% and 40%; the middle quintile includes all percentages between 41% and 60%, the fourth quintile includes all percentages between 61% and 80%, and the top quintile includes all percentages between 81% and 100%. When using four groups these divisions are called quartiles; when using 10 groups they are called deciles (see note 7); and when using 100 groups they are called percentiles, accordingly.

7 A decile is a 10% range used to divide 100% into ten consecutive, essentially equal parts, where the bottom decile includes all percentages between 1% and 10%, the second decile ranges from 11% to 20%, and so on up to the top decile, which includes all percentages between 91% and 100%.

8 See an interesting case about how this occurred with the tests used in one state using the EVAAS® to measure teacher-level value-added in Eckert and Dabrowski (2010).

9 According to AERA et al. (2000), "If a student lacks mastery of the language in which a test is given, then that test becomes, in part, a test of language proficiency." This has implications for validity in that what the test is actually testing (i.e., language proficiency or content mastery) becomes confounded.

10 In general, teachers who teach students who are near the top (or bottom) of achievement distributions tend to have less accurate value-added estimates (Betebenner & Linn, 2010; Cole et al., 2011; Goldhaber et al., 2012; Hermann et al., 2013; Rothstein, 2009; see also Amrein-Beardsley & Collins, 2012; Briggs & Domingue, 2011; Pallas, 2012). This is sometimes due to the ceiling effects that make it very difficult for teachers of gifted students to demonstrate added value, much less get merit pay as a result, because those teachers can only get the best and brightest students "up so much!" (Amrein-Beardsley & Collins, 2012, p. 16; see also Cole et al., 2011; Graue et al., 2013; Kelly & Monczunski, 2007; Koedel & Betts, 2007, 2010; Linn & Haug, 2002; Wright et al., 1997).

11 See AERA et al.'s (2000) statement about the attention students with disabilities deserve when making valid inferences: when "testing individuals with disabilities, steps should be taken to ensure that the test score inferences accurately reflect the intended construct rather than any disabilities and their associated characteristics extraneous to the intent of the measurement." This has implications for validity in that what the test is actually testing (i.e., content mastery with appropriate modifications or an intervening disability that might bias results) becomes confounded, similar to the challenges ELLs may face when tested in English, and resulting test scores are not an accurate representation of true ability. This is likely why special education teachers sometimes tend to have relatively lower value-added scores than their general education peers; their students simply cannot demonstrate their true abilities given the limitations of the test (Baker et al., 2010; Briggs & Domingue, 2011; Hermann et al., 2013; Hill et al., 2011; Newton et al., 2010).

12 Sanders (2003) makes the claim that VAMs must have three elements to be viable [not valid]: (1) close alignment between what is taught and what is tested, (2) sufficient consistency or levels of reliability, which "is usually not a problem" and (3) sufficient "stretch" or variance so that the tests being used to calculate VAM estimates can effectively capture the progress of very low- and very high-achieving students (pp. 3–4; see also Eckert & Dabrowski, 2010). Sanders and his colleagues really pay no attention to and, still, "have no appreciation of the validity question whatsoever" (Glass, 1995).

13 When teachers "teach to the test" students become experts at answering test questions without entirely understanding the concepts justifying their answers. As teachers become familiar with high-stakes testing programs, they analyze the intellectual activities required on tests and use what they learn to give their students an extra edge on upcoming iterations of high-stakes tests. Students may end up spending hours memorizing facts, learning test-taking strategies, discovering how to manipulate test items and response options, making educated guesses, rehearsing test protocols, being coached on test items using items similar to those that will likely reappear on future tests, taking teacher-made and commercial practice tests, or being provided actual test items before official tests are administered. All of these practices replace critical modes of instruction and inquiry-based, higher-order, problem-solving activities and lessons that increase genuine levels of learning (Amrein-Beardsley, 2008b).

14 School curricula are sometimes marginalized or narrowed to ensure that the core subject areas, and the knowledge and concepts within the core subject areas that are typically tested on large-scale standardized achievement tests, become the core subject, knowledge, and concept areas taught, sometimes in isolation, particularly as such tests approach. When this occurs, science, social studies, physical education, the arts, and sometimes even recess are often pushed aside or eliminated, again for varying amounts of time (Amrein-Beardsley, 2008b).

15 Logits or log-odds are the inverse of the "logistic" function used in mathematics, and also in statistics (for more information see http://en.wikipedia.org/wiki/Logit).

16 Interpreting r: $0.8 \leq r \leq 1.0 =$ a very strong correlation; $0.6 \leq r \leq 0.8 =$ a strong correlation; $0.4 \leq r \leq 0.6 =$ a moderate correlation; $0.2 \leq r \leq 0.4 =$ a weak correlation; and $0 \leq r \leq 0.2 =$ a very weak correlation, if any at all.

17 See Chapter 5, note 4 and Harris, 2009c.

7

BIAS AND THE RANDOM ASSIGNMENT OF STUDENTS INTO CLASSROOMS

The most incomprehensible thing about the world is that it is comprehensible.

Albert Einstein

Bias is a huge threat to validity, as biasing factors increase or decrease test scores and test-based estimates, even though the biasing factors are unrelated to what the tests or test-based indicators are meant to represent (e.g., educational effectiveness). Accordingly, if estimates are highly correlated to biasing factors, then it becomes impossible to make valid interpretations about the causes of student achievement gains. Construct-irrelevant variance (CIV; first introduced in Chapter 2) is a technical term representing what is more commonly referred to as bias. More specifically, it is a term first used by Messick (1989) to describe factors that bias the measurement of a variable and distort its interpretation (see also Haladyna & Downing, 2004).

In terms of VAMs, CIV is a serious threat to validity. CIV indicates that VAM estimates make showing growth easier (or tougher) for some educators than others, but in a manner that is wholly irrelevant to the constructs of interest (i.e., teacher or school effects; Harris, 2012b; Messick, 1989, 1995; Rothstein, 2009, 2010b). Put differently, bias occurs when value-added estimates systematically differ when the construct-irrelevant characteristics of the students being investigated correlate with the asserted teacher effects. For example, students who are near the extremes, those at the top or bottom of the score range or the extreme right or left of a normal bell curve or achievement distribution (see Figure 5.2 in Chapter 5) tend to have less accurate value-added estimates for a variety of reasons (Betebenner & Linn, 2010; Cole et al., 2011; Goldhaber et al., 2012; Hermann et al., 2013; Rothstein, 2009; see also Amrein-Beardsley & Collins, 2012; Briggs & Domingue, 2011; Pallas, 2012).

Less accuracy at the top of the score range (or right extreme of the distribution) sometimes occurs because of the ceiling effects[1] that make it difficult for teachers of gifted students to demonstrate added value, much less get merit pay as a result, because teachers of gifted students can only get the best and brightest students "up so much!" (Amrein-Beardsley & Collins, 2012, p. 16). For teachers of gifted students, there is really nowhere else for their students to go on the achievement distribution besides lower on the score range or to the left of the distribution, nearer to the mean or average (i.e., the center of the bell curve). Because gifted students' test scores sometimes "regress towards the mean" in a negatively biased fashion (Amrein-Beardsley & Collins, 2012, p. 16; see also Cole et al., 2011; Graue et al., 2013; Kelly & Monczunski, 2007; Koedel & Betts, 2007, 2010; Linn & Haug, 2002; Wright et al., 1997), this makes determining teachers of gifted students' effects much more difficult. Inversely, floor effects[2] come into play when low achievers score so low (at the bottom of the score range or left of the test score distribution) that, for them, there is really nowhere else to go besides higher on the score range or to the right in the distribution, nearer to the mean or average (i.e., the center of the bell curve). Their scores regress towards the mean in a positively biased fashion, which also makes accurately determining teachers' effects for very low-achieving students much more difficult (Cole et al., 2011; Kelly & Monczunski, 2007; Koedel & Betts, 2007, 2010; Linn & Haug, 2002; Wright et al., 1997). As well (as discussed in Chapter 5), the fewer the students, or the smaller the class size, the more likely it is that teachers' value-added estimates will regress towards the mean (Sanders et al., 1997; see also Baker et al., 2010; Buddin, 2011; Goldhaber & Hansen, 2010; Kersting et al., 2013; Kupermintz, 2003; Lockwood et al., 2008; McCaffrey et al., 2003; Nelson, 2011).

Bias is also an issue for some teachers based on their grade level and/or subject area assignments (as discussed in Chapter 2), whereby some teachers are more (or less) likely to be held accountable depending on whether they teach in tested subject areas and grades. VAM-based estimates cannot be produced for approximately 60–70% of all teachers across America's public schools (Gabriel & Lester, 2013; Harris, 2011; see also Thomas, 2012). In addition, bias is more prevalent in high school (Goldhaber et al., 2013; Jackson, 2012) and middle school settings (Harris & Anderson, 2013; see also Sawchuck, 2012) where students are more likely to be tracked into classrooms within schools.

Taken together, these various sources of bias predispose consumers to make highly erroneous conclusions about teachers with smaller class sizes, teachers teaching extremely low- or high-performing students, teachers in certain subject areas and grade levels, and teachers of other types of students (i.e., ELLs, special education students, children from racial minority backgrounds, students receiving free or reduced-cost lunches, students who have been retained in grade for multiple years, students in remedial or other tracked programs) as these teachers' estimates have more to do with the quantity or type of students they teach rather than their actual qualities as teachers.[3] "Contrary to proponents' claims, these models reward or penalize teachers according to *where* they teach and *what students* they teach, not just *how well* they teach" (Darling-Hammond & Haertel, 2012). This artificially tips the evaluation scale against teachers who consistently teach more homogeneous classes comprising higher risk students.

Furthermore, because some teachers teach very similar sets of students over time, sometimes people are fooled into thinking such teachers have consistent scores (i.e., consistently high or low growth in value-added terms), but the consistency or *reliability* observed is really more of a factor of the types of students the teachers taught over time not a teacher's stable effects. Put differently, when a teacher has a highly consistent value-added score over time, this may not be due to consistency in terms of the *reliability* that is needed as a precondition to supporting validity or truth; rather this might be due to consistency caused by bias. This was the case with the thermometer discussed in Chapter 6. Recall that reliability was not an issue with the thermometer; it yielded consistent readings across observations. However, the other indicators that were observed at the same time (e.g., the forehead radiating heat) contradicted the thermometer's readings, deterring valid inferences from being made *even though* reliable readings were obtained. The thermometer yielded consistent readings, *but* the readings were severely inaccurate. Such can also be the case with value-added estimates.

Take as a VAM-based example, the case of Teacher C discussed in Chapter 2. Consistency was observed across Teacher C's scores (see Table 2.3 in Chapter 2). Again, reliability lent itself to validity, but bias interfered. Teacher C's EVAAS® scores across years and subject areas evidenced that Teacher C detracted value from her students' learning (relative to comparable district peers) 100% of the time across three different subjects. This is what reliability should look like; that is, as illustrated via consistent scores across similar students and subject areas over time. What is illustrated here theoretically supports validity. However, it was later determined by Teacher C's hearing officer that the steady lack of growth she demonstrated was more likely due to the types of students Teacher C persistently taught than her true effects as a teacher. She was given her job back, as her EVAAS® scores were ultimately deemed *stable* yet *invalid* due to *bias*. Her EVAAS® scores were largely biased by the backgrounds of the students she typically taught – the biasing factors that could not be controlled by even the most sophisticated of VAMs (SAS®, 2012a, 2012c).

Take as another example Figure 7.1. Here it is illustrated that three English teachers taught two sections of "identical" content-area courses. One section comprised higher achievers (i.e., tracked) and the other section comprised a mix of students (i.e., untracked). Each teacher's value-added ratings suffered when teaching the lower achievers, not necessarily due to fundamental differences in how the teachers instructed the separate sections, but because the compositions of the two sections were different enough to skew or bias their value-added estimates downwards in the untracked sections. While some teachers are indeed more effective teaching certain types of students, this should not be a trend.

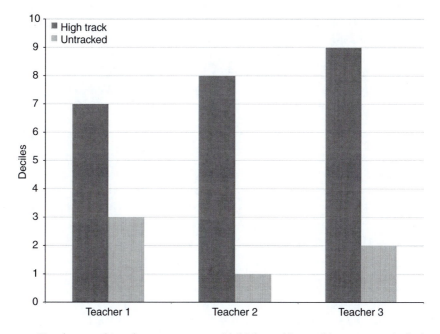

Figure 7.1 Teachers teaching the same courses with high- and low-achievers respectively (source: adapted with permission from Newton et al., 2010).

Or, take as another example a graph that demonstrates, again, how dramatically students' demographics can impact or bias teacher-level value-added estimates (see Figure 6.2 in Chapter 6). Here it is illustrated how a reading/language arts teacher's value-added estimates dramatically changed given how the composition of his/her classroom changed from one year to the next. This teacher's rankings moved from the bottom 10% (decile 1) in Year 1 to the top 10% (decile 10) in Year 2. During this time period (s)he went from teaching a course in which 58% of his/her students were ELLs, 75% were Hispanic, and 42% were from low-income backgrounds to teaching a course in which, by contrast, only 4% of his/her students were ELLs and the proportions of his/her students who were Hispanic or from low-income backgrounds were approximately cut in half. The education levels of the parents of this teacher's students also increased over the same period of time, with parents having at least some college in Year 2 versus having less than a high school education in Year 1.

The main points here, first, are that (1) VAM-based decisions should be accurate and appropriate taking into consideration the types of students a teacher teaches (Messick, 1980), (2) teachers who work with certain populations of students are adversely impacted by bias, and (3) nobody should be fooled by reliability because VAM-based measures might be "stable in their invalidity" or just "consistently wrong" (Baker et al., 2013, p. 9; see also Di Carlo, 2013; Kersting et al., 2013; McCaffrey, 2012; McCaffrey et al., 2004b, 2009).

Second, researchers continue to demonstrate that value-added estimates are biased (Capitol Hill Briefing, 2011; Dills & Mulholland, 2010; Hermann et al., 2013; Hill et al., 2011; Newton et al., 2010; Rothstein, 2009, 2010b; Stacy et al., 2012; Tate, 2004). Researchers continue to demonstrate that this occurs across the cities and states using VAMs for highly consequential purposes (see, for example, Amrein-Beardsley & Collins, 2012; Baker, 2012b; Briggs & Domingue, 2011; Burris as cited in Strauss, 2012b; Darling-Hammond, 2012; Green, Baker, & Oluwole, 2012; Newton et al., 2010). And researchers continue to demonstrate that this occurs most often when relatively homogeneous sets of students (i.e., ELLs, gifted and special education students, children from racial minority backgrounds, students receiving free or reduced-cost lunches, students who have been retained in grade for multiple years, students in remedial or other tracked programs) are non-randomly concentrated into schools, purposefully placed into classrooms, or both (Baker et al., 2010; Capitol Hill Briefing, 2011; Goldhaber et al., 2012; McCaffrey et al., 2004b; Rothstein & Mathis, 2013).

Researchers are therefore increasingly investigating the extent to which the purposeful (non-random) assignment of students biases teacher-level value-added estimates. Students are not randomly assigned to classrooms, and administrators, teachers, and parents play prodigious roles in student placement processes and procedures (Ballou, 2012; Harris & Anderson, 2013; Hill et al., 2011; Ishii & Rivkin, 2009; Kane & Staiger, 2008; McCaffrey et al., 2004b; Player, 2010; Rothstein, 2009, 2010b; Rothstein & Mathis, 2013).

On random assignment

"Random assignment (not to be confused with random selection) allows for the strongest possible causal inferences free of extraneous assumptions" (Wilkinson & Task Force on Statistical Inference, 1999; see also Cook & Campbell, 1979). The purpose of random assignment is to make the probability of the occurrence of any observable differences among treatment groups (e.g., treatment or no treatment) equal at the outset of any experiment or study. Randomized experiments occur when individuals are premeasured on an outcome, randomly assigned to receive different treatments whereby each participant has an equal chance of receiving any treatment (or no treatment), and then measured again on the post-test occasion to determine whether different changes occurred across different treatments. Hence, random assignment is considered the "gold standard" when scientific causal associations and inferences are desired, that control for and are seemingly "free" of the biasing impacts caused by extraneous (i.e., unmeasured or immeasurable) variables (Bausell, 2013; Linn, 2008; Rubin et al., 2004; Schochet & Chiang, 2010; Shaw & Bovaird, 2011).

In the case of VAMs, random assignment would involve using probabilistic methods to assign students to different teachers' classrooms (i.e., treatment groups). This, in effect, would help to ensure that the student characteristics that might bias teacher-level effects (i.e., different treatment effects) are equal across students within classrooms with different teachers (i.e., comparison groups) whereas teachers would be no more or less likely to have been assigned different students than any other comparable teachers teaching the same subjects and grade levels at the same schools. This would help to reduce systematic errors and make better causal statements about teacher effects, (i.e., treatment effects) using output indicators (e.g., growth in student achievement), mainly given the decreased probability of observing differences due to the student characteristics for which random assignment would control.

With value-added analyses, random assignment is the ideal empirical approach if we truly aim to be able to determine whether differences in value-added estimates are due to our main measurement constructs of interest – teacher effects (Ballou, 2012; Bausell, 2013; Ehlert et al., 2012; Glazerman & Potamites, 2011; Raudenbush, 2004; Rothstein & Mathis, 2013). If all students, including ELLs, gifted and special education students, students from racial minority backgrounds, students receiving free or reduced-cost lunches, students retained in grade, students in remedial or other tracked programs, and the like, could be randomly assigned to classrooms (and teachers to classrooms), the confidence with which researchers, policymakers, and practitioners could make valid decisions using value-added scores would be substantially increased (Corcoran, 2010; Guarino, Reckase, et al., 2012; Ishii & Rivkin, 2009; Linn, 2008; Nelson, 2011; Newton et al., 2010; Rothstein, 2009). Random assignment would presumably mitigate the bias present without random assignment (Harris, 2009c; Rothstein, 2010), and therefore help to control for the biasing effects of student background variables (Ballou et al., 2004; Kupermintz, 2003; McCaffrey et al., 2004b; Tekwe et al., 2004).

However, given the fact that value-added estimates are most often calculated when random assignment is not possible, under quasi-experimental conditions (Cook & Campbell, 1979), it is often necessary to assume that even if random assignment practices are not used, assignment practices are "effectively, if not formally, random" (Reardon & Raudenbush, 2009, p. 497). It must be assumed that any school is as likely as any other school, and any teacher is as likely as any other teacher, to be assigned any student who is as likely as any other student to have a similar background, abilities, motivations, attitudes, and the like. This makes it more defensible to make statements about attribution, which is less extreme than direct causation (Ballou, 2012; Goldhaber & Theobald, 2012; Kersting et al., 2013; Raudenbush, 2004).

Perhaps the most central issue here is whether even the most sophisticated VAMs can measure value-added in unbiased ways. "The fundamental concern is that, if making causal attributions is the goal, then no statistical model, however complex, and no method of analysis, however sophisticated, can fully compensate for the lack of randomization ... in the absence of randomization, it is hard to discount alternative explanations for the results that are found" (Braun, 2005, p. 8). Thus, without randomization it is almost if not entirely imposs-ible to even begin making causal statements about teacher effects.

However, as mentioned, value-added statisticians assert that the achievement differences between and among students that occur due to non-random placement and sorting mecha-nisms *can* be controlled for statistically, ultimately making non-random assignment a non-issue (Ballou et al., 2004; Goldhaber & Theobald, 2012; Meyer & Dokumaci, 2010; Sanders, 1998, 2006; Sanders & Horn, 1998; Wright et al., 1997). Yet, along with such an assertion come a series of "heroic assumptions" (Rubin et al., 2004) that, although rarely discussed, researchers are gradually discrediting (Hermann et al., 2013; Marder, 2012; Stacy et al., 2012). These methodological assumptions include, but are not limited to, assumptions about linear-ity, homoskedasticity, and most pertinent here, strongly "ignorable" student assignment (Reardon & Raudenbush, 2009, p. 504; see also Braun, 2005; Scherrer, 2011).

Strongly ignorable student assignment

Researchers continue to argue that students are not randomly assigned to classrooms, and that administrators, and teachers, and parents play prodigious roles in student placement processes and procedures, making student sorting highly non-random (Ballou, 2012; Bausell, 2013; Burris as cited in Strauss, 2012b; Harris & Anderson, 2013; Hill et al., 2011; Ishii & Rivkin, 2009; Kane & Staiger, 2008; McCaffrey et al., 2004b; Player, 2010; Rothstein, 2009, 2010b; Rothstein & Mathis, 2013). However, others sometimes assume and/or argue that this is not necessarily so, or at least that it is not something with which value-added statisticians should be concerned.

Recently, for example, a former director of research and evaluation at the Arizona Depart-ment of Education made public his/her assumptions about random assignment – that, in general, students across the state were randomly assigned to classrooms. The director expressed this during a committee meeting that was about the VAM the state department was to advise legisla-tors to adopt and implement as part of the state's new teacher accountability system. After sharing his/her beliefs, the director was criticized for making what was considered a highly false assumption, as well as a surprising one, considering his/her research background. Attendees who opposed the director argued instead that student assignment practices across the state were highly non-random, and not even effectively random at their best. The director then noted that the state needed more information about the extent to which students were being assigned to classrooms, which inspired the study to be discussed here (Paufler & Amrein-Beardsley, 2013).

However, while the director's comments were made clear, and scrutinized as such, others have supported similar versions of this assumption. Harris (2011), for example, wrote (without supportive evidence) that "in elementary schools, there is typically little tracking across classes (though teachers do track within classes)" (p. 114). He added that, "in middle school, tracking is more common; and in high school, it is almost universal" (p. 114; see similar statements in Harris, 2009c; Harris & Anderson, 2013). Rivkin and Ishii (2008) made an analogous asser-tion (again without supporting evidence) that the systematic sorting of students "is much more prevalent in middle school than in the early grades," which ultimately makes attempts to produce unbiased value-added estimates "more difficult in middle school than in elemen-tary school" (p. 17).

Guarino, Reckase, et al. (2012) claimed (without supportive evidence) that students are typically *not* randomly sorted into classrooms, but rather students are sorted, but using only students' perceived and actual academic abilities. They made explicit their assumptions about how tracking by academic ability is really the only form of student sorting mechanism that exists, and thus academic ability is the main student demographic with which value-added statisticians should chiefly be concerned. Hence, controlling for academically based student placement practices "explicitly controls for the [only] potential source of bias" (p. 30; see also Harris, 2009c).

Elsewhere, many value-added statisticians use VAMs that assume randomness, even though the statisticians themselves do not necessarily believe that actual student assignment practices are, in effect, made at random. Instead, they claim that student assignments need not be made randomly if the most sophisticated models are used to estimate value-added, with controls that account for students' prior achievement(s) and other variables (as needed and according to what control variables are available). Put another way, this set of statisticians suggests that if student placements are not made at random, and even if student placements are made in far from random ways (Braun, 2005; Rothstein, 2009, 2010b), complex statistics (i.e., student, classroom, and school fixed effects and nesting strategies accounting for the nested structures in which students exist; student-level covariates and other sophisticated controls; blocking, shrinkage, and bias compression strategies, ordinary least squares [OLS] estimators) can tolerably counter for the non-random effects and levels of bias that occur outside of experimental conditions.

VARC model developers, for example, explicitly state that their advanced VAM "produces estimates of school productivity – value-added indicators – under the counterfactual assumption that all schools serve the same group of students. This facilitates apples-and-apples school comparisons rather than apples-and-oranges comparisons" (Meyer & Dokumaci, 2010, p. 3). Developers of the EVAAS® note as well that their model is not biased by non-random student placements given the complex systems and controls they too have put into place (Sanders & Horn, 1998; Sanders et al., 2009). They, and others, argue that the random assignment of students to teachers' classrooms, while a nicety, is for the most part unnecessary (see also Bill & Melinda Gates Foundation, 2013; Glazerman & Potamites, 2011; Goldhaber & Chaplin, 2011). The complex statistical strategies and controls they use allegedly make the biasing effects of non-random student placement practices effectively "ignorable" (Reardon & Raudenbush, 2009, p. 504). As for the errors that cannot be controlled, statisticians claim that they can use confidence intervals to better situate value-added estimates and their (often sizeable) random errors, so at the least the errors can be better understood.

Recall from Chapter 6, however, that the typical confidence intervals used in statistics give or take about 5 percentage points (i.e., given standard 95% confidence intervals). In New York, however, the confidence intervals around 18,000 teachers' value-added ratings spanned 35 percentile points in mathematics and 53 percentile points in reading/language arts (Santos & Gebeloff, 2012). This meant that in mathematics a teacher who ranked at the 50th percentile could have actually had a true score anywhere between the 33rd and 68th percentile rank. In reading/language arts a teacher who ranked at the 50th percentile could have had an observed score anywhere between the 24th and 77th percentile rank. While 95% confidence intervals are typically used, with VAMs these standard error ranges are typically much, much larger.

Simply put, some believe random assignment is not an issue in certain grade levels versus others, some believe random assignment is not an issue because student sorting systematically occurs using only students' prior academic achievements that can be controlled, and some believe random assignment is not necessary regardless of what happens when students are assigned to classrooms (and teachers to classrooms) because the statistical strategies and controls used are advanced enough to control for most if not all of the bias that might occur.

Advanced statistical strategies and controls

To reduce the errors often caused by bias, value-added statisticians always control for at least one, and preferably more years of students' previous test scores (e.g., using or exploiting covariates in lieu of randomized experimental conditions) to help adjust for the starting abilities of the students non-randomly sorted into classrooms and schools. Most agree that the most critical variable and the most important VAM-based adjustment is students' prior achievement (Glazerman et al., 2011; Glazerman & Potamites, 2011; Harris, 2009c; Milanowski, Kimball, & White, 2004). Therefore, controlling for prior student achievement helps to "level the playing field," and ameliorate the biasing impact that extraneous variables have on student achievement over time (Sanders et al., 2009, p. 4; see also Ballou et al., 2004; Ehlert et al., 2012; Sanders, 1998; Sanders & Horn, 1998). However, the extent to which this works is yet another source of contention and dispute (Ballou, 2012; Cody et al., 2010; Dorn, 1994; Gabriel & Allington, 2011; Glass, 1995; Graue et al., 2013; McCaffrey, 2012; Rothstein, 2009).

For example, Sanders et al. (2009) argue that controlling for such extraneous variables is unnecessary because including students' prior test scores inherently controls for the variables intentionally excluded. They also argue that controlling for student background and other environmental variables is not only unnecessary, but such practices would create inequitable learning expectations for students at risk (e.g., students from racial minority or high poverty backgrounds). These are the students about whom the "to control or not to control" debate continues. EVAAS® statisticians and others argue that adjustment practices (i.e., "to control") might cause teachers to focus less on high-risk students because these students would be given a statistical accommodation, or artificial boost, given their individual characteristics (Ballou et al., 2004; Ross, Sanders, et al., 2001; Sanders, 2003; Tekwe, et al., 2004).

Sanders et al. (2009) also purport to have evidence to show that allowing students to serve as their own controls successfully accounts for all of the demographic characteristics not controlled. Academic growth, when properly assessed at the teacher or school level, using only students' test prior scores, is not highly correlated with students' backgrounds (mainly race and poverty) in their EVAAS® model.[4] However, they do not provide statistical evidence of this assertion (e.g., correlations among levels of growth and race/poverty). Instead, they write, "correlations are modest at worst and essentially zero at best" (p. 6; see also Ross, Sanders, et al., 2001; Sanders, 1998; Sanders & Horn, 1998; Wright et al., 1997), leaving "modest" correlations open to interpretation (see a similar discussion in Kupermintz, 2003).

Recall, however, from Chapter 5, that historically universal risk factors (e.g., poverty, ELL status, disability) are highly correlated with all achievement measures, more so than anything else. "[T]he socioeconomic disadvantages that affect children's test scores … also affect the rates at which they show progress" (Baker et al., 2010, p. 10). This too should be taken into consideration when contextualizing what "modest" might mean, especially considering that measuring growth is supposed to mediate these historical and universal truths.

Again, because perfect correlations (i.e., $r = +/-1.0$) are almost never attainable, researchers sometimes follow a set of commonly used and purposefully ambiguous categories to help guide their interpretations of correlation coefficients. As described in more detail in Chapter 6, perfect positive correlations (i.e., $r = +1.0$) are almost never attainable, so researchers sometimes follow a set of commonly used, yet purposefully ambiguous, set of categories to help guide their interpretations of correlation coefficients. Again, as per Merrigan and Huston (2004), a representative interpretive framework to help interpret correlation coefficients in the social sciences (e.g., educational research) is available (see Figure 6.1 in Chapter 6); this might be used here to help us better understand what "modest" (i.e., moderate) might mean in terms of the EVAAS®'s commensurate levels of bias.

Put another way, when Sanders et al. (2009) wrote that, "correlations are modest [or moderate] at worst and essentially zero at best" (p. 6; see also Sanders, 1998), this might have actually meant something more than what was implied as inconsequential or irrelevant (i.e., $0.4 \leq r \leq 0.6 =$ a moderate correlation; see also Staiger as cited in Otterman, 2010). In addition, researchers conducting secondary analyses of EVAAS® data have noted that bias still exists within the EVAAS® model, especially when highly homogenous sets of students (including large proportions of racial minority students) are not randomly assigned to classrooms (Kupermintz, 2003; see also Goldhaber et al., 2012; Guarino, Maxfield, et al., 2012; Guarino, Reckase, et al., 2012; Newton et al., 2010).

Allowing students to serve as their own controls only accounts for bias in starting ability due to student traits. Doing this does not, however, address the differential probabilities that students with diverse background characteristics (e.g., language proficiency, familial support, dissimilar motivations, access to technologies and resources outside of school) might have for making discrepant gains from one year to the next.

That said, some value-added statisticians do integrate additional controls to account for some of these other, uncontrollable extraneous influences. They do this under the assumption that by controlling for some additional observable factors they might also control for other factors, particularly those that might be more difficult or impossible to capture. Control variables most often incorporated across most VAMs include, but are not limited to, student-level variables (e.g., race, ethnicity, students' eligibility for free or reduced-cost lunches, ELL status, involvement in special education and gifted programs), and classroom- and school-level variables (e.g., daily attendance rates, prior teachers' residual effects, multiple teachers' fractional effects), when available.[5] The inclusion of combinations of these additional controls seemingly facilitates better model adjustments, again to make output more accurate and less subject to bias (Braun, 2005; Glazerman & Potamites, 2011; Goldhaber & Theobald, 2012; Hill et al., 2011; McCaffrey et al., 2004b; Meyer and Dokumaci, 2010; Newton et al., 2010; Thum & Byrk, 1997).

What is still widely contested, however, is whether including these variables works well to control for the other, *non-observable*, yet potentially biasing variables as well. Some researchers claim that the observable variables typically included within VAMs tend to be imperfect because they are very rudimentary proxies of the wider group of variables causing bias. So while including additional variables helps strengthen VAMs, this does not and might not ever control for or limit bias down to acceptable levels of independence and neutrality (Ehlert et al., 2012; Glazerman & Potamites, 2011; Kersting et al., 2013; McCaffrey et al., 2008).

These researchers also fundamentally question, for example, whether using binary (i.e., using 1 and 0) and categorical variables (i.e., using a range of numbers to represent categories without inherent values) can correctly capture students' ELL status, poverty-based realities, ranges of disabilities, and the like. Reducing highly complex phenomena into mathematical representations and codes is much less exacting than it might seem. While gender might be the most reasonable use of a dichotomous variable (i.e., male and female), of primary interest here is whether numeric classifications and categorizations of other characteristics, such as students' disabilities, can effectively differentiate amongst and accurately capture the learning trajectories of students who might be intellectually challenged, emotionally disabled, autistic, or any combination of these. Similarly, whether race can be isolated and effectively captured using categorical variables (e.g., 1 = American Indian/Alaskan Native, 2 = Asian American/Pacific Islander, 3 = Black/African American, and so on) and whether these categories can be used to account for their influence on different students' learning trajectories as well (Baker et al., 2013; Briggs & Domingue, 2011).

Nevertheless, value-added statisticians often employ these variables, or a combination of those to which they have access, to also implicitly control for the other non-observable variables at play. The non-observable variables not typically available in the large-scale datasets used to conduct these analyses include, but are not limited to, students' behavior, discipline, or suspension records; students' self-handicapping and other dispositional, personality, motivational, attitudinal, or behavioral measures; students' family support systems including their access to resources, books, and technologies within the home; students' parental support, parents' levels of education, and parents' direct and indirect involvement in their children's learning; whether students attend summer school, access libraries or other public sources of learning, or have access to tutors; and the like (Anderman et al., 2010; Briggs & Domingue, 2011; Darling-Hammond, 2010; Gansle et al., 2011; Harris & Anderson, 2013; Lockwood & McCaffrey, 2009; Misco, 2008; Rivkin & Ishii, 2008; Rubin et al., 2004; Wilson, Hallman, Pecheone, & Moss, 2007). These factors ultimately cause disparities in learning, both during the school year and over the summer months (Alexander et al., 2001, 2007a; Baker et al., 2010; Corcoran, 2010; Fairchild, 2009; Gabriel & Allington, 2011; Harris, 2011; Northwest Evaluation Association, 2006; Papay, 2011).

Because all of these variables impact student learning over time, the question then becomes whether what is available and typically included can realistically account for all that is not available and regularly excluded. While the general rule here is to account for as many variables as possible (Baker et al., 2013; Harris, 2011), the factors that undoubtedly impact student achievement and growth over time but are not included when estimating value-added still seem to be causing bias (Glazerman & Potamites, 2011; Newton et al., 2010; Rothstein, 2009, 2010b). This is true even when the most sophisticated controls have been deployed (Capitol Hill Briefing, 2011; Chingos & Peterson, 2011; Dills & Mulholland, 2010; Guarino, Maxfield, et al., 2012: Guarino, Reckase, et al. 2012; Hermann et al., 2013; Koedel & Betts, 2009, 2010; Newton et al., 2010; Stacy et al., 2012; Tate, 2004).

Last, whether missing data are indeed missing at random (Bracey, 2004a; Braun, 2005; Harris, 2008; Lockwood, McCaffrey, Mariano, et al., 2007; Rubin et al., 2004; Sanders, 2006; Sanders et al., 2009; Wilson et al., 2007; Wright et al., 1997), regardless of whether the missing data are replaced via methods of data imputation, is also of concern (as discussed in Chapter 5). Students who are often absent or highly transient are most likely to be missing data; these students are also often from low-income households, have English language deficiencies, are enrolled in special education or remedial programs, etc. These are the very risk variables at issue in terms of VAM-based bias.

Lockwood, McCaffrey, Mariano, et al. (2007), for example, found that for the five years of student achievement data they used to estimate teacher-level value-added, only 20% of students had complete testing data for reading/language arts and mathematics. This is yet another huge problem for VAMs. Corcoran (2010) found that approximately 14% of the students in a large, high-needs district (the Houston Independent School District) were missing test scores for any typical year; African American, ELLs, and recent immigrants were missing data at significantly higher rates. When these students are not randomly placed into classes and their missing scores are treated as "any other unknown parameter" (Lockwood, McCaffrey, Mariano, et al., 2007, p. 135), this too contributes to the bias present across VAMs (Bausell, 2013; Braun, 2004, 2005; Corcoran, 2010; Harris, 2008; Lockwood & McCaffrey, 2009; McCaffrey et al., 2004b; Rubin et al., 2004; Wright et al., 1997).

That said, what is known, and pretty much agreed upon, is that VAMs altogether function better and yield less bias when more statistical controls are used (Ehlert et al., 2012; Harris, 2011; Hill et al., 2011; Koedel & Betts, 2007, 2009, 2010; Newton et al., 2010). Clearly, however, "value-added models do not account for every factor that might contribute to student learning." The question then becomes "whether [VAMs] account for enough variables so that any factors not controlled by the model are not persistently associated with teachers" in terms of bias (McCaffrey, 2012). Without a better understanding and possible accounting for student placement decisions when producing model estimates, we are left with a series of "tentative causal conclusion[s] based on partial evidence drawn from … uncontrolled stud[ies] of [classrooms], schools and districts" (Braun, 2008; see also Bausell, 2013).

What must be understood better is the extent to which student placement practices are effectively, if not formally, random; whether student achievement matters as much as some assume it does when students are assigned to classrooms; in what ways students are otherwise assigned to classrooms; and what all of this might mean for value-added. We must better understand how placement occurs in practice to better determine whether what VAM researchers are typically accounting for can reasonably account for selection bias, and make non-random assignment as strongly ignorable as is so often assumed (Reardon & Raudenbush, 2009; Rosenbaum & Rubin, 1983; see also Ballou et al., 2004; Bill & Melinda Gates Foundation, 2013; Glazerman & Potamites, 2011; Goldhaber & Chaplin, 2011; Guarino, Reckase, et al., 2012; Harris, 2011; McCaffrey, 2012; McCaffrey et al., 2004b; Meyer & Dokumaci, 2010).

Student placement practices

Whether students have been randomly assigned to schools and classrooms has not mattered much in the past, because, until recently, teachers were not typically held accountable for the test scores their students attained (i.e., once per year on traditional "snapshot" standardized tests). Most administrators who evaluated teachers, as well as the teachers themselves, realized that the non-random placement of students into classrooms could not be accounted for and thus should neither be used to gauge the teachers' effectiveness nor influence ratings of their performance, positively or negatively. It did not make sense, for example, to penalize teachers whose classes were populated with more "difficult to teach" students, nor to reward teachers of classes disproportionately filled with higher-achieving students. All of this, of course, also assumes that using a single test derived via a large-scale standardized achievement test that is not representative of the entire curriculum is okay as well. But it isn't.

Relatively limited research has been conducted to explore how students are assigned to classrooms in schools, particularly in the context of value-added (Burns & Mason, 1995;

Center for Education Policy Research, 2012; Dills & Mulholland, 2010; Monk, 1987; Player, 2010; Praisner, 2003). In chronological order, Monk (1987) found that the use of categories, often based on student demographic variables and previous academic performance, was the most common method used to assign students to classrooms. Burns and Mason (1995) concluded that principals of traditional or single-track schools had greater flexibility in creating heterogeneous classrooms based on students' ethnicity, gender, behaviors, language proficiency, parental requests, and previous interactions with teachers or other students. In multi-track schools, however, principals attempted to cluster students homogeneously with consideration given to students' giftedness, special education needs, and language proficiency, in efforts to alleviate instructional and behavioral challenges.

Praisner (2003) found that placement decisions, especially for students with disabilities, were largely affected by principals' attitudes, values, and professional coursework and training. Dills and Mulholland (2010) demonstrated issues with the ways students are placed into certain classes with certain class sizes using students' demographic variables (e.g., prior student behaviors). Player (2010) found that, especially as a form of non-monetary compensation or benefit, principals had an incentive to assign higher-achieving students into the classes of the teachers they favored most and to assign lower-achieving students (i.e., students eligible for free or reduced-cost lunches, or with disabilities) into the classes of the teachers they favored less. The Center for Education Policy Research (2012) found that lower-achieving students are disproportionately placed into classrooms with first-year and other novice teachers (see also Clotfelter, Ladd, & Vigdor, 2006; Player, 2010).

However, as stated, no studies exist in which researchers have systematically explored how non-random student placement practices might be linked to bias in value-added estimates. Again, it is evident that non-random student placement practices occur, but how, why, and to what extent non-random student placements bias value-added estimates still warrants further research. While researchers are increasingly demonstrating evidence that suggests non-random assignment and sorting practices continue to bias value-added estimates, even when the most sophisticated statistics and controls are used, how, why, and to what extent all of this occurs remains uncertain (Hermann et al., 2013; Hill et al., 2011; McCaffrey et al., 2004b; Newton et al., 2010; Rothstein, 2009, 2010b; Stacy et al., 2012; see also Baker et al., 2010).

Most recently, and perhaps most notably, Mathematica Policy Research statisticians demonstrated that the VAM-based estimates for teachers who teach inordinate numbers of students with "harder-to-predict" achievement (i.e., students with relatively lower prior levels of achievement and who receive free or reduced-cost lunches) are less precise, despite the sophisticated controls used (Hermann et al., 2013; see also McCaffrey, 2012). They also evidenced that the methods typically employed to control for the non-random placement of students into classrooms across most VAMs (e.g., shrinkage estimation methods like the Empirical Bayes approach) do not work effectively (Hermann et al., 2013; see also Guarino, Reckase, et al., 2012; Tate, 2004). This was also supported by Guarino, Maxfield, et al. (2012) who wrote that, "although these estimators generally perform well under random assignment of teachers to classrooms, their performance generally suffers under non-random assignment when students are grouped based on prior achievement" (p. 1).

Hill et al. (2011) demonstrated that within-school sorting of higher achieving students into the classes of more effective teachers biased estimates even when the biasing variables were statistically accounted for in the models. While this was more evident among the more simplistic VAMs used, this also occurred when more sophisticated models were employed.

McCaffrey et al. (2004b) demonstrated that the same teachers consistently demonstrated more measurable effectiveness when they taught higher-achieving students, fewer ELLs, and fewer students from low-income backgrounds. They concluded that, "student characteristics are likely to confound estimated teacher effects when schools serve distinctly different populations" (p. 67; see also Baker et al., 2010; McCaffrey et al., 2004a). Stacy et al. (2012) evidenced that students from low socioeconomic backgrounds and with relatively lower levels of past achievement yielded less accurate teacher-level value-added estimates than their more advantaged peers.

Linn (2001), Ballou (2002), and Kupermintz (2003) demonstrated that the blocking strategies statisticians use with the EVAAS® do not effectively eliminate bias either, as teachers in classrooms and schools with highly homogenous and relatively higher racial minority populations still tended to exhibit lower value-added after the strategies were applied (see also Goldhaber et al., 2012; McCaffrey, 2012; McCaffrey et al., 2004b; Stacy et al., 2012). Guarino, Reckase, et al. (2012) supported this as well (see also Guarino, Maxfield, et al., 2012).

Newton et al. (2010) found that teachers' value-added estimates were significantly and negatively correlated with whether teachers taught inordinate proportions of ELLs, students who came from low socioeconomic backgrounds, and Hispanic students. Inversely, teachers' value-added estimates were significantly and positively correlated with whether teachers taught inordinate proportions of Asian American students and students with more educated parents (see Table 7.1). Researchers also found that teachers' value-added estimates were significantly and positively correlated with whether teachers taught inordinate proportions of girls in reading/language arts and students who were tracked in mathematics. Generally speaking, these biasing factors also seemed to yield more bias with less sophisticated value-added models (with Model 1 being the least "sophisticated" and Model 5 being the most "sophisticated"). While the models that controlled for student demographics (Models 2, 4, and 5) seemed to lower the magnitude of the correlations, these correlations were still statistically significant.

Also notable, Rothstein (2009, 2010b) conducted a falsification test by which he tested, counter-intuitively, whether a teacher in the future could have an impact on his/her students' levels of achievement in the past. He demonstrated that, given non-random student placement (and tracking) practices, value-added estimates of future teachers could be used to predict students' past levels of achievement. More generally, he demonstrated that both typical and complex VAMs demonstrate counterfactual effects and do not mitigate bias because students are systematically grouped in ways that explicitly bias value-added estimates. Otherwise, the backwards predictions Rothstein demonstrated could not have been made (see also Briggs & Domingue, 2011; Scherrer, 2011), although Rothstein's work is not without its critics either (Goldhaber & Chaplin, 2011; Koedel & Betts, 2009).

Otherwise, only two studies to date have actually used (or attempted to use) randomized methods to test for selection bias. Kane & Staiger (2008) asserted that accounting for student's prior achievement histories was "sufficient" to control for selection bias or selection on non-observable variables. However, the definition of "sufficient" was left open to interpretation (as it was in the case of the EVAAS®). The VAM estimates were produced using the imperfect Empirical Bayes methods (Hermann et al., 2013; Stacy et al., 2012; see also Chetty et al., 2011). Results applied to a narrow sample of compliant schools (Guarino, Reckase, et al., 2012; Harris & Anderson, 2013). More importantly, results were not generated via a true randomized experiment. Students were not randomly assigned to classrooms, but "principals

Table 7.1 Statistically significant correlations among teachers' VAM estimates and classroom composition

	ELL		Low-income		Asian		Hispanic		Parent education	
	Math	*ELA*	*Math*	*ELA*	*Math*	*ELA*	*Math*	*ELA*	*Math*	*ELA*
Model 1	−.38***	−.48***	−.27*	−.45***	+.27*	+.31***	−.33**	−.43***	+.34**	+.48***
Model 2	−.37***	−.31***	−.25*	−.20*	+.18	+.24*	−.27*	−.26**	+.28**	+.32**
Model 3	−.37***	−.42***	−.30**	−.30**	+.31**	+.30**	−.35**	−.39***	+.35**	+.38***
Model 4	−.31**	−.31**	−.31**	−.18	+.24*	+.31**	−.32**	−.30**	+.32**	+.31**
Model 5	−.29**	−.36***	−.34***	−.22*	+.29**	+.29**	−.34**	−.34***	+.34**	+.32**

Source: Adapted with permission from Newton et al. 2010.

Notes
★ *p* < 0.10.
★★ *p* < 0.05.
★★★ *p* < 0.01.

in each of the schools were asked to draw up two classrooms they would be equally happy to have assigned to each of [78 pairs of] teachers.... The school district office then randomly assigned the classrooms to [each pair of] teachers" (Kane & Staiger, 2008, p. 2).

Related, in the final Bill and Melinda Gates Foundation Measures of Effective Teaching (MET) study (2013), again, "principals created rosters of students for each class in the study, and then researchers randomly assigned each roster to a participating teacher from among those who could teach the class" (Bill & Melinda Gates Foundation, 2013, p. 6). However, a large majority of participating schools and teachers backed out of their agreements to safeguard and follow through with the study's randomized design, leaving only about one quarter to two thirds of the students randomly placed in the classrooms to which they were assigned. This impeded the validity of the study findings (Banchero, 2013; Rothstein & Mathis, 2013; Sawchuck, 2013b; Simon, 2013), although study statisticians argued that they could statistically control for this attrition as well using "instrumental variables" regardless (Bill & Melinda Gates Foundation, 2013; Sawchuck, 2013b).

Nonetheless, the majority of the aforementioned researchers have evidenced that the value-added estimates of teachers who teach largely homogenous groups of students, students who are often non-randomly placed or sorted into classrooms, are still biased despite the sophistication of the controls and estimators used to eliminate bias. As major studies continue to evidence that non-random sorting practices complicate unbiased estimates, and as preliminary evidence suggests that principals are beginning to use even more non-random methods to assign students to the teachers they want to protect (or dismiss) (Amrein-Beardsley & Collins, 2012; Banchero & Kesmodel, 2011; Burris as cited in Strauss, 2012b; Monk, 1987; Ravitch, 2012c; Springer et al., 2010; see also Burris & Welner, 2011; Ishii & Rivkin, 2009; Koedel & Betts, 2009; Rothstein, 2010b, 2011), value-added researchers must continue to acknowledge that this issue deserves even more serious attention (Capitol Hill Briefing, 2011; Corcoran, 2010; Hermann et al., 2013; Hill et al., 2011; Ishii & Rivkin, 2009; Linn, 2008; McCaffrey et al., 2004b; Nelson, 2011; Newton et al., 2010; Rothstein, 2009, 2010b; Stacy et al., 2012), and that it is especially concerning in terms of the potential lawsuits bound to come (Baker, 2011; Baker et al., 2013; Pullin, 2013; Sawchuck, 2013c).

Arizona study

In this study,[6] we investigated the methods that elementary school principals in Arizona typically use to assign students to classrooms. As described, while some things are known regarding how students are placed into classrooms in general, researchers sought to more fully explicate and understand this in the context of value-added. The specific goals here were to add to our collective thinking in terms of the methods elementary school principals currently and typically use to assign students to classrooms, to better understand to what extent teachers and parents play a role in assignment processes and procedures, and to draw implications regarding how such practices might impact value-added estimates and inferences.

The question of whether certain placement practices indeed impacted value-added estimates under varying conditions was not directly examined or explored given a lack of comparable statewide data. Rather, researchers conducted this study on the previously stated assumptions that value-added statisticians often make when controlling for prior student achievement, student background variables, and the other observable variables often used as proxies for the non-observable variables also in play. The fundamental question here was whether the non-random student assignment practices discovered might logically lead to biased VAM estimates, if the non-random student sorting practices went beyond that which is typically controlled for in most VAM models (e.g., students' testing histories, special education status, English language proficiency, gender, giftedness, race/ethnicity, socioeconomic status).

For example, if student behaviors are frequently used to sort students into classrooms but student behaviors are not typically accounted for, as in most VAMs, it is reasonable to assert that sorting students by their past and anticipated future behaviors could be contributing to at least some of the bias being observed. This is especially salient taking into consideration that the records that might effectively capture students' behavior, discipline histories, suspension records, and other self-handicapping behaviors are not often available for inclusion in statistical controls, not to mention how inconsistent these records can be across classrooms, schools, and districts with varying student discipline policies and procedures. Accordingly, it is reasonable to suspect that sorting practices using student attributes outside of the scope of the VAM datasets might bias estimates, even if other sophisticated controls are in place.

Arizona study results

Researchers found that, for most principals,[7] the assignment of students was not discussed during their professional or administrative coursework or during any other professional development they had received. Most principals noted, as well, that their district policy manuals did not prescribe or mention a procedure for placing students into classrooms. This has implications for value-added given the heightened policy and pragmatic interest in VAMs and the amplified attention given to the degree to which the non-random sorting of students into classrooms matters (Bill & Melinda Gates Foundation, 2013; Harris, 2011; Meyer & Dokumaci, 2010; Rivkin & Ishii, 2008).

Variables that matter

If anything, principals reported being advised to consider student background characteristics during the student assignment process, citing as most important: students' prior academic achievement, prior behavioral issues, language status and/or levels of proficiency, perceived behavioral needs, and prior grades and/or scores on large-scale standardized tests, all of which could ostensibly be accounted for using the most sophisticated VAMs. Principals also somewhat considered students' disciplinary records and minimally considered students' racial/ethnic backgrounds, rates of absenteeism, transience, and least often reported considering students' socioeconomic status when making placement decisions. Almost all of these, besides perhaps student transience, behavior, and disciplinary records, are observable variables typically controlled for across most VAMs.

Otherwise, principals identified students' prior behaviors and interactions with other students as critical factors that influence the placement process. Principals indicated that interactions among students, whether positive or negative, significantly impacted the learning environment in classrooms and, as such, played a significant role in determining where students were to be placed in the following school year. For example, one principal described a commonly reported practice, whereby teachers provide "information on behavior issues and/or students that should be placed in separate classes. Anything useful that can assist in the best placement for their students into the next grade" is important. Another principal noted that a student's peer-to-peer interactions can dramatically change classroom dynamics; "if students do have some behavior issues when they are with [certain] peers, they may be assigned to separate classes the next year."

Related, principals stated that placement decisions often depend upon students' learning styles and interactions with their prior teachers as critical factors too. One principal explained:

> Teachers are generally asked to build class loads. We do this to balance out the character of the teacher and students. We believe that this is helpful to have the best model to help kids do well within a class setting. Sometimes we get it wrong, and we change it as needed.

The practice of placing students based on their behaviors in addition to their prior interactions with their teachers, their teachers' varying instructional and management styles, and general personality matches was also often informed by the comments and recommendations made by teachers. For example, principals noted that teachers "assist [in] matching student personalities to teacher personalities" because "students may relate better to a specific teacher." Principals reported that they relied heavily on teachers' input and advice when making recommendations, especially in regards to how students responded to them as teachers in the past. Placing a student with a "particular teacher that [a prior teacher felt] the child would be most successful with" or "who would best fit [the] learning needs [of the student]" was also often the norm.

The fundamental question here was whether the variables used when non-randomly assigning students to classrooms might logically lead to biased VAM estimates, especially if the variables used went beyond those which are typically controlled for in most VAM models. Researchers found that while the factors that are typically controlled for in most VAMs are typically valued when students are assigned to classrooms, the use of these variables to sort students into classrooms is done in highly subjective ways. It is not that teachers and principals, for example, reported using students' prior academic achievement records and systematically sorting students into classrooms objectively on that factor alone. Rather, principals reported subjectively considering achievement, prior grades,[8] or both, but doing so loosely alongside teachers (and sometimes parents) and using a wide variety of other factors and variables, including variables for which VAM researchers typically do not control (i.e., students' prior behaviors, their behavior issues with certain other students, their prior interactions with their teachers, students' being more successful with certain teachers using varying instructional and management styles, and general teacher–student personality matches).

Homogeneous and heterogeneous classrooms

Complicating things further, principals often reported using student information cards for general student placement procedures. Some of these procedures were used to create more heterogeneous classes and others were used to support homogeneity; all were viewed as being in students' best learning interests.

One principal explained:

> We fill out Pink/Blue cards with a detailed description of each child from reading/math scores to behaviors and other pertinent information. We also use an environment

form we give parents to feel out what best describes the needs of their child so if possible we can match personalities of child and teacher. We look to have a "balanced" classroom for each teacher.

Another principal described using student information cards in a different context:

> Our feeder schools have each teacher complete a "card" with some brief data about the student (i.e., high [or] low skills in reading and math). [Teachers] list any behavior concerns as well as any other important information.... Students are then randomly placed into classes based on gender and the above areas balancing the number of IEP students [students with individualized education programs], males/females, etc.

In these cases, it could be argued that the use of student information cards to create heterogeneous or seemingly similar classrooms would make bias less likely in value-added estimates. Perhaps this is true. However, other principals reported using different methods, namely cluster grouping models, with other goals in mind. These principals described the use of prescribed cluster grouping models, such as The Schoolwide Cluster Grouping Method (SCGM) (Winebrenner, Brulles, & Kingore, 2008), when placing students into groups or tracks, to yield more homogeneous groupings. For example, one respondent wrote, "We are a gifted cluster school which means [that] students identified as gifted go into one class at each grade level. The rest of the students in that class are approaching or meeting the standards." Other principals noted valuing clusters for students with special needs as part of the inclusion models at their schools. As mentioned, and as per the current research on bias in value-added estimates, this would be more likely to create bias in value-added estimates (Baker et al., 2010; Capitol Hill Briefing, 2011; Goldhaber et al., 2012; Kupermintz, 2003; McCaffrey et al., 2004b; Newton et al., 2010; Rothstein & Mathis, 2013; Stacy et al., 2012).

Results here suggest that, while principals often seek to "balance" classrooms as much as possible regarding student characteristics, in an effort to create more heterogeneous, harmonious learning environments, there are many noteworthy exceptions. These inconsistencies imply that principals across the state use very different and even contradictory methods for the same purpose – to place students in a manner that they, often idiosyncratically and highly unsystematically, view as fair and equitable and in their students' (and teachers') best educational interests. Again, these assignment methods often involved teachers, as well as parents if parental input was acknowledged or received.

Teacher involvement

As mentioned, results indicated that teachers are highly involved in the student placement process. Principal respondents provided detailed descriptions of the role that teachers typically play in the placement process, where teachers, working individually or collaboratively within grade level teams, were sometimes charged with creating preliminary class lists based on the aforementioned characteristics. It is important to note, as well, that many principals specifically expressed their confidence in their teaching staff, describing their teachers as those best equipped to make such student placement decisions.

A principal captured this by writing:

> They [the teachers] may know which teacher would be the best fit for their student moving to the next grade level. They also know which students may/may not work well together in the same class. They know the student best in the educational setting.

When placing students with the assistance of teachers, though, principals often reviewed these lists to make changes as needed. Principals never reported that it was solely the teachers' responsibility to make placement decisions and principals frequently reported that they provided guidelines for teachers when constructing the preliminary lists. For example, principals noted that they often ask teachers to take into consideration students' behaviors and the learning needs of students with their forthcoming teachers' instructional and classroom management styles, personalities, and other strengths/weaknesses. One principal explained that teachers "complete a paper on each student . . . [and] list which, if any, particular teachers they feel the child would be most successful with and why." Another principal noted the importance of teachers providing "learning modality information about students that helps in assigning students to match teaching strengths of teachers." Another wrote that (s)he has "some teachers who have strengths regarding language who can more effectively work with some demographics or even request [to] work with some of the most in need."

When reviewing these preliminary assignments, however, several principals again noted the need for "balanced," "equal," and "fair" classes. One principal noted, for example, that (s)he worked to ensure that "no classes are 'stacked' for a particular teacher." Respondents frequently suggested that, by making changes to class lists as needed, mismatched placements could be remedied before the school year began as well. Notably, as well, about one in ten respondents emphasized the need for input from others, including special education and special area teachers as well as support staff. While this is appropriately inclusive, in terms of value-added and attempts to control for the bias that seemingly comes about as a result of non-random student placement procedures, this also makes things even more complicated.

Parental involvement

A majority (60%) of responding principals noted that parents request specific placements for their children; more than one third of principals noted that they honored more than 80% of such parental requests. When asked to describe the circumstances under which the principal would consider the parents' requests legitimate, principals most often cited requests based on students' learning styles, prior or current negative experiences between parents, students' siblings/relatives, and teachers, or prior or current issues with students and the student's peers.

In terms of students' learning styles, some principals noted that they would honor a parent request regarding what the parent perceived was the best learning environment for his/her child. One principal described a situation as follows:

> I will always meet and discuss [placements] with parents at their request. Occasionally the request is driven by a medical need or an IEP need. We attempt to provide input to the process for parents via parent input forms though there is a low rate of completion . . . as [the form] does not specify [a] teacher but rather [the] learning needs of the

child. I'd always consider a request for a type of assignment . . . though we do not enter-
tain requests for particular teachers.

Second, principals also cited prior or current negative interactions as legitimate reasons to
honor parental requests. One principal explained that (s)he would move a student to another
class if unable to "remediate [the] problem between [the] parent and teacher even after [a]
discussion [as a result of] a previous problem with the teacher with an older sibling." While a
few principals expressed a willingness to make a placement change under such circumstances,
they also expressed their desire to attempt to resolve any issues prior to moving the student,
however.

For example, a principal explained his/her response to such requests:

> Once teacher assignments are made, I typically have 8 to 10 change requests from
> parents. I meet with the parent and listen to their concern. Typically, I require the
> parent to try the assigned teacher. If after a two-week trial period, the concern remains,
> we meet with the teacher and try to resolve the issue within the classroom. If the issue
> then remains unresolved, I make a classroom change.

Another principal explained:

> Current-year teachers supply the information used to balance out the classes. Teachers
> of the incoming classes only have input regarding students of families with whom they
> have had prior negative experiences. Avoiding situations that are predestined for prob-
> lems is much easier before the classroom assignment has been made.

Another principal stated that he or she would change a student's placement "when all parties
agree and it's truly in the best interest of the child."

Finally, some principals referred to past or current conflicts between students as a legitimate reason to honor parental requests and place students in separate classrooms or change a
placement once the school year had begun. One principal, for example, described a rare
instance where (s)he might consider a new placement, explaining that a change might be
necessary "if there is a bullying issue in the classroom or conflict with another student that
[could not] be resolved with regular inventions."

In sum, principals frequently noted that parents cared about their children's learning styles,
personalities, and interpersonal interactions with other students and teachers. From the
parents' perspectives, as well as the teachers' and principals' perspectives, these were critical
factors that influenced the student placement process.

The implications here stem from the fact that we can logically assume that when parents
are actively involved in their children's classroom placements, they are likely to be more
involved in their children's educations outside of the classroom too (e.g., they might contribute more time and money to support their children's academics, perhaps in general or
even more so if they perceive their children's teachers are inadequate or of low quality). Such
increased parental involvement also biases VAM-based estimates (Bausell, 2013; Reardon &
Raudenbush, 2009; Rivkin & Ishii, 2008).

Moreover, it is uncertain what variables might ever be able to effectively capture these
considerations when attempting to account for the non-random placement of students into

classrooms, or, more specifically, the extent to which controlling for behaviors, learning styles, personalities, and interpersonal interactions might cause bias in value-added estimates. For example, how might methodologists control for students being placed with a particular teacher that others felt "the child[ren] would be most successful with." Or how might methodologists take into consideration that more than one third of principals who noted that they honored more than 80% of parents' requests, also honored what parents' subjectively perceived as their children's best interests? Indeed, most data sets have very limited information that is related "both to commitment to schooling and home resources available to support education" (Ishii & Rivkin, 2009, p. 522).

As such, "[a]ny failure to account adequately for family [and other similar] differences contaminates estimates of teacher quality *unless* students are randomly sorted into classrooms" (Ishii & Rivkin, 2009, p. 522 [emphasis added]; see also Briggs & Domingue, 2011; Corcoran, 2010; Harris, 2009c). It is clear that "value-added models do not account for every factor that might contribute to student learning; the question is whether they account for *enough* variables so that any factors not controlled by the model are not persistently associated with teachers" (McCaffrey, 2012). It seems clear, from these and other research findings, that *enough* variables will likely *never* be controlled for, given the very virtue of the highly idiosyncratic, subjective, interactive, complex, and disparate ways students are assigned to classrooms, beyond considerations of achievement and the other observable variables included within most VAMs. Until the uncontrollable variables become observable, and hence controllable, one can only speculate about how the exclusion of the plethora of unobservable variables might bias value-added estimates in both positive and negative ways.

On random assignment

Lastly, and also importantly, by matching students with teachers in ways that principals thought created the best outcomes for their students, principals rejected the idea of random assignment. Almost all (98.0%) of responding principals, noted that random assignment to classrooms was not general practice, very few principals included the term "random" in their written responses describing their student placement practices, and the majority (68%) of respondents suggested that the use of random methods of assignment would be nonsensical, even if random assignment produced more valid value-added estimates. Almost half of the respondents (48.0%) also believed that random assignment methods, if ever mandated or required for research purposes, would prove impractical and even detrimental. This finding may represent what occurred with the Bill and Melinda Gates Foundation's (2013) MET study, where the large majority of participating schools and teachers backed out of their agreements to safeguard and follow through with the study's randomized design (Banchero, 2013; Rothstein & Mathis, 2013; Sawchuck, 2013a; Simon, 2013).

While a quarter (25%) of responding principals acknowledged that random placement methods might have some potential benefits, specifically acknowledging that random placement methods would be necessary if teacher evaluations were based, at least in part, on the collective test score gains posted by students over time, they also noted that the random placement of students contradicted their own educational philosophies. However, they never appeared to consider the inequitable learning environments that may be resulting otherwise, given their perceived view of their non-random student placement practices as the more appropriate procedures. Regardless, principals thought that random assignment would be inappropriate and even harmful to students. One respondent noted that a "luck of the draw" approach would only "build inequity." Another summarized his/her commitment to indi-vidualized, albeit time-consuming placement procedures, noting: "I would much rather take the time and find a good match between a student and teacher . . . it is very important that we have a suitable match that is a win-win for everyone." Another explained:

> You get what effort you put in. That is if you just shuffle the deck and assign them, you are in for a big mess. Put in the hard work up front and receive the benefits in the end. Plus, one teacher may be strong in reading instruction and that is what certain students need. Why would you not give them that teacher?

Echoing this sentiment another added:

> I think that random assignment to a classroom is unthinkable. This day and age when we have so much information (data) on students, we need to use that information to make all decisions in order to offer the best education possible for each student.

Another expressed his/her disapproval of random assignment by stating, "I prefer careful, thoughtful, and intentional placement [of students] to random. I've never considered using random placement. These are children, human beings." And another respondent explained that, "anything done randomly will get random results. If assignment of students is done stra-tegically with a goal in mind (student success) then there is a higher likelihood of meeting that goal." This presents an interesting conundrum whereby random assignment is necessary to improve VAM-based analyses, but random assignment is overwhelmingly viewed as harmful to children.

That said, it is evident here that even if principals value fairness, equity, and justice, which most if not all of them certainly do, the random assignment of students into classrooms will probably never be the professionals' practice of choice (see also Burns & Mason, 1995). Prin-cipals emphasized the importance of classrooms that could be constructed purposefully, and they insisted that what they deemed purposeful placement ensured classrooms that were in students' best educational and developmental interests, encouraged teacher success, and ulti-mately promoted student learning and achievement. This unquestionably has implications, particularly for researchers who repeatedly debate and argue (in many ways correctly) that value-added analyses will likely never be done well without random assignment practices in place (Corcoran, 2010; Glazerman & Potamites, 2011; Harris, 2009c, 2011; Ishii & Rivkin, 2009; Linn, 2008; Nelson, 2011; Reardon & Raudenbush, 2009; Rothstein, 2009, 2010b; Schochet & Chiang, 2010).

Conclusions

It is argued here that the purposeful, non-random assignment of students into classrooms indeed biases value-added estimates and the interpretation of teachers' value-added scores. Many researchers agree, also noting that if all students, including general, ELLs, and main-streamed special education students, could be randomly assigned to classes, the validity and the confidence with which researchers, policymakers, and practitioners could make conse-quential decisions using value-added scores would be substantially increased (Corcoran, 2010;

Ishii & Rivkin, 2009; Linn, 2008; Nelson, 2011; Rothstein, 2009). As the random assignment of students presumably mitigates bias in teacher effectiveness estimates, such assignment practices would *help* to control for varying student populations and their impact on value-added scores (Ballou et al., 2004; Kupermintz, 2003; McCaffrey et al., 2004b; Tekwe et al., 2004).

Researchers found, however, that principals were greatly opposed to using random methods in lieu of placement practices based on human judgment, practices they collectively agreed were in students' best interests. Random assignment was deemed highly nonsensical, even if it would provide more valid (and more reliable) value-added estimates.

Researchers also found that teachers and parents play a prodigious role in the placement process, in almost nine out of ten schools. They provide both appreciated and sometimes unwelcome insights regarding what they perceive to be the best learning environments for their students or children.

Otherwise, student characteristics, namely prior academic achievement, special education needs, and giftedness heavily influence placement decisions. However, students' prior behaviors, students' interactions with their teachers and peers, students' and parents' current and/or prior negative experiences with teachers, and the like (all of which are not typically controlled for within VAMs) are also frequently taken into consideration when placing students. These factors also serve as legitimate reasons for class changes during the school year, although whether these factors might ever be captured and controlled for in VAM analyses is tentative at best.

Given the widespread use of purposeful, non-random methods of placement as evidenced, value-added researchers, policymakers, and educators, particularly those whose effectiveness is being measured, should carefully consider the implications of their placement decisions, since the myriad of assignment practices will likely continue to bias the value-added estimates now being used in so many teacher and school evaluation systems across the nation.

"There is no other device for excluding biases in social sciences than to face the valuations and to introduce them as explicitly stated, specific, and sufficiently concretized value premises" (Myrdal, 1944, p. 1043). While science does not require that we eliminate 100% of bias, it does demand that we take bias into account when making valid interpretations (Messick, 1975; see also Hill, 2009; McCaffrey, 2012; Rothstein, 2009). This is especially important when highly consequential decisions are to be made using biased, in this case, value-added estimates. This is when logic, or a lack thereof, "demands a careful look under the hood. This is just due diligence" (Braun, 2005, p. 16).

Box 7.1 Top 10 assertions

1 Individual VAM-based estimates cannot be produced for approximately 60–70% of all teachers across America's public schools. This is an issue of VAM-related fairness, or a lack thereof.

2 The 60–70% of teachers who are not eligible for individual VAM estimates are often assigned aggregated school-level VAM estimates instead, sometimes for consequential purposes (e.g., merit pay) even though their estimates are based on even more factors outside of their control.

3   Teachers at the top or bottom of typical VAM distributions (i.e., bell curves) tend to have less accurate value-added estimates for a variety of reasons, while teachers in the middle of the distribution might also be susceptible to invalid interpretations due to inaccuracies.

4   VAM-based estimates for teachers who over time teach more homogeneous populations of certain students (e.g., ELLs, special education students, students receiving free or reduced-cost lunches, students retained in grade for multiple years) are most adversely impacted by bias.

5   Bias is even more prevalent in high school and middle school settings where students are more likely to be tracked into specialized classrooms within schools.

6   VAM-based decisions should be accurate and appropriate, all the while taking into consideration the type of students a teacher teaches. This will forever require human judgment.

7   When teachers yield consistent value-added estimates over time, this may not be due to consistency in terms of the reliability desired and needed as a precondition to validity, but may be due to consistency that might instead be caused by bias.

8   With value-added analyses, the random assignment of students into classrooms (and students into schools) is the ideal empirical approach if valid causal estimates are to be realized and if ever differences in value-added estimates are to be attributed to true teacher effects.

9   Students are not randomly assigned to classrooms, however, and administrators, teachers, and parents play prodigious roles in student placement processes, making student sorting highly non-random and true causal statements all the more elusive.

10   While science does not require that researchers eliminate 100% of bias, science does demand that researchers take bias into account, using human judgment, when making the most valid interpretations possible, all things considered.

Notes

1 Ceiling effects are observed when students score extremely high on their first observation (e.g., in the case of gifted students). Then, because there is no place higher to go in the test score distribution, the test scores hit a "ceiling" and regress backwards towards the mean or average.

2 Test scores also "regress to the mean" when they are extremely low on their first observation (e.g., in the case of very low–performing students), and because there is no place lower to go in the test score distribution, the test scores hit a "floor" and regress forward towards the mean or average instead.

3 This is one reason why value-added technicians encourage using shrunken estimates to account for such measurement errors, as well as multiple years of estimates over time to theoretically generate more accurate classifications (Harris, 2011; McCaffrey et al., 2008; Sanders et al., 2009).

4 In 1995, Gene V. Glass asked TVAAS (now EVAAS®) developers,

> how it could be fair to compare the gains in achievement of students from one teacher to the next if the abilities (on average) of the students in the classes differed substantially [due to non-random assignment]. To this question, TVAAS ... gave the incredible answer that it was an empirical fact that in their data there is no difference in the gains of bright children and slow children.... This artifact is not because bright and slow children actually learn at the same rates; it is because the TVAAS system of calculating gains surely uses a form of least-squares estimation that forces the pre-year measures to be uncorrelated with the post-year measures.

(Glass, 1995)

5 Probably the most sophisticated VAM, when it comes to the control variables that might be used if available, is the VARC system. Conducting their (controversial) research in New York City, VARC statisticians reportedly controlled for (at the student and classroom levels) students' prior year test score(s), gender, race/ethnicity, ELL and former ELL status, disabilities, free or reduced-cost lunch status, summer school attendance, absences, suspensions, retention in grade before the tested year, whether students attended the same school or switched schools, and whether students were new to the city in the pre- or post-test year (Briggs & Domingue, 2011).

6 The major pieces of this research were first published in Paufler & Amrein-Beardsley, 2013.

7 In this survey, a statistically representative sample of principals participated in this study ($n = 378/1,265$, 30.0%). While the sample of respondents was large enough to draw conclusions given statistical power and acceptable/low levels of standard errors, without representativeness ensured, researchers still could not make a strong case that the results of this study generalize across similar settings, people, and other like samples, for example, across other states. For more specifics about this study or this study's methods, see Paufler & Amrein-Beardsley, 2013.

8 Some principals reported using students' prior grades to make placement decisions, but whether students' grades can be effectively captured using students' prior test scores is questionable given the lower than expected correlations among grades and test scores, which are often the result of major discrepancies caused by grading variation across classrooms, schools, and districts (Ricketts, 2010; Willingham, Pollack, & Lewis, 2000). This might also cause concerns about bias in this context as well.

PART IV

Alternatives, Solutions, and Conclusions

8

ALTERNATIVES, SOLUTIONS, AND CONCLUSIONS

Any intelligent fool can make things bigger and more complex.... It takes a touch of genius – and a lot of courage to move in the opposite direction.

Albert Einstein

Measurement purists continue to promote number-dominant approaches for teacher (and school/district) accountability purposes using a "faulty analogy" that this is how the private sector evaluates its employees (Baker et al., 2010, p. 6). If it works for the private sector, it should work for the education sector as well, or so it is too often implied. However, this faulty analogy is based on even more faulty assumptions. For example, managers working in the most successful companies around the world do not publicly rate their employees from far-removed locations, examining only spreadsheets about employees' sales and net profits. Instead, they rely *mainly* on human judgment, as well as judgment about the quantitative indicators of effectiveness (e.g., growth in sales) on which the successes and profit-abilities of their businesses depend (see also Cronbach & Gleser, 1965).

The CEOs of these companies trust their managers, and they especially trust them to make human judgments and high-stakes decisions about their employees as needed. The CEOs of these companies do not view their companies as machines. Nor do they view their employees as lab rats vying for pellets or other external motivators, with inputs and outputs to be objectively measured using a variety of valid indicators of competency, and those responsible for sufficient or insufficient outputs are to be rewarded or penalized, respectively. Rather, the CEOs of the most successful companies throughout the world consider their companies as communities of professionals in which managers inspire, serve, and work with their colleagues as the professionals they, for the most part, are (James, 2012; see also Baker et al., 2010).

Alternatives

So what are alternatives for evaluating teachers that might be more in line with this way of thinking? What are the alternatives that not only fit the current policy and political contexts, but which also move us away from inordinately relying on the value-added estimates high-lighted (and deconstructed) in the chapters heretofore? In this final chapter, I discuss what alternatives exist and what the best research-based alternative might be. As well, instead of recommending that teachers should not be evaluated for increasing student learning and achievement over time (which many view as an impossible option), I suggest differently that there might be a better alternative that takes these indicators into consideration given their strengths and weaknesses.

This alternative is based on the soon to be released *Standards for Educational and Psychological Testing* (AERA, APA, & NCME, 2014) developed by the prominent national associations on educational measurement and testing. This alternative is based on using more than simply large-scale standardized test scores for measurement purposes, but measuring more compre-hensively what it means to be an effective teacher. This alternative is also based on years of experience and some research evidence that it would be a more appropriate, reliable, and valid approach. It would also be a fairer, less biased, probably equally efficient, and as such, viable system, even though it relies on human judgment.

Mead, Rotherham, and Brown (2012) of the conservative American Enterprise Institute in Washington, DC recently recommended that we move away from highly objective evalu-ative systems (and our illusions of what such systems might be) because a series of unintended consequences (discussed in Chapter 6) come about when objectivity is the desired end, and sometimes pursued at all costs. They, too, noted that there is a great need for a good deal of human judgment when developing new and better teacher evaluation systems. Put differ-ently, we cannot continue to strip VAM estimates from the contexts in which they are created and think that without this contextual information we might understand why there are such issues with VAM reliability, validity, bias, and fairness. We can, however, interpret the data using a variety of indicators along with human judgments to make more reliable, valid, unbiased, and fairer determinations about teacher quality, teacher quality over time, and teacher quality for more than the current 30–40% of teachers who are currently VAM-eligible across the country (Gabriel & Lester, 2013; Harris, 2011; Thomas, 2012). As well, such systems would be more useful in terms of teacher reflection and improvement, particu-larly given that human judgment would be valued at the core of information comprehension, interpretation, and use.

Multiple measures and more holistic evaluation systems

As noted by AERA et al. (2000), decisions that affect individual's lives, life chances, or educa-tional opportunities "should not be made on the basis of test scores alone." Other relevant information should *always* be taken into account to (hopefully) enhance reliability and, hence, the validity of any inference or decision that is to be made using estimates based on test scores (e.g., VAM estimates). The leading argument for using multiple measures is that no indicator derived via any one evaluative measure needs to be a perfect indicator, and because all of the indicators currently used for evaluative purposes are imperfect, the weaknesses of any one indicator can be offset by the strengths of the other(s) (National Education Policy Center, 2010; see also McMillan, 1988). In addition, using multiple measures helps to reduce bias; reduces misclassification rates; lessens tendencies to manipulate and distort the measures used; provides a fuller representation of what it means to be an effective teacher; promotes more formative use; and does all of this in fairer and more inclusive terms (Chester, 2003;

Gordon et al., 2006; Harris, 2009b, 2010; Hill, 2009; Koedel & Betts, 2009; Nelson, 2011; Papay, 2011; Rothstein, 2011; Sawchuck, 2011; Schochet & Chiang, 2010; Toch & Rothman, 2008).

Again, when discussing truth, or validity, we are really talking about concurrent-related evidence of validity (discussed in Chapter 6) or "the degree of empirical correlation between the test scores and [the other] criterion scores" (Messick, 1989, p. 7) derived via the additional measures that might be used to represent the teacher (or school/district) effectiveness construct. Additional measures might include, for example, teachers' supervisor and/or peer observation scores, student and parent satisfaction indicators, and student work samples that, when put together, represent the "network of relations derived" (Messick, 1975, p. 956). Making sure that VAM estimates and the other criteria used to assess teacher effectiveness are all "in the same boat," at the same time and over time is also important. This is important not only for purposes of making valid inferences from which valid decisions might be made, but also in terms of credibility and trust. Credibility and trust are the most important features of any successful evaluation system, because with credibility, teachers and administrators are more likely to trust and ultimately use the output to advance student learning and achievement (Hill et al., 2011; Milanowski et al., 2004).

The main drawback to using multiple measures, however, is that when used alongside one another in complementary ways, they are too often assumed to have adequate levels of reliability and validity. The fact of the matter is, however, that any multi-measure evaluation system is only as reliable and valid as the reliability and validity of the system's weakest measure (Baker, 2012a; Baker et al., 2013; Papay, 2011; Rothstein & Mathis, 2013). Contrary to what some believe, and what some perpetuate under such false assumptions, "additional measures will [not] increase both validity and reliability" (Harris, 2012; see also Harris, 2011). As explained by Chester (2003), there is "a common misconception that simply employing multiple measures increases the reliability [and validity] of the decision[s] to be made" (p. 33). However, this is not the case (see also Schochet & Chiang, 2010). While decision errors might be reduced, as they are based on human judgment, statistical errors are not reduced whatsoever. Nonetheless, some still argue that using multiple measures along with value-added estimates is our best, and hence only, option because systems with value-added measures are still better than the outmoded systems used for decades past (Baeder, 2010; Glazerman et al., 2011; Harris, 2009b, 2012b; Wilkins, 2010).

Toward these ends, the best and best-funded study in the world on this topic thus far came out of the recently completed Bill and Melinda Gates Foundation's (2013) MET studies. Researchers examined how best to combine value-added estimates with, in this case, classroom observations and student surveys, but fell far short in terms of supporting what some argued were predetermined conclusions (Camburn, 2012; Rothstein, 2011; Rothstein & Mathis, 2013). One of their a priori conclusions was that relying on multiple measures to construct better teacher evaluation systems was indeed the best way to go. With this, most educational measurement experts and researchers would agree (see also AERA et al., 2000; Harris, 2011). However, MET researchers also embraced an a priori conclusion that multiple measurement systems should include, as a significant and substantially weighted component, value-added estimates, despite their prevailing faults (Rothstein & Mathis, 2013; see also Baker, 2012a, 2013; Baker et al., 2010; Gabriel & Lester, 2013; Harris, 2012a; Liu & Teddlie, 2005; Ravitch, 2012c; Simon, 2013; Sparks, 2012a). Unfortunately, however, the surprisingly weak data revealed across all of the MET studies (Bill & Melinda Gates Foundation,

2010, 2012, 2013) that the low to moderate correlations demonstrated (e.g., $0.2 \leq r \leq 0.6$; see Figure 6.1 in Chapter 6) among and between the multiple measures examined did not support their second conclusion. VAM measures were not suitably related to the other measures they recommended should be used for evaluation systems based on multiple measures (see also Camburn, 2012; Rothstein, 2011; Rothstein & Mathis, 2013).

Instead, what MET researchers did evidence was that the "independent methods for assessing the same construct or trait [were not] substantially interrelated" (Messick, 1975, p. 956). Furthermore, they were certainly not interrelated enough to support increased levels of reliability and validity, or valid interpretations or decisions using their three measures together (Rothstein & Mathis, 2013). Likewise, the MET data revealed in their final study (Bill & Melinda Gates Foundation, 2013) did not support the MET researchers' overall conclusion that, despite the underwhelming correlations, they and others could still "force the fit" of the multiple measures used and apply different numerical weighting systems[1] regardless (e.g., value-added estimates = 50%, teacher observations = 30%, and student surveys = 20%; see Figure 8.1).

More specifically, MET researchers recommended that value-added estimates count for between 33% and 50% of a teacher's overall evaluation score (see also Simon, 2013). As mentioned, and as per Baker (2012b), "when you require that all other measures be correlated with this suspect measure [i.e., VAM estimates] – you've stacked the deck to be substantially if not entirely built on a flawed foundation." This is precisely what occurred here (see also Baker, 2012a, 2013a). This is also what researchers conducting studies in this area for years prior would have predicted, even before MET researchers became involved, but I digress.

Conventional options

So what are some other options beyond what MET researchers suggested? I start with what I have termed some conventional options, conventional in that these options are often and customarily offered by other researchers conducting and disseminating research in this area. I

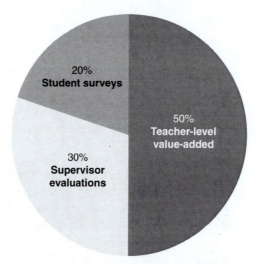

Figure 8.1 A pie chart illustrating how MET researchers recommended value-added estimates might be used for weighted teacher evaluation systems based on multiple measures.

end with an even more conventional solution that I believe, with some research evidence in support, might be the best solution available for evaluating and holding teachers accountable for their effectiveness as the professionals they presumably are, and as we the taxpayers pay them to be.

First, researchers (and others), acknowledging the weaknesses that come along with using VAM-estimates (as critiqued in the previous chapters), suggest that for the time being, until we can make VAM-estimates more consistent and accurate (assuming this is possible), VAM-estimates should "trigger" other interventions, closer looks at, and further screenings of the teachers deemed most ineffective according to their value-added estimates (Baker, 2012a; Baker et al., 2013; Goe, 2008; Hanushek & Rivkin, 2010; Harris, 2012a; Jacob & Lefgren, 2008; Medina, 2009; Raudenbush & Jean, 2012; Schafer et al., 2012). Unfortunately, this option overlooks the fact that value-added estimates can emit false information up to 50% of the time. Using value-added estimates as trigger mechanisms has the potential to motivate the decisions of administrators to conduct further investigations of low value-added teachers as randomly as a flip of a coin (see also Hill, 2009). This approach also leaves in its wake an equal probability that ineffective teachers, who, for whatever reasons, post average or above estimates, might go unnoticed and without the attention both they and their students deserve. These "initial signals [will prove themselves] not to be particularly useful" (Baker, 2012a; see also Hill, 2009; Hill et al., 2011).

Second, researchers (and others) recommend that VAM-based estimates be used for only those teachers who are the outliers, whose value-added estimates fall on either end of the bell curve. More simply put, these researchers recommend that only the teachers who demonstrate extreme levels of negative or positive growth are those about whom low- and high-stakes decisions should be made, either in isolation from or in conjunction with what the other measures indicate (Baker, 2012a; Glazerman et al., 2011; Harris, 2011, 2012a; Hill et al., 2011; Jacob & Lefgren, 2005; Schafer et al., 2012; Toch & Rothman, 2008; Weingarten, 2011). This is probably more reasonable than the first option described above, but it is only reasonable if the other indicators are considered in conjunction with the VAM-based estimates and the other indicators hold a good deal of weight so that they might outright counter what the VAM-based estimates might imply. The drawback here, though, is that this approach leaves nothing in terms of distinguishing among the majority of teachers whose value-added estimates hang around average. As well, this approach disregards how bias might force some teachers to the extremes.[2] Again, this is why human judgment is so important when making valid inferences and decisions.

An even more conventional solution

Highlighted at the beginning of this chapter is another of Albert Einstein's best-known quotes: "Any intelligent fool can make things bigger and more complex.... It takes a touch of genius – and a lot of courage to move in the opposite direction." It is in line with his thinking that I present an even more conventional solution with both logical justification and some research evidence in support.

As stated by Cronbach and Gleser (1965), when testing for pragmatic purposes, "a quantitative estimate is not the real desideratum" (p. 136). Quantitative estimates are valuable only insofar as they aid in making more qualitative, holistic, descriptive, and hence valid inferences from which better decisions can be made. This presumes that those involved understand that consistency and accuracy in the quantitative estimates used are, of course, desired; the quantitative estimates cannot be used to infer much of anything about causation (Rubin et al., 2004); more realistic and context-based information may help make better decisions; and no procedures, no matter how complementary or inclusive they might be, will ever yield precise assessments of "the whole personality" (p. 149), or in this case, the whole construct of interest (i.e., teacher effectiveness). "Instead, it is necessary to distill from a limited quantity of information the most intelligent [inferences] possible" (p. 149), from which the most intelligent possible decisions might be made. This is where human judgment is absolutely required.

Educators' professional judgments should not be removed from personnel decisions, especially when legislating or regulating consequential actions may be taken as a result. If teachers are to be rewarded, promoted, or dismissed, or may have their tenure revoked, they should be involved in the processes used to make such determinations, both collectively on behalf of one another and as individuals on behalf of themselves. Human judgment, when interpreting value-added estimates alongside other multiple measures, is necessary at all times, especially when the decisions to be made may have been privileged or compromised by extenuating circumstances (Baker, 2013; Baker et al., 2013; Betebenner & Linn, 2010; Camburn, 2012; Darling-Hammond, 2010; Rothstein & Mathis, 2013). Science demands that human judgment takes this into account (Kaplan, 1964, p. 376), and so it should be here if we are to uphold the standards of science. Attention must be paid to the "value" of the system of which the value-added data are a part (McMillan, 1988). That said, an effective teacher evaluation system should ensure that:

> All participants in an assessment are involved in its design, and have an opportunity to learn and to fully understand the system that is implemented; Assessments [should be] informed by a full spectrum of tools, rather than a single measurement, such as test scores; and [t]he design of the assessment system [should be] based on high-quality research and supported by adequate resources.
>
> *(National Education Policy Center, 2010)*

All of the measures and statistical maneuvers involved should be taken at face value unless research evidence suggests otherwise, and states and/or districts should be given considerable discretion when developing their own measures, or choosing research-based measures that have been externally vetted and validated for the uses at hand (Baker et al., 2010). This also presumes that the measures developed or chosen align with what local players agree matter within and across the contexts in which they work. Again, while value-added measures might serve as a component of such evaluative systems (and I say this with extreme caution), choice should be permitted in terms of what other measures might be used in both complementary and supplementary ways, as there is not (and will likely never be) consensus regarding the best ways to evaluate teacher (and school/district) quality. In some ways, particularly if local control is appreciated and esteemed, this is actually a nice problem to have.

Before delving into "what measures" should be included, however, the theory[3] behind the evaluative models must be developed as this should drive all of the decisions to be made thereafter. Local players must collaborate to construct a theory about, in this case, what it means to be an effective teacher given the "extensive range of activities, skills, and knowledge [and strategies] involved in teachers' daily work" (Mathis, 2012, p. 2). This theory must be developed in context, as locally defined, even if there are some universal truths that local players agree might apply to them. For example, the core propositions developed by the National Board for Professional Teaching Standards (NBPTS) might offer a good starting point in terms of defining what teacher effectiveness might mean at a more universal level (see Table 8.1).

Also considered might be the other things that matter across schools, districts, and contexts (e.g., leadership). With or without a starting theoretical framework, theory building must nonetheless be done in constructive and transparent ways while those involved think about what it means to be an effective teacher in context. Without a theory, it would be difficult if not impossible to move towards system development and validation, or an assessment of how responsive the system might be to the needs of the local players involved (Gabriel & Allington, 2011; Martineau, 2010; Misco, 2008; Rubin et al., 2004; Schafer et al., 2012).

Ten criteria for assessing teacher effectiveness that might be considered as part of defining such a theory include: (1) how important student performance on value-added and other district-, school-, and teacher-created test-based measures might be; (2) whether the measures should be used within a "weighted" system[4] (see also Baker, 2013a; Rothstein & Mathis, 2103; Yuan et al., 2013); (3) what other quantifiable measures might matter (e.g., number of students and subject areas taught, student promotion or graduation rates, student attendance and other participation rates, course completion rates, and suspension, discipline, and other behavioral referrals); (4) whether things that are typically included within traditional teacher evaluation protocols (e.g., subject knowledge expertise, instructional and pedagogical practices, attention to time-on-task, classroom and safety management, classroom organization, accessibility, responsiveness, motivation, and teachers' caring behaviors) matter more or less than others that are typically valued but not always included on traditional instruments (e.g., teachers' facilitation of students' creativity, critical thinking, curiosity, exploration, and self-motivated and self-directed learning behaviors); (5) whether teachers experiment, take risks, and value new, innovative, and perhaps technologically integrated strategies; (6) whether teachers participate in professional development, within or beyond the district; (7) whether teachers fulfill their job responsibilities and, better yet, fulfill additional roles and responsibilities including but not limited to taking on mentoring and other leadership roles within and outside of normal school hours; (8) whether taking on more difficult teaching assignments, with more difficult-to-teach students (e.g., ELLs, special education students, students retained in grades multiple times) should be acknowledged, or even accounted for in light of the potential for bias; (9) whether teachers are present and generally good citizens in their schools, districts, and communities at large; and related, (10) whether teachers' interpersonal relationships with their students, parents, other teachers, school staff and administrators, and the like

Table 8.1 The five core propositions of the National Board for Professional Teaching Standards (NBPTS)

Proposition 1	Teachers are committed to students and their learning.
Proposition 2	Teachers know the subjects they teach and how to teach those subjects to students.
Proposition 3	Teachers are responsible for managing and monitoring student learning.
Proposition 4	Teachers think systematically about their practice and learn from experience.
Proposition 5	Teachers are members of learning communities.

Source: www.nbpts.org/five-core-propositions.

should matter as well (Glazerman et al., 2011; Graue et al., 2013; Harris, 2009a; Harris & Sass, 2009; Hill, 2009; Misco, 2008; Sawchuck, 2011; Toch & Rothman, 2008; Watanabe, 2013; Wells, 2011; Yuan et al., 2013).

Conventional measures

From here, it must then be determined what measures might best capture what has been locally defined to matter the most, as listed above or otherwise, all the while considering what is realistic, not overly nettlesome, and balanced as per the theory developed. "Any sound evaluation will necessarily involve a balancing of many factors that provide a more accurate view of what teachers in fact do in the classroom and how that contributes to student learning" in context (Baker et al., 2010, p. 2). Discussed next are all of the measurement options of which I am aware, as well as what research has to say about each option's strengths and weaknesses – the weaknesses that are to be offset by the strengths of the other measures included in an evaluative system based on multiple measures. These measures include: test-based measures that might be used in value-added ways (again, I say this with extreme caution); supervisor and/or peer evaluations of live or recorded observations; student and parent surveys; portfolios including teacher artifacts (e.g., lesson plans and student work samples); and teacher self-reports and reflections.

Tests

Test-based measures might be included in value-added evaluative systems under the following five conditions: (1) they do not play the principal or trumping role[5] among the other measures included; (2) teachers and administrators have a say when determining which test-based measures (and perhaps statistical controls) are used in value-added calculations; (3) how, when, for how long, and for what teachers' value-added estimates are to be included; (4) how estimates are to be reported, interpreted, and ultimately used; and (5) that all involved interpret value-added estimates in consideration of those estimates' major, prevailing issues – mainly the issues with reliability, validity, bias, and fairness that should fully constrain their use until research suggests otherwise.

Accordingly, test-based measures from which value-added estimates might be derived include the following, in quasi-order from most to least optimal. End of course exams[6] that are administered at least twice within the same school year (e.g., fall and spring[7]) to control for (without using fancy statistics) students' prior teachers' carry-over or residual effects and the differential summer learning gains and losses continuously distorting the reliability and validity of all current value-added systems might be used (Baker, 2011; Baker et al., 2010; Battelle for Kids, 2013; Harris & Anderson, 2013; Nelson, 2011; Newton et al., 2010; Papay, 2011). Related, district benchmark tests (that might also be end of course exams) can be used to do much of the same thing (see also Harris & Anderson, 2013), if externally validated and also if used at least twice per academic year, although most district benchmark tests are currently more traditional (i.e., tests based largely on multiple choice items and sometimes limited in terms of subject area and content coverage) than might be ideal (Linn, 2008). Finally, other more traditional tests, including most state tests and also other commercially developed tests that might be locally used for both customary (e.g., the SAT-9, Terra Nova, and Galileo tests[8]), alternative, and accommodating purposes (e.g., the Aprenda, Wechsler, and Stanford-Binet[9]) might also be considered. While some teachers might have data on all of such measures, others might not. This complicates things, but only if the goal is to reach a highly elusive level of objectivity.

The bottom line here is that tests might be used as part of any evaluative system, but only in consideration of all of the tests' and test-based strategies' (e.g., VAM-based analyses) limitations. All of the tests included should be reported, interpreted, and used at face-value, within reason, and with their limitations known, and at this point strictly for descriptive, formative, and non-causal purposes (Carter, 2004; Papay, 2011; Rubin et al., 2004). At the same time, however, we want to be sure we do not become overly reliant on tests, largely given their aforementioned weaknesses and in some cases fatal flaws, and given that current estimates are that a total of between 200 and 300 tests are expected with the oncoming Common Core State Standards (Gabriel & Lester, 2013; Richardson, 2012). We must also be cognizant of this as impulses and temptations to test are always lingering nearby.

Whether evaluation systems might use school-wide value-added estimates for teacher evaluation systems should also be considered, here, knowing that while school-level estimates are more precise due to the larger samples of student test scores included within calculations, they also capture in their results even more contributory factors, making the case for direct causation at the teacher-level even more nonsensical (Cody et al., 2010; Hill, 2009; Linn, 2008; Toch & Rothman, 2008). Nonetheless, if those involved believe that school-wide value-added estimates yield something important, they might also be considered as part of a system based on multiple measures.

Supervisor and peer observations

Observational measures might also be included in such evaluative systems, again under another five conditions: (1) teachers and administrators have a say in determining how observational data are to be collected, with what instruments, by whom (e.g., supervisors and peers), how often, and how data are to be used in terms of summative and formative functionality; (2) the instruments used to conduct observations are research-based; (3) the instruments used have been externally examined and validated; (4) evidence suggests that the instruments yield acceptable levels of reliability and validity; and (5) the instruments do not play a principal or trumping role in the overall system. As most if not all school districts currently rely at least in part on observational methods as part of their evaluation systems, and there is really nothing new or innovative in this area (except, maybe, for new and improved instruments, as advertised), including observational data in such systems *should be* quite easy to do.

However, the most noteworthy concern here is that not all observational systems currently in use are reliable and valid, largely because of the instruments themselves and the people using the instruments to score observations. In terms of the instruments, educational professionals (unaware of the basics in educational measurement) too often string together random items that they believe might matter, for example, in terms of student learning and achievement. They often do this without an underlying theory or theoretical framework driving the major and minor factors and items ultimately included within the instruments they develop. They also often include too many items, many of which are redundant or superfluous, and do not add much "value" to the instrument. A simple solution here, particularly for homegrown models, is that those constructing observational instruments without expertise in educational measurement consult with others with the expertise to help them, at the very least, develop and refine their instruments before they are used for inferential and decision-making purposes (Hill et al., 2012; see also McKenna, 2012; Martineau, 2010; Nelson, 2011).

A simpler option might be to choose an "off-the-shelf" observational instrument, for example, like Charlotte Danielson's *Framework for Teaching*[10] (Danielson, 1996; Danielson & McGreal, 2000). However, doing this also often comes with annual fees and removes some of the local liberties realized when developing homegrown systems. Noted here, however, is that, should educators choose this approach, they need to fully understand whether the instruments they purchase have been externally validated and how, as well as what the evidence from the validation study/ies suggests. Many observational instruments (similar to some of the VAM systems discussed in Chapter 3) are internally, not externally, "validated." They are also usually lauded as "research-based." Being "research-based," though, typically only means that the instruments were developed using research to inform their development, but the instruments themselves were not validated otherwise. In other words, not all observational instruments, despite widespread use and despite how their vendors pitch them to consumers, are as established and validated as is often advertised and assumed.[11] A key thing to watch for is external research that supports, with evidence, the statements being made.

It also should be noted here that pulling items from validated instruments is also common, but also not good practice. Doing so is highly random and, again, is atheoretical and misaligned with whatever theory might or should be driving the evaluative system and its use. As well, doing so requires the same testing and validation procedures that a brand new instrument would require, as mentioned above, simply because combining different items from the same or different instruments alters the levels of reliability and validity present before items were pulled.

Related are questions about who is to conduct the observations; principals,[12] other administrators (e.g., assistant principals), and more "neutral" teacher leaders, mentor teachers, and peers must all be considered. Also up for consideration should be how robust the training should be for the human scoring and other data collection procedures (e.g., note-taking for evidence) to support inter-rater reliability.[13] Other considerations include: how to mediate the levels of bias often caused by the interpersonal relationships between the observers and the observed; how processes and procedures might be implemented to ensure that all evaluators are objective; how many observations should be conducted and whether this is enough;[14] and what all the associated costs and human resource constraints are. Attention to all of these questions and details supports the overall integrity and rigor of the observational system (Harris, 2010; Harris & Sass, 2009; Hill et al., 2012), some argue so much so that instead of relying on value-added estimates perhaps we should rely more on observational data to do this work (see, for example, Hill, 2009).

Student and parent surveys

Using student- and parent-level feedback might also be a worthwhile endeavor, again under certain conditions (e.g., in terms of the weight they carry) and with clear understandings about their limitations. These understandings are informed by the research coming mainly from the higher education literature where survey instruments have been used for decades to evaluate instructor satisfaction, instructor quality, and instructors' perceived levels of effectiveness in college classrooms, through the responses of instructors' students.

According to Marsh (2007), using surveys to evaluate instructional, or in this case teaching, effectiveness, serves two purposes. First, and perhaps most importantly, survey results provide diagnostic information so that the instructors being evaluated might continuously access context-rich information from which they can learn and then, hopefully, improve. Second, survey results fulfill a summative role when results are used to make decisions, sometimes high-stakes decisions, about instructors, although, again, survey results are sometimes used for more consequential purposes than is warranted, given their limitations (Amrein-Beardsley & Haladyna, 2009, 2012; Gabriel & Allington, 2011; Liu & Teddlie, 2005).

These measurement tools also bring with them their own issues. As with the observational methods, when student-based survey results are used along with VAM-based estimates, the results also do not correlate well with value-added estimates. While survey responses do seem to produce more internally consistent results than do classroom observations or VAM estimates, in and of themselves (Bill & Melinda Gates Foundation, 2012; see also Camburn, 2012), this is likely due to the halo effects that are pretty much ever-present when using survey methods to gather such feedback.

Halo effects, or halo rating errors, are observed when survey participants give holistic ratings for most or all of the survey items included on an instrument, instead of focusing on and discriminating among the particular items' content. For example, a teacher who might be personable, funny, good-looking, or generally liked, but who might not really be effective in the classroom, might be rated similarly well across all items, regardless of whether the specific items were intended to measure their personality and likeability or effectiveness as an instructor. This yields a high overall impression score versus the valid and uniquely different scores across individual items, which are desired for both summative and formative purposes. Inversely, a teacher who might be very good and very effective, but who makes his/her students work very hard, might be subjected to the opposite, reverse-halo effect. This yields a low overall impression score, again, that neither is valid nor discriminates across items as needed.

In terms of reliability, this falsely increases levels of internal consistency reliability as well (e.g., $r \geq 0.90$; Hobson & Talbot, 2001; Schmelkin, Spencer, & Gellman, 1997). In terms of concurrent-related validity, this also decreases the variance, or range in scores, needed to examine score distributions and their alignment with the other criteria of interest (e.g., value-added estimates), further inhibiting such validity investigations.

Also in terms of validity, survey-based ratings such as these are largely susceptible to other instances of construct-irrelevant variance (CIV) introduced in Chapter 2. These are the factors that are wholly unrelated to the construct of interest that distort, in this case, survey ratings, and ultimately pull scores away from what the instruments are to measure. Here, instances of CIV occur when the following account for at least some of the variance in the ratings produced: (1) survey participant variables (e.g., age, gender, race, ethnicity, nationality, language background, whether participants are capable of understanding that the survey is important, students' grade level, students' expected grades, students' desires for artificial praise or revenge); (2) instructor variables (e.g., gender as it interacts with student participants' gender, age, race, ethnicity, nationality, language background, popularity, physical attractiveness, personality, charisma); (3) course variables (e.g., class size, whether the course is required, course content, course delivery, course workload, perceived course difficulty); and (4) survey instrument variables (e.g., the mode of administration, response rates, the numerical scales used, perceived anonymity, instructors' influences on or "gaming of" participants' ratings,[15] whether participants believe instructors will benefit from their feedback; Block, 1998; Davies, Hirschberg, Lye, Johnston, & McDonald, 2007; Gamliel & Davidovitz, 2005; Liu & Teddlie, 2005;

Sedlmeier, 2006; Trout, 1997; Williams & Ceci, 1997). Even the open-ended, free-response items often included on such survey instruments are threatened by CIV (i.e., females may be more likely to respond, as is the case in higher education; Darby, 2006).

Also of concern here are response rates, or the proportion of participants who must respond in order to yield valuable and valid information for both formative and summative purposes. Contrary to what is often and sometimes perpetually assumed (Bill & Melinda Gates Foundation, 2012; Kyriakides, 2005), acceptable response rates are very difficult to obtain. This is due to many of the factors listed above, as well as how surveys are administered (e.g., online), and whether surveys are or can be administered to captive audiences (e.g., in class).

Nonetheless, the beauty of using survey instruments to gather perceptual data from students and/or teachers, as with observational systems, is that surveys can be used for almost all teachers, except perhaps for teachers of early childhood and some primary grade levels. As such, these methods are still looking promising (Baeder, 2010; Bill & Melinda Gates Foundation, 2013; Harris, 2011; Kyriakides, 2005; Rothstein, 2011; Toch & Rothman, 2008), even though decades of higher education research on these systems foreshadow the major and minor limitations such survey research methods will likely never overcome (Amrein-Beardsley & Haladyna, 2009, 2012; Block, 1998; Davies et al., 2007; Gamliel & Davidovitz, 2005; Sedlmeier, 2006; Trout, 1997; Williams & Ceci, 1997).

Portfolios

Albeit less frequently, sometimes portfolios including teacher artifacts (e.g., lesson plans and student work samples) are used in evaluation systems based on multiple measures (Milanowski, 2004; Wilson et al., 2007). Some portfolio systems, like the one put in place to evaluate teachers who want to become National Board Certified Teachers (NBCTs), have been validated (Bond, Smith, Baker, & Hattie, 2000; Cantrell, Fullerton, Kane, & Staiger, 2008; Cavalluzzo, 2004; Clotfelter, Ladd, and Vigdor, 2007; Goldhaber & Anthony, 2007; National Research Council, 2008; Smith, Gordon, Colby, & Wang, 2005; Vandevoort, Amrein-Beardsley, & Berliner, 2004; Wilson et al., 2007). However, most, if not all, other portfolio systems have not been validated. Consequently, they are not nearly as strong.

However, the purpose of the NBPTS portfolio system is different than the purpose here. Teachers desiring to become NBCTs submit portfolios that include lesson plans, instructional materials, student work samples, videos illustrating work with students, evidence of pertinent accomplishments outside of the classroom, and written self-reflections, and they do this so that they can demonstrate that they are extraordinary teachers according to the five core propositions developed by the NBPTS (see Table 8.1). Portfolios for everyday evaluation systems could be designed for yearly use, perhaps using some of the same measures above. This might help teachers demonstrate that they are effective in their own distinct ways. These measures might also serve supplementary roles; whereas they might not be considered at the core of a yearly evaluation system, depending on the locally defined theory driving what might matter when evaluating teaching effectiveness, they might instead be submitted as needed and at the discretion of individual teachers, their supervisors, and whoever their other evaluators might be.

Teacher self-reports and reflections

Finally, becoming more common in contemporary evaluation systems, albeit still rare, are teacher self-reports and reflections (Liu & Teddlie, 2005; Toch & Rothman, 2008). Self-reports and reflections include a few pages of prose, written by the teachers being evaluated, about themselves as effective teachers. Of course, however effective teaching has been defined at the local level (i.e., the theory) should also be used here to frame or loosely standardize what each teacher is to write as an evaluation.

For example, if a local district values the five core propositions of the NBPTS (see Table 8.1), they might develop a template that is aligned with the five core propositions and then give all teachers (across all grades) directions to develop a narrative to explain how they demonstrated teaching effectiveness in those five areas. How those narratives are to be scored (e.g., using a rubric), by whom (e.g., a team of teacher-elected teachers; see discussion forthcoming), when (e.g., every year[16]), and on what scale (e.g., a scale similar to those used for the other measures included), would also need to be determined, again, locally. This process may sound familiar, as it is similar to some career ladder programs used by districts in the past (Darling-Hammond, 2010; Scharrer & Bureau, 2011).

Importantly, though, including a self-report and reflection component within such a system allows teachers to help contextualize and process their own data, their data being all of the data valued and included in any evaluation system. This is a beneficial exercise in itself, as research suggests that, "feedback from this kind of evaluation improves student achievement, because it helps teachers get better at what they do" (Darling-Hammond, 2012; see also Mathis, 2012; Milanowski, 2004; Toch & Rothman, 2008). For example, if a teacher continuously presents low value-added scores, but the scores do not match the other scores (e.g., benchmark test gains) also valued within the system, the teacher would be given the opportunity to explain why this may be the case. As discussed, it may have occurred due to variables that were beyond the control of the teacher. Here, teachers, in all fairness and in the spirit of due process (Baker et al., 2010, 2013; Pullin, 2013; see also Goldhaber, 2009), should be given the opportunity to explain the situations that impact whichever of the indicators included need contextual information (Yuan et al., 2013). If a teacher posts low value-added scores across the board, however, and his/her observational scores are not much higher, while the teacher might retain the right to explain him/herself, (s)he might have a more difficult time convincing others (e.g., his/her peers or supervisors) that this was out of his/her professional hands. The risk here is that including self-reports and reflections might permit too many excuses. The benefit, though, is that sometimes explanations, especially when understood in context, are necessary.

That said, the weights allocated to self-reports and reflections should be appropriately and proportionally balanced, with designers, scorers, and users well aware that if weighted or valued too much, temptations for teachers to falsely represent themselves as more effective than they indeed are might be too alluring for some. As well, who scores the narratives, and perhaps analyzes the rest of the data included in the system, about which the teachers also might write their narratives, is of the utmost importance. In actuality, the best candidates to evaluate the measures included, along with the narratives teachers might submit on their own behalves, might be teachers' peers. If elected and appointed by the faculty at large, they might certainly be the most rigorous representatives who might collectively keep their colleagues in check. This is the method used in many institutions of higher education. To see each of the measures along with their research-based strengths and weaknesses, see Table 8.2.

Table 8.2 Multiple measures that might be used in holistic evaluation systems and their strengths and weaknesses

Measures	Strengths	Weaknesses
Value-added estimates	• Perceptibly better than test-based "snapshot" estimates administered once per year • Yield indicators of growth over time • Better for school-level and institutional analyses	• Unreliable, and hence invalid • Potentially biased • Unfair given 30% of teachers typically VAM-eligible • Of limited formative value • Difficult to understand and use • Once per year administration contaminates pre-to-post test assessments further
Other test-based indicators	• Typically more reliable and valid • Less biased in terms of actual content tested • Fairer and more inclusive with more teachers (e.g., social studies and science, high school and elementary teachers) and students (e.g., ELLs) involved • Of more formative use and value • More instructionally sensitive • Easier to understand output • More than once per year administration contaminates pre-to-post test assessments less	• Sometimes unreliable and invalid if homegrown (e.g., teacher-developed) • Still issues with fairness with some teachers (e.g., music, PE) • Not typically used to measure growth over time • Different measures for different teachers increases confusion • Often impossible to assess output across teachers for comparative purposes
Supervisor and peer observations	• Instruments capture many more things that "matter" in terms of assessing teacher effectiveness (e.g., student and teacher relationships) • Fair in that all teachers can be observed • Instruments yield instructionally useful information and feedback • Processes involved (e.g., post-observation conferences) instructionally, professionally, and formatively valuable • Educators have much experience using observational methods • Assessment methods occur in real time, over time, throughout the year, and during the instructional day	• Instruments used sometimes unreliable in terms of inter-rater reliability • Require extensive training for observers • Takes a lot of instructional time to do correctly and objectively • Instruments used are sometimes not research-based or externally validated • Issues with validity when compared with value-added estimates • Issues with bias when personal relationships between observers and observed distort scores • Risk for score inflation and lack of variation in subsequent scores • Instruments often too long with superfluous items • Instruments sometimes atheoretical

continued

Measures	Strengths	Weaknesses
Student and parent surveys	• Context-rich data come directly from students and those closest to students • Data yield overall impressions about many constructs of interest • Fair in that students and parents of all teachers can be solicited and obtained • Useful for summative purposes • Open-ended feedback provides diagnostic and formatively useful data • Gives students and parents a voice in the educational process • Gives supervisors an overall impression about such perceptions	• Internal consistency (e.g., reliability) often caused by halo rating errors • Risk for score inflation and lack of variation in subsequent scores • Low response rates threaten validity • Highly invalid for certain populations (e.g., younger students who are generally happy and indiscriminate) • Highly susceptible to construct-irrelevant variance (CIV; e.g., scores distorted by students' expected grades) • Easily gamed (e.g., excluding certain students/parents from participating) • Issues with validity when compared with value-added estimates • Instruments sometimes atheoretical
Portfolios	• Rarely used and educators with limited experience using • Capture student work samples, lesson plans, and other classroom-based products • Highly holistic • Fair in that all teachers can submit such information regardless of courses taught • Useful for supplementary purposes including providing evidence to support certain assertions	• Different artifacts submitted by different teachers for different purposes increase confusion • Often impossible to assess output across teachers for comparative purposes • Time-consuming to score • Scoring highly subjective unless reliable and valid rubric developed, tested, and used • Very few valid portfolio systems exist • Inefficient unless advanced organizational and technological systems used
Self-reports and reflections	• Standardized for scoring purposes if framed consistently across teachers and submitted in uniform ways • Fair in that all teachers report about and reflect upon themselves as teachers • Values teachers' voices more than any other measure • Helps to explain all of the data submitted as evidence of teachers' overall effectiveness in context and with reason • Human scorers with capabilities and levels of trust consume information yielding inter-rater reliability, validity, objectivity • Yields more variance in terms of score distributions (e.g., evidence of procedural rigor)	• Potential to distort or inflate self is high • Potential to lie also exists (although risk of embarrassment among peers also exists) • Might permit too much "excuse making" • Ineffective if ineffectively framed (yielding random notes about this and that) • Scoring rubrics imperfect (although balanced by multiple human raters and procedures involving case-by-case discussions and consensus building)

The conventional solution defined

Unlike the current public school evaluation models that purposely sideline the perspectives of the people being evaluated and the contexts in which their evaluation scores are constructed, evaluation models in many higher education institutions take these factors into consideration when assessing college professors. Actually, evaluation systems in many other professions value rigorous, ongoing assessments of activities that are conducted by experts who review multiple indicators and use human judgment to make low- and high-stakes decisions. Rather than fixating on replacing human judgments with formulaic, inconsistent, imprecise, and sometimes biased statistical techniques (i.e., VAMs), the better approach might be to figure out what will help evaluators make the best and the most democratic judgments, all things considered (Baeder, 2010; Baker et al., 2010; Darling-Hammond, 2012; Darling-Hammond & Haertel, 2012; Liu & Teddlie, 2005; McKenna, 2012; Marder, 2012; Papay, 2011; Rothstein & Mathis, 2013; Weems & Rogers, 2010).

In higher education, the general theory of effectiveness, particularly in Research I institutions, revolves around whether college faculty actively engage in a triad of criteria that define success in the areas of scholarship, teaching, and service. Aside from the overarching theory capturing what matters in higher education, however, it is typically the responsibility of each distinctly different college to determine what each major area means for it. Accordingly, for each college, this is typically defined in a set of standards that faculty collectively and democratically create (and continuously revise). These standards serve as the governing documents that drive pretty much everything faculty are to do.

For a more concrete example of what this looks like, and speaking more from experience in terms of the college in which I am a professor, we value, according to our standards: scholarship, teaching, and service. Scholarship is evaluated in terms of the extent to which faculty demonstrate, with evidence, that they are accomplished scholars whose academic culminations (e.g., books and publications) are consistent over time, focused, deal with significant issues and problems, and have an impact on society at large. The evidence provided here includes books and the reputations of the publishers of the books; journal publications and the reputations of the journals in which articles are published; the number of readers of the books and/or journal articles (i.e., readership); the rates with which books or articles are accepted for publication (i.e., acceptance rates); invited, international, and national scholarly presentations, and the like.

Teaching is a highly valued activity as well, albeit likely more valued in a college of education than in most other colleges across the university. As such, this too is a substantive part of each faculty member's total professional responsibilities. All faculty members are expected to be accomplished teachers. Accordingly, all faculty members are evaluated according to their efforts that result in increased levels of student learning and achievement, however that might be defined. Outcomes used as evidence might include instructor-developed tests, supervisor and peer evaluations, and other forms of evidence (e.g., innovative research projects in which students are engaged). Here, though, the university mandates that faculty also include as evidence of their instructional effectiveness, results from student evaluations. While this is a university-based mandate, each college reserves the right to develop and validate its own student survey instruments as per what faculty members within the college collectively value and believe is important in terms of teaching effectiveness in higher education. As well, each college reserves the right to use the resulting data in context, with the survey's strengths and weaknesses interpreted in context (see, for example, Amrein-Beardsley & Haladyna, 2009, 2012).

Service includes the activities in which faculty engage that contribute to the institutions of which they are a part (i.e., the university and college), the profession in which they are members (e.g., at the national and state levels), and the greater communities in which they are citizens. Excellence in service must be demonstrated with evidence that faculty members take on leadership roles in their institutions, the profession, and their greater communities; that they contribute significantly to the betterment of local agencies; and that they offer their intellectual property and professional time to each constituency, for free. This is all in line with university goals and objectives, but again, each college reserves the right to define how they value the ways in which services might be provided. As well, they reserve the right to define how service is to be demonstrated and evaluated.

Thereafter, all faculty are evaluated by their performance, progress, potential, and whether they met their pre-established and agreed-upon goals, in all three areas, once per year, by both their peers (i.e., via a Personnel Evaluation Committee [PEC]) and their direct supervisors. The PEC includes five tenured faculty members who are elected by their peers to serve three years on this committee. They are responsible for evaluating all of their peers, and themselves when excused from deliberations, every year, after which they send their agreed scores for each faculty member to that member's direct supervisors. After supervisors rank and score the faculty members, as informed by the PEC, summative decisions are made, for example, about probation, promotion, and merit pay. As well, formative feedback provided by the PEC and directors is delivered back to those who were evaluated. This, along with putting together and interpreting the evaluative evidence for the narrative needed per evaluation, satisfies the formative functions and needs of the evaluative system.

Thereafter, this follows what would appear to be a weighted system, whereby scholarship (typically) counts for 40%, teaching (typically) counts for 40%, and service (typically) counts for 20% of a faculty member's total effort and productivity (see Figure 8.2). I say typically

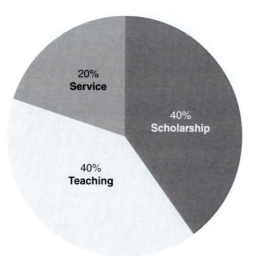

Figure 8.2 A pie chart illustrating how college faculty are sometimes evaluated according to their three main professional responsibilities.

because everything is negotiated on an individual basis, according to each faculty member's strengths, weaknesses, and yearly goals. As well, the final scores per area are treated as distinct scores, but they are also often collapsed as needed and as appropriate whereas numerically weighted averages are almost never used. For example, if a faculty member gets a score of 4 in scholarship, a 3 in teaching, and a 3 in service, the overall score might still be a 4, if, for the individual faculty member, scholarship is the priority and the evaluators making consensus decisions are given the appropriate liberties to adjust the scores accordingly. Otherwise, using strict mathematics to calculate a weighted average, the score would have been a three ($[(4 \times 40\%) + (3 \times 40\%) + (3 \times 20\%)] / 3 = 3$).

Finally, one might ask whether there are data that support with evidence that this might be a better approach? The answer is yes! While writing this book, I gained confidential access to the anonymous personnel files of my colleagues. I did this to test this assertion, in particular to see how faculty members' evaluation scores in my college ($n = 50$) have fared over the last three years, from 2010–2012, having been evaluated yearly by both the PEC and faculty supervisors, and in terms of reliability and validity. Running simple correlational analyses, the data yielded the following findings.

In terms of reliability (see Figure 6.1 in Chapter 6), the consistency with which the PEC ranked faculty members over this three-year period was very strong ($r = 0.75$). The consistency with which faculty members' supervisors ranked the same 50 faculty members over the same period of time was also very strong ($r = 0.75$). In terms of criterion-related evidence of validity, the correlations among scores, independently derived by both the PEC and faculty members' supervised, yielded strong to very strong correlations across all years of analysis (i.e., 2010: $r = 0.68$; 2011: $r = 0.84$; 2012: $r = 0.83$) and very strong correlations across all of the constructs of interest as well (i.e., scholarship: $r = 0.85$; teaching: $r = 0.76$; service: $r = 0.78$; overall: $r = 0.76$).

Some might wonder, however, if the strong correlations yielded via this system are due to a lack of rigor yielding a lack of variation in the scores. To demonstrate that this was not the case, or rather that the scores were quite evenly distributed across faculty as evaluated by both the PEC and faculty members' supervisors, see Figure 8.3. This figure illustrates that the distribution of faculty scores was well dispersed, over the same three-year period (2010–2012), using a 4-to-1 point scale with 4 being the highest, whereby a score of 4 means that the faculty member exceeded the responsibilities of the position in a sustained and outstanding manner; a score of 3 means that the faculty member met the responsibilities of the position; a score of 2 means that the faculty member only marginally met the responsibilities of the position; and a score of 1 means that the faculty member did not meet the responsibilities of the position. Note, as well, that while there is a positive skew to the data (i.e., that there are more 4s allocated than there are 3s, and that there are more 3s allocated than there are 2s, etc.), this also makes sense as faculty members who do not receive tenure after demonstrating a lack of success and promise are almost always filtered out of the system (i.e., terminated or denied continuous probation). This, appropriately, results in a positive skew because these faculty, along with their low evaluation scores, are continuously removed from the college, and hence from the evaluation system and its archived scores. Also importantly, what is demonstrated here is that *not* "All [99% of the] teachers are rated good or great," the fear perpetuated by some (Weisberg et al., 2009). As well, excellence does not go unrecognized (see also Weisberg et al., 2009), as those with the top scores are often rewarded monetarily and otherwise.

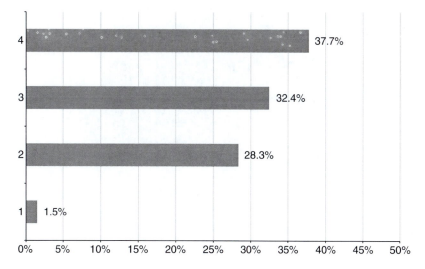

Figure 8.3 A distribution of faculty members' evaluation scores ($n = 50$) within one college of education over three separate evaluation periods (2010–2012).

While these data represent findings from one college's evaluation system, within one university, systems are often similar across institutions. As such, it is important to note that the correlation coefficients demonstrated here, as compared to the correlation coefficients illustrated and discussed throughout the chapters heretofore, suggest that relying on human judgment versus fixed and fixated notions about what mathematics can or should be used to do under such conditions is remiss. When attempting to capture and evaluate complex constructs (i.e., teaching effectiveness), it simply does not have to be that difficult.

Data from this simple albeit rigorous system have illustrated this here, via simple correlations analyses. Accordingly, as also evidenced, this type of system might be more promising than all of the current evaluation systems being mandated and implemented across the country as we speak. I would bet my good arm that teachers in America's public schools could welcome, adopt, and cooperate with a similar system, if given the authority, permission, and trust to do so. (For an example of such a system, that is not over reliant on VAM-based measures, and that can be used for teachers who are both VAM-eligible and not VAM-eligible, see Figures 8.4 and 8.5 respectively; see also the model being used in Connecticut; Thomas, 2012.)

For an example of such a system, that is not explicitly reliant on VAM-based measures, and that is even more holistic and based on a theory capturing what it might mean to be an effective teacher, see Figure 8.6. A system like this would be even fairer as it is potentially useful for all teachers regardless of the subject areas they teach, and the information that could be submitted per area could be much more individualized but also standardized according to subject area, grade level, and the decisions of all of the educators involved (e.g., observational data as evidence of good teaching).

Recall Einstein's quote: "Any intelligent fool can make things bigger and more complex.... It takes a touch of genius – and a lot of courage to move in the opposite direction." This is precisely the type of system which I advocate here. This is a system that relies on multiple measures that are locally developed, and possibly externally validated, that all align with a

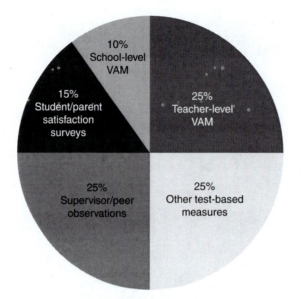

Figure 8.4 A pie chart illustrating how a better, more holistic, evaluation system *might* look for teachers who are VAM–eligible.

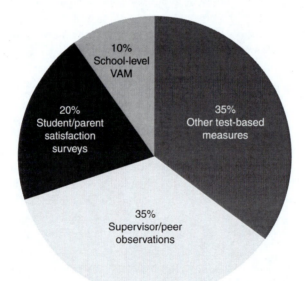

Figure 8.5 A pie chart illustrating how a better, more holistic, evaluation system *might* look for teachers who are *not* VAM-eligible.

locally defined theory capturing what it means to be an effective teacher. This is a system that relies on competent and professional supervisors and a set of peer-elected colleagues who represent the evaluated, but also independently and together review, evaluate, and rate their colleagues every year, and do so often with more rigor (McKenna, 2012; see also Baker et al., 2010, p. 20; Eckert, 2010; Lander & Pautsch, 2011). This is a system in which evaluators

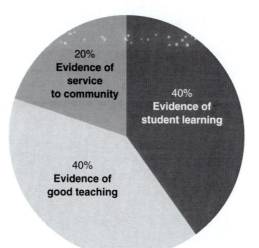

■ Teachers are committed to (and responsible for) students and their learning

■ Teachers know their subject areas, how to teach them, and continuously
    strive to improve

■ Teachers are good citizens and active participants within their communities

Figure 8.6 A pie chart illustrating how a better, more holistic, evaluation system *might* look for all teachers.

interpret each measure in context, and take into consideration each measure's strengths and weaknesses, how each strength and weakness might offset the strengths and weaknesses of the other measures included, how the measures might altogether capture what it means to be an effective teacher, and how the measures might be used in independent, complementary, and supplementary ways (see also Chester, 2003). This is a system that values what the evaluated have to say about the measures being used to evaluate them and what they can add to what the measures being used do not and possibly cannot capture. All of this is accomplished using narratives written by those being evaluated, on their own behalves.

As well, this is a summative system in that it yields scores, whereby the data yielded *per* multiple measure might ultimately be assigned a score as per a pre-determined ordinal scale (e.g., a four-point scale). While one final score representing teaching as one theoretical construct might not be the desired end, scores per measure representing teaching as a complex set of activities that represent a predetermined and locally defined theory might be desired instead (Messick, 1975; see also Baeder, 2010; Campbell, Kyriakides, Muijs, & Robinson, 2012; Gabriel & Allington, 2011). Nonetheless, reducing evaluators' assessments into scores ultimately permits low- and high-stakes summative decision-making (Cronbach & Gleser, 1965), at multiple levels, and, if collectively desired, about things like merit-based bonuses or salary increases, promotions and demotions, granting and revoking tenure, probation, professional growth plans, hiring, and firing (Baker et al., 2010, p. 20; Braun, 2005; Darling-Hammond, 2012; Liu & Teddlie, 2005; McKenna, 2012; Weisberg et al., 2009).

This is also a formative system that can be used for making determinations about weaknesses, or who might need immediate intervention, attention, and professional development.

It can also be used to identify strengths, from which those involved can make better deter-minations about who might best serve the institution in additional roles as peer assistance team members, teacher coaches, teacher mentors, and teacher leaders. Decision-makers here on both ends (i.e., those making summative and formative decisions) might include the peer evaluation teams, but more often it is the (hopefully active, skillful, professional, effective, and visionary) school leaders and administrators who make the final decisions as they are ulti-mately responsible for moving schools forward towards meeting the goals and objectives of the school each year, and they are most privy to their schools' human and financial resources and capabilities. All of this must be considered as well (Sparks, 2013; see also Eckert, 2010).

Finally, what also ultimately matter are the intended and unintended consequences of the evaluative system, and more specifically the evaluative system's implementation and use. Investigating system consequences requires at least a quasi-robust research plan to evaluate and refine the system to make it better and determine whether it is meeting the needs and desires of those involved. Questions to keep in mind, as aligned with the general research premises discussed in the previous chapters, might include: whether the model identifies teachers essentially the same from year to year and how consistent scores are over time against each measure in the system (i.e., evidence of reliability); whether the scores derived via the multiple measures seem to be appraising the same things, and whether major or minor changes in the evaluation system might dramatically impact results (i.e., evidence of validity); whether trends exist whereby teachers teaching certain sets of students (e.g., ELLs, gifted and special education students, children from racial minority backgrounds, students receiving free or reduced-cost lunches, students who have been retained in grade for multiple years, students in remedial or other tracked programs) consistently demonstrate higher or lower scores on average, and on any of the measurement's scores (i.e., evidence of bias); whether all teachers involved have enough, good evaluative information that can be used to appropriately evaluate them, and whether certain teachers (e.g., by subject area or grade level) benefit more than others as a result of having different types of evidence to support their effectiveness (i.e., fair-ness). What additional sources of evidence might help to continuously support system improvement (i.e., summative and formative functionality)? And, of course, what might the intended and unintended consequences of the system and system implementation be? More specifically, does system use incite gaming techniques, and what does all of this mean in terms of promoting student learning and achievement (Baker et al., 2010; Chester, 2003; Hill, 2009; Sass, 2008)?

"If we set out to be *methodologists*, we set out to be experts in problems and, hopefully, inventors of solutions" (Campbell, 1979, p. 69). This is the best conventional, and as such, time-tested and research-based solution of which I am aware. As well, it is a solution with which I have great personal experience, as I have both been evaluated within such a system as a college professor and been elected (and trusted) by my peers as a college professor to evaluate them as well. That said, I firmly believe, as aligned with Albert Shanker (1985), without such a system we do not otherwise "have the right to be called professionals – and we will never convince the public that we are … unless we are prepared honestly to decide what constitutes competence in our profession and what constitutes incompetence and apply those definitions to ourselves and our colleagues" (as cited in Toch & Rothman, 2008, p. 15). This is precisely what I am calling for here and for teachers across America's public schools.

Overall summary

Humankind has a rich history of using extreme social engineering methods to methodically sway public attitudes and behaviors to achieve idealized ends. By definition, a public policy is a tool used by governments to define a course of action that will ultimately lead to a high-level, supreme, and desirable end. In 1983, the U.S. Department of Education released *A Nation at Risk* – a report that harshly condemned the failing conditions of the American public schools. Despite scholars' discrediting of the report (Berliner & Biddle, 1995), fear had set into the public, and, under a Measure and Punish (M&P) Theory of Change, three decades of measurement-driven education policies ensued. The M&P Theory of Change argues that by holding districts, schools, teachers, and students accountable for performance on states' large-scale standardized achievement tests, administrators would supervise the schools better, teachers would teach better, and students would learn more, particularly in the nation's lowest performing schools, and all with disregard of the other agents at play (e.g., poverty).

However, the fact of the matter is that this theory of change is grossly flawed and misguided, and correspondingly, it has not yielded its intended effects (i.e., increased levels of student achievement). Likewise, many early proponents of this M&P Theory of Change have since become its strongest opponents. Nonetheless, the most recent school reform effort, *Race to the Top* (RttT; 2011), followed the same misguided logic of the M&P Theory of Change, requiring that states receiving RttT funds use students' test scores for even more consequential purposes and adopt even stronger accountability mechanisms than those required by the policy's predecessor, *No Child Left Behind* (NCLB), this time to hold teachers even more accountable than their students for increased levels of student learning and achievement. Though such policies have had detrimental effects on students, primarily by denying many students proper, appropriate, fair, and equal opportunities to learn, private corporations have fared quite well putting such initiatives into play, as the initiatives have delivered substantial benefits. Recent estimates indicate that we as a nation now spend well over $1.7 billion on tests, excluding the costs that come along with tests' associated resources (e.g., test preparation packets, workbooks, and materials) and other related costs (e.g., administrative and instructional time costs for test preparation and administration). We now spend more so that these test scores can be evaluated using advanced statistics, which is also requiring states to spend more as they develop or more often adopt (often with fees) value-added models to conduct these analyses.

In order to meet the demands of RttT, 44 states and the District of Columbia have since developed or more often adopted some form of a value-added model to statistically and more objectively measure the amount of "value" that a teacher adds to a student's learning over the course of each school year. While even the U.S. Department of Education found mixed results after sponsoring a series of state pilots to test how VAMs might be integrated into statewide accountability policies, and despite the warnings of most VAM researchers at the time, federal policymakers have still funneled billions in taxpayer revenues to incentivize all states to integrate VAMs into their state accountability policies. Accordingly, 30 states and DC now have state legislation or regulations that require student achievement data be used to substantively inform both the evaluation of teacher effectiveness and subsequent decision-making efforts.

The use of VAMs has faced harsh criticism from educators and education scholars, and nearly all (i.e., approximately 95%) of value-added researchers are academically protesting the misuse of VAMs. The 5% that are VAM supporters include VAM statisticians, economists, politicians, policymakers, and business savvy philanthropists, who continue to promote the overstated power and potential of VAMs, often using their own research to support their positions. Also included in the 5% of VAM supporters are entrepreneurs, statisticians, and economists affiliated with the biggest testing, research, and educational measurement companies and non-profit organizations offering their value-added services, models, and systems to state and district leaders for sizable profits and gains, again using publicly subsidized monies. They continue to immortalize the view that VAMs provide a statistical sophistication that can effectively measure teacher impact on student learning. They do so by utilizing a series of unchecked assumptions to preserve their stands and promote their positions.

VAM advocates will have people believe that if only teachers could be measured, evaluated, and held accountable, students would learn more and achieve higher; but the truth of the matter is that teachers only account for 10–20% of the differences in student achievement test scores. Even though teachers are strong *in-school* factors, they do not have nearly as much impact on student achievement as is commonly assumed. In fact, 80–90% of the difference in students' test scores is related to out-of-school factors (e.g., students' home lives, parents, access to resources) over which teachers have no control. Additionally, there is an assumption that schools are failing because of exorbitant numbers of bad teachers; when actually, not nearly as many teachers are in fact ineffectual, particularly when "teacher effectiveness" is quantified in normative terms, as is the case with VAM estimates that identify 50% of any given set of teachers as relatively ineffective.

VAM logic also assumes that monetary incentives will encourage teachers to work harder and teach better; but the truth is that merit-based reforms have been proposed time and time again as a way to boost student achievement, and there is no evidence to suggest that such systems have ever worked. In fact, research suggests that merit-based systems such as these have had detrimental effects on students and teachers, inciting teachers to teach to the test, narrow the curriculum, and so forth, particularly around the times that high-stakes tests count (Amrein-Beardsley & Collins, 2012; Capitol Hill Briefing, 2011; Collins, 2012; Darling-Hammond et al., 2012; Player, 2010; Vogell et al., 2012). There is also no evidence that using VAM-based data in formative ways will help increase student learning and achievement because VAM formulas are often perceived as being confusing, overly obscure, and complex, so much so that few teachers, few administrators, and few people in general understand the output or how to interpret and use VAM estimates. Also, because the data are typically designed for summative, not formative, purposes, this also (obviously) limits formative use.

Not only do unwarranted assumptions pervade the rationales behind the need for VAMs, however, there are statistical and methodological problems that are often dismissed or ignored by VAM advocates as well. For example, all VAM methods and statistics are based on large-scale standardized achievement test scores, even though it is well known that scores taken from these tests do *not* provide wholly accurate indicators of educational effectiveness as often assumed. In addition, large-scale standardized achievement tests were designed to measure students' levels of achievement, but they were never designed to estimate teachers' causal effects on student learning. The fact remains that VAMs are meant only to measure changes in student achievement over time but NOT to attribute this growth to some cause (i.e., teacher, administrator, school, district, state, or program quality). Yet VAMs are being used for these purposes regardless.

This is further complicated by the fact that achievement tests in and of themselves are laden with validity issues, primarily caused by outside factors that distort or contaminate students' test scores. Correlations between student test scores and students' demographic and environmental backgrounds are so strong that one (i.e., students' demographics) can effectively be used to predict the other (i.e., students' test scores), even before students take the tests, with near perfect precision. This is complicated further when VAMs use two or more sets of these test scores to measure growth over time. While VAM statisticians claim that by controlling for certain student-, classroom-, and school-level factors they can isolate students' learning and attribute the learning directly to their teachers of record, it is (and will likely remain) impossible to account for all of the factors that affect student achievement and learning over time even if the fanciest of statistics are used. Hence, VAM-based bias still exists, particularly for teachers who teach more homogeneous sets of students (e.g., ELLs, special education, and gifted students). This is all contaminated by the fact that VAMs also cannot account for the effects that prior teachers' residual effects, summer gains and losses, and the impacts other team teachers, counselors, classroom aides, tutors, and administrators might also have on student test scores.

The ideal empirical approach to lessening these issues would be to randomly assign students to classrooms (and teachers to classrooms), but this has also been shown to be highly unlikely and unrealistic. Perhaps the "explicit balancing of student characteristics across classrooms and the assignment of each teacher to multiple classes per year [might help] … [V]alue-added measures [might serve as] a less error-prone component of the overall 'toolbox'" (Schochet & Chiang, 2010, p. 36). Perhaps not.

Though different models vary in terms of how precisely estimates are made, it is becoming increasingly evident that all forms of VAMs are, in the end, unreliable, and hence invalid, biased at least for some, and unfair in that 60–70% of teachers are not even VAM-eligible. This is because their students do not take state achievement tests. But, really, which teachers are worse off? Those who are VAM-eligible run the risk of being misclassified 25% to 33% of the time, depending on how many years of prior test scores can be used to measure growth over time. Another persistent validity problem is that value-added scores often do not align well with other measures of teacher quality, such as classroom observation scores, student surveys, teacher honors, and other more subjective indicators. Also, students who take similar subject area tests at the same time within the same grade levels have been found to post vastly different scores. This also has implications for validity in that a teacher's value-added score largely depends on which test their students take. If valid, the test, even if similar, should not matter; really any test should yield a similar score per teacher regardless. Nonetheless, objective teacher evaluation systems are so much desired that the quantification of the teacher effectiveness is increasingly being positioned to supersede, if not replace, traditional evaluation systems based, even in part, on subjective human judgments.

The conventional solution offered in this book, and detailed in this chapter, instead, relies heavily on human judgment. This is an evaluative approach that values rigorous, ongoing assessments of activities that are conducted by experts who review multiple indicators and use human judgment to make low- and high-stakes decisions about those being evaluated. Rather than fixating on replacing human judgments with formulaic, inconsistent, imprecise, and sometimes biased statistical techniques (i.e., VAMs), the approach I suggest here, with research in support, is to figure out what will help evaluators make the best, most rigorous, most rational, and most democratic judgments, all things considered. Again, this would be based on multiple measures that capture the construct of interest (teaching effectiveness), narratives written by the evaluated on their own behalves explaining the multiple measures within context, and other supplementary material as needed. All of this would be examined and assessed by a representative, elected, and appointed team of colleagues who have also evidenced themselves as fair, accurate, and discriminate, according to the goals and objectives of the institution. At the end of the day, VAMs should never be used to measure anything in isolation, particularly in consequential ways.

VAMs are the instruments in which too many are unwisely trusting, and VAMs are the instruments many are pitching, and in some cases selling, for profit, to a naïve, uncritical, and highly assuming public. Statistics are being used to convey authority and intimidate others into accepting VAMs simply because VAMs are based on statistics and their mystique, despite statistics' gross limitations. Metaphorically speaking, America's public schools are being silenced, given the educational opportunities and experiences that high-stakes tests are in many cases annihilating, particularly in the schools most in need of genuine guidance and support. Educational reform in this case is failing, ironically due to a lack of accountability to its own history.

Overall conclusions

The summer before I finished writing this book, one summer after having spent time with my family traveling throughout Asia and, as discussed in the introduction of this book, Cambodia, I spent time with my family traveling throughout northern Europe. What I found most inspiring here, one year later, in contrast to what I learned to my chagrin about the Cambodian Holocaust in Siem Reap, was what I learned to my delight about the Finnish education system. I essentially voyaged from a wonderfully inspiring country with a tragic history in one summer to a literally life-giving country in the summer following. In Finland, while reading *Finnish Lessons* (Sahlberg, 2011), I learned more about its education system and why its education system makes Finland one of the best and most educated countries in the world.

"[U]nlike many other contemporary systems of education, the Finnish education system has not been infected by market-like competition and high-stakes testing policies" (Sahlberg, 2011, p. 39). Finland relies very little on testing, *and* it continues to be considered the highest-achieving nation in the world. What the Finnish do is indeed different (e.g., they value their teachers as they do their doctors and lawyers), and what they do (and do not do) should be used to change if not get over our country's complete and utter love affair with testing schools on the assumption that this will improve the students, teachers, and others within them.

"If education is ever to make serious generational progress, educators must somehow stop the pendulum by focusing their efforts to improve education on programs that are effective, rather than on those that are merely new and sound good" (Slavin, 1989, p. 752). Correspondingly, educational policymakers and others cannot continue to address the supposed plight of America's schools by promoting and adopting an empirically and morally void accountability mechanism, one based largely on false assumptions, myths, and overly simplistic fixes to highly complex problems (Berliner, 2010, 2011, 2012; Carter, 2004; Kozol, 2005).

This approach simply does not work, nor has it worked for the last 30 years we have tried it in the U.S., and elsewhere. Hence, there is really no reason to be optimistic about this movement, again, even with the addition of new and improved value-added metrics and models to conduct better analyses using, yet again, test scores. As it still stands, as also stated over one decade ago, "Those who look to value-added assessment as the solution to the problem of educational accountability are likely to be disappointed" (Ballou, 2002). Decades of disappointment about right captures it. Using value-added methods is, still, "above all, not a panacea, or even a *solution* to be recommended widely" (Baird, 1987, p. 214 [emphasis added]; see also Baker, 2011; Bracey, 2004b; Pickering & Bowers, 1990; Schaeffer, 2004; Slavin, 1989).

Some things simply have to change, within and beyond America's public schools, and given the economic and social conditions of the communities in which America's public schools exist and function. "[A] recognition of the broader nature of root causes, which cannot all be eliminated simply by holding schools and teachers more accountable" (Carter, 2004, p. 135) is a step in the right direction. As is valuing and understanding teacher (and school/district) evaluation for what it is, for what it is worth, and for what it can and cannot do.

Box 8.1 Top 10 assertions

1 Educational policymakers and others cannot continue to address the supposed plight of America's schools by promoting and adopting an empirically and morally void accountability mechanism, one based largely on false assumptions, myths, and overly simplistic fixes to highly complex problems.

2 Stripping VAM estimates of the context from which they were created leads to problems with interpreting and fully understanding reliability, validity, bias, and fairness.

3 The data yielded via multiple measures should be interpreted using human judgments to make more reliable, valid, unbiased, and fairer determinations and decisions, even if for high-stakes purposes (e.g., merit pay, termination), about teacher quality and effectiveness.

4 Using multiple measures ensures that no indicator derived via any one evaluative measure needs to be a perfect indicator; the weaknesses of each indicator can be offset by the strengths of the other(s), although this does not increase overall levels of reliability and validity.

5 Credibility and trust are the most important features of any successful evaluation system, because with credibility, teachers and administrators are more likely to trust and ultimately use the output that is based on the measures used for evaluative purposes.

6 Educators' professional judgments should not be removed from personnel decisions, especially when legislating or regulating consequential actions be taken as a result.

7 States and/or districts should be given considerable discretion when developing their own measures, or choosing research-based measures that have been externally vetted and validated for the uses at hand.

8 The recommended evaluation system should rely on multiple measures that are also aligned with a locally defined theory capturing what it means to be an effective teacher.

9 The best alternative might rely on competent and professional supervisors and a set of peer-elected colleagues who represent the evaluated, but also independently and together review, evaluate, and rate their colleagues each year.

10 Investigating system consequences requires at least a quasi-robust research plan to evaluate and refine the evaluative system to make it better and to determine whether the system is meeting the needs and desires of those involved.

Notes

1 Baker et al. (2013, p. 5) wrote:

> Placing the measures alongside one another in a weighting scheme assumes all measures in the scheme to be of equal validity and reliability but of varied importance (utility) – varied weight. Validity in this case means that the assigned values or statistical estimates in question measure what they claim to – the effect a teacher has on her students' achievement growth over the course of the year. . . . Under common evaluation frameworks, each measure *must* be included, and must be assigned the prescribed weight – with no opportunity to question the validity of any measure. . . . Such a system also assumes that the various measures included in the system are each scaled such that they can vary to similar degrees. That is, that the obser-vational evaluations will be scaled to produce similar variation to the student growth meas-ures; and that the variance in both measures is equally valid – not compromised by random error or bias.

2 Recall that when teachers yield consistent value-added estimates over time, this may not be due to consistency in terms of the reliability desired and needed as a precondition to validity, but may rather be due to consistency that might by caused by bias. Recall as well that students are not ran-domly assigned to classrooms, and administrators, teachers, and parents play prodigious roles in student placement processes, making student sorting highly non-random and consistent value-added estimates sometimes even more problematic. Because of this, VAM-based estimates for teachers who teach more homogeneous populations of students over time (e.g., ELLs, special education students, students who receive free or reduced-cost lunches, students retained in grade for multiple years) are more adversely impacted by bias. It is this bias that must be investigated before any infer-ences or decisions are made about even the, supposedly, most excellent or most ineffective teachers (Baker et al., 2010; Briggs & Domingue, 2011; Hermann et al., 2013; Hill et al., 2011; McCaffrey, 2012; Newton et al., 2010).

3 "A theory is a well-substantiated set of interrelated conjectures about a group of concepts that help people understand phenomena" (Amrein-Beardsley & Haladyna, 2012, p. 18). Put differently, theo-ries guide how people react to and make sense of the phenomena of interest, and theories should also help frame how people understand and explain the same phenomena.

4 I would recommend that human judgment, not strict mathematics, is used to make evaluative judg-ments about which components are most important in a so-called "weighted" system. In a numeri-cally weighted system, think about whether the value-added estimates might be weighted over time as an example of why this will not necessarily work here. Averaging value-added estimates over time means, essentially, that you would take an average of scores that have the potential to jump around from the 20th to the 80th and back to the 20th percentile again. Your average score might reveal some level of mathematical certainty (i.e., an average at the 40th percentile), but this average would be highly misleading and would also mask the lack of stability at issue with VAMs (see also Baker, 2013a).

5 In New York, for example, 40% of teachers' evaluation scores are to be based on the value they add to or detract from student learning, and the other 60% is to be based on other measures including teachers' supervisor and/or peer evaluation scores and feedback from students and/or parents. But one sentence in their policy indicates what truly matters, regardless of their seemingly holistic approach based on multiple measures. Here it is written that teachers who are rated as "ineffective" on student performance alone must be rated as "ineffective" overall. Simply put, however a teacher might have done in the eyes of his/her students, students' parents, supervisors, or peers would not matter whatsoever, *if* the growth or value-added demonstrated by the teacher was poor. This would in effect generate a teacher evaluation system that, while theoretically based on multiple measures, is rather a system that is in actuality based only on the one measure that counts for 100% of the teacher's alleged effectiveness – the teacher's value-added. In New York, the plan is also that if a teacher demonstrates two years of ineffectiveness, that teacher is to be terminated (Ravitch, 2012c; see also Giordano, 2012; Turque, 2012).

6 End of course exams are criterion-referenced tests that are given at the end of a course to test student mastery of the content of that course. They are typically administered at the high school levels and accordingly include more tests of more subject areas (e.g., Algebra I, Physics, English Literature, World History, Art, Physical Education) than most state-administered tests (unless states mandate

state-level end of course exams). In addition, they are typically more representative of the content taught as there are more items permitted to cover the concept areas to be tested; they are typically more informative because of the levels of specificity about what students have learned; and they increase fairness in that more (though still typically high school) teachers can be included in evaluation systems that use these tests. End of course exams do not have to be limited to just high school grades, however, and with the adoption of the tests aligned with the Common Core State Standards under way, this should help improve the testing situation in this area. In addition, districts can develop/adopt their own end of course exams as a part of their district accountability systems; states do not have to develop/adopt or mandate that they be used.

7 When using tests to measure gains within one academic year, caution is required to ensure that those involved, as yet another gaming technique, do not work to artificially decrease the pre-test scores to manufacture high levels of growth from the pre- to post-test occasion.

8 For more information about the SAT-9 see http://hobel.org/lwved/id71.htm. For more information about the Terra Nova see www.ctb.com/ctb.com/control/productFamilyViewAction?producttFamilyId=449&p=products. For more information about the Galileo tests see www.ati-online.com/.

9 The Aprenda is a "culturally inclusive" mathematics and reading/language arts test written in Spanish for Spanish speakers. For more information, see www.pearsonassessments.com/HAIWEB/Cultures/en-us/Productdetail.htm?Pid=Aprenda3. The Wechsler Individual Achievement Test® is a test designed to measure the academic strengths and weaknesses of students, particularly special education students. For more information see www.pearsonassessments.com/HAIWEB/Cultures/en-us/Productdetail.htm?Pid=015-8984-609. The Stanford-Binet Intelligence Scale tests fluid reasoning, knowledge, quantitative reasoning, visual-spatial processing, and working memory, also often for special education students. For more information see www.riverpub.com/products/sb5/.

10 For more information about Danielson's Framework for Teaching, see www.danielsongroup.org/article.aspx?page=frameworkforteaching. Other instruments also available include protocols that are a part of TAP: The System for Teacher and Student Advancement supported by the Milken Foundation (for more information see www.talentedteachers.org/); the Classroom Assessment Scoring System (CLASS) from Teachstone Training, LLC (for more information see www.teachstone.org/about-the-class/); California's Performance Assessment for California Teachers (PACT) program (for more information see www.pacttpa.org/_main/hub.php?pageName=Home; Colorado's Peer Assistance and Review (PAR) 10 approach (for more information see www.coloradoea.org/TeachingLearning/EdEffective/peerassist.aspx), Connecticut's Beginning Educator's Support and Training (BEST) system (for more information see www.sde.ct.gov/sde/lib/sde/pdf/commish/BEST_MAP_TaskForceReport.pdf), and the system developed by the National Board for Professional Teaching Standards (NBPTS; for more information see www.nbpts.org/).

11 For example, research-based criticisms about the TAP System for Teacher and Student Advancement are becoming increasingly prevalent (e.g., Glazerman & Seifullah, 2010; Sawchuck, 2010; see also Gratz, 2010) despite the results some internal research studies have suggested (e.g., Schacter & Thum, 2004; Solomon, White, Cohen, & Woo, 2007).

12 Research suggests that principals demonstrate less reliable and valid evaluation scores when compared to teachers who conduct the same evaluations. Principals' ratings are based on fewer observations; their analyses of teachers' practice tend to focus on fewer areas of interest in terms of how one defines teaching effectiveness; and the documentation of evidence provided by principals tends to be scarce (Koppich & Humphrey, 2011).

13 Inter-rater reliability represents the degree to which raters, in this case conducting observations, agree in terms of the scores they assign per observations. Research suggests that including the perspectives of two or more observers per observation enhances reliability, and hence supports validity (Bill & Melinda Gates Foundation, 2013; Harris, 2010; Toch & Rothman, 2008).

14 Research suggests that two to four observations per academic year is common, although limited research suggests that four observations is the optimal number (Harris, 2012b).

15 Any instrument, in this case survey instruments, can be distorted quite easily when stakes are attached to instrument output. As Campbell's Law would have it, for example, young adults might take advantage of opportunities to influence their teachers' lives and careers and, accordingly, may not answer honestly. As well, and as is common, teachers might express more lenience, alter their attitudes and/or practices to cater to student demands, present other artificial inflators (e.g., pizza or

donut parties, extra credit points, point deductions, idle threats, discouraging all or certain respondents from participating, and other incentives, rewards, or sanctions) to artificially inflate their scores (see also Rothstein, 2011).

16 This is an important consideration knowing that teachers might reduce their effort in years they are not evaluated (Milanowski, 2004). Conversely, they might not. But if stakes (e.g., merit pay) are attached to yearly evaluations, then conducting evaluations yearly might be the only feasible and fair option, or again not (e.g., teachers might prefer to alternate or rotate evaluation years and adjust merit pay decisions to follow a similar schedule).

REFERENCES

Aaronson, D., Barrow, L., & Sanders, W. (2007). Teachers and student achievement in the Chicago Public High Schools. *Journal of Labor Economics, 25*, 95–135. doi:10.1086/508733

Adler, M. (2013, February 1). Findings vs. interpretations in "The long-term impacts of teachers" by Chetty et al. *Education Policy Analysis Archives, 21*(10), 1–14. Retrieved from epaa.asu.edu/ojs/article/download/1264/1033

Ahmed-Ullah, J. S., Hood, J., & Mack, K. (2012, September 10). Picket lines up after CPS, teachers fail to prevent strike. *Chicago Tribune.* Retrieved from http://articles.chicagotribune.com/2012–09–10/news/chi-chicago-public-schools-chicago-teachers-union-contract-talks-strike_1_picket-lines-teachers-strike-president-david-vitale

Alexander, K. L., Entwisle, D. R., & Olson, L. S. (2001). Schools, achievement, and inequality: A seasonal perspective. *Educational Evaluation and Policy Analysis, 23*(2), 171–191. doi:10.3102/01623737023002171

Alexander, K. L., Entwisle, D. R., & Olson, L. S. (2007a). Lasting consequences of the summer learning gap. *American Sociological Review, 72*, 167–180. doi:10.1177/000312240707200202

Alexander, K. L., Entwisle, D. R., & Olson, L. S. (2007b). Summer learning and its implications: Insights from the Beginning School Study. *New Directions for Youth Development, 114*, 11–32. doi:10.1002/yd.210

American Educational Research Association (AERA) (2000). *Position statement on high-stakes testing in PreK–12 education.* Retrieved from www.aera.net/AboutAERA/AERARulesPolicies/AERAPolicyStatements/PositionStatementonHighStakesTesting/tabid/11083/Default.aspx

American Educational Research Association (AERA), American Psychological Association (APA), & National Council on Measurement in Education (NCME). (2000). *Standards for educational and psychological testing.* Washington, DC: American Educational Research Association.

Ames, C. A. (1992). Classrooms: Goals, structures, and student motivation. *Journal of Educational Psychology, 84*(3), 261–271. doi:10.1037//0022–0663.84.3.261

Amrein, A. L., & Berliner, D. C. (2002). High-stakes testing, uncertainty, and student learning. *Education Policy Analysis Archives, 10*(18), 1–74. Retrieved from http://epaa.asu.edu/epaa/v10n18/

Amrein-Beardsley, A. (2008a). Methodological concerns about the Education Value-Added Assessment System (EVAAS®). *Educational Researcher, 37*(2), 65–75. doi:10.3102/0013189X08316420

Amrein-Beardsley, A. (2008b). "This is Jeopardy": A veritable potpourri of answers to the assaults on America's public schools. *School Administrator, 6*(65), 24–26.

Amrein-Beardsley, A. (2009a). Buyers be-aware: What you don't know can hurt you. *Educational Leadership, 67*(3), 38–42.

Amrein-Beardsley, A. (2009b. October 13). Controlling schools using high-stakes tests: Moral imperatives inspired by Rachel Carson. *Teachers College Record*. Retrieved from www.tcrecord.org/Content. asp?ContentId=15804

Amrein-Beardsley, A. (2012, January 12). Value-added measures in education: The best of the alternatives is simply not good enough. (Commentary). *Teachers College Record*. Retrieved from www. tcrecord.org/content.asp?contentid=16648

Amrein-Beardsley, A., & Barnett, J. H. (2012). Working with error and uncertainty to increase measurement validity. *Educational Assessment, Evaluation and Accountability*, 1–11. doi:10.1007/ s11092-012-9146-6

Amrein-Beardsley, A., Barnett, J. H., & Ganesh, T. (2013). Seven legitimate apprehensions about evaluating teacher education programs and seven "beyond excuses" imperatives. *Teachers College Record, 115*(2). Retrieved from www.tcrecord.org/content.asp?contentid=17251

Amrein-Beardsley, A., Berliner, D. C., & Rideau, S. (2010). Cheating in the first, second, and third degree: Educators' responses to high-stakes testing. *Education Policy Analysis Archives, 18*(14), 1–36. Retrieved from http://epaa.asu.edu/ojs/article/view/714

Amrein-Beardsley, A., & Collins, C. (2012). The SAS Education Value-Added Assessment System (SAS® EVAAS®) in the Houston Independent School District (HISD): Intended and unintended consequences. *Education Policy Analysis Archives, 20*(12), 1–36. Retrieved from http://epaa.asu.edu/ ojs/article/view/1096

Amrein-Beardsley, A., Collins, C., Polasky, S. A., & Sloat, E. (Eds.). (2013). Special issue on value-added models: What America's policy-makers need to know. *Education Policy Analysis Archives, 21*. Retrieved from http://epaa.asu.edu/ojs/article/view/1311

Amrein-Beardsley, A., & Haladyna, T. (2009). Tinkering with the traditional to assess and promote quality instruction: Learning from a new and unimproved instructional evaluation instrument. *Journal of College Teaching and Learning, 6*(4), 51–64.

Amrein-Beardsley, A., & Haladyna, T. M. (2012). Validating a theory-based survey to evaluate teaching effectiveness in higher education. *Journal on Excellence in College Teaching, 23*(1), 17–42.

Anderman, E. M., Anderman, L. Y., Yough, M. S., & Gimbert, B. G. (2010). Value-added models of assessment: Implications for motivation and accountability. *Educational Psychologist, 45*(2), 123–137. doi:10.1080/00461521003703045

Anderson, J. (2013, March 30). Curious grade for teachers: Nearly all pass. *New York Times*. Retrieved from www.nytimes.com/2013/03/31/education/curious-grade-for-teachers-nearly-all-pass.html? ref=nyregion&_r=1&

Andrejko, L. (2004). Value-added assessment: A view from a practitioner. *Journal of Educational and Behavioral Statistics, 29*(1), 7–9. doi:10.3102/10769986029001007

Andreoni, J., Harbaugh, W., & Versterlund, L. (2003). The carrot or the stick: Rewards, punishments, and cooperation. *American Economic Review, 93*(3), 893–902. doi:10.1257/000282803322157142

Anyon, J. (1997). *Ghetto schooling: A political economy of urban school reform*. New York, NY: Teachers College Press.

Arizona Department of Education. (2012). *State of Arizona race to the top*. Retrieved from www.azed. gov/racetothetop

Associated Press. (2013, May 22). Apple case seen as possible spur to tax action. *National Public Radio* (NPR). Retrieved from www.npr.org/templates/story/story.php?storyId=185742803

Attkisson, S. (2012, October 7). Behind the closed doors of Washington lobbyists. CBS News *Sunday Morning*. Retrieved from www.cbsnews.com/news/behind-the-closed-doors-of-washington- lobbyists/

Au, W. (2009). *Unequal by design: High-stakes testing and the standardization of inequality*. New York, NY: Routledge.

Au, W. (2011, Winter). Neither fair nor accurate: Research-based reasons why high-stakes tests should not be used to evaluate teachers. *Rethinking Schools*. Retrieved from www.rethinkingschools.org/ archive/25_02/25_02_au.shtml

Baeder, J. (2010, December 21). Gates' Measures of Effective Teaching study: More value-added madness. *Education Week.* Retrieved from http://blogs.edweek.org/edweek/on_performance/2010/12/gates_measures_of_effective_ teaching_study_more_value-added_madness.html

Baird, L. L. (1987). Value-added: Using student gains as yardsticks of learning. In C. Adelman (Ed.), *Performance and judgement: Essays on principles and practice in the assessment of college student learning* (pp. 205–216). Washington, DC: U.S. Government Printing Office.

Baker, B. D. (2011). Take your SGP and VAMit, Damn it! [Blog post]. Retrieved from http://school-finance101.wordpress.com/2011/09/02/take-your-sgp-and-vamit-damn-it/

Baker, B. D. (2012a, March 31). Firing teachers based on bad (VAM) versus wrong (SGP) measures of effectiveness: Legal note [Blog post]. Retrieved from http://schoolfinance101.wordpress.com/2012/03/31/firing-teachers-based-on-bad-vam-versus-wrong-sgp-measures-of-effectiveness-legal-note

Baker, B. (2012b, December 12). It's good to be King: More misguided rhetoric on the NY State Eval System. (Blog). Retrieved from http://schoolfinance101.wordpress.com/2012/12/12/its-good-to-be-king-more-misguided-rhetoric-on-the-ny-state-eval-system/

Baker, B. D. (2013a, January 9). Gates still doesn't get it! Trapped in a world of circular reasoning & flawed frameworks [Blog post]. Retrieved from http://schoolfinance101.wordpress.com/2013/01/09/gates-still-doesnt-get-it-trapped-in-a-world-of-circular-reasoning-flawed-frameworks/

Baker, B. D. (2013b, January 9). *Revisiting the Chetty, Rockoff, & Friedman molehill.* Boulder, CO: National Education Policy Center (NEPC). Retrieved from http://nepc.colorado.edu/blog/revisiting-chetty-rockoff-friedman-molehill

Baker, B. D., Oluwole, J. O., & Green, P. C. (2013). The legal consequences of mandating high stakes decisions based on low quality information: Teacher evaluation in the Race-to-the-Top era. *Education Policy Analysis Archives, 21*(5), 1–71. Retrieved from http://epaa.asu.edu/ojs/article/view/1298

Baker, E. L., Barton, P. E., Darling-Hammond, L., Haertel, E., Ladd, H. F., Linn, R. L. … Shepard, L. A. (2010). *Problems with the use of student test scores to evaluate teachers.* Washington, DC: Economic Policy Institute. Retrieved from www.epi.org/publications/entry/bp278

Ballou, D. (2002, Summer). Sizing up test scores. *Education Next.* Retrieved from educationnext.org/files/ednext20022_10.pdf

Ballou, D. (2004). Rejoinder. *Journal of Educational and Behavioral Statistics, 29*(1), 131–134. doi:10.3102/10769986029001131

Ballou, D. (2005). Value-added assessment: Lessons from Tennessee. In R. Lissetz (Ed.), *Value-added models in education: Theory and applications* (pp. 272–303). Maple Grove, MN: Journal of Applied Measurement (JAM) Press.

Ballou, D. (2009). Test scaling and value-added measurement. *Education Finance and Policy, 4*(4), 351–383. doi:10.1162/edfp2009.4.4.351

Ballou, D. (2012, February 16). Review of *The long-term impacts of teachers: Teacher value-added and student outcomes in adulthood,* by R. Chetty, J. Friedman, & J. Rockoff. Boulder, CO: National Education Policy Center. Retrieved from http://nepc.colorado.edu/thinktank/review-long-term-impacts

Ballou, D., Sanders, W. L., & Wright, P. (2004). Controlling for student background in value-added assessment of teachers. *Journal of Educational and Behavioral Statistics, 29*(1), 37–65.

Banchero, S. (2013, January 8). Good teachers linked to test success. *Wall Street Journal.* Retrieved from http://online.wsj.com/article/SB10001424127887323706704578230121388712506.html?mod=WSJ_WSJ_US_News_5

Banchero, S., & Kesmodel, D. (2011, September 13). Teachers are put to the test: More states tie tenure, bonuses to new formulas for measuring test scores. *Wall Street Journal.* Retrieved from http://online.wsj.com/article/SB10001424053111903895904576544523666669018.html

Barlevy, G., & Neal, D. (2012). Pay for percentile. *American Economic Review, 102*(5), 1805–1831. doi:10.1257/aer.102.5.1805

Battelle for Kids. (2013). *Leading collaborative change.* Retrieved from http://battelleforkids.org/how-we-help/communications-collaborative-change/leading-collaborative-change

Bausell, R. B. (2013, January 15). Probing the science of value-added evaluation. (Commentary). *Education Week.* Retrieved from www.edweek.org/ew/articles/2013/01/16/17bausell.h32.html?tkn=WYSFJQFebIaF9bGl0ZWx7G4%2BumWl9a5m58e9&cmp=ENL-EU-NEWS2&intc=es

Bellwether Education Partners. (2011, August). *Recent teacher effectiveness legislation: How do the states stack up?* Retrieved from http://bellwethereducation.org/

Berliner, D. C. (2002). Educational research: The hardest science of all. *Educational Researcher, 31*(8), 18–20. doi:10.3102/0013189X031008018

Berliner, D. C. (2005). The place of process–product research in developing the agenda for research on teacher thinking. In P. M. Denicolo and M. Kompf (Eds.), *Teacher thinking and professional action* (pp. 3–15). New York, NY: Routledge.

Berliner, D. C. (2010). New analysis of achievement gap: ½ × ½ = 1½. *Washington Post.* Retrieved from http://voices.washingtonpost.com/answer-sheet/guest-bloggers/new-analysis-of-achievement-ga.html#more

Berliner, D. C. (2011, May 1). The manufactured crisis revisited. *School Leadership Briefing.* Retrieved from www.schoolbriefing.com/1967/the-manufactured-crisis-revisited/

Berliner, D. C. (2012, October 16). Effects of inequality and poverty vs. teachers and schooling on America's youth. *Teachers College Record, 116*(1). Retrieved from www.tcrecord.org/Content.asp?ContentID=16889

Berliner, D. C. (2013). Exogenous variables and value-added assessments: A fatal flaw. *Teachers College Record 116*(1). Retrieved from www.tcrecord.org/Content.asp?ContentId=17293

Berliner, D. C., & Biddle, B. J. (1995). *The manufactured crisis: Myths, fraud, and the attack on America's public schools.* Reading, MA: Addison-Wesley Publishing Company, Inc.

Berry, B. (2004). Recruiting and retaining "high quality teachers" for hard to staff schools. *NASSP Bulletin, 88*(638), pp. 5–27. doi:10.1177/019263650408863802

Berry, B. (2008). *Recruiting and retaining quality teachers for high-needs schools: Insights from NBCT summits and other policy initiatives.* Washington, DC: Center for Teaching Quality. Retrieved from www.nbpts.org/index.cfm?t=downloader.cfm&id=757

Betebenner, D. W. (2008). *Norm- and criterion-referenced student growth.* Report of the National Center for the Improvement of Educational Assessment. Retrieved from Colorado Department of Education website: www.cde.state.co.us/cdedocs/Research/PDF/betebenner_norm_crit_measuresofgrowth.pdf

Betebenner, D. W. (2009a, April 6). *Growth, standards and accountability.* Dover, NH: The Center for Assessment. Retrieved from www.nciea.org/publication_PDFs/growthandStandard_DB09.pdf

Betebenner, D. W. (2009b). Norm- and criterion-referenced student growth. *Education Measurement: Issues and Practice, 28*(4), 42–51. doi:10.1111/j.1745–3992.2009.00161.x

Betebenner, D. W. (2011, April). *Student growth percentiles.* National Council on Measurement in Education (NCME) Training Session presented at the Annual Conference of the American Educational Research Association, New Orleans, LA.

Betebenner, D. W., & Linn, R. L. (2010). *Growth in student achievement: Issues of measurement, longitudinal data analysis, and accountability.* Exploratory Seminar: Measurement Challenges within the *Race to the Top* Agenda: Center for K–12 Assessment and Performance Management. Retrieved from www.k12center.org/rsc/pdf/BetebennerandLinnPolicyBrief.pdf

Biddle, B. J. (2001). *Social class, poverty, and education.* New York, NY: RoutledgeFalmer.

Bill & Melinda Gates Foundation. (2010, December). *Learning about teaching: Initial findings from the Measures of Effective Teaching project.* Seattle, WA. Retrieved from www.gatesfoundation.org/college-ready-education/Documents/preliminary-findings-research-paper.pdf

Bill & Melinda Gates Foundation. (2012, September). *Asking students about teaching: Student perception surveys and their implementation.* Seattle, WA: Measures of Effective Teaching (MET) project. Retrieved from www.metproject.org/downloads/Asking_Students_Practitioner_Brief.pdf

Bill & Melinda Gates Foundation. (2013, January 8). *Ensuring fair and reliable measures of effective teaching: Culminating findings from the MET project's three-year study.* Seattle, WA. Retrieved from www.gatesfoundation.org/press-releases/Pages/MET-Announcement.aspx

Block, D. (1998). Exploring interpretations of questionnaire items. *System, 26*(3), 403–425.

Bloom, H. S., Hill, C. J., Black, A. R., & Lipsey, M. W. (2008). Performance trajectories and performance gaps as achievement effect-size benchmarks for educational interventions. *Journal of Research on Educational Effectiveness, 1,* 289–328. doi:10.1080/19345740802400072

Boardman, A. E., & Murnane, R. J. (1979). Using panel data to improve estimates of the determinants of educational achievement. *Sociology of Education, 52*(2), 113–121. doi:10.2307/2112449

Bock, R. D., Wolfe, R., & Fisher, T. H. (1996). *A review and analysis of the Tennessee Value-Added Assessment System: Summary and recommendations.* Nashville: Tennessee Office of Education Accountability.

Bond, L., Smith, T., Baker, W. K., & Hattie. J. (2000). *The certification system of the National Board for Professional Teaching Standards: A construct and consequential validity study.* Greensboro, NC: Center for Educational Research and Evaluation.

Bonk, W. (2011). *District and school use of Colorado Growth Model results.* Report prepared for the Unit of Accountability and Improvement. Denver, CO: Colorado Department of Education. Retrieved from www.cde.state.co.us/.../GrowthStandardsAccountability.pdf

Bosworth, R., & Caliendo, F. (2007). Educational production and teacher preferences. *Economics of Education Review, 26*(4), 487–500. doi:10.1016/j.econedurev.2005.04.004

Boustan, L. P. (2011). Racial residential segregation in American cities. In N. Brooks & G. Knapp (Eds.), *Oxford Handbook of Urban Economics and Planning* (pp. 318–339). New York, NY: Oxford University Press.

Boyd, D., Grossman, P., Lankford, H., Loeb, S., & Wyckoff, J. (2008, May). *Who leaves? Teacher attrition and student achievement.* Cambridge, MA: National Bureau of Economic Research. Retrieved from www.nber.org/papers/w14022

Boyd, D., Lankford, H., Loeb, S., Ronfeldt, M., & Wyckoff, J. (2011). The role of teacher quality in retention and hiring: Using applications to transfer to uncover preferences of teachers and schools. *Journal of Policy Analysis and Management, 30*(1), 88–110. doi:10.1002/pam.20545

Bracey, G. W. (1995). Variance happens: Get over it! *Technos, 4*(3), 22–29.

Bracey, G. W. (2000). Value-added, value lost? *Rethinking Schools 15*(1). Retrieved from www.rethinkingschools.org/archive/15_01/Val151.shtml

Bracey, G. W. (2004a). Serious questions about the Tennessee Value-Added Assessment System. *Phi Delta Kappan, 85*(9), 716–717.

Bracey, G. W. (2004b). Value-added assessment findings: Poor kids get poor teachers. *Phi Delta Kappan, 86*(4), 331–333.

Bracey, G. W. (2007, May 1). Value subtracted: A "debate" with William Sanders. *Huffington Post.* Retrieved from www.huffingtonpost.com/gerald-bracey/value-subtracted-a-deba_b_47404.html

Branch, G. F., Rivkin, S. G., & Hanushek, E. A. (2013, Winter). School leaders matter. *Education Next, 13*(1). Retrieved from http://educationnext.org

Braun, H. I. (2004). *Value-added modeling: What does due diligence require?* Princeton, NJ: Educational Testing Service.

Braun, H. I. (2005). *Using student progress to evaluate teachers: A primer on value-added models.* Princeton, NJ: Educational Testing Service. Retrieved from www.ets.org/Media/Research/pdf/PICVAM.pdf

Braun, H. I. (2008). *Vicissitudes of the validators.* Paper presented at the 2008 Reidy Interactive Lecture Series, Portsmouth, NH. Retrieved from www.cde.state.co.us/cdedocs/OPP/HenryBraunLectureReidy2008.ppt

Braun, H., Goldschmidt, P., McCaffrey, D., & Lissitz, R. (2012). *Graduate student council Division D fireside chat: VA modeling in educational research and evaluation.* Paper presented at Annual Conference of the American Educational Research Association (AERA), Vancouver, Canada.

Brennan, R. L. (2006) *Perspectives on the evolution and future of educational measurement.* In R. L. Brennan (Ed.) *Educational measurement* (4th ed., pp. 1–16). Westport, CT: American Council on Education/Praeger.

Brennan, R. L. (2013). Commentary on "Validating interpretations and uses of test scores." *Journal of Educational Measurement, 50*(1), 74–83. doi:10.1111/jedm.12001

Briggs, D. (2012, April). Understanding the Colorado Growth Model. *New Jersey Education Association (NJEA) Review.* Retrieved from www.njea.org/news-and-publications/njea-review/april-2012/understanding-the-colorado-growth-model

Briggs, D. C., & Betebenner, D. (2009). *Is growth in student achievement scale dependent?* Paper presented at the annual meeting of the National Council for Measurement in Education, San Diego, CA.

Briggs, D. C., & Domingue, B. (2011, February). *Due diligence and the evaluation of teachers: A review of the value-added analysis underlying the effectiveness rankings of Los Angeles Unified School District Teachers by the Los Angeles Times.* Boulder, CO: National Education Policy Center. Retrieved from nepc. colorado.edu/publication/due-diligence

Briggs, D. C., & Weeks, J. P. (2009). The sensitivity of value-added modeling to the creation of a vertical scale score. *Education Finance and Policy, 4*(4), 384–414. doi:10.1162/edfp.2009.4.4.384

Brill, S. (2009, August 31). The rubber room. *New Yorker.* Retrieved from www.newyorker.com/ reporting/2009/08/31/090831fa_fact_brill

Brooks, D. (2012, April 19). Testing the teachers. *New York Times.* Retrieved from www.nytimes. com/2012/04/20/opinion/brooks-testing-the-teachers.html?_r=2&

Brophy, J. (1973). Stability of teacher effectiveness. *American Educational Research Journal, 10*(3), 245–252. doi:10.2307/1161888

Buddin, R. J. (2011). *How effective are Los Angeles elementary teachers and schools?* MPRA Paper, University Library of Munich, Germany. Retrieved from http://econpapers.repec.org/scripts/showcites. pf?h=repec:pra:mprapa:27366

Buddin, R., & Zamarro, G. (2008). *Teacher quality, teacher licensure tests and student achievement.* Santa Monica, CA: RAND Corporation. Retrieved from http://ideas.repec.org/p/ran/wpaper/555.html

Buffett, W. (2008). Annual letter to shareholders: Berkshire's corporate performance vs. the S&P 500. Retrieved from www.vanityfair.com/online/daily/2009/03/buffett

Burns, R. B., & Mason, D. A. (1995). Organizational constraints on the formation of elementary school classes. *American Journal of Education, 103*(2), 185–212. doi:10.1086/444096

Burns, R. B., & Mason, D. A. (2002). Class composition and student achievement in elementary schools. *American Educational Research Journal, 39*(1), 207–233. doi:10.3102/00028312039001207

Burris, C. C., & Welner, K. G. (2011). *Letter to Secretary of Education Arne Duncan concerning evaluation of teachers and principals.* Boulder, CO: National Education Policy Center. Retrieved from http://nepc. colorado.edu/publication/letter-to-Arne-Duncan

Bushaw, W. J., & Lopez, S. J. (2012). The 44th annual Phi Delta Kappa/Gallup poll of the public's attitudes toward the public schools. *Phi Delta Kappan.* Retrieved from www.pdkintl.org/poll/index. htm

Callendar, J. (2004). Value-added student assessment. *Journal of Educational and Behavioral Statistics, 29*(1), 5. doi:10.3102/10769986029001005

Camburn, E. M. (2012, November). *Review of "Asking students about teaching."* Boulder, CO: National Education Policy Center. Retrieved from http://nepc.colorado.edu/thinktank/review-asking-students

Campanile, C. (2012, February 25). Formula uncovers the "value-added." *New York Post.* Retrieved from www.nypost.com/p/news/local/formula_uncovers_the_value_added_xbOcUSqIqXCXDZ GlgOTZ2N

Campbell, D. T. (1976). *Assessing the impact of planned social change.* Hanover, NH: The Public Affairs Center, Dartmouth College.

Campbell, D. T. (1979). Assessing the impact of planned social change. *Evaluation and Program Planning, 2*(1), 67–90. doi:10.1016/0149-7189(79)90048-X

Campbell, D. T., & Stanley, J. C. (1963). *Experimental and quasi-experimental designs for research.* Chicago, IL: Rand McNally & Company.

Campbell, J., Kyriakides, L., Muijs, D., & Robinson, W. (2012). *Assessing teacher effectiveness: Different models.* New York, NY: Routledge.

Capitol Hill Briefing. (2011, September 14). *Getting teacher evaluation right: A challenge for policymakers.* A briefing by E. Haertel, J. Rothstein, A. Amrein-Beardsley, and L. Darling-Hammond. Washington, DC: Dirksen Senate Office Building (research in brief). Retrieved from www.aera.net/Default. aspx?id=12856

Cantrell, S., Fullerton, J., Kane, T. J., & Staiger, D. O. (2008). *National Board Certification and teacher effectiveness: Evidence from a random assignment experiment.* Retrieved from www.gse.harvard. edu/~pfpie/pdf/National_Board_Certification.pdf

Carey, K. (2006). *Evidence suggests otherwise. Hot air: How states inflate their educational progress under NCLB.* Washington, DC: Education Sector.

Carey, K., & Manwaring, R. (2011). *Growth models and accountability: A recipe for remaking ESEA.* Washington, DC: Education Sector.

Caro, R. A. (1975). *The power broker: Robert Moses and the fall of New York.* New York, NY: Random House.

Carolina Journal Weekly Report (2003, April 28). *In this issue.* Raleigh, NC: John Locke Foundation. Retrieved from www.johnlocke.org/cj_weekly/2003042855.html

Carson, R. (1962). *Silent spring.* New York, NY: Houghton Mifflin Co.

Carter, R. L. (2004). Rejoinder. *Journal of Educational and Behavioral Statistics, 29*(1), 135–137. doi:10.3102/10769986029001135

Cavalluzzo, L. (2004). *Is National Board Certification an effective signal of teacher quality?* Alexandria, VA: CAN Analysis Solutions. Retrieved from www.cna.org/solution-centers/cnas-institute-public-research/education/publications/reports

Center for Education Policy Research. (2012). *Do low-performing students get placed with novice teachers?* The Strategic Data Project Human Capital Diagnostic Strategic Performance Indicators. Cambridge, MA: Harvard University. Retrieved from www.gse.harvard.edu/.../Placement_Pattern_Memo_07102012.pdf

Center on Organization and Restructuring of Schools. (1995). *Successful school restructuring.* Madison, WI: Newmann & Wehlage.

Cesarani, D. (2004). *Holocaust: Critical concepts in historical studies.* New York, NY: Routledge.

Chakrabarti, R., & Shwartz, N. (2013). *Unintended consequences of school accountability policies: Evidence from Florida and implications for New York.* New York, NY: Federal Reserve Bank of New York. Retrieved from www.newyorkfed.org/research/epr/2013/0513chak.pdf

Chamberlain, A. (2005, December 16). *Tax reform and "social engineering." The Tax Foundation.* Retrieved from http://taxfoundation.org/blog/tax-reform-and-social-engineering

Chilcott, L., & Guggenheim, D. (2011). *Waiting for "Superman"* [documentary]. Hollywood, CA: Paramount Home Entertainment.

Chester, M. D. (2003). Multiple measures and high-stakes decisions: A framework for combining measures. *Educational Measurement: Issues and Practice, 22*(2), 32–41. doi:10.1111/j.1745–3992.2003. tb00126.x

Chetty, R., Friedman, J. N., & Rockoff, J. E. (2011, December). *The long-term impacts of teachers: Teacher value-added and student outcomes in adulthood.* Cambridge, MA: National Bureau of Economic Research. Retrieved from http://obs.rc.fas.harvard.edu/chetty/value_added.pdf

Chicago Tribune (2012, March 3). Illinois parents demand this vital data [Editorial]. Retrieved from www. chicagotribune.com/news/opinion/editorials/ct-edit-teacher-0303–20120303,0,6644359.story

Chingos, M. M., & Peterson, P. E. (2011). It's easier to pick a good teacher than to train one: Familiar and new results on the correlates of teacher effectiveness. *Economics of Teacher Effectiveness, 30*(3), 449–465. doi:10.1016/j.econedurev.2010.12.010

Clotfelter, C. T., Ladd, H. F., & Vigdor, J. L. (2006). Teacher–student matching and the assessment of teacher effectiveness. *Journal of Human Resources, 41*(4), 778–820.

Clotfelter, C. T., Ladd, H. F., & Vigdor, J. L. (2007). *How and why do teacher credentials matter for student achievement?* Cambridge, MA: National Bureau of Economic Research. Retrieved from www.nber. org/papers/w12828

Cody, A. (2012, December 5). How many billions are we REALLY spending on testing? *Education Week.* Retrieved from http://blogs.edweek.org/teachers/living-in-dialogue/2012/12/how_many_billions_are_we_reall.html

Cody, C. A., McFarland, J., Moore, J. E., & Preston, J. (2010, August). *The evolution of growth models.* Raleigh, NC: Public Schools of North Carolina. Retrieved from www.dpi.state.nc.us/docs/intern-research/reports/growth.pdf

Cohen, J. (1988). *Statistical power analysis for the behavioral sciences* (2nd ed.). Hillsdale, NJ: Lawrence Erlbaum.

Cole, R., Haimson, J., Perez-Johnson, I., & May, H. (2011, September). *Variability in pretest–posttest correlation coefficients by student achievement level*. Washington, DC: National Center for Education Evaluation and Regional Assistance, Institute of Education Sciences, U.S. Department of Education. Retrieved from ies.ed.gov/ncee/pubs/20114033/pdf/20114033.pdf

Coleman, J. S., Campbell, E. Q., Hobson, C. J., McPartland, J., Mood, A. M., Weinfeld, F. D., & York, R. L. (1966). *Equality of educational opportunity*. Washington, DC: US Department of Health, Education & Welfare. doi:10.3886/ICPSR06389.v3

Collins, C. (2012). *Houston, we have a problem: Studying the SAS® Education Value-Added Assessment System (EVAAS®) from teachers' perspectives in the Houston Independent School District (HISD)*. (Doctoral dissertation). Retrieved from http://repository.asu.edu/items/16043

Collins, C., & Amrein-Beardsley, A. (2011, November 23). Review of the book *Value-added measures in education: What every educator needs to know* by Douglas N. Harris. *Education Review, 14*. Retrieved from www.edrev.info/reviews/rev1126.pdf

Collins, C., & Amrein-Beardsley, A. (2014). Putting growth and value-added models on the map: A national overview. *Teachers College Record, 16*(1). Retrieved from www.tcrecord.org/Content. asp?ContentId=17291

Constantine, J., Player, D., Silva, T., Hallgren, K., Grider, M., Deke, J., & Warner, E. (2009). *An evaluation of teachers trained through different routes to certification: Final report*. National Center for Education Evaluation and Regional Assistance. Retrieved from www.mathematica-mpr.com/publications/pdfs/education/teacherstrained09.pdf

Cook, T. D., & Campbell, D. T. (1979). *Quasi-experimentation: Design and analysis issues for field settings*. Chicago, IL: Rand McNally.

Cooper, G., & Sweller, J. (1987). Effects of schema acquisition and rule automation on mathematical problem-solving transfer. *Journal of Educational Psychology, 79*(4), 347–362. doi:10.1037//0022–0663.79.4.347

Cooper, H., Valentine, J. C., Charlton, K., & Melson, A. (2003). The effects of modified school calendars on student achievement and school community attitudes: A research synthesis. *Review of Educational Research, 73*(1), 1–52. doi:10.3102/00346543073001001

Corcoran, S. P. (2010). *Can teachers be evaluated by their students' test scores? Should they be? The use of value-added measures of teacher effectiveness in policy and practice*. Providence, RI: Annenberg Institute for School Reform. Retrieved from http://annenberginstitute.org/publication/can-teachers-be-evaluated-their-students%E2%80%99-test-scores-should-they-be-use-value-added-mea

Corcoran, S. P., Jennings, J. L., & Beveridge, A. A. (2011). *Teacher effectiveness on high- and low-stakes tests*. New York, NY: New York University. Retrieved from https://files.nyu.edu/sc129/public/papers/corcoran_jennings_beveridge_2011_wkg_teacher_effects.pdf

Council of Chief State School Officers (CCSSO). (2005, June). *Policymakers' guide to growth models for school accountability: How do accountability models differ?* Washington, DC: Council of Chief State School Officers. Retrieved from www.ccsso.org/Resources/Publications/Policymakers%E2%80%99_Guide_to_Growth_Models_for_School_Accountability_How_Do_Accountability_Models_Differ. html

Cronbach, L. J. (1971). Test validation. In R. L. Thorndike (Ed.), *Educational measurement* (2nd ed., pp. 443–507). Washington, DC: American Council on Education.

Cronbach, L. J., & Gleser, G. C. (1965). *Pscyhological tests and personnel decisions*. Urbana, IL: University of Illinois Press.

Cronbach, L. J., & Meehl, P. E. (1955). Construct validity in psychological tests. *Psychological Bulletin, 52*, 281–302. doi:10.1037/h0040957

Croninger, R. G., & Valli, L. (2009). "Where is the action?" Challenges to studying the teaching of reading in elementary classrooms. *Educational Researcher, 38*(2), 100–108. doi:10.3102/0013189X09333206

Crony capitalism. (n.d.). In *Wikipedia*. Retrieved from, http://en.wikipedia.org/wiki/Crony_capitalism

Curtis, R. (2011). *District of Columbia public Schools: Defining instructional expectations and aligning accountability and support*. Washington, DC: The Aspen Institute. Retrieved from www.nctq.org/docs/Impact_1_15579.pdf

Danielson, C. (1996). *Enhancing professional practice: A framework for teaching*. Alexandria, VA: Association for Supervision and Curriculum Development.

Danielson, C., & McGreal, T. L. (2000). *Teacher evaluation to enhance professional practice*. Alexandria, VA: Association for Supervision and Curriculum Development (ASCD).

Darby, J. A. (2006). Evaluating courses: An examination of the impact of student gender. *Educational Studies, 32*(2), 187–199. doi:10.1080/03055690600631093

Darling-Hammond, L. (1990). Instructional policy into practice: "The power of the bottom over the top." *Educational Evaluation and Policy Analysis, 12*, 339–347.

Darling-Hammond, L. (1995). Inequality and access to knowledge. In J. A. Banks & C. A. M. Banks (Eds.) *Handbook of research on multicultural education* (pp. 465–483). New York, NY: Simon & Schuster Macmillan.

Darling-Hammond, L. (2010, September, 7). Too unreliable. *New York Times*. Retrieved from www.nytimes.com/roomfordebate/2010/09/06/assessing-a-teachers-value/value-added-assessment-is-too-unreliable-to-be-useful

Darling-Hammond, L. (2012, March 5). Value-added evaluation hurts teaching. *Education Week*. Retrieved from www.edweek.org/ew/articles/2012/03/05/24darlinghammond_ep.h31.html?print=1

Darling-Hammond, L., Amrein-Beardsley, A., Haertel, E., & Rothstein, J. (2012). Evaluating teacher evaluation. *Phi Delta Kappan, 93*(6), 8–15. Retrieved from www.kappanmagazine.org/content/93/6/8.full.pdf+html

Darling-Hammond, L., & Haertel, E. (2012, November 5). A better way to grade teachers. *Los Angeles Times*. Retrieved from www.latimes.com/news/opinion/commentary/la-oe-darling-teacher-evaluations-20121105,0,650639.story

Darling-Hammond, L., Holtzman, D. J., Gatlin, S. J., & Heilig, J. V. (2005). Does teacher preparation matter? Evidence about teacher certification, Teach for America, and teacher effectiveness. *Education Policy Analysis Archives, 13*(42), 1–51. Retrieved from http://epaa.asu.edu/ojs/article/view/147

Davies, M., Hirschberg, J., Lye, J., Johnston, C., & McDonald, I. (2007). Systematic influences on teaching evaluations: The case for caution. *Australian Economic Papers, 46*(1), 18–38.

Davis, A. (1994). [Message posted to online discussion forum of Tennessee Value-Added Assessment System.] Retrieved from http://epaa.asu.edu/tvaas.html

De Long, J. B., & Lang, K. (1992). Are all economic hypotheses false? *Journal of Political Economy, 100*(6), 1257–72.

Denby, D. (2012, November 19). Public defender: Diane Ravitch takes on a movement. *New Yorker*. Retrieved from www.newyorker.com/reporting/2012/11/19/121119fa_fact_denby

Derby, M. S. (2013, May 10). Schools game system to meet standards, paper finds. *Wall Street Journal*. Retrieved from http://blogs.wsj.com/economics/2013/05/10/schools-game-system-to-meet-standards-paper-finds/

Derringer, P. (2010, August). RTT in Tennessee: Assessment done right. *Technology and Learning, 31*(1), 40. Retrieved from www.techlearning.com/article/31572

Dewey, J. (1916) *Democracy and education. An introduction to the philosophy of education*. New York, NY: Free Press.

Di Carlo, M. (2013, January 17). A few points about the instability of value-added estimates. *The Shanker Blog*. Retrieved from http://shankerblog.org/?p=7446

Dillon, S. (2010a, August 31). Formula to grade teachers' skill gains acceptance, and critics. *New York Times*. Retrieved from www.nytimes.com/2010/09/01/education/01teacher.html?pagewanted=all&_r=0

Dillon, S. (2010b, January 31). Obama to seek sweeping change in "No Child" law. *New York Times*. Retrieved from www.nytimes.com/2010/02/01/education/01child.html?pagewanted=all

Dills, A. K., & Mulholland, S. E. (2010). A comparative look at private and public schools' class size determinants. *Education Economics, 18*(4), 435–454. doi:10.1080/09645290903546397

Dith Pran. (2004). *Encyclopedia of World Biography*. Retrieved from www.encyclopedia.com/topic/Dith_Pran.aspx

Doran, H. C., & Fleischman, S. (2005, November). Challenges of value-added assessment. *Assessment to Promote Learning, 63*(3), 85–87.

Dorn, S. (1994, September 9). [Message posted to online discussion forum of Tennessee Value-Added Assessment System.] Retrieved from http://epaa.asu.edu/tvaas.html

Duffrin, E. (2011). What's the value in value-added? *District Administration, 47*(1), 48–50, 52.

Duncan, A. (2009a, July 4). The Race to the Top begins: Remarks by Secretary Arne Duncan. Retrieved from www.ed.gov/news/speeches/2009/07/07242009.html

Duncan, A. (2009b, October 22). Teacher preparation: Reforming the uncertain profession. Retrieved from www.ed.gov/news/speeches/2009/10/10222009.html

Duncan, A. (2011, March 9). Winning the future with education: Responsibility, reform and results. Testimony given to the U.S. Congress, Washington, DC: Retrieved from www.ed.gov/news/speeches/winning-future-education-responsibility-reform-and-results

Dunn, M. C., Kadane, J. B., & Garrow, J. R. (2003). Comparing harm done by mobility and class absence: Missing students and missing data. *Journal of Educational and Behavioral Statistics, 28*(3), 269–288. doi:10.3102/10769986028003269

Durso, C. S. (2011). *An analysis of the use and validity of test-based teacher evaluations reported by the* Los Angeles Times: *2011.* Boulder, CO: National Education Policy Center. Retrieved from nepc.colorado.edu/files/FactSheet_0.pdf

Eaton, S. (2007). *The children in Room E4: American education on trial.* Chapel Hill, NC: Algonquin Books.

Eaton, S., & Rivkin, S. (2010). Is desegregation dead? Parsing the relationship between achievement and demographics. *Education Next, 10*(4). Retrieved from http://educationnext.org/is-desegregation-dead/

Eckert, J. (2010, August). *Performance-based compensation: Design and implementation at six Teacher Incentive Fund sites.* Seattle, WA: Bill & Melinda Gates Foundation. Retrieved from www.tapsystem.org/publications/eck_tif.pdf

Eckert, J. M., & Dabrowski, J. (2010, May). Should value-added measures be used for performance pay? *Phi Delta Kappan, 91*(8), 88–92.

Education Week (2006, December). William L. Sanders on value-added methodology and the Tennessee Value-Added Accountability System. Retrieved from www.edweek.org/media/sanders.pdf

Education Week (2011, February 1). Houston pays $42 million in value-added bonuses. Retrieved from www.edweek.org/ew/articles/2011/02/02/19brief-6.h30.html?r=288217486

Ehlert, M., Koedel, C., Parsons, E., & Podgursky, M. (2012, August). *Selecting growth measures for school and teacher evaluations.* Washington, DC: National Center for Analysis of Longitudinal Data in Education Research. Retrieved from www.caldercenter.org/publications/upload/WP-80.pdf

Epstein, J. (1988). Effective schools or effective students: Dealing with diversity. In R. Haskins and D. MacRae (Eds.), *Policies for America's public schools: Teachers, equity, indicators* (pp. 89–126). Norwood, NJ: Ablex.

Evans, H. (2008). *Use of value-added in English schools.* Paper presented at the National Conference on Value-Added Modeling, sponsored by the Wisconsin Center for Education Research, Madison, WI.

Ewing, D. (2011, May 9). Leading mathematician debunks "value-added." *Washington Post.* Retrieved from www.washingtonpost.com/blogs/answer-sheet/post/leading-mathematician-debunks-value-added/2011/05/08/AFb999UG_blog.html

Fairchild, R. (2009, November 4). *Reducing summer learning loss: Implementing successful programs.* New York, NY: The Wallace Foundation. Retrieved from www.wallacefoundation.org/view-latest-news/events-and-presentations/Pages/Reducing-Summer-Learning-Loss-Implementing-Successful-Programs.aspx

FairTest. (2013). *FairTest: The national center for fair and open testing.* Retrieved from www.fairtest.org/

Fang, L. (2011, November 16). How online learning companies bought America's schools. *The Nation.* Retrieved from www.thenation.com/article/164651/how-online-learning-companies-bought-americas-schools

Fang, L. (2013, January 30). E-mails show Jeb Bush foundation lobbied for businesses, including one tied to Bush. *The Nation*. Retrieved from www.thenation.com/blog/172551/jeb-bush-uses-his-education-reform-foundation-corporate-personal-gain-e-mails-show#

Farrell, P., & Rummel, D. (2008, June 8). The last word: Dith Pran. *New York Times*. Retrieved from www.nytimes.com/packages/html/multimedia/20080320_DITH_PRAN_LAST_WORD_FEATURE/#section1

Felch, J. (2011, February 7). Separate study confirms many *Los Angeles Times* findings on teacher effectiveness. *Los Angeles Times*. Retrieved from www.latimes.com/news/local/la-me-teacher-study-20110207,0,2144294.story

Felch, J., Song, J., & Smith, D. (2010, August 14). Who's teaching L.A.'s kids? *Los Angeles Times*. Retrieved from www.latimes.com/news/local/la-me-teachers-value-20100815,0,258862,full.story

Ferguson, G. A., & Takane, Y. (1989). *Statistical analysis in psychology and education*. New York, NY: McGraw Hill.

Fessenden, F. (2012, May 11). A portrait of segregation in New York City's schools. *New York Times*. Retrieved from www.nytimes.com/interactive/2012/05/11/nyregion/segregation-in-new-york-city-public-schools.html

Fincher, C. (1985). What is value-added education? *Research in Higher Education, 22*, 395–398.

Flynn, K. (2012, January 11). Teachers hold the key: They always have. *Education Week*. Retrieved from http://blogs.edweek.org/teachers/living-in-dialogue/2012/01/kelly_flynn_teachers_hold_the.html?intc=es

Foundation for Excellence in Education. (2012). *Chiefs for Change*. Retrieved from www.excelined.org/Pages/Excellence_in_Action/Chiefs_for_Change.aspx

Fraenkel, J. R., & Wallen, N. E. (1996). *How to design and evaluate research in education* (3rd ed.). New York, NY: McGraw Hill.

Freedman, D. H. (2010, December 10). Why scientific studies are so often wrong: The streetlight effect. *Discover Magazine*. Retrieved from http://discovermagazine.com/2010/jul-aug/29-why-scientific-studies-often-wrong-streetlight-effect

Gabriel, R., & Allington, R. (2011, April). *Teacher effectiveness research and the spectacle of effectiveness policy*. Paper Presented at Annual Conference of the American Educational Research Association, New Orleans, LA.

Gabriel, R. & Lester, J. (2010, December 15). Public displays of teacher effectiveness. *Education Week*. Retrieved from www.edweek.org/ew/articles/2010/12/15/15gabriel.h30.html

Gabriel, R., & Lester, J. (2012). *Constructions of value-added measurement and teacher effectiveness in the* Los Angeles Times: *A discourse analysis of the talk of surrounding measures of teacher effectiveness*. Paper presented at the Annual Conference of the American Educational Research Association, Vancouver, Canada.

Gabriel, R., & Lester, J. N. (2013). Sentinels guarding the grail: Value-added measurement and the quest for education reform. *Education Policy Analysis Archives, 21*(9), 1–30. Retrieved from http://epaa.asu.edu/ojs/article/view/1165

Gamliel, E., & Davidovitz, L. (2005). Online versus traditional teaching evaluation: Mode can matter. *Assessment and Evaluation in Higher Education, 30*(6), 581–592. doi:10.1080/02602930500260647

Gansle, K. A., Burns, J. M., & Noell, G. (2011, September 22). *Value-added assessment of teacher preparation programs in Louisiana: 2007–08 to 2009–10. Overview of 2010–11 results*. Louisiana Teacher Quality Initiative. Retrieved from http://tntp.org/assets/documents/LABoR_2011_Report.pdf?files/LABoR_2011_Report.pdf

Garland, S. (2012, February 7). Tennessee teacher evaluation systems have rough road ahead. *Huffington Post*. Retrieved from www.huffingtonpost.com/2012/02/07/tennessee-teacher-evaluat_n_1260790.html?page=1

Garlikov, R. (1995, January 10). [Message posted to online discussion forum of Tennessee Value-Added Assessment System.] Retrieved from http://epaa.asu.edu/tvaas.html

Gates, B. (2012, February 22). Shame is not the solution. *New York Times*. Retrieved from www.nytimes.com/2012/02/23/opinion/for-teachers-shame-is-no-solution.html?_r=3&smid=FB-nytimes&WT.mc_id=OP-E-FB-SM-LIN-SIN-022312-NYT-NA&WT.mc_ev=click

Gates, B. (2013, April 3). A fairer way to evaluate teachers. *Washington Post*. Retrieved from www. washingtonpost.com/opinions/bill-gates-a-fairer-way-to-evaluate-teachers/2013/04/03/c99fd1bc-98c2–11e2–814b-063623d80a60_story.html

George, D., & Mallery, P. (2003). *SPSS for Windows step by step: A simple guide and reference* (4th ed.). Boston, MA: Allyn & Bacon.

Ginsberg, R., & Kingston, N. (2013, January 11). Caught in a vise: The challenges facing teacher preparation in an era of accountability. Paper presented at *The High-Stakes Teacher Evaluation: High Cost – Big Losses Conference*, Tucson, AZ. Retrieved from www.youtube.com/watch?v=uELqx3X U1hw&feature=youtu.be

Giordano, M. A. (2012, March 13). Fallout continues over teacher rankings. *New York Times*. Retrieved from www.nytimes.com/schoolbook/2012/03/13/fallout-continues-over-teacher-rankings/

Glass, G. V. (1995). [Message posted to online discussion forum of Tennessee Value-Added Assessment System.] Retrieved from http://epaa.asu.edu/tvaas.html

Glass, G. V. & Hopkins, K. D. (1989). *Statistical methods in education and psychology* (3rd ed.). Needham Heights, MA: Allyn and Bacon.

Glazerman, S., Goldhaber, D., Loeb, S., Staiger, D., Raudenbush, S., & Whitehurst, G. (2010, December 15). Value-added: It's not perfect, but it makes sense. *Education Week*. Retrieved from www.edweek.org/ew/articles/2010/12/15/15whitehurst.h30.html

Glazerman, S., Goldhaber, D., Loeb, S., Raudenbush, S., Staiger, D. O., & Whitehurst, G. J. (2011, April 26). *Passing muster: Evaluating teacher evaluation systems*. Washington, DC: The Brookings Institution. Retrieved from www.brookings.edu/reports/2011/0426_evaluating_teachers.aspx

Glazerman, S. M., & Potamites, L. (2011, December). *False performance gains: A critique of successive cohort indicators*. Washington, DC: Mathematica Policy Research. Retrieved from www.mathematica-mpr.com/publications/PDFs/education/false_perf.pdf

Glazerman, S., & Seifullah, A. (2010, May). *An evaluation of the Teacher Advancement Program (TAP) in Chicago: Year two impact report*. Washington, DC: Mathematica Policy Research. Retrieved from www.mathematica-mpr.com/newsroom/releases/2010/TAP_5_10.asp

Goe, L. (2008). *Using value-added models to identify and support highly effective teachers*. Washington, DC: National Comprehensive Center for Teacher Quality. Retrieved from www2.tqsource.org/strategies/het/UsingValueAddedModels.pdf

Goldhaber, D. (2009, May). *Teacher pay reforms: The political implications of recent research*. Washington, DC: Center for American Progress. Retrieved from www.americanprogress.org/issues/education/report/2006/12/11/2387/teacher-pay-reforms/

Goldhaber, D., & Anthony, E. (2007). Can teacher quality be effectively assessed? National Board Certification as a signal of effective teaching. *Review of Economics and Statistics, 89*(1), 134–150. doi:10.1162/rest.89.1.134

Goldhaber, D., & Chaplin, D. (2011, October 31). *Assessing the "Rothstein Test": Does it really show teacher value-added models are biased?* Seattle, WA: Center for Education Data and Research. Retrieved from www.mathematica-mpr.com/publications/pdfs/education/rothstein_wp.pdf

Goldhaber, D., Gabele, B., & Walch, J. (2012, August). *Does the model matter? Exploring the relationship between different student achievement-based teacher assessments*. Seattle, WA: Center for Education Data & Research. Retrieved from http://cedr.us/papers/working/CEDR%20WP%202012–6_Does%20the%20Model%20Matter.pdf

Goldhaber, D. D., Goldschmidt, P., & Tseng, F. (2013). Teacher value-added at the high-school level: Different models, different answers? *Educational Evaluation and Policy Analysis, 35*(2), 220–236. doi:10.3102/0162373712466938

Goldhaber, D., & Hansen, M. (2010). *Is it just a bad class? Assessing the stability of measured teacher performance* (CEDR Working Paper 2010-3). Seattle, WA: Center for Education Data & Research. Retrieved from www.cedr.us/publications.html

Goldhaber, D., & Theobald, R. (2012, October 15). Do different value-added models tell us the same things? *Carnegie Knowledge Network*. Retrieved from www.carnegieknowledgenetwork.org/briefs/value-added/different-growth-models/

Goldschmidt, P., Choi, K., & Beaudoin, J. B. (2012, February). *Growth model comparison study: Practical implications of alternative models for evaluating school performance*. Washington, DC: Council of Chief State School Officers. Retrieved from www.ccsso.org/Documents/2012/Growth_Model_Comparison_Study_Evaluating_School_Performance_2012.pdf

Goldstein, D. (2012, February 24). NYC to release teachers' "value-added" ratings: Why it's not fair. *The Nation*. Retrieved from www.thenation.com/blog/166453/nyc-release-teachers-value-added-ratings-why-its-not-fair#

Goodman, J. (2006). School discipline in moral disarray. *Journal of Moral Education, 35*(2), 213–230. doi:10.1080/03057240600681736

Gordon, R., Kane, T. J., & Staiger, D. O. (2006, April). *Identifying effective teachers using performance on the job*. Washington, DC: The Brookings Institution. Retrieved from www.brookings.edu/papers/2006/04education_gordon.aspx

Gottlieb, A. (2011, September 13). Student growth percentiles and shoe leather. *Education News Colorado*. Retrieved from www.ednewscolorado.org/2011/09/13/24400-student-growth-percentiles-and-shoe-leather

Gould, S. J. (1996). *The mismeasure of man*. New York, NY: W. W. Norton Company.

Gratz, D. B. (2010, March). *Review of district awards for teacher excellence program: Final report*. Boulder, CO: National Education Policy Center. Retrieved from http://nepc.colorado.edu/thinktank/review-district-awards

Graue, M. E., Delaney, K. K., & Karch, A. S. (2013). Ecologies of education quality. *Education Policy Analysis Archives, 21*(8), 1–36. Retrieved from http://epaa.asu.edu/ojs/article/view/1163

Graue, B., Delaney, K., Karch, A., & Romero, C. (2011, April). *Data use as a reform strategy*. Paper presented at the Annual Convention of the American Educational Research Association , New Orleans, LA.

Graue, B., Gawade, N., Delaney, K., Karch, A., & Romero, C. (2011, April). *Ecologies of education quality*. Paper presented at the Annual Convention of the American Educational Research Association, New Orleans, LA.

Green, P. C., Baker, B. D., & Oluwole, J. (2012). The legal and policy implications of value-added teacher assessment policies. Brigham Young University Education and Law Journal, 1, 1–29. Retrieved from http://heinonline.org/HOL/LandingPage?handle=hein.journals/byuelj2012&div=5&id=&page=

Green, S. B., & Salkind, N. J. (2010). *Using SPSS for Windows and Macintosh: Analyzing and understanding data* (6th ed.). Upper Saddle River, NJ: Pearson.

Grier, T. B., & Holcombe, A. A. (2008). Mission possible. *Educational Leadership, 65*(7), 25–30.

Griswold, E. (2012, September 21). How *Silent Spring* ignited the environmental movement. *New York Times*. Retrieved from www.nytimes.com/2012/09/23/magazine/how-silent-spring-ignited-the-environmental-movement.html?pagewanted=all&_moc.semityn.www

Grodsky, E. S., Warren, J. R., & Kalogrides, D. (2009). State high school exit examinations and NAEP long-term trends in reading and mathematics, 1971–2004. *Educational Policy, 23*, 589–614. doi:10.1177/0395909808320678

Gualtieri, M. (2013, January 3). *The Forrester Wave™: Big data predictive analytics solutions, Q1 2013*. Cambridge, MA: Forrester Research Inc. Retrieved from www.forrester.com/pimages/rws/reprints/document/85601/oid/1-KWYFVB

Guarino, C. M., Maxfield, M., Reckase, M. D., Thompson, P., & Wooldridge, J. M. (2012, March 1). *An evaluation of Empirical Bayes' estimation of value-added teacher performance measures*. East Lansing, MI: Education Policy Center at Michigan State University. Retrieved from www.aefpweb.org/sites/default/files/webform/empirical_bayes_20120301_AEFP.pdf

Guarino, C. M., Reckase, M. D., & Wooldridge, J. M. (2012, December 12). *Can value-added measures of teacher education performance be trusted?* East Lansing, MI: The Education Policy Center at Michigan State University. Retrieved from http://education.msu.edu/epc/library/documents/WP18 Guarino-Reckase-Wooldridge-2012-Can-Value-Added-Measures-of-Teacher-Performance-Be-T_000.pdf

Guba, E. G., & Lincoln, Y. S. (1981). *Effective evaluation: Improving the usefulness of evaluation results through responsive and naturalistic approaches*. San Francisco, CA: Jossey-Bass.

Haertel, E. (2011, April). *Using student test scores to distinguish good teachers from bad.* Paper presented at the Annual Conference of the American Educational Research Association, New Orleans, LA.

Haladyna, T. M., & Downing, S. M. (2004). Construct-irrelevant variance in high-stakes testing. *Educational Measurement: Issues and Practice, 23*(1), 17–27. doi:10.1111/j.1745–3992.2004.tb00149.x

Haladyna, T. M., Nolen, N. S., & Haas, S. B. (1991). Raising standardized achievement test scores and the origins of test score pollution. *Educational Researcher, 20*(5), 2–7. doi:10.2307/1176395

Haney, W. (2000). The myth of the Texas miracle in education. *Education Analysis Policy Archives, 8*(41). Retrieved from http://epaa.asu.edu/epaa/v8n41

Hanifan, L. J. (1916). The rural school community center. *Annals of the American Academy of Political and Social Science, 67*, 130–138. doi:10.1177/000271621606700118

Hanushek, E. A. (1970). *The value of teachers in teaching.* Santa Monica, CA: RAND Corporation.

Hanushek, E. A. (1971). Teacher characteristics and gains in student achievement: Estimation using micro data. *American Economic Review, 61*(2), 280–288.

Hanushek, E. A. (1979). Conceptual and empirical issues in estimating educational production function issues. *Journal of Human Resources, 14*(3), 351–388.

Hanushek, E. (2009). Teacher deselection. In D. Goldhaber & J. Hannaway (Eds.), *Creating a new teaching profession* (pp. 165–80). Washington, DC: Urban Institute Press.

Hanushek, E. A. (2011). The economic value of higher teacher quality. *Economics of Education Review, 30*, 466–479.

Hanushek, E. A. (2013, February 6). Why educators' wages must be revamped now. *Education Week.* Retrieved from www.edweek.org/ew/articles/2013/02/06/20hanushek_ep.h32.html?r=12319 15840

Hanushek, E. A., & Raymond, M. E. (2005). Does school accountability lead to improved student performance? *Journal of Policy Analysis and Management, 24*(2), 297–327. doi:10.1002/pam.20091

Hanushek, E. A., & Rivkin, S. G. (2010, May). *Using value-added measures of teacher quality.* Washington, DC: National Center for Analysis of Longitudinal Data in Education Research. Retrieved from www.urban.org/uploadedpdf/1001371-teacher-quality.pdf

Harbaugh, L. (2011, June 9). Response to LeClaire. *Raleigh Public Record.* Retrieved from www.raleigh-publicrecord.org/featured/2011/06/01/will-evaas-make-wake-schools--part-ii/

Harris, D. N. (2008). The policy uses and "policy validity" of value-added and other teacher quality measures. In D. H. Gitomer (Ed.), *Measurement Issues and the Assessment of Teacher Quality* (pp. 99–130). Thousand Oaks, CA: SAGE Publications.

Harris, D. N. (2009a). Response to Heather C. Hill. *Journal of Policy Analysis and Management, 28*(4), 709–711. doi:10.1002/pam.20466

Harris, D. N. (2009b). Teacher value-added: Don't end the search before it starts. *Journal of Policy Analysis and Management, 28*(4), 693–700. doi:10.1002/pam.20464

Harris, D. N. (2009c). Would accountability based on teacher value-added be smart policy? An evaluation of the statistical properties and policy alternatives. *Education Finance and Policy, 4*, 319–350. doi:10.1162/edfp2009.4.4.319

Harris, D. N. (2010, May). Clear away the smoke and mirrors of value-added. *Phi Delta Kappan, 91*(8), 66–69.

Harris, D. N. (2011). *Value-added measures in education: What every educator needs to know.* Cambridge, MA: Harvard Education Press.

Harris, D. N. (2012a, November 28). Creating a valid process for using teacher value-added measures. *The Shanker Blog.* Retrieved from http://shankerblog.org/?p=7242

Harris, D. N. (2012b, October 15). How do value-added indicators compare to other measures of teacher effectiveness? *Carnegie Knowledge Network.* Retrieved from www.carnegieknowledgenetwork.org/briefs/value-added/value-added-other-measures/

Harris, D. N., & Anderson, A. (2013). Does value-added work better in elementary than in secondary grades? *Carnegie Knowledge Network.* Retrieved from www.carnegieknowledgenetwork.org/briefs/value-added/grades/

Harris, D. N., & Sass, T. R. (2009). *What makes for a good teacher and who can tell?* Washington, DC:

Center for Analysis of Longitudinal Date in Education Research. Retrieved from www.urban.org/publications/1001431.html

Harville, D. A. (1995). *A review of the Tennessee Value-Added Assessment System (TVAAS)*. Ames: Iowa State University.

Hawkins, B. (2012, January 6). Can a good teacher change a student for life? *Minnesota Post*. Retrieved from www.minnpost.com/learning-curve/2012/01/can-good-teacher-change-student-life

Haycock, K., & Crawford, C. (2008). Closing the teacher quality gap. *Educational Leadership, 65*(7), 14–19.

Henderson, C. R. (1973). Sire evaluation and genetic trends. *Journal of Animal Science, 1973*, 10–41. Retrieved from www.animal-science.org/content/1973/Symposium/10.full.pdf

Hermann, M., Walsh, E., Isenberg, E., & Resch, A. (2013, April 12). *Shrinkage of value-added estimates and characteristics of students with hard-to-predict achievement levels*. Washington, DC: Mathematica Policy Research. Retrieved from www.mathematica-mpr.com/publications/PDFs/education/value-added_shrinkage_wp.pdf

Herrnstein, R. J., & Murray, C. A. (1996). *The bell curve: Intelligence and class structure in American life*. New York, NY: Simon & Schuster.

Heubert, J. P., & Hauser, R. M. (Eds.). (1999). *High stakes: Testing for tracking, promotion, and graduation*. Washington, DC: National Academy Press.

Hill, H. C. (2009). Response to Douglas N. Harris. *Journal of Policy Analysis and Management, 28*(4), 711–712. doi:10.1002/pam.20465

Hill, H. C., Kapitula, L., & Umlan, K. (2011, June). A validity argument approach to evaluating teacher value-added scores. *American Educational Research Journal, 48*(3), 794–831. doi:10.3102/00028312 10387916

Ho, A. D., Lewis, D. M., & Farris, J. L. (2009). The dependence of growth-model results on proficiency cut scores. *Educational Measurement: Issues and Practice, 28*(4), 15–26. doi:10.1111/j.1745-3992.2009.00159.x

Hobson, S. M., & Talbot, D. M. (2001). Understanding student evaluations: What all faculty should know. *College Teaching, 49*(1), 26–31. doi:10.1080/87567550109595842

Hoff, D. J. (2007, February 13). NCLB panel calls for federal role in setting national standards. *Education Week*. Retrieved from www.edweek.org/ew/articles/2007/02/13/23aspen_web.h26.html

hooks, b. (2000). *Where we stand: Class matters*. New York, NY: Routledge.

Houston Independent School District (HISD). (2010). *Accelerating Student Progress and Increasing Results and Expectations (ASPIRE) at HISD: A guide for parents and our community*. Retrieved from www.houstonisd.org/.../PDF/ASPIRE_ParentGuide_2010114web.pdf

Houston Independent School District (HISD). (2011m May 26). *Board of education workshop 2011–12 budget update* [PowerPoint slides]. Retrieved from www2.houstonisd.org/HISDConnectEnglish/Home/Board%20of%20Education/Board%20Meetings-Agendas/Board%20Meetings%20and%20Agendas%20PDFs/Budget_Update_%28May%2026,%202011%29.pdf

Hershberg, T. (2004, December). The revelations of value-added. *School Administrator*. Retrieved from www.aasa.org/publications/saarticledetail.cfm?ItemNumber=1060

Hursh, D. W. (2008). *High-stakes testing and the decline of teaching and learning: The real crisis in education*. Lanham, MD: Rowman & Littlefield.

Ingersoll, R., & May, H. (2012). The magnitude, destinations, and determinants of mathematics and science teacher turnover. *Educational Evaluation and Policy Analysis, 34*(4), 435–464. doi:10.3102/0162373712454326

Institute of Education Sciences (IES). (2012). Review of the report "The long-term impacts of teachers: teacher value-added and student outcomes in adulthood." *What Works Clearinghouse Review*. Retrieved from http://ies.ed.gov/ncee/wwc/quickreview.aspx?sid=209

Ishii, J., & Rivkin, S. G. (2009). Impediments to the estimation of teacher value-added. *Education Finance and Policy, 4*, 520–536. doi:10.1162/edfp2009.4.4.520

Jackson, C. K. (2012) *Teacher quality at the high-school level: The importance of accounting for tracks*. Cambridge, MA: National Bureau of Economic Research. Retrieved from www.nber.org/papers/w17722

Jacob, B. A. (2011). Do principals fire the worst teachers? *Educational Evaluation and Policy Analysis, 33*(4), 403–434. doi:10.3102/0162373711414704

Jacob, B. A., & Lefgren, L. (2005, June). *Principals as agents: Subjective performance measurement in education.* Cambridge, MA: National Bureau of Economic Research. Retrieved from www.nber.org/papers/w11463

Jacob, B. A., & Lefgren, L. (2008). Can principals identify effective teachers? Evidence on subjective performance evaluation in education. *Journal of Labor Economics, 26*(1), 101–136. doi:10.1086/522974.

James, G. (2012, April 23). 8 core beliefs of extraordinary bosses. *Inc.com.* Retrieved from www.inc.com/geoffrey-james/8-core-beliefs-of-extraordinary-bosses.html

Jehlen, A. (2009, January/February). NCLB: Is it working? *NEA Today Magazine.* Retrieved from www.nea.org/home/20755.htm

Jenkins, M. (2012, January). The healing fields. *National Geographic.* Retrieved from http://ngm.nationalgeographic.com/2012/01/landmines/jenkins-text

Jennings, J. L., & Corcoran, S. P. (2009). "Beware of geeks bearing formulas": Reflections on growth models for school accountability. *Phi Delta Kappan, 90*(9), 635–639.

Johnson, D. D., Johnson, B., Farenga, S. J., & Ness, D. (2005). *Stop high-stakes testing: An appeal to America's conscience.* Lanham, MD: Rowman & Littlefield.

Johnson, S. (2013, March 25). Occupying the Department of Education. *Huffington Post.* Retrieved from www.huffingtonpost.com/shaun-johnson/occupying-the-department-_b_1378555.html

Johnson, W. (2012, March 3). Confessions of a "bad" teacher. *New York Times.* www.nytimes.com/2012/03/04/opinion/sunday/confessions-of-a-bad-teacher.html?_r=2&pagewanted=all

Kane, M. T. (2006). *Validation.* In R. L. Brennan (Ed.), *Educational measurement* (4th ed., pp. 17–64). Washington, DC: National Council on Measurement in Education and the American Council on Education.

Kane, M. T. (2013). Validating the interpretations and uses of test scores. *Journal of Educational Measurement, 50*(1), 1–73. doi:10.1111/jedm.12000

Kane, T. J., & Staiger, D. O. (2008). *Estimating teacher impacts on student achievement: An experimental evaluation.* Cambridge, MA: National Bureau of Economic Research. Retrieved from www.nber.org/papers/w14607

Kane, T. J., & Staiger, D. O. (2012). *Gathering feedback for teaching: Combining high-quality observations with student surveys and achievement gains.* Seattle, WA: Bill & Melinda Gates Foundation. Retrieved from www.metproject.org/downloads/MET_Gathering_Feedback_Practioner_Brief.pdf

Kaplan, A. (1964). *The conduct of inquiry: Methodology for behavioral science.* San Francisco, CA: Chandler Publishing Company.

Katz, M. B. (1989). *The undeserving poor: From the war on poverty to the war on welfare.* New York, NY: Pantheon Books.

Keen, J. (2012, November 11). In Chicago strike, teachers' issues not all at stake. *USA Today.* Retrieved from http://usatoday30.usatoday.com/news/nation/story/2012/09/10/chicago-teachers-to-strike-after-talks-fail/57720772/1

Kelly, A., & Downey, C. (2010). Value-added measures for schools in England: Looking inside the "black box" of complex metrics. *Educational Assessment, Evaluation and Accountability, 22*(3), 181–198. doi:10.1007/s11092-010-9100-4

Kelly, S., & Monczunski, L. (2007). Overcoming the volatility in school-level gain scores: A new approach to identifying value-added with cross-sectional data. *Educational Researcher, 36*(5), 279–287. doi:10.3102/0013189X07306557

Kennedy, B. W. (1991). C. R. Henderson: The unfinished legacy. *Journal of Dairy Science, 74,* 4067–4081.

Kennedy, M. M. (2010, November). Attribution error and the quest for teacher quality. *Educational Researcher, 39*(8), 591–598. doi:10.3102/0013189X10390804

Kersting, N. B., Chen, M., & Stigler, J. W. (2013). Value-added added teacher estimates as part of teacher evaluations: Exploring the effects of data and model specifications on the stability of teacher value-added scores. *Education Policy Analysis Archives, 21*(7), 1–39. Retrieved from http://epaa.asu. edu/ojs/article/view/1167

Kim, J. S., & Sunderman, G. L. (2005). Measuring academic proficiency under the No Child Left Behind Act: Implications for educational equity. *Educational Researcher, 43*(8), 3–13. doi:10.3102/ 0013189X034008003

Kimball, S. M., White, B., Milanowski, A. T., & Borman, G. (2004). Examining the relationship between teacher evaluation and student assessment results in Washoe County. *Peabody Journal of Education, 79*(4), 54–78. doi:10.1207/s15327930pje7904_4

Klein, S. P., Hamilton, L. S., McCaffrey, D. F., & Stecher, B. M. (2000). What do test scores in Texas tell us? *Education Policy Analysis Archives, 8*(49), 1–22. Retrieved from http://epaa.asu.edu/epaa/ v8n49

Kline, P. (1999). *The handbook of psychological testing* (2nd ed.). London: Routledge.

Knight, S. L., Lloyd, G. M., & Arbaugh, F. (Eds.). (2012). Examining the complexities of assessment and accountability in teacher education. *Journal of Teacher Education, 63*(5), 301–303. doi: 10.1177/0022487112460200

Koedel, C., & Betts, J. R. (2007, April). *Re-examining the role of teacher quality in the educational production function* (Working Paper No. 2007-03). Nashville, TN: National Center on Performance Initiatives.

Koedel, C., & Betts, J. R. (2009). *Does student sorting invalidate value-added models of teacher effectiveness? An extended analysis of the Rothstein critique* (Working Paper 2009-01). Nashville, TN: National Center on Performance Initiatives. Retrieved from www.performanceincentives.org/data/files/ news/PapersNews/Koedel_and_Betts_2009_REVISED.pdf

Koedel, C., & Betts, J. (2010). Value-added to what? How a ceiling in the testing instrument influences value-added estimation. *Education Finance and Policy, 5*(1), 54–81.

Kohn, A. (1986). *No contest: The case against competition.* Boston, MA: Houghton Mifflin.

Koppich, J. E., & Humphrey, D. C. (2011, October 10). Getting serious about teacher evaluation. *Education Week.* Retrieved from www.edweek.org/ew/articles/2011/10/12/07koppich.h31.html?t kn=SUVFzKwrXILuiIbXc%2FpaWcW7eJr4P5wPRHiR&cmp=ENL-EU-VIEWS1

Koretz, D. M. (1996). Using student assessments for educational accountability. In E. A. Hanushek & D. W. Jorgenson (Eds.), *Improving America's schools: The role of incentives* (pp. 131–157). Washington, DC: National Academy Press.

Koretz, D. M. (2002). Limitations in the use of achievement tests as measures of educators' productivity. *Journal of Human Resources, 37*(4), 752–777. doi:10.2307/3069616

Koretz, D. M., McCaffrey, D. F., & Hamilton, L. S. (2001). *Toward a framework for validating gains under high-stakes conditions* (CSE Technical Report #551). Los Angeles, Center for the Study of Evaluation. Retrieved from www.cse.ucla.edu/products/Reports/TR551.pdf

Kozol, J. (1991). *Savage inequalities: Children in America's schools.* New York, NY: Crown Publishers.

Kozol, J. (1995). *Amazing grace: The lives of children and the conscience of a nation.* New York, NY: Crown Publishers.

Kozol, J. (2000). *Ordinary resurrections: Children in the years of hope.* New York, NY: Crown Publishers.

Kozol, J. (2005). *The shame of the nation: The restoration of apartheid schooling in America.* New York, NY: Crown Publishers.

Kraemer, S. (2011, April). *A human factors engineering framework for effective data use in education reform and accountability.* Paper presented at the Annual Convention of the American Educational Research Association, New Orleans, LA.

Kraemer, S., Geraghty, E., Lindsey, D., & Raven, C. (2010). *School leadership view of human and organizational factors in performance management: A comparative analysis of high- and low-performing schools.* Madison, WI: University of Wisconsin–Madison.

Kress, S. (2011, April 18). On "No Child," no going back: An architect of education reform says Obama's wobbly on accountability. *New York Daily News.* Retrieved from www.nydailynews.com/opinion/ child-back-architect-education-reform-obama-wobbly-accountability-article-1.113184#ixzz27Osjk8Jq

Kupermintz, H. (2003). Teacher effects and teacher effectiveness: A validity investigation of the

Tennessee Value-Added Assessment System. *Educational Evaluation and Policy Analysis, 25*, 287–298. doi:10.3102/01623737025003287

Kyriakides, L. (2005). Drawing from teacher effectiveness research and research into teacher interpersonal behaviour to establish a teacher evaluation system: A study on the use of student ratings to evaluate teacher behaviour. *Journal of Classroom Instruction, 40*(2), 44–66.

Laczko-Kerr, I., & Berliner, D. (2002). The effectiveness of "Teach for America" and other under-certified teachers. *Education Policy Analysis Archives, 10*(37), 1–53. Retrieved from http://epaa.asu.edu/ojs/article/view/316

Lander, R., & Pautsch, C. (2011, April). *Data use in schools: An exploratory study of four schools using value-added sampling.* Paper presented at the Annual Convention of the American Educational Research Association, New Orleans, LA.

Layard, R., & Dunn, J. (2009). *A good childhood: Searching for values in a competitive age.* New York, NY: Penguin Books.

Layton, L. (2012, September 20). Rethinking the classroom: Obama's overhaul of public education. *Washington Post.* Retrieved from www.washingtonpost.com/local/education/rethinking-the-classroom-obamas-overhaul-of-public-education/2012/09/20/a5459346-e171-11e1-ae7f-d2a13e249eb2_print.html

Lazear, E. P. (2001). Educational production. *Quarterly Journal of Economics, 116*(3), 777–803. doi:10.1162/00335530152466232

Lazear, E. P., & Poterba, J. (2006, January 30). That rarest of opportunities. *Hoover Digest, 1.* Stanford, CA: Hoover Institution, Stanford University. Retrieved from www.hoover.org/publications/hoover-digest/article/7883

LeClaire, B. (2011, June 1). Will EVAAS make Wake schools Better? *Raleigh Public Record.* Retrieved from www.raleighpublicrecord.org/featured/2011/06/01/will-evaas-make-wake-schools-better-part-ii/

Lefly, D. L. (2012). *Measuring student growth: The Colorado model.* Report of the Colorado Department of Education. Retrieved from www.ncsl.org/documents/educ/lefly.pdf

Lewin, T. (2012, May 16). Backer of Common Core school curriculum is chosen to lead College Board. *New York Times.* Retrieved from www.nytimes.com/2012/05/16/education/david-coleman-to-lead-college-board.html

Lincoln, Y. S., & Guba, E. G. (1985). *Naturalistic inquiry.* Newbury Park, CA: SAGE.

Linn, R. L. (2000). Assessments and accountability. *Educational Researcher, 29* (2), 4–15. doi:10.2307/1177052

Linn, R. L. (2001). *The design and evaluation of educational assessment and accountability systems.* CSE Technical Report 563. Los Angeles, CA: Center for the Study of Evaluation. Retrieved from www.cse.ucla.edu/products/reports/TR539.pdf

Linn, R. L. (2008). Methodological issues in achieving school accountability. *Journal of Curriculum Studies, 40*, 699–711. doi:10.1080/00220270802105729

Linn, R. L., & Haug, C. (2002). Stability of school-building accountability scores and gains. *Educational Evaluation and Policy Analysis, 24*, 29–36. doi:10.3102/01623737024001029

Liu, S., & Teddlie, C. (2005). A follow-up study on teacher evaluation in China: Historical analysis and latest trends. *Journal of Personnel Evaluation in Education, 18*, 253–272. doi:10.1007/s11092–007–9029–4

Lockwood, J. R., Doran, H., & McCaffrey, D. F. (2003). Using R for estimating longitudinal student achievement models. *R News, 3*(3), 17–23.

Lockwood, J. R., & McCaffrey, D. F. (2009). Exploring student–teacher interactions in longitudinal achievement data. *Education Finance and Policy, 4*(4), 439–467. doi:10.1162/edfp.2009.4.4.439

Lockwood, J. R., McCaffrey, D. F., Hamilton, L. S., Stecher, B., Le, V., & Martinez, J. F. (2007). The sensitivity of value-added teacher effect estimates to different mathematics achievement measures. *Journal of Educational Measurement, 44*(1), 47–67.

Lockwood, J. R., McCaffrey, D. F., Mariano, L. T., & Setodji, C. (2007). Bayesian methods for scalable multivariate value-added assessment. *Journal of Educational and Behavioral Statistics, 32*(2), 125–150. doi:10.3102/1076998606298039

Lockwood, J. R., McCaffrey, D. F., & Sass, T. R. (2008). *The intertemporal stability, of teacher effect estimates.* Paper presented at the National Conference on Value-Added Modeling. Sponsored by the Wisconsin Center for Education Research, Madison, WI. Retrieved from www.wcer.wisc.edu/news/events/VAM%20Conference%20Final%20Papers/IntertemporalStability_McCaffreySass-Lockwood.pdf

Loeb, S., & Candelaria, C. A. (2012, October 15). How stable are value-added estimates across years, subjects, and student groups? *Carnegie Knowledge Network.* Retrieved from www.carnegieknowledgenetwork.org/briefs/value-added/value-added-stability/

Loevinger, J. (1957). Objective tests as instruments of psychological theory. *Psychological Reports, 3*(7), 635–694. doi:10.2466/PR0.3.7.635–694

Lowrey, A. (2012, January 6). Big study links good teachers to lasting gain. *New York Times.* Retrieved from www.nytimes.com/2012/01/06/education/big-study-links-good-teachers-to-lasting-gain.html?emc=eta1#comments

Lozier, C. (2012, July 18). What the PGA can teach us about value-added modeling. *Getting Smart.* Retrieved from http://gettingsmart.com/blog/2012/07/what-pga-can-teach-us-about-value-added-modeling/

March, W. (2013, April 3). Jeb Bush's education foundation under fire for lobbying for laws that benefit corporate donors. *Huffington Post Miami.* Retrieved from www.huffingtonpost.com/2013/03/03/jeb-bush-education-foundation_n_2802536.html

Marder, M. (2012). Measuring teacher quality with value-added modeling. *Kappa Delta Pi Record, 48,* 156–161. doi 10.1080/00228958.2012.733929

Marsh, H. W. (2007). Students' evaluations of university teaching: Dimensionality, reliability, validity, potential biases, and usefulness. In R. P. Perry & J. C. Smart (Eds.), *The scholarship of teaching and learning in higher education: An evidence-based perspective* (pp. 319–383). New York, NY: Springer.

Martin, D. (2008, March 31). Dith Pran, photojournalist and survivor of the Killing Fields, dies at 65. *New York Times.* Retrieved from www.nytimes.com/2008/03/31/nyregion/31dith.html?pagewanted=all

Martineau, J. A. (2010). The validity of value-added models: An allegory. *Phi Delta Kappan, 91*(7), 64–67.

Marx, G. T. (1995). The engineering of social control: The search for the silver bullet. In J. Hagan & R. Peterson (Eds.), *Crime and inequality* (pp. 225–246). Palo Alto, CA: Stanford University Press.

Mathews, J. (2013). Hidden power of teacher awards. *Washington Post.* Retrieved from www.washingtonpost.com/blogs/class-struggle/post/hidden-power-of-teacher-awards/2013/04/08/15b7afcc-9e66-11e2-9a79-eb5280c81c63_blog.html

Mathis, W. (2011). *Review of "Florida Formula for Student Achievement: Lessons for the Nation."* Boulder, CO: National Education Policy Center. Retrieved from http://nepc.colorado.edu/thinktank/review-florida-formula

Mathis, W. (2012, September). *Research-based options for education policymaking: Teacher evaluation.* Boulder, CO: National Education Policy Center. Retrieved from http://nepc.colorado.edu/publication/options-teacher-evaluations

McCaffrey, D. F. (2012, October 15). Do value-added methods level the playing field for teachers? *Carnegie Knowledge Network.* Retrieved from www.carnegieknowledgenetwork.org/briefs/value-added/level-playing-field/

McCaffrey, D. F., & Hamilton, L. (2007). *Value-added assessment in practice lessons from the Pennsylvania Value-Added Assessment System: Pilot project.* Santa Monica, CA: RAND Corporation. Retrieved from www.rand.org/pubs/technical_reports/2007/RAND_TR506.sum.pdf

McCaffrey, D. F., Han, B., & Lockwood, J. R. (2008). *From data to bonuses: A case study of the issues related to awarding teachers pay on the basis of their student's progress* (Working Paper 2008-14). Nashville, TN: National Center on Performance Incentives. Retrieved from https://my.vanderbilt.edu/performanceincentives/ncpi-publications/design-and-implementation-of-incentive-pay-systems/from-data-to-bonuses-a-case-study-of-the-issues-related-to-awarding-teachers-pay-on-the-basis-of-their-students-progress/

McCaffrey, D. F., Lockwood, J. R., Koretz, D. M., & Hamilton, L. S. (2003). *Evaluating value-added models for teacher accountability*. Santa Monica, CA: RAND Corporation. Retrieved from www.rand.org/pubs/monographs/2004/RAND_MG158.pdf

McCaffrey, D. F., Lockwood, J. R., Koretz, D., Louis, T. A., & Hamilton, L. (2004a). Let's see more empirical studies on value-added modeling of teacher effects: A reply to Raudenbush, Rubin, Stuart and Zanutto, and Reckase. *Journal of Educational and Behavioral Statistics, 29*(1), 139–143. doi:10.3102/10769986029001139

McCaffrey, D. F., Lockwood, J. R., Koretz, D., Louis, T. A., & Hamilton, L. (2004b). Models for value-added modeling of teacher effects. *Journal of Educational and Behavioral Statistics, 29*(1), 67–101. Retrieved from www.rand.org/pubs/reprints/2005/RAND_RP1165.pdf

McCaffrey, D. F., Sass, T. R., Lockwood, J. R., & Mihaly, K. (2009). The intertemporal variability of teacher effect estimates. *Education Finance and Policy, 4*(4), 572–606. doi:10.1162/edfp2009.4.4.572

McKenna, L. (2012, November 30). Extra pay for great teachers: Newark's simple idea is a breakthrough. *The Atlantic.* Retrieved from www.theatlantic.com/business/archive/2012/11/extra-pay-for-great-teachers-newarks-simple-idea-is-a-breakthrough/265759/

McMillan, J. H. (1988). Beyond value-added education: Improvement alone is not enough. *Journal of Higher Education, 59*(5), 564–579. doi:10.2307/1981704

McNeil, M. (2012, January 31). School chiefs' group elbows into policy fight. *Education Week.* Retrieved from www.edweek.org/ew/articles/2012/02/01/19chiefs_ep.h31.html

Mead, S., Rotherham, A. J., & Brown, R. (2012, September 26). *The hangover: Thinking about the unintended consequences of the nation's teacher evaluation binge.* Washington, DC: American Enterprise Institute. Retrieved from www.aei.org/files/2012/09/25/-the-hangover-thinking-about-the-unintended-consequences-of-the-nations-teacher-evaluation-binge_144008786960.pdf

Medina, J. (2009, September 8). 12,000 teacher reports, but what to do? *New York Times.* Retrieved from www.nytimes.com/2009/09/09/nyregion/09teachers.html

Mellon, E. (2010, January 14). HISD moves ahead on dismissal policy: In the past, teachers were rarely let go over poor performance, data show. *Houston Chronicle.* Retrieved from www.chron.com/disp/story.mpl/metropolitan/6816752.html

Mellon, E. (2012, September 12). HISD considers revised teacher bonus plan. *Houston Chronicle.* Retrieved from www.chron.com/news/houston-texas/article/HISD-considers-revised-teacher-bonus-plan-3861041.php

Merrigan, G., & Huston, C. L. (2004). *Communication research methods.* New York, NY: Oxford University Press.

Messick, S. (1975). The standard problem: Meaning and values in measurement and evaluation. *American Psychologist, 30*, 955–966.

Messick, S. (1980). Test validity and the ethics of assessment. *American Psychologist, 35*, 1012–1027.

Messick, S. (1989). *Validity.* In R. L. Linn (Ed.), *Educational Measurement* (3rd ed.; pp. 13–103). New York, NY: American Council on Education and Macmillan.

Messick, S. (1995). Validity of psychological assessment: Validation of inferences from persons' responses and performances as scientific inquiry into score meaning. *American Psychologist, 50*, 741–749.

Meyer, R. H. (1997). Value-added indicators of school performance: A primer. *Economics of Education Review, 16*(3), 283–301. doi:10.1016/S0272–7757(96)00081–7

Meyer, R. H. (2012). Robert H. Meyer [Curriculum vitae]. Retrieved from www.lafollette.wisc.edu/facultystaff/.../meyer-robert-cv.pdf

Meyer, R. H., & Dokumaci, E. (2011). *Value-added models and the next generation of assessments.* Austin, TX: Center for K–12 Assessment and Performance Management. Retrieved from www.k12center.org/rsc/pdf/MeyerDokumaciPresenterSession4.pdf

Michie, G. (2012, March 7). What value is added by publicly shaming teachers? *Huffington Post Blog.* Retrieved from www.huffingtonpost.com/gregory-michie/what-value-is-added-by-pu_b_1325487.html

Milanowski, A. T. (2004). The relationship between teacher performance evaluation scores and student achievement: Evidence from Cincinnati. *Peabody Journal of Education, 79*, 33–53. doi:10.1207/s15327930pje7904_3

Milanowski, A., Kimball, S. M., & White, B. (2004). *The relationship between standards-based teacher evaluation scores and student achievement: Replication and extensions at three sites.* Madison, WI: University of Wisconsin-Madison, Center for Education Research, Consortium for Policy Research in Education. Retrieved from www.cpre-wisconsin.org/papers/3site_long_TE_SA_AERA04TE.pdf

Miller, M. H., & Modigliani, F. (1961). Dividend policy, growth and the valuation of shares. *Journal of Business, 34*(4), 411–433. doi:10.1086/294442

Misco, T. (2008). Was that a result of my teaching? A brief exploration of value-added assessment. *Clearing House: A Journal of Educational Strategies, Issues and Ideas, 82*(1), 11–14.

Monk, D. H. (1987). Assigning elementary pupils to their teachers. *Elementary School Journal, 88*(2), 167–187.

Moore-Johnson, S. (1984). Merit pay for teachers: A poor prescription for reform. *Harvard Educational Review, 54*, 175–185.

Morgan, J. P. (2002). *Multiple choices: Testing students in Tennessee.* Nashville, TN: Comptroller of the Treasury, Office of Education Accountability. Retrieved from www.comptroller1.state.tn.us/repository/RE/testing.pdf

Myrdal, G. (1944). *An American dilemma.* New York, NY: Harper and Row.

National Education Policy Center. (2010, July 12). *High-quality teacher evaluation or "fetishization" of tests? New report offers clear guidance for policymakers.* Boulder, CO: National Education Policy Center. Retrieved from www.educationnews.org/ed_reports/education_organizations/104052.html

National Education Policy Center. (2011, January 13). *Gates report touting "value-added" reached wrong conclusion.* Boulder, CO: National Education Policy Center. Retrieved from http://nepc.colorado.edu/newsletter/2011/01/study-released-last-month-gates-foundation-has-been-touted-%E2%80%9Csome-strongest-eviden

National Governors Association (NGA) Center for Best Practices and the Council of Chief State School Officers (CCSSO). (2010). *Common Core State Standards initiative: Frequently asked questions.* Retrieved from corestandards.org/frequently-asked-questions

National Research Council. (2008). *Assessing accomplished teaching: Advanced-level certification programs.* Washington, DC: National Academies Press. Retrieved from www.nap.edu/openbook.php?record_id=12224

Nelson, F. H. (2011, April). *A guide for developing growth models for teacher development and evaluation.* Paper presented at the Annual Conference of the American Educational Research Association, New Orleans, LA.

Newton, X., Darling-Hammond, L., Haertel, E., & Thomas, E. (2010). Value-added modeling of teacher effectiveness: An exploration of stability across models and contexts. *Educational Policy Analysis Archives, 18* (23), 1–27. Retrieved from http://epaa.asu.edu/ojs/article/view/810

Nichols, S. L., & Berliner, D. C. (2007). *Collateral damage: How high-stakes testing corrupts America's schools.* Cambridge, MA: Harvard Education Press.

Nichols, S., Glass, G. V., Berliner, D. C. (2012, July). High-stakes testing and student achievement: Updated analyses with NAEP data. *Education Policy Analysis Archives, 20*(20), 1–35. Retrieved from http://epaa.asu.edu/ojs/article/view/1048

Nicholson, M. R., & Brown, J. R. (2010). Value-added analysis in instruction. *School Administrator, 67*(2), 26–30.

Nieto, S., & Bode, P. (2008). *Affirming diversity. The sociopolitical context of multicultural education* (5th ed.). Boston, MA: Allyn & Bacon.

No Child Left Behind (NCLB) Act of 2001, Pub. L. No. 107–110, § 115 Stat. 1425. (2002). Retrieved from www.ed.gov/legislation/ESEA02/

Northwest Evaluation Association (NWEA). (2006). *Achievement gaps: An examination of differences in student achievement and growth.* Lake Oswego, OR. Retrieved from www.nwea.org/research/achievementgap.asp

New York State Educational Conference Board. (2004). *Bio: William (Bill) L. Sanders.* Albany, NY: Investment and Accountability for Student Success Policy Conference of the Educational Conference Board. Retrieved from www.nysecb.org/2004conference/04sanders.html

Nye, B., Konstantopoulos, S., & Hedges, L. V. (2004). How large are teacher effects? *Educational Evaluation and Policy Analysis, 26*(3), 237–257. doi:10.3102/01623737026003237

Obama, B. (2009, July 24). *Remarks by the President on education.* (Press release). Washington, DC: U.S. Department of Education and Office of the Press Secretary. Retrieved from www.whitehouse.gov/the_press_office/Remarks-by-the-President-at-the-Department-of-Education

Olson, L. (2002, November 20). Education scholars finding new "value" in student test data. *Education Week, 22*(12), 1–14. Retrieved from www.edweek.org

Orfield, G. (2009). *Reviving the goal of an integrated society: A 21st-century challenge.* Los Angeles, CA: The Civil Rights Project, UCLA.

Orfield, G., & Kornhaber, M. L. (Eds.). (2001). *Raising standards or raising barriers? Inequality and high-stakes testing in public education.* New York, NY: Century Foundation Press.

Organization for Economic Cooperation and Development (OECD). (2005). *Teachers matter: Attracting, developing, and retaining effective teachers.* Washington, DC: OECD. Retrieved from www.oecd.org/edu/preschoolandschool/attractingdevelopingandretainingeffectiveteachers-finalreportteachersmatter.htm

Otterman, S. (2010, December 26). Hurdles emerge in rising effort to rate teachers. *New York Times.* Retrieved from www.nytimes.com/2010/12/27/nyregion/27teachers.html

Pallas, A. (2012, May 16). Meet the "worst" 8th grade math teacher in NYC. *Washington Post.* Retrieved from www.washingtonpost.com/blogs/answer-sheet/post/meet-the-worst-8th-grade-math-teacher-in-nyc/2012/05/15/gIQArmlbSU_blog.html?tid=pm_pop

Papay, J. P. (2011). Different tests, different answers: The stability of teacher value-added estimates across outcome measures. *American Educational Research Journal, 48*(1), 163–193. doi:10.3102/0002831210362589

Paufler, N. A., & Amrein-Beardsley, A. (2013, October 22). The random assignment of students into elementary classrooms: Implications for value-added analyses and interpretations. *American Educational Research Journal.* doi: 10.3102/0002831213508299

Pauken, T. (2013, January 23). Texas vs. No Child Left Behind. *American Conservative.* Retrieved from www.theamericanconservative.com/articles/texas-vs-no-child-left-behind/

Perry, J., & Vogell, H. (2009, October 19). Are drastic swings in CRCT scores valid? *Atlanta Journal-Constitution.* Retrieved from www.ajc.com/news/news/local/are-drastic-swings-in-crct-scores-valid/nQYQm

Phelps, R. P. (2011, April). The effect of testing on achievement: Meta-analyses and research summary, 1910–2010. *Nonpartisan Education Review, 7*(3), 1–23.

Philips, R. H. (2012, Sept. 10). No Child Left Behind waiver sought by Alabama, six other states. *Press Register.* Retrieved from http://blog.al.com/live/2012/09/no_child_left_behind_waiver_so.html

Pickering, J. W., & Bowers, J. C. (1990). Assessing value-added outcomes assessment. *Measurement & Evaluation in Counseling & Development, 22*(4), 215–221.

Pies, S. (2013). The nine methods of propaganda. *eHow.* Retrieved from www.ehow.com/info_10000962_nine-methods-propaganda.html

Player, D. (2010). Nonmonetary compensation in the public teacher labor market. *Education Finance and Policy, 5*(1), pp. 82–103. doi:10.1162/edfp2009.5.1.5105

Popham, W. J. (1997). The moth and the flame: Student learning as a criterion of instructional competence. In J. Millman, (Ed.), *Grading teachers, grading schools. Is student achievement a valid evaluation measure?* (pp. 264–274). Thousand Oaks, CA: Corwin.

Popham, W. J. (2011). *Classroom assessment: What teachers need to know* (6th ed.). Boston, MA: Pearson.

Popham, W. J. (2013, January 8). Waving the flag for formative assessment. *Education Week.* Retrieved from www.edweek.org/ew/articles/2013/01/09/15popham.h32.html?tkn=LMSFalVt%2FzHY2790%2FCNw88VfniWfZ8Aa8EIS&cmp=ENL-EU-NEWS2&intc=es

Postal, L. (2013, April 16). Teachers' union suit: Florida's merit-pay law violates U.S. Constitution. *Orlando Sentinel.* Retrieved from http://articles.orlandosentinel.com/2013–04–16/features/os-teacher-evaluations-union-challenge-20130416_1_teachers-union-suit-evaluation-system-test-score-data

Praisner, C. (2003). Attitudes of elementary school principals toward the inclusion of students with disabilities. *Exceptional Children, 69*(2), 135–145.

Pullin, D. (2013). Legal issues in the use of student test scores and value-added models (VAM) to determine educational quality. *Education Policy Analysis Archives, 21*(6), 1–27. Retrieved from http://epaa. asu.edu/ojs/article/view/1160

Putnam, D., & Smith, I. (producers), & Joffé, R. (director). (1984, November 2). *The killing fields* [Motion picture]. United Kingdom: Warner Bros.

Quintero, E. (2012, October 22). The data-driven education movement. *Shanker Blog*. Retrieved from http://shankerblog.org/?p=7015

R Development Core Team (2009) *R: A Language and Environment for Statistical Computing*. Vienna, Austria: R Foundation for Statistical Computing.

Race to the Top (RttT) Act of 2011, S. 844–112th Congress. (2011). Retrieved from www.govtrack. us/congress/bills/112/s844

Raudenbush, S. W. (2004). What are value-added models estimating and what does this imply for statistical practice? *Journal of Educational and Behavioral Statistics, 29*(1), 121–129. doi:10.3102/10769986029001121

Raudenbush, S. W., & Jean, M. (2012, October 15). How should educators interpret value-added scores? *Carnegie Knowledge Network*. Retrieved from www.carnegieknowledgenetwork.org/briefs/value-added/interpreting-value-added/

Ravitch, D. (2007) *EdSpeak: A glossary of education terms, phases, buzzwords, jargon*. Alexandria, VA: ASCD.

Ravitch, D. (2010a). *The death and life of the great American school system: How testing and choice are undermining education*. New York, NY: Basic Books.

Ravitch, D. (2010b, October). Ravitch: Why teachers should never be rated by test scores. *Washington Post* (reporter Valerie Strauss). Retrieved from http://voices.washingtonpost.com/answer-sheet/diane-ravitch/ravitch-why-teachers-should-ne.html?wprss=answer-sheet

Ravitch, D. (2011, May 6). *Standardized testing undermines teaching* [Radio broadcast]. National Public Radio. Retrieved from www.npr.org/2011/04/28/135142895/ravitch-standardized-testing-undermines-teaching?ft=1&f=13&sc=17

Ravitch, D. (2012a). Does the average TFA teacher stay for 8 years? [Blog post]. Retrieved from http://dianeravitch.net/2012/12/17/does-the-average-tfa-teacher-stay-for-8-years/

Ravitch, D. (2012b, March 7). Flunking Arne Duncan. *New York Review of Books*. Retrieved from www.nybooks.com/blogs/nyrblog/2012/mar/07/flunking-arne-duncan/

Ravitch, D. (2012c, February 21). No student left untested. *New York Review of Books*. http://www.nybooks.com/blogs/nyrblog/2012/feb/21/no-student-left-untested/

Ravitch, D. (2012d, January 17). Problems with the big teacher evaluation study. *Washington Post*. Retrieved from www.washingtonpost.com/blogs/answer-sheet/post/ravitch-problems-with-the-big-teacher-evaluation-study/2012/01/17/gIQAjGPl5P_blog.html

Ravitch, D. (2013a, October 13). Teacher: Why I am leaving teaching [Blog post]. Retrieved from http://dianeravitch.net/2013/10/23/teacher-why-i-am-leaving-teaching

Ravitch, D. (2013b, May 11). On merit pay [Blog post]. Retrieved from http://dianeravitch.net/2013/05/11/on-merit-pay/

Ravitch, D. (2013c, June 1). Why I oppose merit pay [Blog post]. Retrieved from http://dianeravitch.net/2013/06/01/teacher-why-i-oppose-merit-pay/

Ravitch, D. (2014, January 5). English teacher: Why I had to leave a profession I loved [Blog post]. Diane Ravitch's blog. Retrieved from http://dianeravitch.net/2014/01/05/english-teacher-why-i-had-to-leave-a-profession-i-loved/

Raymond. M. E., & Hanushek, E. A. (2003, Summer). High-stakes research. *Education Next, 3*(3). Retrieved from http://hanushek.stanford.edu/sites/default/files/publications/Raymond%2BHanushek%202003%20Ednext%203%283%29.pdf

Reardon, S. F., Atteberry, A., Arshan, N., & Kurlaender, M. (2009, April 21). *Effects of the California high school exit exam on student persistence, achievement and graduation* (Working Paper 2009–12). Stanford, CA: Stanford University, Institute for Research on Education Policy and Practice.

Reardon, S. F., & Raudenbush, S. W. (2009). Assumptions of value-added models for estimating school effects. *Education Finance and Policy, 4*(4), 492–519. doi:10.1162/edfp2009.4.4.492

Reckase, M. D. (2004). The real world is more complicated than we would like. *Journal of Educational and Behavioral Statistics, 29*(1), 117–120. doi:10.3102/10769986029001117

Region 13 (2004). *Professional Development Appraisal System (PDAS)*. Austin, TX: Region 13 Education Service Center. Retrieved from http://www5.esc13.net/pdas/

Rhee, M. (2011, April 6). The evidence is clear: Test scores must accurately reflect students' learning. *Huffington Post*. Retrieved from www.huffingtonpost.com/michelle-rhee/michelle-rhee-dc-schools_b_845286.html

Rhoades, K., & Madaus, G. (2003). *Errors in standardized tests: A systemic problem* (Report of the National Board on Educational Testing and Public Policy). Chestnut Hill, MA: Boston College Center for the Study of Testing, Evaluation and Educational Policy. Retrieved from www.bc.edu/research/nbetpp/statements/M1N4.pdf

Richardson, W. (2012, September 27). Do parents really want more than 200 separate state-mandated assessments for their children? *Huffington Post*. Retrieved from www.huffingtonpost.com/will-richardson/do-parents-really-want-ov_b_1913704.html

Ricketts, C. R. (2010). *End of course grades and standardized test scores: Are grades predictive of student achievement?* (Doctoral dissertation). Capella University, Minneapolis, MN. Retrieved from http://search.proquest.com/docview/755303452

Rivkin, S. G. (2007, November). *Value-added analysis and education policy*. Washington, DC: National Center for Analysis of Longitudinal Data in Education Research, Urban Institute. Retrieved from www.urban.org/UploadedPDF/411577_value-added_analysis.pdf

Rivkin, S. G., Hanushek, E. A., & Kain, J. F. (2005). Teachers, schools, and academic achievement. *Econometrica, 73*(2), 417–458. doi:10.1111/j.1468–0262.2005.00584.x

Rivkin, S. G., & Ishii, J. (2008). *Impediments to the estimation of teacher value-added*. Paper presented at the National Conference on Value-Added Modeling. Sponsored by the Wisconsin Center for Education Research (WCER), Madison, WI.

Robelen, E. W. (2012, January 9). Yardsticks vary by nation in calling education to account. *Education Week*. Retrieved from www.edweek.org/ew/articles/2012/01/12/16testing.h31.html?tkn=ZRXFgiQ5krPVo%2FsHmf1v%2Bh33GqSq%2ByE1LBEQ&cmp=ENL-EU-NEWS1&intc=EW-QC12-ENL

Roberts, G. (2012, February 26). Queens parents demand answers following teacher's low grades. *New York Post*. Retrieved from www.nypost.com/p/news/local/cursed_with_the_worst_in_queens_f5wLhEdDRN1Wl9h1GQgxAM

Roberts, J. (2012, March 8). Tenn. teacher evaluations to be made public this summer. *Education Week*. Retrieved from www.edweek.org/ew/articles/2012/03/08/24mct_tnevalsonline.h31.html?tkn=SNMFO7v9uXfg%2FDThT7r%2Fu4NaI7oquyzl2J%2B%2B&cmp=ENL-EU-NEWS2

Roche, W. F. (2006, October 22). Bush's family profits from "No Child" Act. *Los Angeles Times*. Retrieved from http://articles.latimes.com/2006/oct/22/nation/na-ignite22

Rockoff, J. E., Staiger, D. O., Kane, T. J., & Taylor, E. S. (2010). *Information and employee evaluation: Evidence from a randomized intervention in public schools*. Cambridge, MA: The National Bureau of Economic Research. Retrieved from www.nber.org/papers/w16240

Rose, L. C., & Gallup. (2007, September). The 39th Annual Phi Delta Kappa/Gallup Poll of the public's attitudes toward the public schools. *Phi Delta Kappan, 88*(1), 33–48. Retrieved from www.kappanmagazine.org/content/89/1/33.abstract

Rosenbaum, P., & Rubin, D. B. (1983). The central role of the propensity score in observational studies for causal effects. *Biometrika, 70*(1), 41–55. doi:10.2307/2335942

Ross, S. M., Sanders, W. L., Wright, S. P., Stringfield, S., Wang, W. L., & Alberg, M. (2001). Two- and three-year results from the Memphis Restructuring Initiative. *School Effectiveness and School Improvement, 12*(3), 323–346. doi:10.1076/sesi.12.3.323.3451

Ross, S. M., Wang, L. W., Alberg, M., Sanders, W. L., Wright, S. P., & Stringfield, S. (2001). *Fourth-year achievement results on the Tennessee Value-Added Assessment System for restructuring schools in Memphis*.

Paper presented at the Annual Meeting of the American Educational Research Association: Seattle, WA.

Rotherham, A. J. (2011, January 6). School of thought: 11 education activists for 2011. David Coleman: The architect. *Time*. Retrieved from www.time.com/time/specials/packages/article/0,28804,2040 867_2040871_2040925,00.html

Rothstein, J. (2009). Student sorting and bias in value-added estimation: Selection on observables and unobservables. *Education Finance and Policy, 4*(4), 537–571. doi:http://dx.doi.org/10.1162/edfp.2009.4.4.537

Rothstein, J. (2010a, September 7). More harm than good. *New York Times*. Retrieved from www.nytimes.com/roomfordebate/2010/09/06/assessing-a-teachers-value/dont-be-too-quick-to-embrace-value-added-assessments

Rothstein, J. (2010b, February). Teacher quality in educational production: Tracking, decay, and student achievement. *Quarterly Journal of Economics, 125*(1), 175–214. doi:10.1162/qjec.2010.125.1.175

Rothstein, J. (2011, January). *Review of learning about teaching*. Boulder, CO: National Education Policy Center. Retrieved from http://nepc.colorado.edu/thinktank/review-learning-about-teaching

Rothstein, J., & Mathis, W. J. (2013, January). *Review of two culminating reports from the MET Project*. Boulder, CO: National Education Policy Center. Retrieved from http://nepc.colorado.edu/think-tank/review-MET-final-2013

Rubenstein, G. (2012a, February 26). Analyzing released NYC value-added data: Part 2 [Blog post]. *Teach for Us*. Retrieved from http://garyrubinstein.teachforus.org/2012/02/28/analyzing-released-nyc-value-added-data-part-2/

Rubenstein, G. (2012b, February 26). Analyzing released NYC value-added data: Part 4 [Blog post]. *Teach For Us*. Retrieved from http://garyrubinstein.teachforus.org/2012/03/10/analyzing-released-nyc-value-added-data-part-4/

Rubin, D. B., Stuart, E. A., & Zanutto, E. L. (2004). A potential outcomes view of value-added assessment in education. *Journal of Educational and Behavioral Statistics, 29*(1), 103–116. doi:10.3102/10769986029001103

Rutkoff, A. (2012, February 24). Testing teachers: Origins of NYC's evaluation system. *Wall Street Journal*. Retrieved from http://blogs.wsj.com/metropolis/2012/02/24/testing-teachers-origins-of-nycs-evaluation-system/?mod=google_news_blog

Sachs, J. D. (2011, November 12). The new progressive movement. *New York Times*. Retrieved from www.nytimes.com/2011/11/13/opinion/sunday/the-new-progressive-movement.html

Sahlberg, P. (2011). *Finnish lessons: What can the world learn from educational change in Finland?* New York, NY: Teachers College Press.

Sahlberg, P. (2012, April 2). Global educational reform movement is here! [Blog post]. Retrieved from www.pasisahlberg.com/blog/?p=68

Sanders, W. (1994, October 27). [Message posted to online discussion forum of Tennessee Value-Added Assessment System.] Retrieved from http://epaa.asu.edu/tvaas.html

Sanders, W. L. (1998). Value-added assessment. *School Administrator, 55*(11), 24–27.

Sanders W. L. (2000). Value-added assessment from student achievement data: Opportunities and hurdles. *Journal of Personnel Evaluation in Education, 14*(4), 329–339.

Sanders, W. L. (2003, April). *Beyond "No Child Left Behind."* Paper presented at the Annual Meeting of the American Educational Research Association: Chicago. Retrieved from www.sas.com/govedu/edu/no-child.pdf

Sanders, W. L. (2004). *How can value-added assessment lead to greater accountability?* Report presented at the First Annual Policy Conference of the New York State Educational Conference Board (Investment and Accountability for Student Success), Albany, NY.

Sanders, W. L. (2006). *Comparisons among various educational assessment value-added models*. Paper presented at *The Power of Two – National Value-Added Conference*, October 16, 2006, Columbus, Ohio. Retrieved from www.sas.com/govedu/edu/services/vaconferencepaper.pdf

Sanders, W. J., Ashton, J. J., & Wright, S. P. (2005, March 7). *Comparison of the effects of NBPTS certified teachers with other teachers on the rate of student academic progress*. Cary, NC: SAS EVAAS Group, SAS

Institute, Inc. Retrieved from www.eric.ed.gov/ERICWebPortal/search/detailmini.jsp?_nfpb=true&_&ERICExtSearch_SearchValue_0=ED491846&ERICExtSearch_SearchType_0=no&accno=ED491846

Sanders, W. L., & Horn, S. (1994). The Tennessee Value-Added Assessment System (TVAAS): Mixed-model methodology in educational assessment. *Journal of Personnel Evaluation in Education, 8*(3), 299–311.

Sanders, W. L., & Horn, S. (1998). Research findings from the Tennessee Value-Added Assessment System (TVAAS) database: Implications for educational evaluation and research. *Journal of Personnel Evaluation in Education, 12*(3), 247–256.

Sanders, W. L., & Rivers, J. C. (1996). *Cummulative and residual effects of teachers on future student academic achievement*. Knoxville, TN: University of Tennessee Value-Added Research and Assessment Center. Retrieved from http://heartland.org/policy-documents/cumulative-and-residual-effects-teachers-future-student-academic-achievement

Sanders, W. L., Saxton, A. M., & Horn, S. P. (1997). The Tennessee Value-Added Accountability System: A quantitative, outcomes-based approach to educational assessment. In J. Millman (Ed.), *Grading teachers, grading schools: Is student achievement a valid evaluation measure?* (pp. 137–162). Thousand Oaks, CA: Corwin Press.

Sanders, W. L., & Wright, S. P. (2008). *A response to Amrein-Beardsley (2008): "Methodological concerns about the Education Value-Added Assessment System."* Cary, NC: SAS Institute, Inc. Retrieved from www.sas.com/govedu/edu/services/Sanders_Wright_response_to_Amrein-Beardsley_4_14_2008.pdf

Sanders, W. L., Wright, S. P., Rivers, J. C., & Leandro, J. G. (2009, November). *A response to criticisms of SAS EVAAS*. Cary, NC: SAS Institute, Inc. Retrieved from www.sas.com/resources/asset/Response_to_Criticisms_of_SAS_EVAAS_11–13–09.pdf

Santos, F., & Gebeloff, R. (2012, February 24). Teacher quality widely diffused, ratings indicate. *New York Times*. Retrieved from www.nytimes.com/2012/02/25/education/teacher-quality-widely-diffused-nyc-ratings-indicate.html?_r=1&hpw

SAS. (2007). *Resource guide for value-added reporting*. Cary, NC. SAS Institute, Inc. Retrieved from www.dpi.state.nc.us/docs/evaas/guide/resourceguide.pdf

SAS. (2012a). *SAS® EVAAS® for K–12: Assess and predict student performance with precision and reliability*. Cary, NC. SAS Institute, Inc. Retrieved from www.sas.com/govedu/edu/k12/evaas/customers.html

SAS. (2012b). *SAS® EVAAS® for K–12 fact sheet*. Cary, NC. SAS Institute, Inc. Retrieved from www.sas.com/resources/factsheet/education-evaas-factsheet.pdf

SAS. (2012c). *SAS® EVAAS® for K–12: Reliably assess and predict student performance*. Cary, NC. SAS Institute, Inc. Retrieved from www.sas.com/govedu/edu/k12/evaas/index.html

Sass, T. R. (2008). *The stability of value-added measures of teacher quality and implications for teacher compensation policy*. Washington, DC: National Center for Analysis of Longitudinal Data in Education Research. Retrieved from www.urban.org/UploadedPDF/1001266_stabilityofvalue.pdf

Sass, T., & Harris, D. (2012, March 1). *Skills, productivity and the evaluation of teacher performance* (W. Andrew Young School of Policy Studies Research Paper series No. 12-11). Retrieved from http://papers.ssrn.com/sol3/papers.cfm?abstract_id=2020717

Sawchuck, S. (2010, June 1). Performance-pay model shows no achievement edge. *Education Week*. Retrieved from www.edweek.org/ew/articles/2010/06/01/33tap.h29.html

Sawchuck, S. (2011, May 11). NEA leaders propose teacher-evaluation shift. *Education Week*. Retrieved from www.edweek.org/ew/articles/2011/05/11/31nea.h30.html?tkn=WOUFtVRsnkjub0%2B9AFmpN8POyNm4azmYGNPk&intc=es

Sawchuck, S. (2012, October 23). "Value-added" measures at secondary level questioned. *Education Week*. Retrieved from www.edweek.org/ew/articles/2012/10/24/09tracking_ep.h32.html?tkn=YNQFfkvNAG%2B96E0UtCsDl8v5KmxATsSBWeuD&cmp=ENL-EU-NEWS2

Sawchuck, S. (2013a, May 6). Are teacher evaluations public? Assessing the landscape. *Education Week*. Retrieved from http://blogs.edweek.org/edweek/teacherbeat/2013/05/are_teacher_evaluations_public.html?cmp=ENL-EU-NEWS2

Sawchuck, S. (2013b, January 8). Combined measures better at gauging teacher effectiveness, study finds. *Education Week*. Retrieved from www.edweek.org/ew/articles/2013/01/08/17teach_ep.h32. html?tkn=XQSF%2FRt5Y0QfRrL10tg5JOZyRSdR2Eozgzl6&cmp=ENL-EU-NEWS2

Sawchuck, S. (2013c, April 16). Florida unions sue over test-score-based evaluations. *Education Week*. Retrieved from www.edweek.org/ew/articles/2013/04/16/29lawsuit.h32.html?tkn=UMPFGDca E1zq%2FdRs4eOyDBFRRZBNPPBnrsY4&cmp=ENL-EU-NEWS1&intc=es

Sawchuck, S. (2013d, February 5). Teachers' rating still high despite new measures: Changes to evaluation systems yield only subtle differences. *Education Week*. Retrieved from www.edweek.org/ew/ articles/2013/02/06/20evaluate_ep.h32.html?tkn=ZSTF0t1L9D3DuLKhRwCfNuY2HyYg2z2zS JUw&cmp=ENL-EU-NEWS1&intc=es

Schacter, J., & Thum, Y. M. (2004). Paying for high and low quality teachers. *Economics in Education Review, 23*, 411–430.

Schaeffer, B. (2004, December). Districts pilot value-added assessment. *School Administrator*. Retrieved from www.aasa.org/publications/saarticledetail.cfm?ItemNumber=1066

Schafer, W. D., Lissitz, R. W., Zhu, X., Zhang, Y., Hou, X., & Li, Y. (2012, December). Evaluating teachers and schools using student growth models. *Practical Assessment, Research & Evaluation, 17*(17), 1–21. Retrieved from pareonline.net/getvn.asp?v=17&n=17

Scharrer, G., & Bureau, A. (2011, February 8). Should performance dictate teachers' pay? Rod Paige and other reformers say it shouldn't be on seniority. *Houston Chronicle*. Retrieved from www.chron. com/disp/story.mpl/metropolitan/7417299.html

Scherrer, J. (2011). Measuring teaching using value-added modeling: The imperfect panacea. *NASSP Bulletin, 95*(2), 122–140. doi:10.1177/0192636511410052

Schmelkin, L. P., Spencer, K. J., & Gellman, E. S. (1997). Faculty perspectives on course and teacher evaluations. *Research in Higher Education, 38*(5), 575–592. doi:10.1023/A:1024996413417

Schneider, M. (2013, March 21). Like spokes to a hub: Chiefs for Change in Bush's service [Blog post]. Retrieved from http://deutsch29.wordpress.com/2013/03/21/like-spokes-to-a-hub-chiefs-for-change-in-bushs-service/

Schochet, P. Z., & Chiang, H. S. (2010, July). *Error rates in measuring teacher and school performance based on student test score gains*. Washington, DC: U.S. Department of Education. Retrieved from http:// ies.ed.gov/ncee/pubs/20104004/

Schochet, P. Z., & Chiang, H. S. (2013). What are error rates for classifying teacher and school performance using value-added models? *Journal of Educational and Behavioral Statistics, 38*, 142–171. doi:10.3102/1076998611432174

Sedlmeier, P. (2006). The role of scales in student ratings. *Learning and Instruction, 16*(5), 401–415. doi:10.1016/j.learninstruc.2006.09.002

Serow, R. C. (1984). Effects of minimum competency testing for minority students: A review of expectations and outcomes. *Urban Review, 16* (2), 67–75. doi:10.1007/BF01142699

Shaw, L. H., & Bovaird, J. A. (2011, April). *The impact of latent variable outcomes on value-added models of intervention efficacy*. Paper presented at the Annual Conference of the American Educational Research Association, New Orleans, LA.

Shea, C. (2012, December). The data vigilante. *The Atlantic*. Retrieved from www.theatlantic.com/ magazine/archive/2012/12/the-data-vigilante/309172/

Simon, S. (2013, January 8). What measures the best teacher? More than scores, study shows. *Reuters*. Retrieved from www.reuters.com/article/2013/01/08/us-education-teachers-idUSBRE90713O 20130108

Simonson, M. E. (1998, March). School uniforms: A blueprint for legal challenges. *Inquiry & Analysis*, 1–7.

Slavin, R. E. (1989). PET and the pendulum: Faddism in education and how to stop it. *Phi Delta Kappan, 70*(10), 752–758.

Sloat, E. (2012, April). *Implementing teacher effectiveness measures under loosely defined state mandates: Practitioner considerations at the LEA level*. Paper presented at the annual meeting of the American Education Research Association, Vancouver, Canada.

Smith, D. S. (2013, May 5). America's "Forgotten War," south of the border. *CBS News Sunday Morning*. Retrieved from www.cbsnews.com/8301–3445_162–57582787/americas-forgotten-war-south-of-the-border/

Smith, M. L., & Noble, A. (1997). *Reforming schools by reforming assessment: Consequences of the Arizona Student Assessment Program (ASAP)*. Los Angeles, CA: National Center for Research on Evaluation, Standards, and Student Testing.

Smith, T. W., Gordon, B., Colby, S. A., & Wang, J. (2005). *An examination of the relationship between depth of student learning and National Board certification status*. Boone, NC: Appalachian State University. Retrieved from www.news.appstate.edu/releases/091905NBPTS%20Manuscrip.pdf

Solomon, L., White, J. T., Cohen, D., & Woo, D. (2007). *The effectiveness of the teacher advancement program*. Santa Monica, CA: National Institute for Excellence in Teaching. Retrieved from www.fldoe.org/dpe/pdf/effective-ness-of-TAP.pdf

Song, J., & Felch, J. (2011, May 7). Times updates and expands value-added ratings for Los Angeles elementary school teachers. *Los Angeles Times*. Retrieved from www.latimes.com/news/local/la-me-value-added-20110508,0,930050.story

Sparks, S. D. (2011, November 15). Value-added formulas strain collaboration. *Education Week*. Retrieved from www.edweek.org/ew/articles/2011/11/16/12collab-changes.h31.html?tkn=OVMFb8PQXxQi4wN6vpelNIr7%2BNhOFCbi71mI&intc=es

Sparks, S. D. (2012a, October 25). Caution urged in using "value-added" evaluation. *Education Week*. Retrieved from www.edweek.org/ew/articles/2012/10/25/10valueadd.h32.html?tkn=TMQFnzeyR8nxRed1VGn2bAchfRL0fw7WDKm7&cmp=ENL-EU-NEWS2

Sparks, S. D. (2012b, November 13). Today's tests seen as bar to better assessment. *Education Week*. Retrieved from www.edweek.org/ew/articles/2012/11/14/12tests.h32.html?tkn=NZOFSka1jXyHbB18S5vixNgKvFALFQQZTj18&cmp=ENL-EU-NEWS2

Sparks, D. (2013, March 11). Improved teacher evaluation may be necessary, but it's far from sufficient [Blog post]. Retrieved from http://dennissparks.wordpress.com/2013/03/11/improved-teacher-evaluation-may-be-necessary-but-its-far-from-sufficient/

Spellings, M. (2012, September 25). What if? *Huffington Post*. Retrieved from www.huffingtonpost.com/margaret-spellings/what-if_5_b_1910679.html

Springer, M. G., Ballou, D., Hamilton, L. S., Le, V., Lockwood, J. R., McCaffrey, … Stecher, B. M. (2010). *Teacher pay for performance: Experimental evidence from the Project on Incentives in Teaching (POINT)*. Nashville, TN: Vanderbilt University. Retrieved from www.rand.org/pubs/reprints/RP1416.html

Stacy, B., Guarino, C., Reckase, M., & Wooldridge, J. (2012, November 10). *Does the precision and stability of value-added estimates of teacher performance depend on the types of students they serve?* East Lansing, MI: Education Policy Center at Michigan State University. Retrieved from https://appam.confex.com/appam/2012/webprogram/Paper3327.html

Stanford Encyclopedia of Philosophy (2006). The Uncertainty Principle. Retrieved from http://plato.stanford.edu/entries/qt-uncertainty/

Stephens, S. (2008, August 24). Value-added evaluation being tried in Ohio schools. *Cleveland Metro*. Retrieved from http://blog.cleveland.com/metro/2008/08/valueadded_evaluation_being_tr.html

Stone, D. (1997). *Policy paradox: The art of political decision making*. New York, NY: Norton.

Stotsky, S., Bradley, R., & Warren, E. (2005). School-related influences on Grade 8 mathematics performance in Massachusetts. *Third Education Group Review, 1*(1), 1–32.

Strauss, V. (2011, December 13). Teach for America "research" questioned. *Washington Post*. Retrieved from www.washingtonpost.com/blogs/answer-sheet/post/teach-for-america-research-questioned/2011/12/12/gIQANb40rO_blog.html

Strauss, V. (2012a, April 23). Ed Dept seeks to bring test-based assessment to teacher prep programs. *Washington Post*. www.washingtonpost.com/blogs/answer-sheet/post/ed-dept-seeks-to-bring-test-based-assessment-to-teacher-prep-programs/2012/04/22/gIQAmdAxaT_blog.html

Strauss, V. (2012b, September 30). New teacher evaluations start to hurt students. *Washington Post*. Retrieved from www.washingtonpost.com/blogs/answer-sheet/post/new-teacher-evaluations-start-to-hurt-students/2012/09/29/f6d1b038–0aa6–11e2-afff-d6c7f20a83bf_blog.html

Strauss, V. (2013, January 6). The secret emails about Mark Zuckerberg's $100 million donation to Newark schools. *Washington Post*. Retrieved from www.washingtonpost.com/blogs/answer-sheet/wp/2013/01/06/the-secret-e-mails-about-mark-zuckerbergs-100-million-to-newark-schools/

Street, P. L. (2005). *Segregated schools: Educational apartheid in post-civil rights America*. New York, NY: Routledge.

Stroup, W. (1995). *Assessment of the statistical methodology used in the Tennessee Value-Added Assessment System*. Knoxville, TN: Tennessee Value-Added Research and Assessment Center. Retrieved from www.cgp.upenn.edu/pdf/Stroup-Statistical_Methodology_used_in_TVASS.PDF

Takahashi, P. (2012, October 30). Teachers union refuses to support school district's Race to the Top bid. *Las Vegas Sun*. Retrieved from www.lasvegassun.com/news/2012/oct/30/teachers-union-refuses-support-school-districts-ra/

Tate, R. L. (2004). A cautionary note on shrinkage estimates of school and teacher effects. *Florida Journal of Educational Research, 42*, 1–21. Retrieved from www.coedu.usf.edu/fjer/2004/FJERV42P0121.pdf

Tekwe, C. D., Carter, R. L., Ma, C., Algina, J., Lucas, M. E., Roth, J. ... Resnick, M. B. (2004). An empirical comparison of statistical models for value-added assessment of school performance. *Journal of Educational and Behavioral Statistics, 29*(1), 11–36. doi:10.3102/10769986029001011

The New Teacher Project (TNTP). (2012). *The irreplaceables: Understanding the real retention crisis in America's Urban Schools*. Brooklyn, NY: TNTP. Retrieved from http://tntp.org/assets/documents/TNTP_Irreplaceables_2012.pdf

Thomas, J. R. (2012, January 25). Coming soon: Teacher report cards based on student performance. *CT Mirror*. Retrieved from http://ctmirror.org/story/15172/coming-soon-teacher-report-cards-based-student-performance

Thum, Y. M., & Byrk, A. S. (1997). Value-added productivity indicators. In J. Millman (Ed.), *Grading teachers, grading schools: Is student achievement a valid evaluation measure?* (pp. 100–110). Thousand Oaks, CA: Corwin Press.

Timar, T. B., & Maxwell-Jolly, J. (Eds.). (2012). *Narrowing the achievement gap: Perspectives and strategies for challenging times*. Cambridge, MA: Harvard Education Press.

Toch, T., & Rothman, R. (2008). *Rush to judgment: Teacher evaluation in public education*. Washington, DC: Education Sector. Retrieved from www.educationsector.org/usr_doc/RushToJudgment_ES_Jan08.pdf

Tomassini, J., & Venugopal, N. (2012, November 13). Common-core deal in Florida sparks legal feud. *Education Week*. Retrieved from www.edweek.org/ew/articles/2012/11/14/12infinity.h32.html?tkn=VYLFasCwbjXSWMCRiG3DMYWUeXRJKd2%2BYOMK&cmp=ENL-EU-NEWS1

Topping, K. J., & Sanders, W. L. (2000). Teacher effectiveness and computer assessment of reading: Relating value-added and learning information system data. *School Effectiveness and School Improvement, 11*(13), 305–337. doi:10.1076/0924–3453(200009)11:3;1-G;FT305

Toppo, G. (2005, January 7). Education Dept. paid commentator to promote law. *USA Today*. Retrieved from www.usatoday.com/news/washington/2005–01–06-williams-whitehouse_x.htm

Toppo, G., Amos, D., Gillum, J., & Upton, J. (2011). When test scores seem too good to believe. *USA Today*. Retrieved from www.usatoday.com/news/education/2011–03–06-school-testing_N.htm

Trout, P. A. (1997). What the numbers mean: Providing a context for numerical student evaluations of courses. *Change, 29*(5), 24–30.

Turque, B. (2012, March 6). "Creative ... motivating" and fired. *Washington Post*. www.washingtonpost.com/local/education/creative–motivating-and-fired/2012/02/04/gIQAwzZpvR_story.html

Tyack, D., & Cuban, L. (1995). *Tinkering toward utopia: A century of public school reform*. Cambridge, MA: Harvard University Press.

Underwood, J., & Mead, J. F. (2012, February 29). A smart ALEC threatens public education. *Education Week*. Retrieved from www.edweek.org/ew/articles/2012/03/01/kappan_underwood.html

United Opt Out National. (2013, February 11). Occupy the U.S. Department of Education: The battle for public schools. Retrieved from http://unitedoptout.com/wp-content/uploads/2013/02/Occupy-DOE-2.0-Press-Release-FINAL-PDF.pdf

Upton, J. (2011). For teachers, many ways and reasons to cheat on tests. *USA Today*. Retrieved from www.usatoday.com/news/education/2011–03–10–1Aschooltesting10_CV_N.htm

U.S. Department of Education. (1983). *A nation at risk: The imperative for educational reform*. Washington, DC: U.S. Department of Education. Retrieved from http://datacenter.spps.org/uploads/SOTW_A_Nation_at_Risk_1983.pdf

U.S. Department of Education. (2006a, May 17). *Secretary Spellings approves Tennessee and North Carolina growth model pilots for 2005–2006* [Press release]. Retrieved from www2.ed.gov/news/pressreleases/2006/05/05172006a.html

U.S. Department of Education. (2006b, November 9). *Secretary Spellings approves additional growth model pilots for 2006–2007* [Press release]. Retrieved from www2.ed.gov/news/pressreleases/2007/05/05242007.html

U.S. Department of Education. (2010a). *A blueprint for reform: The reauthorization of the Elementary and Secondary Education Act*. Washington, DC: U.S. Department of Education. Retrieved from www2.ed.gov/policy/elsec/leg/blueprint/index.html

U.S. Department of Education. (2010b, December 8). International education rankings suggest reform can lift U.S. [Blog post]. *Homeroom: the official blog of the U. S. Department of Education*. Retrieved from www.ed.gov/blog/2010/12/international-education-rankings-suggest-reform-can-lift-u-s/

U.S. Department of Education. (2011). *Great teachers and leaders: State considerations on building systems of educator effectiveness* (ED-ESE-10-O-0087). Washington, DC: U.S. Department of Education. Retrieved from www2.ed.gov/programs/racetothetop/great-teachers.doc

U.S. Department of Education. (2012). *ESEA flexibility*. Washington, DC: U.S. Department of Education. Retrieved from www.ed.gov/esea/flexibility

Value-Added Research Center (VARC). (2012a). *About VARC*. Madison, WI: VARC. Retrieved from http://varc.wceruw.org/about.php

Value-Added Research Center (VARC). (2012b). *Current projects*. Madison, WI: VARC. Retrieved from http://varc.wceruw.org/projects.php

Value-Added Research Center (VARC). (2012c). *Methodology*. Madison, WI: VAR C. Retrieved from http://varc.wceruw.org/methodology.php

Value-Added Research Center (VARC). (2012d). *Value-added research center*. Madison, WI: VARC. Retrieved from http://varc.wceruw.org/

Value-Added Research Center (VARC). (2012e). *Value-added tutorials*. Madison, WI: VARC. Retrieved from http://varc.wceruw.org/tutorials/index.php

Vandevoort, L. G., Amrein-Beardsley, A., & Berliner, D. C. (2004). National Board Certified teachers and their students' achievement. *Education Policy Analysis Archives, 12*(46). Retrieved from http://epaa.asu.edu/epaa/v12n46/

Vogell, H., Perry, J., Judd, A., & Pell, M. B. (2012, March 25). Cheating our children: Suspicious school test scores across the nation. *Atlanta Journal Constitution*. Retrieved from www.ajc.com/news/cheating-our-children-suspicious-1397022.html

Vu, P. (2008, January 17). Do state tests make the grade? *Stateline*. Retrieved from www.pewstates.org/projects/stateline/headlines/do-state-tests-make-the-grade-85899387452

Wainer, H. (2004). Introduction to a special issue of the *Journal of Educational and Behavioral Statistics* on value-added assessment. *Journal of Educational and Behavioral Statistics, 29*(1), 1–3. doi:10.3102/10769986029001001

Walberg, H. J., & Paik, S. J. (1997). Assessment requires incentives to add value: A review of the Tennessee Value-Added Assessment System. In J. Millman (Ed.), *Grading teachers, grading schools: Is student achievement a valid evaluation measure?* (pp. 169–178). Thousand Oaks, CA: Corwin Press.

Watanabe, T. (2012, October 28). Measuring the worth of a teacher? *Los Angeles Times*. Retrieved from http://articles.latimes.com/2012/oct/28/local/la-me-teacher-evals-20121029

Watanabe, T. (2013, January 19). L.A. teachers' union members OK new evaluation method. *Los Angeles Times*. Retrieved from www.latimes.com/news/local/la-me-utla-evals-20130120,0,5009372.story

Weems, D. M., & Rogers, C. B. H. (2010). Are U.S. teachers making the grade? A proposed framework for teacher evaluation and professional growth. *Management in Education, 24,* 19–24. doi:10.1177/0892020609354959

Weingarten, R. (2011) Foreword. In D. N. Harris (Ed.), *Value-added measures in education: What every educator needs to know* (pp. vi–ix). Cambridge, MA: Harvard Education Press.

Weisberg, D., Sexton, S., Mulhern, J., & Keeling, D. (2009). "The Widget Effect." *Education Digest, 75*(2), 31–35.

Weisman, J., & Paley, A. R. (2007). Dozens in GOP turn against Bush's prized "No Child" Act. *Washington Post*. Retrieved from www.washingtonpost.com/wp-dyn/content/article/2007/03/14/AR2007031402741.html

Wells, J. (2011, April). *Teacher responses to pay-for-performance policies: Survey results from four high-poverty, urban school districts*. Paper presented at the Annual Meeting of the American Educational Research Association, New Orleans, LA.

Wheatley, M. J. (1992). *Leadership and the new science: Learning about organizations from an orderly universe.* San Francisco, CA: Berrett-Koehler Publishers.

Wilkins, A. (2010, September 7). Valuable feedback. *New York Times*. Retrieved from www.nytimes.com/roomfordebate/2010/09/06/assessing-a-teachers-value/valuable-feedback-for-teachers

Wilkinson, L., & Task Force on Statistical Inference. (1999). Statistical methods in psychology journals: Guidelines and explanations. *American Psychologist, 54*(8), 594–604. doi:10.1037//0003-066X.54.8.594

Williams, W. M., & Ceci, S. J. (1997). "How'm I doing?" Problems with student ratings of instructors and courses. *Change, 29*(5), 12–23. doi:10.1080/00091389709602331

Willingham, W. W., Pollack, J. M., & Lewis, C. (2000, September). *Grades and test scores: Accounting for observed differences*. Princeton, NJ: Education Testing Service. Retrieved from www.ets.org/Media/Research/pdf/RR-00-15-Willingham.pdf

Wilson, M. (author/music/lyrics), and Lacey, F. (co-author). (1957). *The music man* [musical]. New York.

Wilson, M., Hallman, P. J., Pecheone, R., & Moss, P. (2007, October). *Using student achievement test scores as evidence of external validity for indicators of teacher quality: Connecticut's Beginning Educator Support and Training [BEST] Program*. Palo Alto, CA: Stanford Center for Assessment, Learning and Equity. Retrieved from http://edpolicy.stanford.edu/publications/pubs/107

Winebrenner, S., Brulles, D., & Kingore, B. (2008). *The cluster grouping handbook: A schoolwide model: How to challenge gifted students and improve achievement for all*. Minneapolis, MN: Free Spirit Publishing.

Winerip, M. (2011, March 6). Evaluating New York teachers, perhaps the numbers do lie. *New York Times*. Retrieved from www.nytimes.com/2011/03/07/education/07winerip.html?_r=1&emc=eta1

Winerip, M. (2012, January 15). Study on teacher value uses data from before teach-to-test era. *New York Times*. Retrieved from www.nytimes.com/2012/01/16/us/study-on-teacher-value-uses-data-from-before-teach-to-test-era.html?emc=eta1

Winters, M. A., Trivitt, J. R., & Greene, J. P. (2010). The impact of high-stakes testing on student proficiency in low-stakes subjects: Evidence from Florida's elementary science exam. *Economics of Education Review, 29,* 138–146.

Witham, P. (2011, April). *Applying performance management framework to data use in an urban district's professional development program*. Paper presented at the Annual Convention of the American Educational Research Association, New Orleans, LA.

Wright, P., Horn, S., & Sanders, W. L. (1997). Teachers and classroom heterogeneity: Their effects on educational outcomes. *Journal of Personnel Evaluation in Education, 11*(1), 57–67.

Wright, S. P., Sanders, W. L., and Rivers, J. C. (2006). Measurement of academic growth of individual students toward variable and meaningful academic standards. In R. Lissitz (Ed.), *Longitudinal and value-added models of student performance* (pp. 385–406). Maple Grove, MN: JAM Press. Retrieved from www.sas.com/govedu/edu/wrightsandersrivers.pdf

Wright, S. P., White, J. T., Sanders, W. L., & Rivers, J. C. (2010, March 25). *SAS® EVAAS® statistical models*. Retrieved from www.sas.com/resources/asset/SAS-EVAAS-Statistical-Models.pdf

Xu, Z., Ozek, U., & Corritore, M. (2012, June). *Portability of teacher effectiveness across schools*. Washington, DC: National Center for Analysis of Longitudinal Data in Education Research. Retrieved from www.caldercenter.org/publications/upload/wp77.pdf

Yeh, S. S. (2011). *The cost-effectiveness of 22 approaches for raising student achievement*. Charlotte, NC: Information Age Publishing, Inc.

Yin, R. (1994). *Case study research: Design and methods* (2nd ed.). Beverly Hills, CA: SAGE Publishing.

Yuan, K., Le, V., McCaffrey, D. F., Marsh, J. A., Hamilton, L. S., Stecher, B. M., & Springer, M. G. (2013). Incentive pay programs do not affect teacher motivation or reported practices: Results from three randomized studies. *Educational Evaluation and Policy Analysis, 35*(1), 3–22. doi:10.3102/0162373712462625

Zavis, A., & Barboza, T. (2010, September 28). Teacher's suicide shocks school: Rigoberto Ruelas, a fifth-grade teacher at Miramonte Elementary in South L.A., was hailed as a caring teacher. *Los Angeles Times*. Retrieved from http://articles.latimes.com/2010/sep/28/local/la-me-south-gate-teacher-20100928

Zeis, C., Waronska, A. K., & Fuller, R. (2009). Value-added program assessment using nationally standardized tests: Insights into internal validity issues. *Journal of Business and Economics, 9*(1), 114–127.

INDEX

Page numbers in *italics* denote tables, those in **bold** denote figures.

Accelerating Student Progress and Increasing Results and Expectations (ASPIRE) program 25, 27–8, 30–2

accountability systems 47, 51, 52, 54, 83, 162; new and improved data systems 20; technologies for improving 20, 53; value-added models (VAMs) *see* value-added models (VAMs)

Adequate Yearly Progress (AYP) measures 20

adult education schools 14

American Association of Retired Persons (AARP) 80

American educational policy, social engineering in 8–9

American Educational Research Association (AERA) 47, 68, 155n11

American Enterprise Institute 186

American Institutes for Research and Mathematica Policy Research 71

American Legislative Exchange Council (ALEC) 53–4, 73n3

American Psychological Association (APA) 47, 68

America's public schools 10, 14–16, 24, 41, 63, 83, 85, 203, 210–11; academic achievement in 52; betterment of 54; corporate and for-profit education reforms 51; educational accountability system 52, 87; educational reforms in *see* educational reforms; faulty human evaluation systems 88–90; ratings of teachers 89; "reform" initiatives 53; student learning and performance in 102; teachers as antagonists in 86–8; teachers as protagonists in 84–6

Ames, C. A. 95

analysis of covariance (ANCOVA) 57, 74n19

analysis of variance (ANOVA) 57, 74n17

Arizona Department of Education 75n29, 162

Arizona study, for investigating students placements 171–2; cluster grouping models for 174; homogeneous and heterogeneous classrooms 173–4; "luck of the draw" approach 178; parental involvement, issue of 175–7; on random assignment 177–8; results of 172–8; student's peer-to-peer interactions 173; teacher involvement, issue of 174–5; value-added estimates 171; variables influencing 172–3

Asian American students 169

assumptions: about value-added models 82–4; legitimacy of 81–2; "missing at random" 123; statistical and methodological *see* statistical assumptions, about VAMs; used to further advance VAM implementation 93–101; used to justify VAM adoption 84–93

Battelle for Kids 53, 64

bell curve 87, 89, *92*, 110–11, *114*, 142, 157–8, 189

best linear unbiased prediction (BLUP) methods 56, 74n15

Betebenner, Damian 25, 66, 69–70

bias: Arizona study 171–8; random assignment and 160–2; statistical strategies and controls for reducing 164–7; in student assignments 162–4; in student placement practices 167–71; in test-based estimates 38–41, 157

Bill and Melinda Gates Foundation 53, 116, 163; Measures of Effective Teaching (MET) study 116, 146–7, 171, 177, 187
binary coding system 124
box-and-whisker plot **109**, 110, 142
B-spline technique 67, 75n31
Buffett, Warren 95
burden of proof 148

carrots and sticks, ideas about 95–8, 102
Carson, Rachel 6, 15, 54
ceiling effects 40, 49n12, 155n10, 157, 180n1
Center for Education Policy Research 168
Chester, M. D. 187
chief executive officers (CEOs) 50
classrooms: based on students' ethnicity 168; homogeneous and heterogeneous 173–4
cluster grouping models 174
Coleman Report (1966) 57, 85
college faculty: distribution of scores **203**; evaluation of **201**
Collins, Clarin 24, 37, 40–1, 43
Colorado Growth Model *see* Student Growth Percentiles (SGP) model
Common Core State Standards 19, 51, 100, 109, 193; implementation of 53
confidence intervals 33, 163; definition of 133–4
consequence-related evidence, of validity 148–52
construct-irrelevant variance (CIV) 38, 107, 118, 143, 157, 195
construct-related evidence, of validity 152–3
content-related evidence, of validity 141–4
Corcoran, S. P. 72, 82, 137, 147, 167
Council of Chief State School Officers 19
credibility and trust, issue of 187
criterion-related evidence, of validity 144–8
crony capitalism, in educational economy 54
curriculum, school 85, 97, 142, 150, 156n14

Dallas Independent School District 71
data interpretation: sample size 124–5; skills for 110
data systems, for linking students' test scores 20
decision-making purposes *84*, 107, 132–3, 135, 194
Delaware model 71
"devil's bargain" 70, 100
Duncan, Arne 52, 65, 93, 95, 99, 141, 148

educational inputs and outputs, measurement of 21
educational quality 112, *114*; indicators of 70; large-scale standardized test scores 152; measurement of 24, 51
educational reforms: carrots and sticks, ideas about 95–8; economics-based beliefs about 93–5; initiatives for 53; measures for 15–16;

merit-based policies 96; performance-pay plans 96; VAM-based reforms 97
educational "value", measurement of 118
Einstein, Albert 12, 189, 203
Elementary and Secondary Education Act (2010) 11–12
Emancipation Proclamation of 1863 5
emotional/learning disabilities 11, 85, 111
Empirical Bayes methods 169
English Language Learners (ELLs) 25, 33, 37, 39, 67, 123, 139, 147, 151, 160, 165, 178, 191, 206
English-language proficiency 85, 172
Environmental Protection Agency 6
Epstein, J. 95
evaluation systems, used in education 88–90; VAM-based 141

fairness issues, in VAM-based estimates 41–2
falsification test 169
"feedback loop" 98–101; for common use **99**; for VAM-based educational use **99**
Foundation for Excellence in Education (FEE) 53
Freedom of Information Act 73n4

gain score index 27
Galileo tests 192
"garbage in, garbage out" systems 70, 148
Gates, Bill 53, 87, 141
General Education Diplomas (GEDs) 14
Gordon, Edmund 108

halo effects (halo rating errors) 195
Harris, Doug 127
Heisenberg, Werner 106; uncertainty principle 106
hierarchical linear model (HLM) 57, 63, 74n20
Houston Federation of Teachers 26
Houston Independent School District (HISD) 24, 38, 41–2, 61; Accelerating Student Progress and Increasing Results and Expectations (ASPIRE) program 25, 27–8, 30–2; Alternative Teaching Certificate program 26, 30, 32; SAS® Education Value-Added Assessment System (EVAAS®) 25, 42, 46; teacher termination 26; teachers' performance pay 97
human factors, influence on value-added models 24–5

incentives, financial 97
intellectual genocide 5, 13–16
intelligence quotients (IQs) 110; distribution of scores, under bell curve **111**

job responsibilities 191
job-related stress 97

knowledge production, teachers' levels of 94

language proficiency 58, 63, 85, 165, 168, 172
large-scale standardized achievement tests 85–6,
142–3, 146, 153; attribution and causation
112; bell curve 110–11; box-and-whisker plot
109, 110; errors associated with 106–8; impact
and bias 111–12; as measurement tools
105–12; No Child Left Behind Act (NCLB,
2002) 106; problems with construction of
108–10; scientific inferences derived via 108;
statistical assumptions, about VAMs *113–14*
learning behaviors, self-motivated and self-
directed 191
Limited English Proficiency (LEP) 25
Lincoln, Abraham 5
litigations, challenging teacher dismissals 26

Manifest Destiny 5
Marsh, H. W. 194–5
Mathematica Policy Research 71, 168
mean squared error (MSE) 74n15
Measure and Punish (M&P) Theory of Change
14–16, 19–20, 23, 152, 207; America's
educational policy 10–11; educational
accountability system 52; for improving
education condition 13; intellectual genocide
13–16; interpretation of 11; logic map **10**;
policy actions based on 50; proponents of 12;
regenerating policies based on 12; statistical
tools 20
Measures of Effective Teaching (MET) study
116, 146–7, 171, 177, 187
merit pay, idea of 96
Messick, S. 38, 141–4, 148, 152, 157
metric systems, for measuring teacher
effectiveness 20
Meyer, Robert H. 62, 64, 66
Milwaukee model 71
multivariate response model (MRM) 57, 74n16;
teacher-level equation 57, **58**; use of 59–60

Nation at Risk, A (1983) 9, 11–13, 16, 50, 207
National Board Certified Teachers (NBCTs) 196
National Board for Professional Teaching
Standards (NBPTS) 191, 213n10
National Center for the Improvement of
Educational Assessment (NCIEA) 66, 70
National Commission on Education 9
National Council on Measurement in Education
(NCME) 47, 68
National Governors Association 19
National Rifle Association (NRA) 80
New Teacher Project's "Widget Effect" report
88–9, 146, 152
"New York City's Worst Teacher" 147
No Child Left Behind Act (NCLB, 2002) 11–13,

19, 48n1, 50, 54, 80, 152, 207;
implementation of 20; standardized
achievement tests 106
normal curve equivalent (NCE) 27, 143
not detectably different (NDD) scores 27, 60

Obama, Barack 11, 51–2, 60, 65, 80, 152
Open Records Request 26
ordinary least squares (OLS) estimators 163
out-of-subject teachers 121

parental involvement, in students placement
175–7
Partnership for Assessment of Readiness for
College and Careers (PARCC) Consortium
51, 100
pay-for-performance plan 97–8
Personnel Evaluation Committee (PEC) 201–2
political sciences, social engineering in 5–8
Popham, W. J. 100
portfolios, used in evaluation systems 196
problem solving, skills for 108
Professional Development and Appraisal System
(PDAS) 28–9, 31, 35–6, 38, 44–7

quantile regression 67, 75n30

Race to the Top (RttT) initiative (2011) 11–12,
19, 61, 80, 90, 207; federal incentives 24;
funding for 52; guiding principle of 20
random assignment technique 116–18, 160–2;
Arizona study on 177–8; to assign students to
different teachers' classrooms 161; purpose of
160
reading teachers 121
reciprocity, law of 80
reliability, issue of: complementary anecdotes
137–9; complications causing 139; confidence
intervals 133–4; correct and incorrect
interpretations **136**; and r factor 134–5; and R^2
correlation coefficient 135–7; relation with
validity 132–3; research on 133–40; of student
achievement data 134–5; of test scores 33–5
Rothstein, J. 169

Sanders, William L. 35, 56–7, 61, 65, 123–4, 164
SAS® Education Value-Added Assessment
System (EVAAS®) 24, 55, 67–8, 139, 143,
145, 148, 150, 164–5, 169; bias 38–41; "black
box" model 61; "blocking factors" 41; claims
and realities 60–2; current and planned growth
model **56**; data and results 28–33; education
policy implications 62; history of 56–7; in
Houston Independent School District 25;
multivariate response model (MRM) teacher-
level equation 57, **58**; operating budget of 64;
reliability of 33–5; Reports for Teacher

SAS® *continued*
Reflection 27; specifics of 57–9; teacher termination 26; Teacher Value-Added Reports 26–7, 44; training sessions 43; transparency and formative use 42–4; univariate response model (URM) projection equation 57, **58**; validity of 35–8; VAM-based use 44–6, **56,** 59–60

SAS® Institute, Inc. 25, 44, 47, 56–7

Sass, T. R. 136–7

SAT-9 test 192

scare tactics 5, 9, 12, 50, 53

school administrators 8, 26, 102; as co-conspirators 91–3

Schoolwide Cluster Grouping Method (SCGM) 174

science teachers 34, 121

"selective seating" practices 14–15

Shanker, Albert 206

Silent Spring (1962) 6, 15, 54

Smarter Balanced Assessment Consortium (SBAC) tests 51, 100

social engineering 207; accountability movement 9–11; in American educational policy 8–9; federal and state tax policies, via use of 6; by genocide 4–5; not-so-temporary insanity 12–13; paradigm case of 9; in political sciences 5–8

social studies teachers 121

special education: students 39, 158, 191; teachers 124

standardized achievement tests *see* large-scale standardized achievement tests

Standards for Educational and Psychological Testing 47, 68, 148, 186

Stanford/Aprenda achievement tests 27

statistical assumptions, about VAMs 112–26; chaos and disorder, control of 114–16; large-scale standardized achievement tests *113–14*; random assignment technique 116–18

statistical strategies and controls 164–7

status changes of students, measurement of 20

student assignments 162–4, 172

Student Growth Percentiles (SGP) model 25, 55, 66, 144; claims and realities 68–70; classification of 22; difference with value-added models 22; education policy implications of 70–1; equations **67**; history of 66; levels of reliability 69; specifics of 66–8; use of 68

student information cards 173–4

student learning: and ability to think critically 108; and achievement 84, 94, 148, 150; data interpretation skills 110; determinants of 83; with "harder-to-predict" achievement 168; levels of 91, 200; linear, consistent, and persistent 118–19; merit-based policies for improving 96; missing data, impact of 122–4;

perceived and actual academic abilities 163; problem solving, skills for 108; quality of the teachers, effect of 84–5, 146; residual and interaction effects on 120–2; sample size 124–5; styles of 175; summer learning growth and decay 119–20; trajectories of achievement **120**; VAM-based inferences 115

student motivation 85

student placement practices 177; academically based 163; administrative control over 117; bias in 167–71

student risk factors 85

students' test scores 96; classroom- or school-level variables 22; control of 22; criterion scores, relation with 144; factors influencing variance in 85; measurement of 20; not detectably different (NDD) scores 60; risk variables 22; validity, issue of 142

StudentsFirst (non-profit organization) 18n3, 53, 73n5

summer academic programs 119–20

Tax Reform Act (1986) 6

Teach for America (TFA) 88

teacher certification program 26

teacher effectiveness 28, 31, 36, 46, 55, 69, 87–9, 95, 105–6, 135, 139, 144–6, 152, 167, 187, 190–1; criteria for assessing 191; EVAAS® system for measuring 35; evaluation of *see* teachers evaluation system; general theory of 200; levels of 112; perception for 144; quantitative and qualitative measures of 145–6, 209; state legislation requiring **55**; VAM estimates of 33, 41, 133, 153

Teacher Incentive Funds (TIF) 52, 65

teacher unions 51

teachers: accountability, for meeting higher standards 20, 86, 162; as antagonists 86–8; befriending with school principals 151; dismissal rules and regulations 91; EVAAS® scores 26; evaluation systems *see* teachers evaluation system; influence on student learning and achievement 85; inter- and intra-teacher value-added comparisons 116; involvement in students placement in classroom 174–5; job responsibilities 191, 200; levels of knowledge production 94; missing data, issue of 122–4; monetary awards 96; normal curve equivalent (NCE) 27; performance-pay plans 96; Professional Development and Appraisal System (PDAS) 28–9, 31, 35–6, 38, 44–7; as protagonists 84–6; quality distribution 137; quality of 84–5, 88, 95; ratings of 89; Report for Teacher Reflection **27**; SAS® EVAAS®, and PDAS scores and ASPIRE bonuses 28–33; self-reports and reflections 197; student learning and growth, impact on 26; teaching the same courses with high- and low-achievers **159**; termination of *see* teachers termination; value-added categorizations 147; value-added decile **138**; value-added rankings 137; Value-Added Reports 26–7; value-added score 134; VAM estimates and classroom composition *170*

teachers evaluation system 33, 35, 46, 55, 62, 88–90; alternatives for 185–6; conventional measures for 192–7; conventional options for 188–9; conventional solution for 189–92, 200–6; credibility and trust 187; halo effects (halo rating errors) 195; human judgment 190; methods for assessment 188; multiple measures and holistic 186–8, *198–9*; pie chart **188**; portfolios 196; quantitative estimates 189–92; student and parent surveys 194–6; supervisor and peer observations 193–4; teacher self-reports and reflections 197; test-based measures 192–3; value-added estimates 186–9

teachers' future performance, predictors of 145

teachers termination 26, 94; barriers preventing 91; four terminated teachers, story of 26–8; school administrators as co-conspirators in 91–3; for subpar EVAAS® scores 35–6

Tennessee Value-Added Assessment System (TVAAS) 42, 57, 66, 144, 180n4; implementation and use 61

Terra Nova test 192

test interpretation and use, social consequences of 148

test participation, rates of 14

Texas's Assessment of Knowledge and Skills (TAKS) 27, 37, 39, 46

transparency, in VAM-based measurement system 42–4

univariate response model (URM) 57, 74n18; projection equation **58**

U.S. Department of Education 21, 64, 136, 152, 207; approval of Tennessee's use of the EVAAS® 61; value-added systems, evaluation of 65

validity, issue of 140–1; consequence-related evidence of 148–52; construct-related evidence of 152–3; content-related evidence of 141–4; criterion-related evidence of 144–8; of measurement of test scores 35–8; research on 141–53; test-based inferences 143; VAMs' concurrent-related evidence of 145; VAMs' predictive-related evidence of 144

value-added assessment 57, 210

value-added comparisons, inter- and intra-teacher 116

value-added indicators 116, 163

value-added models (VAMs) 20–1, 165; and bias in test-based estimates 38–41; control for students' test scores 22; defined 21–3, 49n2; difference with student growth models 22; educational issues 21; as education's iconic charging bull 51–4; estimates of school productivity 163; fairness issues 41–2; general assumptions about 82–4; gold-painted watches and glass diamond rings scenario 81–2; human factor 24–5; integration with accountability policies and systems 21; manufactured crisis scenario 81; misuse of 51; national landscape 54–6; other statistical and methodological assumptions about *125–6*; outcomes-based information 98–101; powers and potentials 52; SAS® Education Value-Added Assessment System (EVAAS®) 24–5; statistical and methodological assumptions about 112–26; statistical equation, for calculating value-added **21,** 22; teacher effectiveness, estimates of 33, 35, 46, **55**; value-added estimates, for students' test scores 23–4

Value-added Research Center (VARC), Wisconsin 25, 55, 70, 163, 181n5; claims and realities 65; education policy implications 65–6; history of 62–3; specifics of 63–4; two-period value-added model for school/district **63**; use of 64

"Widget Effect" report, on teacher effectiveness 88–9, 146, 152

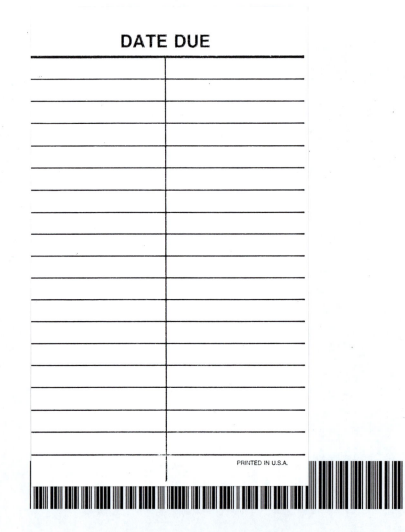

DATE DUE